306.2 ScA 1 ST

CULTURE AND POWER

The Media, Culture & Society Series

Series editors: John Corner, Nicholas Garnham, Paddy Scannell, Philip Schlesinger, Colin Sparks, Nancy Wood

The Economics of Television
The UK Case

Richard Collins, Nicholas Garnham and Gareth Locksley

Media, Culture and Society
A Critical Reader

edited by
Richard Collins, James Curran, Nicholas Garnham,
Paddy Scannell, Philip Schlesinger and Colin Sparks

Capitalism and Communication
Global Culture and the Economics
of Information

Nicholas Garnham, edited by Fred Inglis

Media, State and Nation
Political Violence and
Collective Identities

Philip Schlesinger

Broadcast Talk
edited by
Paddy Scannell

**Journalism and
Popular Culture**
edited by
Peter Dahlgren and
Colin Sparks

Media, Crisis and Democracy
edited by
Marc Raboy and Bernard Dagenais

CULTURE AND POWER

A *Media, Culture & Society* Reader

edited by

**Paddy Scannell, Philip Schlesinger
and Colin Sparks**

SAGE Publications
London · Newbury Park · New Delhi

First published 1992

SAGE Publications Ltd
6 Bonhill Street
London EC2A 4PU

SAGE Publications Inc
2455 Teller Road
Newbury Park, California 91320

SAGE Publications India Pvt Ltd
32, M-Block Market
Greater Kailash – I
New Delhi 110 048

British Library Cataloguing in Publication data

Culture and Power: Media, Culture &
Society Reader. – (Media, Culture &
Society Series)
  I. Scannell, Paddy   II. Series
  302.23

  ISBN 0–8039–8630–0
  ISBN 0–8039–8631–9 (pbk)

Library of Congress catalog card number 92–050168

Typeset by The Word Shop, Bury, Lancs.
Printed in Great Britain by The Cromwell Press Ltd,
Broughton Gifford, Melksham, Wiltshire

Contents

Notes on contributors

Klaus Bruhn Jensen is Associate Professor in the Department of Film, TV and Communication, University of Copenhagen. He is the author of *Making Sense of the News* (Aarhus University Press, 1986) and first co-editor of *A Handbook of Qualitative Methodologies for Mass Communication Research* (Routledge, 1991). His current research focuses on media history, the reception of TV news in different cultural contexts, and a theory of social semiotics.

Néstor García Canclini teaches at the National Institute of Anthropology and History, Tlalpan, Mexico. He is an authority on communication and culture in South America.

Kuan-Hsing Chen is an Associate Professor in the Institute of Literature, National Tsing Hua University, Taiwan. He has published essays on minority discourse, postmodernism and cultural studies, and is working on a book project linking social movement, intellectuals and cultural politics in Taiwan.

John Corner is Senior Lecturer in the School of Politics and Communication Studies at the University of Liverpool and an editor of *Media, Culture & Society*. He has written many articles on media history, forms and audiences, and has edited and co-edited a number of books including *Communication Studies* (Arnold, 3rd edn, 1989), *Documentary and the Mass Media* (Arnold, 1986) and *Popular Television in Britain* (BFI, 1991). He is currently working on a study of the politics of communicative form.

Peter Dahlgren is Principal Lecturer in the Department of Journalism, Media and Communication, Stockholm University. His recent publications include two collections, *Communication and Citizenship* (Routledge, 1991) and *Journalism and Popular Culture* (Sage, 1992), both edited with Colin Sparks. His current research is in the area of television, modernity and modes of subjectivity.

John D.H. Downing is Professor and Chair of the Radio, Television and Film Department, University of Texas at Austin. Recent edited books include *Film and Politics in the Third World* (1987), *Questioning the Media* (1990) and *Computers in Social Change and Community Organizing* (1991). He is currently preparing books on media and democratic transitions in Eastern Europe and on ethnic minorities and media in the USA.

Thomas K. Fitzgerald is Professor of Anthropology at the University of North Carolina at Greensborough. He is primarily interested in culture, identity and communication. His publications on these themes include *Education and Identity* (1977) and *Aspirations and Identity among Second-Generation Cook Islanders in New Zealand* (1988). He is currently finishing a book, *Metaphors of Identity: A Culture–Communication Dialogue*.

Sarah Franklin, Celia Lury and Jackie Stacey lecture in the Department of Sociology at Lancaster University. They are co-editors of *Off-Centre: Feminism and Cultural Studies* (Routledge, 1991).

Elizabeth Frazer is Fellow and Tutor in Politics at New College, Oxford. She teaches and researches in social and political theory.

Susan Kippax is Associate Professor in Psychology in the School of Behavioural Sciences, Macquarie University. She is the co-author of *Emotion and Gender* (Sage, 1992), and has published a number of papers on sexuality and sexual behaviour change in the context of the HIV epidemic. Her current areas of interest are the social aspects of the prevention of HIV/AIDS, and the social construction of emotions.

Shaun Moores is Lecturer in Media and Cultural Studies at the Polytechnic of Wales. His research, both on early radio and satellite television, has been concerned with the place of new communication technologies in everyday life. He is currently writing a book, *Interpreting Audiences: Ethnography and Media Consumption*, to be published in the *Media, Culture & Society* series by Sage Publications.

Kay Richardson teaches Communication Studies at the University of Liverpool. She has published several articles analysing political discourse and (with John Corner and Natalie Fenton) has contributed to research in the field of television audiences, notably in *Nuclear Reactions* (John Libby, 1990).

Paddy Scannell is Senior Lecturer in the School of Communication, Polytechnic of Central London, and a founding editor of *Media, Culture & Society*. He is the co-author, with David Cardiff, of the first volume of *A Social History of British Broadcasting*: 'Serving the Nation 1922–1939' (Blackwell, 1991) and editor of *Broadcast Talk* (Sage, 1991). His current research is into British radio in World War Two and the impact of broadcasting on modern life.

Philip Schlesinger is Professor of Film and Media Studies at the University of Stirling, Scotland and an editor of *Media, Culture & Society*. He is the author of *Putting 'Reality' Together* (2nd edn, 1987) and *Media, State and Nation* (1991), and has co-authored *Televising 'Terrorism'* (1983) and *Women Viewing Violence* (1992). Current research includes theoretical work on the question of collective identity and an empirical study of crime, criminal justice and the media.

Colin Sparks teaches in the School of Communication, Polytechnic of Central London and is a founding editor of *Media, Culture & Society*. He has written widely in the field of mass communication and is currently interested in the problematic relationship between the media and democracy.

David Tetzlaff teaches media production at Miami University in Oxford, Ohio. Now and then he also makes documentary films for public television, and writes about the politics of popular culture.

Introduction

Our title for this collection of articles underlines the importance of the question of power in the study of culture. The meaning of both terms has, of course, been much debated. In a recent issue of the analysis of 'culture' [*MCS*, 13(2)], John Corner has reiterated the basic duality at its core, a duality embodied in Raymond Williams's groundbreaking study, *Culture and Society*. On the one hand there is a concern with artistic expression and creative, aesthetic, representational activity, and on the other with ways of living, the organization and nature of social activity. In both there is a concern with the transmission and reception of values and meanings, but the focus of attention and methods of approach are very different. The study of the arts as culture, drawing on literary and aesthetic traditions, tends to a top-down view of culture embodied in the division between high and low culture. The study of culture as a way of life draws more on social history, anthropology and sociology, and focuses on the structures of everyday life and its forms of interactions – 'popular' culture.

The strength of cultural studies, as it developed in the UK, was its resolutely political stance in relation to its object of study. In Marxist aesthetics the concept of ideology came to be of central importance as a means of explaining how the dominant class remained in dominance through the control and imposition of their 'ruling ideas'. No concept in the field has been more exhaustively examined and none has proved more elusive on close scrutiny. Althusser's theses on ideology and subjectivity deeply influenced a generation of work in cultural studies and, applied to the study of television or film for instance, led to a split about the ideological effectivity of film or TV texts. There were those, particularly film analysts, who argued for the power of the text in organizing spectators' 'subject positions'. Stuart Hall and his research students at the Centre for Contemporary Cultural Studies, more concerned with television, argued for a negotiated view of meaning. They proposed that viewers could read different, possibly oppositional, meanings from the preferred, dominant meaning encoded in programmes by the broadcasters.

This conceptual difference can, in part, be understood in relation to the different positions of cinema and television vis à vis their cultural status and power. Cinema has been appropriated into the domain of high culture (at an early stage it was decked out with an *auteur* theory as its rite of passage), whereas television remains rooted in mass (low) or popular culture. Cinema, that is, could be assimilated more easily than television into traditional aesthetic debates that privileged texts and their meanings. Television posed more immediate questions about reception, about how people made sense of what they heard and saw in the contexts of viewing and listening, and it was here that a significant turn took place away from the study of texts to the study of how audiences made sense of them. This perhaps has been the main development in media studies in the last few years and is represented in the second section of this reader.

In our first reader we republished an article by Stuart Hall, first written in 1980, on 'two paradigms' in cultural studies – the 'structuralist' and the 'culturalist' as he called them (Hall, 1986a). At the time Hall was writing, the structuralist paradigm was in dominance, 'decentering' the culturalist stress on the category of 'lived experience' and replacing it with the category of ideology. Hall offered a third, Gramscian position, in which 'hegemony' – with its stress on class domination as a historically situated struggle – was negotiated through the institutions of state and civil society. This, he predicted, was the way forward.

At the end of the 1980s, the over-deterministic emphases of structuralism were increasingly rejected as too simplistic to explain highly complex social phenomena. The pendulum has now swung back in favour of culturalism again, with its emphasis on the ordinary and mundane, with its attention to how people live; but it is braced with a new stress on how, in such contexts, power relations are routinely reproduced. In different ways, the writings of Foucault, Gramsci and Bourdieu have contributed to replacing an interest in ideology with an interest in the operations of power not simply as operating from the top down through state-apparatuses, but as articulated in and through the culture of daily life, the organization of identities and the production and consumption of life-styles. These developments have, however, increasingly been situated within a new, and much contested, conceptual framework, namely postmodernism.

Whether postmodernism represents a sharp break from modernity or simply a late stage in that historical development is the crux of the matter. Debates have focused on three overlapping terrains: the *experience* of contemporary reality (subjectivity and identity); the *representation* of the contemporary (in the arts, architecture, the media, advertising and consumer goods); and the *analysis* of the contemporary (the state of knowledge in postmodern society). Much attention has focused on contemporary consumer culture as expressive of a postmodern sensibility or structure of feeling, and this has led to renewed attention to the construction of individual and social identities, using the media and popular culture as 'identikits', as registers of subjective responses to the world today.

At the level of theory, postmodernism is characterized by the rejection of 'grand narratives' which attempt to totalize the social structures, to grasp society as a whole. Such attempts – most notably Marxist-structuralist theory – are now thought of as terroristic attempts to impose a unitary meaning or truth on societies whose continuously evolving and changing complexity must inevitably elude all efforts to constrain and comprehend them. History-as-progress, as the working-out of some unitary divine or human goal (salvation, socialism) is one casualty of the postmodern critique. So, too, are the Enlightenment and its political project of human emancipation from political and religious absolutism. The 'dark side' of that historical project – notably examined by Adorno and Horkheimer in *Dialectic of Enlightenment* (1979) – is again empha-sized, and its claims for an emancipatory rationality dismissed. Again, any notion of the individual as a unitary, rational, self-reflecting subject is regarded as delusory. Postmodernism mistrusts all modernist claims to ground an understanding of the contemporary social world in scientific rationality.

Modernism acknowledged the fragmentary, transient, dislocated charac-ter of the social world but tried to overcome it, to retrieve a lost unity, whereas postmodernism is content to accept and celebrate a de-centred political, economic and cultural global environment. It rejects deep structures, any notion of an underlying, determining reality. It accepts a world of appearances, a surface reality without depth. The meaning of postmodernism has been much discussed in cultural studies, as most of the contributions to the first section of this collection make plain. Here we would note that this journal has always been deeply suspicious of the retreat from reason that postmodernism represents. Within the broad spectrum of work represented in *Media, Culture & Society*, one unifying emphasis is on the possibility of rational social enquiry producing valid knowledge of the workings of the social world. This project, in line with that commitment of the Enlightenment to a critique of the present in the name of a better tomorrow, is incompatible with the philosophical basis of postmodernism.

The emergence of postmodernism in the 1980s must be understood not simply as a set of academic debates but also in relation to what was happening in the wider society. This is not the place to attempt an account of the 1980s. It will suffice to note that the collapse of Marxist-structuralist 'grand narratives' in cultural and media studies was preceded by the growing crisis of Marxism as a political system. On the one hand there was the manifest decay of post-Stalinist state socialism. The regimes in the Soviet Union and the Eastern bloc as a whole were patently becoming more politically bankrupt and economically decrepit, and their intelligentsia and working classes more openly disenchanted. By the end of the 1970s this underlying reality of structural crisis had begun to have greater impact on Marxist theorizing in the West. In Western Europe there was a brief moment of optimism that some 'Eurocommunist' third way might be available between welfare capitalism and the command economy. The failure of leading Western communist parties to devise such a programme dealt a further blow to Western Marxism.

This downturn in Marxism's fortunes coincided with the rapid retreat from welfarism and public ownership that went under the banner of liberalism and deregulation. This period, which stretched across the whole of the 1980s, was symbolized by the presidency of Ronald Reagan and the premiership of Margaret Thatcher. The emphasis on rolling back the state, on cutting back the public sector, on revitalizing a private, 'enterprise' culture – all this tilted the balance in the state/society dichotomy away from a notion of the former as all-powerful and the latter as powerless. Indeed the notion of civil society against the state took on new significance in the light of the revolutions of 1989. Of course 'civil society' has functioned rather differently as a critical concept, depending on whether we are talking about East or West. In the East it was part of a positive critique aimed at bringing an end to the total dominance of the party-state over everyday life, of recapturing some space for voluntary association and personal moral responsibility. In the West it tended to be annexed to left-liberal projects dedicated towards resisting encroachments on civil liberties and the ideals of welfarism and the public sector.

If, in our field, the last ten years have seen a shift away from the study of the production of culture to its consumption, this too makes sense in relation to concurrent economic and political developments. Attention has shifted from the institutions and their products to the contexts in which they are consumed, to the ways in which they articulate social identities, and the manner in which they are interpreted. Hall (1986a) pointed to the strengths and weaknesses of the culturalist concern with lived experience. While it emphasized human agency, it tended to lose sight of all those processes that shaped and constrained the conditions of existence for people. There was, and is, a danger of popular culture tending towards, say, celebrating consumer power as people power. This problem is addressed in the final section of the reader where we take up a discussion of the character of contemporary, mediatized public life in relation to Habermas's study of the public sphere. We attend in particular to the historically situated argument that an older critical-discussing public has been replaced by a spectacle-consuming public, a process largely brought about by the complicity of the press and broadcasting in what Habermas calls the 're-feudalization' of politics as display (Habermas, 1989).

It remains to say, in this introduction, that while the material published here deals with a set of interlocking concerns that have been and remain central to the work of the journal, other consistently pursued lines of enquiry have been excluded to achieve an overall thematic unity. Our continuing concerns with the political economy of the media, with policy and the new information society, and with media and language have been well represented both in past issues in the last five years and in our expanding book series (cf. Collins et al., 1988; Garnham, 1990; Scannell, 1991). One welcome recent trend is the increasingly international range of contributions to *Media, Culture & Society* which reflects our growing worldwide readership. In this respect it is appropriate to start with a contribution from Mexico that reviews recent developments in the field of media and cultural studies from a Latin American perspective.

Culture and power

The connections between culture and power are discussed by Néstor García Canclini, who offers a systematic critique of what he sees as the prevailing approaches to the study of popular culture and outlines an alternative related to the specific conditions of Latin American societies – an alternative that finds an echo in the other chapters in this section. He describes two dominant theoretical traditions as 'deductive' and 'inductive' that broadly correspond with Hall's structuralist/culturalist paradigms. The former, characterized by Marxist structuralist and semiotic approaches and the media imperialism thesis, conceptualizes all aspects of popular daily life as formed by and explicable in terms of dominant economic and political forces. Its effect is to reduce subordinate social groups to the status of the passive products of dominant social processes with no independent sphere of action. Inductive approaches – ethnographic or anthropological – while respecting the indigenous cultures of native peoples or subordinate social groups and celebrating their specificity are inherently conservative, for they affirm their spontaneous, surface features without conceptualizing the relations of power that give them their meaning in the wider social structure.

In sketching out his own approach Canclini argues that indigenous cultures need to be analysed both in terms of their historical formation and in the structural context of dependent capitalism. He emphasizes the capacity of popular cultures to resist, absorb and transform threats to their continued existence. Furthermore, a detailed examination of consumption patterns demonstrates the range of variation in the ways in which political discourse and media messages are interpreted. A thorough understanding of the politics of everyday transformations is a precondition for any programme of democratic advance.

The next three chapters would agree with that last proposition, though their perspectives are rather different. All engage with the impact of postmodernism on contemporary cultural studies. David Tetzlaff develops the interesting thesis that 'the collapse of meaning' which postmodernism celebrates may be a more accurate way of accounting for how late capitalism operates on the terrain of culture than the older dominant ideology thesis which saw mass-culture as achieving social control through ideological unity. Capitalism, he argues, has always worked by dividing and fragmenting dominated social groups. Today the proliferation of consumer goods, the ever-increasing diversity of tastes and life-styles, and the ever-decreasing timescale of turnovers in fashion all point to the ways in which popular culture precludes the possibility of forms of collective organization and protest, reducing it to mere individual rebellion. In short, postmodernism is capitalism's best friend, the realization of long-term tendencies in a totally commodified culture.

Kuang-Hsing Chen attempts to reconcile postmodernism and (post) Marxism in contemporary cultural studies. Where Tetzlaff sees postmodernism as symptomatic of the workings of global capitalism today, Chen sees it as having a critical, diagnostic function which it shares with cultural studies. He develops his argument by attempting to show that both have a similar perspective on history, cultural politics and the mass media. But postmodernism decisively rejects Marxism, whereas cultural studies clings to it still, in name at least. Chen ingeniously proposes that this seemingly unbridgeable gulf can be overcome by uniting them under the name of postmarxism. This, as defined by Stuart Hall (1986b), means going beyond orthodox Marxism (the laws of history) while still using it as a reference point – though what is retained from Marx himself remains unclear.

Cultural studies is next considered from a contemporary feminist perspective by Sarah Franklin, Celia Lury and Jackie Stacey. In their wide-ranging review of feminist studies they note the shared concerns, and the divergences, between it and cultural studies while noting the impact on both of poststructuralism and postmodernism. The concern with radical politics, with the analysis of inequalities of power and with strategies to overcome them, is common to cultural studies and women's studies, though the former was (originally) more concerned with class inequalities while the latter has stressed the neglected issue of male (patriarchal) domination and in so doing has made a major contribution to broadening the terms in which the relations between culture and power are considered.

Thomas Fitzgerald offers an anthropological perspective on the relationship between culture and society in relation to questions of ethnicity and identity and the effect of modern media. He explores the seeming paradox that today cultural homogenization and social diversification seem to be happening simultaneously: whereas more and more people of different backgrounds share an overlapping culture influenced by the media, there is a strong tendency for certain groups to insist that they are at least symbolically distinct. People, that is, can be different socially while still sharing the same culture. This proposition is examined in relation to what Fitzgerald calls *ethnogenesis*, the emergence of new ethnic groups claiming an identity that is not grounded in a traditional, authentic culture. He illustrates this in a brief account of his study of second-generation Cook Islanders who have settled in New Zealand.

The interrelations between culture and identity have become increasingly central to contemporary debate, and their analysis looks likely to become one of the key themes of the 1990s, not least because of the renewed salience of nationalism and supranationalism in Europe and elsewhere in the world. As the Cold War era vanishes, new markers of identity will be sought to fill the vacuum. As nation and national culture become more of a focus of interest and of political struggles, the more we shall be obliged to discuss other collective cultural formations framed in terms of race, class, ethnicity, religion and sexuality. One form of identity inevitably articulates with others; hence, dislocation in one field has consequences elsewhere. Thus identities are negotiated and processual in character rather than essences from which there is no escape, as all the contributions in this section confirm.

The audience and everyday life

A renewed interest in the study of media audiences has been a major recent development in the field. Rethinking consumption, in relation to media output, has led to a rejection of the prevailing view of passive audiences manipulated by the culture industries. There has been an explosion of studies in the last few years, all of which express dissatisfaction with that over-deterministic conceptualization of the power of cultural 'texts' that underlie the theorization of their ideological effect. The articles we republish here all argue, based on their own empirical research, for people's capacity to produce their own interpretations of media output (and for significant divergences in those interpretations amongst the range of individuals sampled). Equally, all are concerned to specify the boundaries that determine the scope and character of individual interpretations of cultural products. None wishes to replace an over-deterministic view of the power of texts with a radically indeterminate view of audience interpretation in which meaning is purely subjective and all interpretations are of equal value.

Shaun Moores offers a succinct review of recent developments in the study of media audiences, in the context of text–reader theory as developed in British cultural studies. He begins with the split, in the 1970s, between *Screen* (the British journal of film theory) and the Centre for Contemporary Cultural Studies over the ideological effect of film and television that we have discussed above. A theory of the determinacy of (film) texts was replaced by one which acknowledged their complexity – their 'polysemy' – and hence the possibility that different 'readers' might produce different readings of (television) texts. As Hall (1980) argued, the moment of decoding had no necessary correspondence with the moment of encoding. Moores carefully traces the subsequent empirical attempts to explore the truth of that proposition.

In an early case-study of how viewers make sense of what they see, Kay Richardson and John Corner consider how people in Liverpool interpret a television documentary about 'fiddling' the dole in that city. The problem of mediation is at the heart of their analysis, namely the attribution and interpretation by viewers of intention and motive not only on the part of the speakers in the programme, but also on the part of programme makers. They show that some viewers take the discourses of the speakers in the programme at face value (transparent readings) while others display an awareness of the manipulation of those discourses by the programme makers (mediated readings). Different interpretative frames are deployed by viewers depending on whether or not they take the programme at face value.

A similar distinction is noted by Elizabeth Frazer in her study of how *Jackie*, a popular British magazine, is read by teenage girls. In discussing the problems that arise from construing readers as 'in the grip of ideology', she proposes a more useful way of considering the determinacy of texts – the ways they set the agenda for readers – in terms of what she calls 'discourse registers' which she characterizes as 'institutionalized, situationally specific, culturally familiar, public ways of talking'. The force of this concept is neatly demonstrated by her own experiment with the girls in the groups she was working with. Noting that while talking about the problem pages in the magazine the girls tended to laugh – the problems weren't real problems, the advice offered was stupid – she invited some of them to write about their own real problems and others to write helpful replies. The results, in every case, were written in the same style and had the same content as the magazine they rubbished. They were, Frazer suggests, unable to think outside the conceptual frame, the public discourse register, of the magazine. Frazer further notes that the manner in which she discussed *Jackie* with the girls had its own particular discourse register that affected what was (and could) be said.

Peter Dahlgren makes a similar distinction in his discussion of how viewers make sense of TV news. He notes that, in his own small-scale reception research, he found that people tended to talk about news in a particular way, producing responses they felt were appropriate to the situation. It was difficult to get beyond this. It is partly a matter of what is being talked about – news is something serious and important and in talking about it people assume a citizenship role – but it is partly a matter of the interviewing situation and measuring up to the expectations of the professional researcher. When Dahlgren abandoned his initial formal research methods in favour of more unobtrusive approaches, he found that people talked differently. Thus he proposes a distinction between modes of official discourse for public consumption and modes of personal discourse for private interactions. The distinction is, he notes, similar to that drawn by Goffman (1969) between front- and back-stage performances. However Dahlgren's attention is less on the context and performance than on the variations in discourse within the two broad domains of public and private that he proposes.

Dahlgren draws on the concept of 'polysemy', a term deployed by John Fiske (1987: 15 ff.) to refer to the plurality of meanings both in television 'texts' and the ways in which they are interpreted by viewers as makers of meanings. Klaus Bruhn Jensen takes issue with Fiske's claims that the capacity to produce alternative or oppositional readings of television texts is politically 'empowering'. Rather the reverse, Jensen argues. His respondents (mainly American academics) reveal, in their accounts of watching TV news, the extent to which the discourses of news are remote from the actual circumstances of their daily lives. They may attend to news in order to be politically informed or, more vaguely, to feel 'in touch', but the world of public events and discourses that is routinely reproduced in nightly news has no direct connection with the day-to-day lives of viewers who feel disempowered in relation to the public world of politics and its discourses.

The patterns of cultural consumption and their relation to material and symbolic wealth as the expression of social status and life-style has always been a central concern of our journal. The consumption of high cultural forms – opera, ballet, cinema, orchestral music and theatre – may affirm not merely a sense of personal identity and self-worth through their enjoyment but also a public, social entitlement to opinions about them (cf. Bourdieu, 1984: 18 ff.). Not everyone, however, is so entitled as Susan Kippax shows in her sympathetic study of Australian middle-class women – mostly unwaged – for whom the enjoyment of such things has only an inner, private resonance. In public, social contexts they express their views tentatively and with diffidence. They do not possess their opinions because they are not entitled to them.

The media and public life

What emerges from such studies of audience responses is a distinction between public and private, formal and informal, institutional and interpersonal that is embedded in the character of the communicative context and the forms of discourse appropriate to that context. One powerful way of formulating this distinction for analytic purposes is in terms of system- and life-world (Habermas, 1991; White, 1989: 90–127). For Habermas, drawing on Weber's concept of rationalization as central to modernity, the system-world refers to those abstract universal systems of money and power (bureaucratic, legal and political) which organize and sustain contemporary social life, and to which members of modern societies are necessarily subject, not as distinct individuals but as identical and indistinguishable members of a totality. The life-world refers to the domain of everyday existence as it is experienced and made sense of directly, differently and uniquely by every individual human being as an intelligent social actor. The distinction bears some similarity to that between *langue* and *parole* in Saussurian linguistics. In line with the intellectual tradition that runs from Marx, Weber and Lukács to the Frankfurt School, Habermas thinks of these two worlds as separate but interdependent. The logic of the system-world, governed by its in-strumental rationality, is in constant tension with the inherently unstable and unsystematic life-world governed by communicative rationality. Although the process of modernity can be understood as the increasing domination and colonization of the life-world by the system-world, this process can never be completed since it is from the constantly renewed sources of the life-world that human motivations and values, definitions of the good life and legitimations of the social order all ultimately spring.

How do the media fit into Habermas's schematic model? With their feet in both worlds how do they manage the tension between instrumental and communicative rationality? To what extent do they, in their structures and practices, extend the dominance of the system-world by pacifying and systematizing the experiences of the life-world? Or, on the contrary, to what extent do they necessarily, because of their need to ensure continuing audience loyalty by drawing on the experiences of the life-world, foster the change-bearing and value-laden eruption of those experiences and their communicative rationality into the abstract world of the systems? Habermas himself has paid little attention to the media in his recent writings, but their role was central to his early and influential historical analysis of the public sphere or realm (Habermas, 1989), and the critical issues raised in that analysis remain central to his later concerns.

John Downing offers a brief resumé of what Habermas meant by the public realm before turning to the concept of the 'alternative public realm'. Habermas had developed his historical thesis of the public realm as an institution of bourgeois society. In Germany, in the political context of the 1960s and 70s, there was a vigorous debate around this formulation, particularly in relation to the possibilities for alternative, proletarian or oppositional public spheres. The work of Oskar Negt and Alexander Kluge was influential in this respect and Downing critically reviews their position before turning to an examination of the radical media in West Germany as an alternative public realm, with particular emphasis on their opposition to nuclear power. In his discussion Downing draws attention to 'the strange failure' of analysts of the alternative realm to link it to the history of popular culture, for it is from within the ranks of the general public that resistance and opposition to state policy emerges.

Downing argues that in West Germany an oppositional political culture, in which an alternative public realm could flourish, has been better sustained in recent years than in Great Britain. Colin Sparks suggests some reasons why this may be so in his critical analysis of the British press. It was a central part of Habermas's thesis that a political public sphere, in its classic form, developed in Britain between the mid-eighteenth and nineteenth centuries. This political public sphere was nourished by a vigorous political press which constituted an open forum for critical review and reasoned discussion of the activities of the state, and as such was crucial in the formation of rationally informed public opinion. The notion that this is still the role of the press lingers on, but Sparks effectively demolishes it. It is no longer possible to speak of the *news*paper as a unitary category. Rather there are two kinds of journalism in the UK that have developed in the course of this century in response to economic and political pressures (Sparks, 1991). There is the serious broadsheet press that still performs a (more or less critical) informational role and there is the popular tabloid press that supplies little news but much entertainment. It is beside the point to lament the depoliticized character of the tabloid press, Sparks argues. Market conditions, the political realities of bourgeois democracies and the growing internationalization of the media all combine to persuade people to opt out of the political public sphere. Thus the depoliticized nature of contemporary popular culture is not an effect of the passivity of the masses, their lack of education and so on, but a consequence of the irrelevance of politics in the contexts of daily life. 'Most of the things that happen in news are not things that I think are important to me.' That quote, from an American professor of physiology, with which Klaus Bruhn Jensen ends his discussion of television news, everyday consciousness and political action in Chapter 10 neatly points up the riddle that Sparks identifies. It is harder to explain why people should want to be politically informed than why they should prefer fun with the *Sun*.

But how has this depoliticization of the public sphere come about? In his original thesis Habermas pointed to the 'refeudalization' of public life in late capitalism. The power of the state to stage-manage politics through the arts of public relations (appropriated from the techniques of market research and 'image management' in the promotion of consumer goods), crisis management and the control of information combined, he argued, to commodify contemporary politics as public rituals and displays performed for consuming (as distinct from discussing) publics. Philip Schlesinger's review of recent studies of news production links to a wider reassessment that is now taking place in the sociology of journalism, which has a considerable bearing upon how we conceive of the conditions for the very functioning of a critical political public sphere. Increasingly there is a shift away from 'media-centric' analyses of how news media relate to official and other sources of information. A dominant line of argument until recently has been Hall et al.'s (1978) view that the media act as secondary definers of an agenda whose primary definers are the powerful. However, questions are now being posed about the very notion of the coherence of primary definition (Schlesinger, 1990). And, in line with this, studies have been undertaken into the variability of news sources' ability successfully to manage political agendas (Ericson et al., 1989; Tiffen, 1989). Although such work still recognizes the importance of inequality of access to processes of mass communication, it has introduced a greater sense of the negotiated nature of definitional processes, thereby making a break with the essentially structuralist model employed by theorists of ideological hegemony.

Schlesinger's essay considers what we can learn about the conditions for the functioning of a political public sphere by a focus on moments of political crisis. The Vietnam and Falklands wars, or the kidnapping by the Red Brigades of the Italian premier, Aldo Moro, throw into relief the relations between media and the state, and test to the limits the institutional mechanisms of information control and the boundaries of political dissent. Recent research is divided between those who take a nuanced and conjunctural view of the degree of openness or closure that liberal democratic states may concede to the media, and those who perceive an increasing rationalization of state–media relationships. The debate over which direction research should take is set to continue (Schudson, 1989; Curran, 1990).

So can a plausible defence of the contemporary media as a public sphere be mounted? Paddy Scannell attempts to do so for the tradition of public service broadcasting in Britain. He argues, drawing on a wealth of historical evidence, that the real effect of public service broadcasting has been to grant people greater access to the processes of public life than any known broadcasting arrangement, and that it has likewise transformed the language and style of political life into a form more approximate to the norms of everyday life. Broadcasting has not only enormously extended the range of public discourse (what can be talked about in public) but at the same time it has transformed communicative styles of interaction in public, shifting from older authoritarian modes of address to more egalitarian, interpersonal ways of talking. In so doing it has radically demystified politics and granted the possibility of political speech to the majority of the population, and as such it has been a profoundly democratic force.

Nevertheless, Scannell notes the limits within which this historical process has developed. Although broadcasting has given voices to the voiceless and created new communicative entitlements for social groups previously excluded from public discourses, these developments have been subject to the constraints of mass representative democracy whose interests broadcasting must serve as part of its remit from the nation–state. Communicative entitlements in radio and television are unequally distributed between public persons, speaking as authoritative representatives of powerful institutions, who are entitled to opinions in news and current affairs, and private persons, speaking only as themselves, who are merely entitled to their experiences.

Conclusion

The public sphere is a mediating category between the state and civil society, system- and life-world. The press and broadcasting are part of the public world and the general scope of their activity is constrained by the operations of markets and the regulating hand of the state. But the sphere to which they speak and in which they are consumed is that of the private and everyday, the life-world of members of modern societies. The contemporary mediatized public sphere is constituted by the intersection of these two worlds, and its products and discourses articulate their conflicting rationalities. On the one hand the press and broadcasting are caught up in the administration and management of information, a process manipulated not only by the state in relation to the discourses of politics but by capitalism in relation to the discourses of consumption (particularly advertising). On the other hand they provide everyday pleasures and enjoyment that respond to the everyday tastes and needs of whole populations.

At the heart of the concept of the public sphere is a moral concern for communication that is non-dominative, non-manipulative and non-instrumental. A normative social order, grounded in justice and truth, is discovered by consensus-forming debate. It is this, Nicholas Garnham observes, which 'ultimately underlies the concept of the public sphere and of the political centrality of free communication within the western tradition'. At the present time, he concludes, 'there is a growing tension between the globalization of the communications and cultural market at the economic level and the role of the nation–state at a political level. We need to rethink the concept of citizenship in the modern world in relation to a re-examination of the locus and powers of the institutions of representative democracy and their appropriate regulatory relationship to the system of cultural production' (Garnham, 1990: 4, 18–19). Such concerns have been central to the intellectual trajectory of this journal and the contributions that make up the final section of this, our second reader.

References

Adorno, T. and M. Horkheimer (1979) *Dialectic of Enlightenment*. London: Verso.

Bourdieu, P. (1984) *Distinction. A Sociological Critique of the Judgement of Taste*. London: Routledge.

Collins, R., N. Garnham and G. Locksley (1988) *The Economics of Television*. London: Sage Publications.

Curran, J. (1990) 'The new revisionism in mass communication research', *European Journal of Communication*, 5(2–3): 135–64.

Ericson, R.V., P.M. Baranek, and J.B.L. Chan (1989) *Negotiating Control: a Study of News Sources*. Toronto, Buffalo, London: University of Toronto Press.

Fiske, J. (1987) *Television Culture*. London: Methuen.

Garnham, N. (1990) *Capitalism and Communication*. London: Sage Publications.

Goffman, E. (1969) *The Presentation of Self in Everyday Life*. Harmondsworth: Penguin.

Habermas, J. (1989) *The Structural Transformation of the Public Sphere*. Cambridge: Polity Press.

Habermas, J. (1991) *The Theory of Communicative Action*, Vol 2, 'Lifeworld and System: a Critique of Functionalist Reason'. Cambridge: Polity Press.

Hall, S., C. Critcher, T. Jefferson, J. Clarke and B. Roberts (1978) *Policing the Crisis: Mugging, the State and Law and Order*. London: Macmillan.

Hall, S. (1980) 'Encoding/decoding', in S. Hall et al. (eds), *Culture, Media, Language*. London: Hutchinson.

Hall, S. (1986a) 'Cultural studies: two paradigms', in R. Collins et al. (eds), *Media, Culture & Society: A Critical Reader*. London: Sage Publications.

Hall, S. (1986b) 'On postmodernism and articulation: an interview with Stuart Hall', *Journal of Communication Inquiry*, 10(2): 45–60.

Scannell, P. (1991) *Broadcast Talk*. London: Sage Publications.

Schlesinger, P. (1990) 'Rethinking the sociology of journalism: source strategies and the limits of media centrism', in M. Ferguson (ed.) *Public Communication: The New Imperatives. Future Directions for Media Research*. London: Sage Publications.

Schudson, M. (1989) 'The sociology of news production', *Media Culture & Society*, 11(3): 263–82.

Sparks, C. (1991) 'Goodbye Hildy Johnson. The vanishing serious press', in Dahlgren, P. and Sparks, C. (eds) *Communication and Citizenship*. London: Routledge.

Tiffen, R. (1989) *News and Power*. Sydney: Allen & Unwin.

White, S.K. (1989) *The Recent Work of Jürgen Habermas*. Cambridge: Cambridge University Press.

Williams, R. (1958) *Culture and Society*. London: Chatto and Windus.

PART ONE
CULTURE AND POWER

they only exercised political control over some areas of society in order to promote a subordinate and inconsistent development? They claimed to be forming national cultures, yet scarcely constructed elite cultures, leaving outside enormous indigenous and peasant populations who registered their exclusion by means of a thousand revolts and by a migration that turned the city on its head. The populists acted as if they were incorporating these excluded sectors, recovering popular movements and mass culture. But without structural change, their distributivist policy in economics and culture was reversed in a few years, or diluted itself in demogogic clientelisms. Marxism, which produced explanations for the structural obstacles to economic development and social injustice, did not succeed — other than exceptionally — in making its criticism of capitalism shift toward specific studies of Latin American cultures and of their power relations, nor in making large sections of the people feel themselves represented by its proposals.

Perhaps the decisive question is not why popular cultures have now begun to take on a major role, but rather how is it possible that they have been absent from research on hegemony and the state, social change and development? Why, in a continent in which the masses have been decisive in revolutions (at least since Mexico's in 1910) has popular culture almost never been a central problem for political studies? How can we explain the fact that so many frustrated revolutions — Bolivia in 1952, the aspiration of repeating the Cuban experience in this and other countries — have not produced scientific studies of the causes diverting the masses or blocking their responses to the calls of the vanguard? Were the recent 'triumphs' of repression and monetarism necessary to make us recognize the crisis of all the strategies of modernization and social change: the developmentalisms, the populisms, the Marxisms. Since then, several states, and those on the left who take their failures seriously, have been trying to know and understand popular cultures. New conditions for the production of knowledge are arising: for the first time, culture is not just a reason for speculative reflections in literary reviews, but rather a central theme of several of the main social sciences, and at conferences in which national and international organizations analyse its relation to development and power. Above all, interest in popular cultures is growing: museums are built in order to preserve and exhibit them, research centres set up to know them, state and popular organizations created in order to promote their expansion.

If we are going to construct a first cultural map of Latin America, a social history of culture, the lack of theoretical and methodological bases for research becomes an obstacle, a central challenge. How are we to situate this search in terms of the contemporary crisis of philosophy and the social sciences, a crisis which reaches well beyond one or other paradigm, be it liberalism or Marxism, into the very project of modernity itself? How are we to confront this revision in Latin America, where the basic components of modernity have never reached into everything or touched everybody? The majority has not yet had sufficient evidence to believe that our late industrialization will generate economic growth and social improvement. And as for formal and material rationality, which according to Kant and Weber has been the West's common path, the model of democratic public space for citizens, here too we have not reached modernity. For evolutionary progressivism and democratic rationalism are not wont to be amongst our popular causes.

Beyond the epistemological crisis lies a scientific task: to acquire knowledge of Latin American societies and to create the groundwork pertinent to such knowledge. Beyond the crisis of hegemony, we confront the task of constructing states and societies with democratic goals shared by all, in which disaggregation becomes diversity, and inequalities between classes, ethnicities and regions reduce themselves into differences.

However, the debate over modernity does not seem strange to us. We can take part in it if we understand it as the need to rethink the bases of our history. Though Latin American reality differs from that of the metropolitan countries, this revision of the basics includes the process of modernization because our societies — although late, unequal and incomplete — are *also* a result of that process. They continue to be articulated to it, and therefore to its crisis, to the extent that they form a part of the capitalist system. For this reason, a point of departure for this revision must be the critical examination of the paradigms with which modern thought has come to the study of our popular cultures: we may say that the crisis of Western modernity begins (long before recent postmodernism) with the discovery of popular cultures in others' lands. Well before Westerners' lack of faith in their own utopias (of the Enlightenment, of the industrial and social revolutions) the crisis in the paradigm of modernity was born of the dread of different peoples. We have no space here in which to trace the history of the shock of difference and the questions which it engendered. We will simply analyse the tactical responses and how these sedimented themselves into structures of knowledge which persist to this day. These forms of knowing popular culture may be grouped according to two principal theoretical strategies: deductivism and inductivism.

We will call deductivist those who define popular cultures by moving from the general to the particular, according to features which they impose upon them: such as the mode of production, imperialism, the dominant class, the ideological apparatuses or the mass media. Conversely, the inductivists are those who confront the study of the popular by beginning with certain properties which they suppose to be intrinsic to the subordinate classes, or with their genius, or with a creativity that other sectors of the population have lost, or with oppositional power as the basis of their resistance. First of all, we would like to consider why these theoretico-methodological positions (which almost all of us have used a little) obstruct knowledge of popular cultures and of power. Presently, we will attempt to suggest how the logic of research might be reformulated by way of three problems: the confrontation between modernity and tradition, the role of transactions in political resistance, and the analysis of reception and of consumption.

Deduction and induction: the debate over method

How can we rigorously explain society and at the same time widely communicate this knowledge? How can we ally the objectivity of knowledge to the drama of the everyday? These questions have provoked a convergence between methodological concern and expressive quests: novelists who undertake research and social scientists who have recourse to journalism or literature (I am thinking of Rodolfo Walsh, of Darcy Ribeiro), anthropologists who explore the laws of society by means of life histories and historians who make use of popular tales to reconstruct the collective sentiments (Miguel Barnet, Carlos Monsiváis). At times, such works give us a synthetic and condensed vision of some basic problems of social knowledge.

Deductivism

We find these concerns in various theatrical works disseminated in Brazil at the outset of the 1970s by the Popular Culture Centres. One of these, *José da Silva and the Guardian Angel* portrayed an average day in the life of a Brazilian in order to reveal the minute effects of imperialism in everyday life. From the moment he wakes up and switches on the light José pays his dues to foreign companies (Light and Power). And so it goes on when he cleans his teeth (Colgate Palmolive), drinks coffee (American Coffee Company), when he goes to work whether in a Mercedes Benz bus or walking on his Goodyear soles, or when he goes to the cinema to see a western (Hollywood produces more than half the films shown in Brazil). Even inside the cinema, when he simply breathes the air, this is conditioned by Westinghouse. Made desperate by so many royalty payments, he decides to kill himself. But then the Guardian Angel appears, with an English accent, in order to collect Smith and Wesson's royalties from José (Boal, 1982: 23).

This conceptual approach, in which all aspects of popular life derive from macrosocial powers, has characterized the majority of sociological, communications and educational studies during the past two decades. To analyse culture was equivalent to describing the manoeuvres of dominant forces. Marxism, first in its structuralist and then its semiological guise, attempted to make a more astute analysis of the cunning of power, rather than pose questions about these models themselves, which were based on the needs provoked by new objects of study. Dependency theory provided the means for the critique of domination, demystifying imperialism and its manipulation of consciousness — the sole reason for the masses not behaving with the revolutionary energy that corresponds to their historic interests. These new objects of study — television, radio, advertising — as the cultural sectors most closely linked to the North American corporations, confirmed the fertility of dependency theory and contributed to over-estimating the impact of the dominant on popular consciousness.

Critical analyses of imperialism were not the only way of describing reality according to a deductivist methodology. Absolute powers were ascribed to the 'mode of production' when doing scientific work meant applying the categories of *Capital*, invoking the 'ideological apparatuses' during the Althusserian vogue, or pointing to the media or to the underlying codes in studies of mass communication. In all cases, deductivism depended upon two operations: first, it reified the major social actors and attributed the exclusive possession of power to them; next, it deduced effects upon popular cultures from their strategies of domination.

The fields in which this procedure was and is used with most enthusiasm are mass communication and education. Under the influence of the Frankfurt School's account of the cultural industry and Wright Mills's and Paul Baran's works on the manipulation of 'mass society', communicative power was conceived as an attribute of a monopolistic system which, administered by a minority of specialists, could impose bourgeois values and opinions upon the remaining classes. The efficacy of this system resided not only in the broad diffusion of dominant messages through the mass media, but also in the unconscious manipulation of audiences. Social and political history have insistently refuted this notion of overwhelming media power: for instance, the electoral triumph of Peronism in 1973, after eighteen years of bans in politics and communications, and the collapse of the economic and military sectors who controlled the mass media. This can only be understood if we accept that in order to promote new political responses, apart from individual perceptions media messages need 'to obtain positive sanctions from the rest of the group, especially its leaders. An individual's experience and that of his group is just as decisive, or even more so, than the possible influence of mass media' (Muraro, 1974: Ch. 3). Above all, we need to lay bare the 'theoretical' pillars which underpin deductivism in communications research. First, there is a conception of power which we might call 'theological' inasmuch as it is imagined to be omnipotent and omnipresent. Audiences and consumers are seen as passive executants of practices imposed by the dominant, incapable of distinguishing between those messages which benefit and those which harm, between the use value in given goods (which is assumed to be 'authentic') and their exchange or symbolic value (which is considered 'artificial'). The methodological consequence is the belief that purely by studying the mass media's economic aims and the ideological structure of their messages, one might deduce the needs they create in the audience. No autonomy on the part of popular cultures is recognized, nor is the complex relation between consumers, objects and social space.

In educational research, deductivism has become a kind of

common sense for the diffusion of reproductionist theories. The works of Bowles and Gintis, of Baudelot and Establet, of Bourdieu and Passeron, have reshaped the understanding of the schooling system by showing it to be the key locus for the reproduction of the class structure by means of the differential qualifications of the labour force. Demonstrating that scholastic selection and the unequal formation of social strata contribute to reproducing the productive apparatus, the labour market and the differences between classes, has served to banish the illusions of pedagogic liberals who saw the school as a medium for overcoming socio-economic inequalities. However, by subordinating the condition of the popular classes to the place in which they are fixed by social and educational reproduction, all the initiative is reserved for the dominant sectors. It is they who determine the path of development, the possibilities of access for each class, the cultural contents that unite or separate the parts of a nation. In the most radical versions of reproductionism, all aspects of popular cultures, including those well outside the framework of the school — such as artistic tastes, eating habits, the organization of the household — are seen as impoverished imitations of the dominant culture resulting from their subaltern position (Bourdieu, 1979: Chs. 1 and 7).

Juan Carlos Tedesco has made two criticisms of the application of the reproductionist model to Latin America: first, this paradigm organizes relations between dominant and dominated sectors as though it concerned the simple 'imposition of a cultural order focused on the disciplining of the labour force'. However, in our continent educational demands and the expansion of schooling are not purely linked to economic questions, but rather with the formation of national states and the 'achievement of a certain basic cultural homogeneity. In this sense, the most dynamic actor has been the state and not the entrepreneurs, the industrial bourgeoisie or any other "private" sector of society'. As for reproductionist explanations of the construction of consensus and domination, Tedesco says that such theories have more validity in societies with strong ideological and institutional integration. But in Latin America where

> . . . the peculiarity is a hegemonic crisis, instability and structural and cultural heterogeneity . . . a theoretical orientation exclusively centred on the mechanisms of reproduction runs the risk of leaving out of analytical focus the major

developments which are being produced inside the social structure in general
and on the ideological plane in particular. (Tedesco, 1983: 60, 62)

As for those studies that barely see the shadow of the dominant
culture in popular culture, let us recall that the coexistence of
various cultural capitals in every Latin American society (especially
in the multi-ethnic ones) sustains formations different from that
which reproduces the hegemonic order. In huge areas of Bolivia,
Peru, Paraguay, Nicaragua, Guatemala and Mexico, the indigenes
do not speak, or speak little, Spanish, and keep up customs of
production and consumption, feasts and rituals quite alien to
Western modernity. In Brazil, most of the Caribbean and other
areas of the continent, black cultures still maintain their own
cultural forms. The adoption of their handicrafts and works of art
by national cultures simulates an integration that destroys; nor can
we clearly see the daily practices, and in some cases the political
movements, by means of which they defend their autonomy.
Whatever the relative subordination of large sectors, neither these
movements nor these practices nor the major part of their artistic
life may be defined by reference to the dominant culture nor may
they be simply analysed in terms of disadvantages or insufficiencies.

The deductivist tendencies have produced more obstacles to
discovering the life of the popular classes than knowledge about
them. But we shall leave the discussion of how to know the
popular until the next section, when we consider the inductivists.
The critique of deductivism is part of a critique of that which it is
said to investigate: power. Today, we think of this not as blocs of
institutional structures, with pre-established, fixed tasks (to
dominate, to manipulate), nor as mechanisms for imposing order
from the top downwards, but rather as a social relation diffused
throughout all spaces. In Foucault's words, we do not need to
search for power at 'a central point, in one unique focus of
sovereignty from which derivative and dependent forms radiate
outwards'. Given that 'it is not something that may be acquired', it
cannot be trapped inside an institution, in the schools, in the
television channels or in the state. It is not a particular capacity
with which some are endowed: 'it is the name which is applied to a
strategic situation in a given society'. There are multiple relations
of force which are formed and actuated in production, in families
and individuals, which reinforce themselves in their conjoint
operation in all those spaces (Foucault, 1978a: 112–15). Neverthe-

less, unlike Foucaultian analyses, our recognition of this decentring of power must not lead us to ignore how power sediments itself and concentrates itself in social institutions and agents. If all that we see is disseminated power, it is impossible to hierarchize the actions of different 'instances' or 'apparatuses': the power of the transnationals is not the same as that of the head of a family.

A complementary line, running from Gramsci to various recent anthropologists, teaches that each form of domination secures itself by ceasing to be domination as such, by converting itself into hegemony. It is very convenient to condense the responsibility for the material and ideological organization of popular life into abstractions such as 'the bourgeoisie', 'imperialism' or 'the media'. But this conception contains two problems. One is that it suppresses the internal heterogeneity of the hegemonic and subordinate sectors: for the deductivists, the dominant are just one bloc and the dominated another. In consequence, studies emphasize the most obvious acts of subjection, without considering either how the dominant concern themselves with some of the needs of the dominated or the legitimatory responses that they arouse in some sections of the people. Even those who defend the dictatorships know that forced consent is unstable, and so they try to make their actions look useful to the oppressed. We are not denying the amount of violence, actual or virtual, which domination and inequality always imply. What we would like to say, in line with many anthropological examples given by Godelier, is that in order for relations of domination and exploitation to reproduce themselves in lasting form 'they need to present themselves as an exchange, and an exchange of services' between classes (Godelier, 1978: 176–83). Hegemonic classes achieve this position to the extent that, over and above their sectoral interests, they include those aspects of popular cultures in the function and meaning of institutions, objects and messages, that render them useful and significant for the majority. If we do not see the people as a quiescent mass which always submits to illusions about what it wants, we will admit that its dependence is, in part, due to finding that aspects of hegemonic activity meet some of its needs. Take, for example, the peasant migrants who feel that their local culture (language, everyday customs, beliefs about the natural order) makes it difficult for them to participate in urban life. Many of them receive from mass culture the information necessary for them to understand and to act 'correctly' in the new conditions which enables them to come out of isolation, to cease being 'inferior'. Perhaps we can understand why television — including advertising for things they cannot buy — is so attractive to them, if, rather than criticizing domination we examine the service that it offers the popular classes as a 'handbook of urbanity' which tells one how to dress, to eat, to express feelings in the city.

To recognize this does not minimize the fact of exploitation. It merely helps us to understand why the oppressed, who recognize that this service is not entirely illusory, offer their consent, give a certain legitimacy to hegemony. By dealing with hegemony and dominance, the linkage between the classes rests less upon violence than upon contract, an alliance in which the hegemonic and the subaltern covenant 'reciprocal' prestations. The objective and subjective importance of this exchange explains why exploitation does not always appear on the surface of social relations. It also explains the success of populist politics and communication, not so much as a manipulative operation as for its capacity to comprehend this interlocking, this reciprocal necessity, between opposing classes. The fragility of these inter-class alliances in Latin America derives, amongst other things, from the difficulties that the hegemonic classes have in combining the development of the distribution of consumption and the growth of production.

First conclusion. This section could have been titled 'behaviour in lifts'. For in the theories which we have reviewed, social classes are compact groups which either rise or fall; they do not appear to develop other activities apart from aligning themselves inside a bloc which will move upwards or struggle to achieve that end. Often, descriptions of class struggles give the impression that while they are being undertaken it is as if all interaction were suspended — just as in a lift; as though inside each class, relations were impersonal and between persons unknown to one another. There is no drama. It is as if there were no internal differences and conflicts between those who side with those in control and those who basically distance themselves, those who come first or last, those who arrive in family groups or travel alone. We call deductivist those macrosocial theories that use 'the great movements of history' to make sense of what happens in subordinate groups — theories apt to forget that such movements construct themselves according to interactions basic to groups in everyday life, and that they sometimes fail by trying to do without them.

Inductivism

The spread of inductive procedures in studies of the popular in Latin America is due to a convergence of two diverse currents: North American-style anthropological culturalism, and populist doctrines. Anthropology and folklore, which for decades were the only scientific disciplines focused upon knowing the popular — by virtue of their restriction of the object of study — have contributed to identifying it with the traditional, the peasant and the indigenous, isolating supposedly immanent properties of these 'traditional communities'. Whilst populist conceptions, from Third Worldism to those of the left, have over-estimated 'innate' values or a certain impermeability of the popular classes to change.

Anthropology and folklore

The confrontation between colonizing and colonized countries in the nineteenth century and at the beginning of the twentieth demanded that peoples strange to the West be recognized as an object of study. The anthropologists who accompanied the mercantile and political expansion of the metropolises produced knowledge of and reflections upon their own modernity which in part contradicted the imperialist project. In the recovery of forms of thinking and acting, despised until then, anthropology reformulated the Eurocentric notion of culture and the paradigm for its study which was derived from evolutionist utopias. The later industrial and urban expansion of the dependent countries deepened this process, incorporating indigenous groups, 'traditional' communities and ultimately the 'marginalized' sectors of the large cities into each national culture and into scientific culture generally. However, the predominant line in these studies was the minute investigation of isolated communities, as if they did not share in the country's changes or changes in the transnational economic system. Those studies, which are very sensitive to the specificity of each group, tended to mark their *difference* without explaining the *inequality* which confronts them — and links them — to other sectors.

Cultural relativism, with which one conceals the distances between unequal cultures, affirming that all are valuable in their own way, is a form of pride, a sign that the relativists secretly consider themselves superior. (Géza Róheim used to say that to listen to the anthropologists preaching relativism was like hearing 'You are completely different, but I forgive you for it.') Relativist egalitarianism has even less credibility in the study of different groups interacting in the same society; when the issue to be resolved is the conflict between the symphonies of Mozart, jazz, *la salsa* and rock, then it is argued that they are all equally distinctive ways of expressing oneself, all equally worthwhile. Unless we situate some musical forms alongside others, together with the groups which accept or reject them, we will not be able to explain their coexistence, nor the various ways in which audiences are composed. Latin American cultures are not embalmed traditions; they are the conflictual result of relations between highly diverse groups, with common or convergent histories, which may now no longer exist separately. Cultural relativism leaves us two unresolved problems. One is of an epistemological kind: how can we construct a universally valid knowledge which goes beyond each culture's particularities and which isn't simply imposed by the dominant culture on the rest. The other is of a political kind: how, in an increasingly interdependent world may one establish criteria for the cohabitation of and interaction between different classes, ethnic groups and nations? The answers are beginning to emerge in those anthropological studies which go beyond the traditional and atomized conception of the popular, locating indigenous and marginal groups in macrosocial structures and processes. The broadening out of the concept of the popular and the reworking of its problematic are especially evident in studies of urbanization and the working class, and the interaction between traditional cultures and modernity (studies of migrants, the mass consumption of handicrafts, the reception of modern cultural goods amongst the subaltern classes).

Folklore takes anthropological traditionalism to extremes. Not only does it limit the popular to its peasant and native manifestations; with the exception of those who follow Gramsci and a few besides, it reduces research to the gathering of objects and a description of their formal characteristics. Thus, the majority of texts on traditional handicrafts, feasts and music, catalogue and extol popular products without situating them in the current logic of social relations. This decontextualization is particularly palpable in the folklore or popular arts museums which exhibit receptacles and textiles stripped of all references to their daily uses. Those that include contemporary forms of popular culture are exceptional. They limit themselves to listing and classifying fragments that represent traditions and stand out by virtue of their resistance or indifference to change. 'Thinking of "popular culture" as synonymous with "tradition"', states Antonio Augusto Arantes, alluding to Brazil (although this also applies to the rest of Latin America)

> . . . is to reaffirm the idea that its Golden Age is revealed in the past. Consequently, the successive modifications through which those objects, conceptions and practices necessarily pass cannot be understood except as disturbances and an impoverishment. Things that might have had validity in the past may be interpreted today as curiosities. From this point of view, 'popular culture' appears as 'another culture', which by contrast with dominant, cultivated knowledge, appears to be a 'totality', although in reality it has been constructed by means of the juxtaposition of residual and fragmentary elements considered resistant to a 'natural' process of wear and tear. (Arantes, 1981: 17–18)

This conception of the popular is influential in academic circles, but even more so in the production and distribution of knowledge in state institutions and in the mass media. It appears in museums and in books, as we have pointed out, and also in programmes about folklore on radio and television, and in artistic groups that recreate traditional music and dance for urban publics, displaying the product and obscuring the social process that engendered it, selecting what is best adapted to the 'Western' aesthetic and eliminating the signs of poverty or the conflicts that lie at the root of a song or dance. Folklore brings about a double reduction: of the plurality and diversity of popular cultures to the unity of national 'art' or 'music'; and of social processes into objects or the codified expressions that they acquired in the past.

Populism

Although good analyses of the political movements and ideological strategies that fall under this label exist, we know little of that central question for populism — its use of culture to build power. A question that is never asked is what happens to the culture of the popular sectors in populist movements? If we accept the definition that best characterizes these movements as a politico-ideological phenomenon — Ernesto Laclau's (1978: 201) view that 'populism consists in the presentation of the popular–democratic interpellations as a synthetic–antagonistic unity with respect to the dominant ideology' in order to neutralize popular demands (bourgeois populism) or in order to develop them (socialist populism) — we would have to treat it as a deductivist current. Who 'presents' the interpellations? The leadership of the populist movement? Do they constitute the people from the balcony of the government palace, from the dais, from the positions of power? But how do the people participate in this process and what happens to their culture if it is to 'become' populist?

In an earlier study (García Canclini, 1983), I analysed two of the most common positions. The first is what I labelled the biologico-telluric approach which naturalizes culture by assuming that the people are an innate force, a unity constituted through physical bonds (geographical, spacial, racial) or irrational bonds (a love for the same land, a religion that expresses 'natural' truths). This style of thought (which is characteristic of how nature is related to history where the productive forces are at a low stage of development) benefits the oligarchic sectors who are hegemonic in those periods. The other conception, which I have called statist, is generated outside the subaltern classes, and consists in their accepting that the state gives expression to popular values, whether revolutionary or national, and that it conciliates the interests of all and arbitrates their conflicts. The corporatist organization of this popular 'participation' may be supported by the mythologized figure of a leader (Vargas, Perón) or by a party–state structure held together hierarchically (the Mexican system).

What will happen now to the populist movements, as the international economic crisis and the monetarist reorganization of society eliminate their economic bases (there is no surplus to redistribute), as the military dictatorships and/or the loss of representativeness of the great parties make it difficult for the popular sectors to find forms of participation? Populism has become an almost impracticable option from the point of view of hegemony. I say 'almost' because whatever the economic and organizational shortcomings, there are two forms in which it can be revived: authoritarian populism, like Galtieri's ephemeral achievement during the Malvinas War, and populism as a cultural system of the subordinate groups. I should like to point out that the second form of populism is not just a consequence of a cultural 'inertia' that persists when the underlying economic and political conditions have disappeared; but it is actually a line propounded by various leftist tendencies. Given the crisis in the political apparatuses and the ideological models, a belief in the 'natural purity' of the people as the sole recourse is re-emerging amongst 'movements of the base', 'alternatives' and groups emanating from the populist parties. I would like to illustrate this by reference to a recent novel, based on the testimony of a survivor of the Argentinian concentration camps, which both attempts to be a global denunciation of this tragic period and an autocritique of the populist left. I am speaking of Miguel Bonasso's *Recuerdos de la muerte (Reminiscences of Death)*.

Beneath its narrative brilliance and its engrossing, clear-cut plot, Bonasso's book invites a complex debate about the relations between literature and political culture. One polemical point concerns the limits involved in choosing the thriller form for an evaluation of political violence and a rethinking of one's own participation in it: to turn a crime novel into an historical drama is to prefer action to reflection, to concede to action the initiating and self-justifying space given to guerrilla insurrectionism. But let us go on to consider another question, more central to this paper, namely the metaphysical conception upon which the guerrilla bases his populism.

The novel describes the military's repression of the Montoneros and their aim to incorporate them into the order imposed by the dictatorship. The military, quoting Saint Thomas Aquinas, say that the guerrillas must be destroyed, obliterated, for they aim to change a 'natural order' imagined as established for all time, inscribed in the human race. Although the novel attacks this naturalization of the social, it nevertheless makes the same move when characterizing the people. It supposes that the more men are close to nature (for instance, those living in the countryside, or at least in the provinces) the better they preserve their moral purity and a 'clean' intellect: El Pelado, a leading Montonero, kidnapped and afraid of being liquidated, nevertheless, thanks to his 'old provincial guile', knows that he is 'the protagonist of a hidden occult contradiction between those men, and, perhaps, between those two institutions', the church and the navy (Bonasso, 1984: 106). Kidnapped and confused, neither the guerrilla's logistical precautions could stop him from being captured, nor could the ideological and political knowledge proper to a leader enable him to understand what is going on; but the 'old provincial guile' enables him to make sense of the secret contradiction between the main military forces.

Another scene: in the concentration camp at Rosario, almost all
the city's Montonero membership is collaborating with the army
but pretends instead to be working for an alliance with 'nationalist'
soldiers (under military pressure going so far as to publish journals
and leaflets from this 'organization'). All is false, but El Pelado
encounters authenticity in a provincial soldier who is guarding
him. Although this guard is a representative of those who torture
him, ensuring that the rebel guerrilla remains 'shackled to the
metal bed by one hand and one foot', on observing his 'swarthy
complexion' and believing him to be a young man from the
interior, El Pelado thinks that in his oppressor he has found 'a
thousand signs of a life in the open air'; although he criticizes those
who believe in the opportunistic illusion that amongst the military
there were those who 'were seeking the good of the country', El
Pelado says that in this soldier he sees 'the professional bonhomie
of the barracks enriched by the native wit of a man from the
countryside' (Bonasso, 1984: 131).

The novel maintains that from 1952 onwards (which it locates as
the origin of Peronism's and the country's decadence) Argentinian
history has been a series of diversions, betrayals and bitter lessons.
Only the people can save itself from the precipice.

> While the national bourgeoisie began to vacillate and defect, while the Peronist
> Party converted itself into an empty shell, while the big trades unions became
> sclerosed in bureaucratic madness, and power was corrupted by the arrivistes
> and undermined by the military, they remained faithful to their identity. The
> only faithful ones. (Bonasso, 1984: 32–3)

Where do these intuitions and this fidelity come from, that keep
the people's 'naturalness' intact? We become aware of it when
Bonasso (1984: 361) describes the massive mobilization of Novem-
ber 1972, on the day Perón returned from exile: 'The rarefaction
of reality is all-encompassing, the very pampa itself brings forth
the obscure certainty that all is permitted. Anything could
happen.' The social sciences, ironically devalued by the novel, are
no use in understanding popular processes. 'It would be trifling to
say that these are social or political phenomena, because they are
something more: they are better accounted for as atmospheric, or
cosmic.' It is only possible to comprehend them by listening to the
Earth — a telluric and national–popular irrationalism. These two
obstacles need to be overcome for this very valuable denunciation
of military terror to reach the roots of the conflict, for it to be more

than a denunciation of the oppressors and a recognition of some shortcomings of the guerrilla campaign, for interrogating the way in which the Montoneros' politics defined and aimed to represent popular interests.

Second conclusion. What do folklore and populism have in common? Both choose particular or 'concrete' empirical objects, absolutize their immediate and apparent features, and starting with these features, inductively infer the social location and historical destiny of the popular classes. Just as anthropology autonomizes traditional communities, the folklore of archaic objects and the populism of a natural wisdom of the oppressed fail to address the problem of the relative success with which capitalism has reorganized Latin American cultures and societies. Although the inefficacy of hegemony and persistent popular resistance prevent us from deducing how each group lives from imperialist or mass media policies, we should not fall into the opposite error: that of imagining that the oppressed classes conserve intact an ahistorical essence or are capable of determining for themselves, quite independently, the global changes that confront them.

One methodological consequence of this immanentist conception of popular cultures is that it analyses their situation purely from the actors' point of view. Given that the interviewee defines himself as a native, research consists in 'recovering' what he does in his own terms, the anthropological or folkloristic task being reduced to 'faithfully' duplicating the informant's discourse; or, if he defines himself as a worker, since nobody knows better than he what is happening to him, it is necessary to believe that his condition and his class consciousness are as he presents them. This ingenuous empiricism disregards the divergence between what we think and our practices, between the popular classes' self-definition and what we can know of their lives by reference to the laws of society: it acts as if to know means heaping up facts according to their 'spontaneous' appearance, instead of conceptually constructing the relations that give them their meaning in the social logic.

However, it is not only the question of knowledge that is in play. When deductivism and inductivism fail to think about the discrepancy between macrosocial laws and the actual conditions of the popular classes, what they also exclude is the problem of political failure: why hegemony fails to reproduce itself in the everyday life of some sectors, why so many popular projects for transformation do not manage to alter the social structure. To respond to these questions it is necessary to go much further than doctrinaire affirmations such as 'we need dialectically to interrelate the theoretical and the empirical'. What we actually need is to create conceptual tools that articulate the social order to the conditions peculiar to each group. But here we are now discovering several problems on the borders between deductivism and inductivism, in the lacunae left by both. We shall see how far it is worth pursuing these.

Critical itineraries

A first requirement is to delimit the scope of popular culture and the conditions for its study. It is not enough to say that it does not echo the hegemonic culture or that it is not an autonomous creation of the subaltern classes. Research must grasp the three processes through which they constitute themselves: (a) the unequal appropriation of economic and cultural goods on the part of different classes, ethnic and social groups in production and consumption; (b) the characteristic elaboration of their conditions of life and the specific satisfaction of their needs; (c) the conflictual interaction of the popular and hegemonic classes for the appropriation of goods, and the exchanges that counterbalance conflicts and renew interaction. Since this formula does not result in an agreed recognition of those three parallel processes, it is necessary to see how they are articulated in the specific context of research.

Modernity vs. tradition?

One of the most used schemes for defining the situation of popular cultures is to locate them in opposition to modernity. The inductivists, as we have seen, identify the popular with the traditional. Deductivism maintains that capitalist expansion inexorably eliminates traditional cultures. How then can we explain the continued existence of those cultures in advanced countries? What are we to make of the fact that Mexico, for instance, even after rapid industrialization since the 1940s still has the largest number of artisans on the continent — some six million people? Why in recent years has the volume of production been increasing and why has the state been multiplying organizations aimed at promoting work that occupies 10 percent of the population but hardly represents 0.1 percent of the gross national product? (Becerril-Strafon, 1979: 1). In Peru we encounter similar figures: the 1977–8 estimates speak of 700,000 artisans, concentrated not in the low development areas, but with 29 percent of them in the city of Lima (Lauer, 1982: 78). It is impossible to go on maintaining that small workshops are questionable entities in this century and artisans an atavistic sector condemned to dissolve into the industrial proletariat.

In a study we conducted in Mexico, we observed that the growth of artisanal production was caused by the combined action of factors peculiar to the unequal development of capitalism in a dependent country and others that had to do with the history of indigenous and mixed race groups. From a macrosocial point of view, the growth of workshops may be explained by the lack of resources for indigenes and peasants afforded by agricultural production: they therefore need to seek supplementary earnings. Furthermore, the workshops are a tourist attraction and a means for renewing urban consumption by introducing new designs, some variety and imperfection at low cost into the serial production of industrial objects; these permit consumers to differentiate themselves as individuals and to establish symbolic relations with the 'natural', the 'primitive' and the 'popular'. In the Mexican case, workshops additionally serve as a means for making national identity visible, as a locus in which traditions common to all classes are revitalized. For these and other reasons, the state and several sections of the bourgeoisie are interested in promoting artisanry. In the same way as occurs with other popular practices — indigenous festivals, traditional medicine — capitalist develop-ment does not always need to eliminate the economic and cultural forces that do not directly serve its growth, if these forces nevertheless cohere into a significant sector, which satisfies its needs or those of a balanced reproduction of the system.

However, those explanations do not go far enough for us to grasp the advance of artisanal production. Why do the peasants produce handicrafts instead of other kinds of objects? Why do they not emigrate in larger numbers or seek occupations in their own areas in commercial or touristic activities, as some do? The answers can come only from the popular groups themselves. Artisanal production, from labour process to iconography, maintains forms of organization, traditions and beliefs dating from pre-Columbian times. Workshops in many villages represent a continuity of integration between productive activities and (when the workshops are in one's own home) family life; therefore, at times one finds that artisans do not resist changes of design adapted to urban tastes so much as programmes of technical modernization (gas kilns instead of wood-burning ones or mechanical looms) that imply moving into collective workshops on a salaried basis where the unity between family life and work is obliterated (García Canclini, 1982: Ch. 4).

This is precisely to retrieve, in the course of research, the two-sidedness of cultural production: it is *historical* (a process that gives identity to ethnic groups) and *structural* (within the present logic of dependent capitalism). The inductivist temptation is to isolate the ethnic-historical aspect and to consider artisanry purely as an instrument of cultural self-affirmation. The deductivist temptation is the reverse: to attend only to the macrostructural meaning of artisanry, almost always economic, and to study it just like any object regulated by a mercantile logic, or as a twilight survival of disappearing groups.

Indigenous cultures cannot exist in total autonomy, nor are they mere atypical appendages of a capitalism devouring all before it. Although there are situations in which both occur, more as a political project than as effective reality, it seems to us that the most widespread problem in Latin America, especially in multiethnic societies, is how to work with heterogeneous cultural processes that express conflicts between diverse groups. One of these is the persistence of forms of communal and domestic organization in the economy and culture, or their remains (also to be found in urban migrants' districts) whose interaction with the hegemonic system gives rise to highly varied formations. These cultural forms are accompanied by their own structures of power — *mayordomías, compradazgos*, relations of reciprocity and solidarity that complicate the articulation with the bourgeois or national system of representation and power. These structures internal to the groups are evaluated in opposing ways that depend on the observer's position: deductivists see them as obstacles to modernity, as reproducing archaic hierarchies and inequalities; inductivists find in these ancient forms of power the base through which popular groups preserve their autonomy and resist outside domination. Beyond the doctrinaire affirmation of one or other perspective (which may be politically justifiable) for the sake of knowledge (and even perhaps for political purposes) it is interesting to understand what happens during processes of change.

Political resistance and everyday transactions

Aprioristic political positions are wont to result in a Manichean approach. The schematic use of Gramsci and of those Italian anthropologists (Cirese, Lombardi Satriani) who have developed his analysis of culture and power, has contributed to making an intellectual habit of the contraposition between the hegemonic and the subaltern. In fact, in Lombardi Satriani (1975), the schism between both terms or between 'narcotizing' and 'oppositional' acts, reduces rather more complex interactions to a polar scheme. By diminishing the suble Gramscian distinction between domination and hegemony, one neglects 'the network of interchanges, borrowings, reciprocal conditioning' between the cultures of different classes — the 'intermediate formations' identified by Cirese (1979: 53–4).

The model of a polar confrontation between dominant and dominated is a little more pertinent for explaining the conquest of America and much of the colonial period, when the Spaniards and the Portuguese were implanting their patterns of life from the outside. It continues to apply in several regions of Latin America where the indigenous population preserves its political and cultural structures. But even there, the fact that hardly any ethnic groups completely detached from capitalist development now exist, shows the need — in research and in political practice — to consider both strategies of self-defence and independent development as well as the extensive exchange with the hegemonic system. We must take account of the fact that such scientific equanimity is difficult for the politically committed. The thirty million Indians who have been exploited, abused and always only half-included in programmes of integration for centuries think only of defending themselves. The left, at least those sections who respect the legitimacy of ethnic claims, daily confirm that the subordination of the natives to economic, juridico-political and cultural relations, to the labour market and 'modern' consumption, has induced such fundamental (unequal) integration that it is impossible to restore absolute autonomy. In the midst of this opposition perhaps the sole realizable task for researchers — apart from supporting liberation struggles with specific studies — may be to probe into the nodal points of interaction with the greatest possible objectivity. As an instance of the conceptual work needed to advance in this direction, we would like to mention the problem of transactions.

Why do the popular sectors so often support those who oppress them? How, taking account of this malaise, can we explain that the most energetic expressions of protest ('We can't live like this!'; 'The people can bear no more!') seldom become support for the strikes or armed actions advocated by some. Why, Eduardo Menéndez (1981) asks himself in his book on health in the Maya region, do the popular classes most frequently not raise questions but engage in transactions? It is not due to a lack of awareness of their health needs, nor of the oppression that adds to their burdens, nor even of the lack of state services. Even in cases where they do make use of radical action to combat inequality, they then demand only intermediate solutions. Before the economic crisis, they demanded wage rises and at the same time limited their own consumption. Faced with political hegemony, for example, trans-actional behaviour consisted in accepting personal relations as a way of obtaining individual benefits. In the ideological sphere, elements extraneous to the group are incorporated and positively valued (such as criteria of prestige, hierarchies, designs and functions of objects: we have already noted artisans' adaptation to the demands of urban consumers). Faced with problems of health, the normal response is not to impugn exploitation, but rather to accommodate oneself to the exploitation of sickness by private medicine or to make good use of deficient state services. The same combination of scientific and traditional practices — to go to the doctor and to the healer — is a transactional way of confronting the situation. For Menéndez, medical self-treatment is the 'paradigmatic' case: faced with cases of sickness and their economic exploitation, the popular classes 'try to establish minimal forms of efficacy, appropriating techniques generated from "outside" the community and from "on high", without thereby coming to question the system of exploitation'. At times, negotiation is a way of obtaining a certain reciprocity in the midst of subordination, but in general, these transactions are so asymmetrical that they 'suggest not only an unquestioning outlook but resignation and a "solution" of problems from within the limits established by dominant classes' (Menéndez, 1981: 363–81).

The transaction is a constant mechanism in the formation of popular cultural and artistic products. Here, I am thinking of Lloréns Amico's research into the 'urbanization' of the Peruvian creole waltz, a history of stylistic readjustments by means of which the creators of traditional Andean music came to adapt it to radio broadcasting, to the migrants that settled in Lima, at the crossroads with new musical forms. We also come across transactional processes when studying artisanry and the popular arts in Mexico: iconography, dance and rituals are spaces in which social contradictions are symbolically 'resolved'.

Why, at the end of the 1960s, did the inhabitants of Ocumicho, a small village in the Sierra Tarasca, begin to make pottery with diabolic scenes, that rapidly became one of the most widely diffused and prized handicrafts in Mexico?

> The devil passed through Ocumicho and molested everyone. He interfered with the trees and killed them. He entered the dogs, and all they did was to get agitated and howl. Then he persecuted the people, who became ill and demented. It occurred to someone that it was necessary to give him places where he could live without disturbing anybody. So we made clay devils, so that he might have somewhere to stay.

The Tarascans tell that during the period in which they began to produce devils the rains began to diminish, neighbours from other villages took over the more fertile lands, and some of the Ocumicho villagers, being without work, emigrated to the United States. The entire community had to seek supplementary incomes through artisanry and open itself up to major commerce with the national market. The depiction of devils condensed these conflicts in many scenes: they were surrounded by birds, snakes and plants of the region, but in the village they struggled against non-existent elements and personalities from the 'modern' world: policemen, motorcycles, aeroplanes. A great deal of this pottery's attraction derives from the ironic use made of these objects. The devils deform aeroplanes, they take unlikely photographs, speak on the telephone, eat in bed alongside a mermaid. The largest ceramic to be seen in the village represents a bus full of happy devils, bodies leaning out of the windows, bearing this legend on the front: Ocumicho–Mexico–Laredo (the village's name in sequence with two places to which migrants travel when seeking work). In the handicrafts made for sale to outsiders — the villagers do not use them — the world of others appears as threatening to the devils, who in turn treat it parodically. We can also see the clay figures as being a way of controlling the 'devils' — the lack of rain, the robbing of lands, the need to open the community to the outside world, all the evils that have caused them to disintegrate and to become poor; the devils needed a place in which they could safely be contained. Cultural creation is therefore a space for opposition and resistance, and at the same time, the symbolic elaboration of contradictions, of transactions between forces that cannot be reconciled in reality.

The romantic idealization of popular resistance is used to basing itself upon the most spectacular instances of opposition: rebellions, strikes, protest demonstrations. The analysis of everyday life shows that in the long intervals between these explosions the popular classes intertwine their non-conformity with the obligatory reproduction of the hegemonic culture. Resistance is an arduous process of re-elaborating one's own with the alien, of selection and combination, in order to protect and develop oneself in conditions that subaltern classes do not control. The strength of the domination leaves few openings; the guile of hegemony demands a daily, furtive adhesion to heterodox uses of objects, manoeuvres to counteract hierarchy in conversation, the little tactics of survival (de Certeau, 1980, I: 9–28). A study attentive to these transactions and tactics, to the discreet and contradictory expedients by which the popular classes organize their lives, more subtly captures the political possibilities and restrictions of popular movements. The problem posed from the perspective of those movements is how to prevent the adaptations of the oppressed from contributing to the simple reproduction of inequality, how the circle of transactions might be transcended in order to arrive at transformation.

Reception and consumption: power with a small 'p'

The main recent advances in the study of power in Latin America have come about by according space to culture and symbolic processes (Lechner, 1981, 1984; Brunner, 1982, 1983, 1984; and Chaui, 1982 amongst others), by the renewal of the analysis of political discourse (Giménez, 1981; Laclau, 1978; Verón, 1980; de

Ipola, 1982) and by incipient research into cultural policies (Bonfil et al., 1983; Miceli et al., 1984). Even if several of these authors have also conducted research into everyday life, the dominant tendency in work on power is the examination of hegemonic politics and discourses.

Perhaps the main risk in this one-sidedness is that of reproducing in research one of the principal deficiencies of cultural policies: design and application which fails to take account of the real needs of the popular classes. Even if they are formally addressed by government or mass media, even if they are called upon to participate, the actions taken do not rest upon specific knowledge of popular needs. States, whether populist or not, assume that what they do for the people — housing, education, cultural events — must be of use to them; the mass media, under the sway of a statist conception of the audience suppose that if they can reach so many millions of spectators it is because they satisfy their needs. Moreover, hardly any of the left parties study the popular needs in the name of which they engage in opposition and urge proposals for change; it is necessary to ask oneself whether the minority character of practically all these parties on the continent does not in part derive from a lack of knowledge and from a failure to link up progressive ideas with the interests and life-styles of the subaltern classes.

On the other hand, the currents that make claims upon everyday life (phenomenology, symbolic interactionism) reduce it to a discontinuous succession of specific situations, in which it becomes difficult to find traces of broader social determinants. By thus shrinking the scale of observation and by abstracting it from any macrosocial paradigm, studies of the everyday in local cultures limit themselves to a description of elementary forms of sociability and tend to privilege that which is common to distinct strata. It appears to us that the problematic of everyday life might be made more conceptually precise and situated in a framework of greater explanatory power by linking it to social reproduction through the process of consumption. Almost all writing on the popular classes, especially that of Marxist origin, defines and analyses them by starting with their economic exploitation and their subordinate position in production. Consumption is reduced to 'consumerism', associated with passive reception, useless waste and depoliticization. However, there are already several studies in urban sociology and in the sociology of culture that show how differences between classes and the identities of popular sectors are constituted as much in production as in consumption.

Two studies conducted in Brazil and in Argentina suggest how we might reformulate some of the problems discussed earlier so as to conduct more systematic research. While questioning working women in São Paulo about their reading habits, Ecléa Bosi found (as did Richard Hoggart in England) that mass communications are not all-powerful with respect to readers and viewers because their messages have to pass through the filters of social relations with friends, domestic tasks and managing on low wages. The culture promoted by the media coexists in popular life with the structures of family and neighbourhood. The influence of mass communicated messages depends less upon skilful techniques of persuasion than the situation of the recipient, the moral code of her primary group, ingrained attitudes, and working women's selective perception as a function of prior conditioning.

In a study of Argentinian working men, José Nun discovered notable differences between the 'Justicialist ideology' that appeared in Perón's speeches, the common sense of Peronist workers and the diverse ways these worked out in practice. Given the variety of responses, he distinguished five groups with divergent conceptions of the principal forms of social antagonism, those 'responsible for the existence of the poor' and the type of policy that might improve their situation. The vast majority of those surveyed declared themselves to be Peronists, but whereas for one group this meant that there was a president who concerned himself with the poor, for others this represented the existence of a party capable of defending their interests in a constitutional system; a third section saw Peronism as a movement focused on the trades unions and which therefore increased the bargaining power of the workers over the bosses; a fourth group combined an individualistic ideology ('everyone has to fight for his interests') with the hope that solutions might follow by means of a political alliance that might embrace workers, employees, peasants, small industrialists and students; and the fifth group understood Peronism as a class movement in continuous formation. It is obvious that we cannot derive what the workers think from the explicit ideology of the leader or of the party. The hegemonic ideology refracts itself in diverse focuses that go all the way from belief in Peronism because it generated greater economic well-being within the established order to an adherence based on the capacity to change radically that order. Contrary to the metaphysical unity of the 'Peronist people' imagined by Bonasso's novel and by doctrinaire texts from within that movement, empirical research into the reception of political discourses shows a fragmented common sense — hardly common — whose diversity enables us to understand the obstacles to producing transformative collective actions.

The texts by Bosi, Nun and a few others who are empirically researching reception and consumption demonstrate how knowledge of popular cultures and power could change if it would only study the field systematically and arrive at a global theory. It is not just a matter of measuring the distance between the enunciation of messages and their effects, but rather of constructing an integral analysis of consumption, understood as the overall effect of the *social processes of appropriation of products* (Castells, 1980: 499). Defined thus, consumption includes, for example, the use of urban space and the ways of living at home, of dressing and eating, of informing and amusing oneself. It is much broader than the 'consumerist compulsion' problematic to which it is usually reduced and also more fundamental than the repertoire of tastes and attitudes catalogued by market research. It transcends its Marxist characterization as the space in which the cycle of production is completed. Consumption is the locus in which conflicts between classes, caused by unequal participation in the structure of production, continue by way of the distribution of goods and the satisfaction of needs. It is, therefore, one of the spaces in which the culture of the popular classes and its differences from those of others takes shape.

Given the impossibility of going further into that question here, let us at least say what appear to be the theoretical problems that require further elaboration:

(1) to construct a sociocultural theory of *needs* that goes beyond naturalistic definitions and conceives them as the simultaneous result of the internalization of structural determinations and the psycho-social elaboration of desire;

(2) to articulate in a *coherent theory of consumption processes* perspectives that until now have been treated separately: namely, consumption as the locus of the reproduction of the labour force and the expansion of capital (Castells, 1976; Terrail et al., 1977), the space in which classes struggle for the appropriation of the

social product (Castells, 1977), the locus of symbolic differentiation and distinction (Baudrillard, 1974; Bourdieu, 1979), and the system of integration and communication between groups (Leonini, 1982);

(3) to elaborate, well beyond the Marxist conception of consciousness as reflection and the behaviourist stimulus–response scheme, a theory of *how hegemony becomes rooted in everyday life*, interiorizing social structures in subjects, converting them into unconscious dispositions, basic schemes of perception, thought and action, 'habitus' (Bourdieu, 1977) that organize the 'needs' of subjects so that they might be congruent with social reproduction.

Research into these three problems helps us to understand in what *socio-cultural* conditions *political* conflicts between the hegemonic and the subaltern classes operate. From this conception arises a new way of testing out cultural policies in relation to popular demands, and criteria for evaluating relations and disjunctions between policies and needs. The fact that in past decades popular conflicts have extended themselves from classic struggles in production to others located in consumption (the home, inflation, education, medical care), creating forms of organization outside the parties and trades unions (urban social movements, consumers' associations, consumers' cooperatives) reveals not just the scientific but also the political importance of this field.

Final questions

Let us return from this uncertain exploration of the daily territories of consumption, transactions, and popular wisdom to the reality of any given day — today's reality for instance, when the news tells of failures of hegemony and of the determination of those who mean to carry on dominating. Pinochet flattens popular districts, imprisons, closes down, prohibits. The US government refuses all dialogue and insists on harassing Nicaragua and the peoples of Central America. Some carry on refusing to do cultural and political battle and some endeavour to reduce relations to a ferocious military domination.

In addition, some left groups dissolve politics into war and weaken the precarious autonomy of our civil society. Can the struggle of the oppressed be peaceful? What end do symbolic mediations serve in political struggles? Without denying the necessity of popular violence in the processes of liberation — but not that of self-styled visionary elites — we think that one of the key tasks for reinforcing popular causes is to work inside everyday life. We know that struggle by means of cultural mediations offers neither immediate nor spectacular results. But it is the only guarantee that we are not passing from the simulacrum of hegemony to the simulacrum of democracy — a way of avoiding the resurgence of a defeated hegemony in the complicitous habits that hegemony has installed in our ways of thinking and interacting. The political uncertainties of the cultural struggle seem preferable to a revolutionary epic that repudiates culture. All of this is based on the conviction that the uncertainties and the failures might be lessened if we study and know better the wrinkles of everyday life through which politics moves or gets bogged down.

What can be the political effectiveness of everyday transformations, of the cultural renewal of society? If we do not reduce politics to war, if we think that to engage in politics is to reappropriate — more than power — the public exercise of a democratic sociability, the socialization of all goods, then work in spaces and institutions in which cultural changes may be realized is important: through educational centres, artistic movements, struggles for human rights, ethnic, district and popular organizations of every type. There is a persistent question of how to articulate these sectoral struggles with those of parties and classes, of how to give to battles in consumption and in everyday life a transformative effect that generally requires them to be bound up with conflicts in production. But this is not just a problem of the new social movements; it is also one for the parties of the left, which are wont to ignore things unconnected with economic conflicts or that do not serve the conquest of power. If we take the traditional forms of political activity seriously, we will give a central place to tasks as protracted and wearisome as the transformation of daily life in present struggles for the democratic renewal of the parties and their reinsertion into everyday culture.

While the great poet René Char was fighting Nazism in the French Resistance he wrote: 'You bring a match close to the lamp and what is lit gives no light. It is far, far away from you when the circle brings light.'

Note

This paper was originally presented at the symposium on 'Popular Culture and Political Resistance' held at Columbia University, New York, 11–13 April 1985.

References

Arantes, A.A., (1981) *O que é cultura popular*. São Paulo: Brasiliense.
Barnet, M. (n.d.) *Biografía de un cimarrón*. Mexico: Siglo XXI.
Baudelot, C. and Establet, R. (1975) *La Escuela capitalista*. Mexico: Siglo XXI.
Baudrillard, J. (1974) *Crítica de la economía política del signo*. Mexico: Siglo XXI.
Becerril Strafon, R. (1979) 'Intervención', in FONART-SEP, *I Seminario sobre la política artesanal*. Mexico.
Boal, A. (1982) *Técnicas latinoamericanas de teatro popular*. Mexico: Nueva Imagen.
Bonasso, M. (1984) *Recuerdos de la muerte*. Mexico: Era.
Bonfil, G. (1981) *Utopía y revolución*. Mexico: Nueva Imagen.
Bonfil, G. et al. (1982) *Culturas populares y política cultural*. Mexico: Museo de Culturas Populares-SEP.
Bosi, E. (1981) *Cultura de massa e cultura popular: leituras de operárias*. Petrópolis: Vozes.
Bourdieu, P. (1977) *La Reproducción*. Barcelona: Laia.
Bourdieu, P. (1979) *La Distinction*. Paris: Minuit.
Bourdieu, P. (1980) *Le Sens pratique*. Paris: Minuit.
Brunner, J.J. (1982) *Vida cotidiana, sociedad y cultura: Chile, 1973–1982*. Santiago de Chile: FLACSO.
Brunner, J.J. (1983) *Cultura y crisis de hegemonía*. Santiago de Chile: FLACSO.
Brunner, J.J. (1984) *Cultura y política en la lucha por la democracia*. Santiago de Chile: FLACSO.
Bowles, S. and Gintis,H. (1981) *La Instrucción escolar en la América capitalista*. Mexico: Siglo XXI.
Candido, A. (1959) *Formação da literatura brasileira*. São Paulo: Martins.
Castells, M. (1976) *La cuestión urbana*. Mexico: Siglo XXI, 2nd edn.
Castells, M. (1980) *Movimientos sociales urbanos*. Mexico city: Siglo XXI, 6th edn.
Chaui, M. (1982) *Cultura e democracia*. São Paulo: Editora Moderna.
Cirese, A.M. (1979) *Ensayos sobre las culturas subalternas*. Mexico: CISINAH.
de Certeau, M. (1980) *L'Invention du quotidien*. Paris: UGE, vols 1 and 2.
de Ipola, E. (1982) *Ideología y discurso populista*. Mexico: Folios.
Foucault, M. (1978a) *Historia de la sexualidad, I: La voluntad de saber*. Mexico: Siglo XXI.
Foucault, M. (1978b) *Microfísica del poder*. Madrid: La Piqueta.
Fox, E. et al. (n.d.) *Comunicación y democracia en América Latina*. Lima: DESCO–CLACSO.
Franco, J. (1971) *La Cultura moderna en América Latina*. Mexico: J. Mortiz.
Franco, J. (1982) 'What's in a Name? Popular Culture Theories and Their Limitations', *Studies in Latin American Popular Culture* 1.

García Canclini, N. (1982) *Las Culturas populares en el capitalismo*. Mexico: Neuva Imagen.

García Canclini, N. (1983) *Las Políticas culturales en América Latina*. Lima: Materiales para la comunicación popular 1.

Giménez, G. (1981) *Poder, estado y discurso*. Mexico City: UNAM.

Godelier, M. (1978) 'La part idéelle du réel', *L'Homme*, XVIII(3/4).

Graburn, N.H.H. (ed.) (n.d.) *Ethnics and Tourist Art*. Berkeley.

Hoggart, R. (1957) *The Uses of Literacy*. London: Chatto and Windus.

Laclau, E. (1978) *Política e ideología en la teoría marxista*. Mexico: Siglo XXI.

Landi, O. (1981) *Crisis y lenguajes políticos*. Buenos Aires: CEDES.

Lauer, M. (1982) *Crítica de la artesanía: plástica ye sociedad en los Andes Peruanos*. Lima: DESCO.

Lechner, N. (1981) *Estado y política en América Latina*. Mexico: Siglo XXI.

Lechner, N. (1984) *La Conflictiva y nunca acabada construcción del orden deseado*. Santiago de Chile: FLACSO.

Leonini, L. (1982) 'I consumi: desideri, simboli, sostegni', *Rassegna italiana di sociologia*, XXIII(2).

Lombardi Satriani, L.M. (1975) *Antropología cultural: analisís de la cultura subalterna*. Buenos Aires: Galerna.

Lombardo Satriani, L.M. (1978) *Apropriación y destrucción de la cultura de las clases subalterna*. Mexico: Nueva Imagen.

Lloréns Amico, J.A. (1983) *Música popular en Lima: criollos y andinos*. Lima: Instituto de Estudios Peruanos–Instituto Indigenista Interamericana.

Losada, A. (1982) *La Literatura en la sociedad de América Latina*. Frankfurt: Vervuert.

Margulis, M. (n.d.) 'Cultura y desarrollo en México: la reproducción de las unidades domésticas', mimeo.

Martín-Barbero, J. (1984) *Cultura popular y comunicación de masas*. Lima: Materiales para la comunicación popular 3.

Menéndez, E. (1981) *Poder, estraficación y salud*. Mexico: Ediciones de la Casa Chata.

Miceli, S. et al. (1984) *Estado e política cultural no Brasil*. São Paulo: Difel.

Monsiváis, C. (1981) 'Entre el espíritu y el presupuesto: notas sobre difusión y política de la cultura', *Nexos* 41 (May).

Monteforte Toledo, M. (ed.) (1980) *El Discurso político*. Mexico: Nueva Imagen.

Muraro, H. (1974) *Neocapitalismo y comunicación de masa*. Buenos Aires: Eudeba.

Nun, J. (1984) 'Averiguaciones sobre algunos significados del peronismo', *Proceso: crisis y transición democrática* 2. Buenos Aires: Cedal.

Perus, F. (1976) *Literatura y sociedad en América Latina: el modernismo*. Mexico: Siglo XXI.

Ribeiro, D. (1983) *Maira*. Mexico: Nueva Imagen.

Tedesco, J.C. (1983) 'Crítica al reproductivismo educativo', *Cuadernos Políticos* 37.

Terrail, J-P et al. (1977) *Necesidades y consumo en la sociedad capitalista actual*. Mexico: Grijalbo.

Verón, E. (1980) *A produção de sentido*. São Paulo: Cultrix-Universidade São Paulo.

Walsh, R. (1969) *¿Quién mató a rosendo?* Buenos Aires: Tiempo Contemporáneo.

Walsh, R. (1972) *Operación masacre*. Buenos Aires: de la Flor.

2

Popular culture and social control in late capitalism

David Tetzlaff

If we view the world from the Left, what do we make of the continued dominance of capitalism, its ties to racism and patriarchy, and the attendant perpetuation of economic and spiritual injustices? How do we explain the apparent general lack of opposition to this situation, the fact that organized forces of resistance — unions, movements, even left/liberal political parties — seem everywhere to be either in retreat or virtually helpless stagnation?

'Vulgar' Marxists may remain secure in their faith that liberation is written into the dialectical progress of history, that it is only a matter of time before capitalism crumbles under the weight of its own economic contradictions. In more fashionable determinist utopias, the inevitable indeterminacy of language and/or the necessarily open character of textuality stand ready to sunder the semic pillars of the temple of social authority. These positions are sort of the left-theoretical versions of 'Don't worry, be happy!' They relieve us from any responsibility for action. Thus, they are perfect for academics. We need only watch and describe the inexorable forces. There is little at stake in our analyses of the prevailing systems of dominance, for history or epistemology have guaranteed that the oppressors will be swept away when the time is right.

Instead, let us assume that the future is unwritten; there are no political guarantees. The structures of social injustice will not crumble by themselves; we will have to take them apart. This will require us to know how systems of domination preserve themselves, how social order and social control are maintained. I assume we study media and popular culture in large part because we suspect they play an important role in that maintenance. The questions then are: what sort of role? How important is it? Through what mechanisms exactly is it performed?

Media, Culture and Society (SAGE, London, Newbury Park and New Delhi), Vol. 13 (1991), 9–33

Of course, the Left has been trying to answer these questions for some time now. We have even developed standard sorts of answers that now often serve as unstated primary assumptions, starting points from which research, theory and criticism proceed. Unfortunately, I'm afraid some of these standard assumptions are heading us in the wrong direction.

Left theories of communication/media/language/esthetics in this century have almost always conceived of social power as operating through unification, centering, the repression of contradiction. People are controlled by getting them together, doing the same thing, thinking the same thing. The key analytical term here is 'dominant ideology'. The ruling forces of society work to secure their position (consciously or unconsciously) by spreading an ideology that favors their interest, which becomes masked as nature or common sense. Mass-produced culture, of course, is a key agent in the reproduction of this ideological unification. In opposition to the unities of dominant culture, theorists have advocated social and esthetic practices of negation, difference, disjunction. Even as critical theories have developed and diverged, disagreeing vigorously on many important points (see Grossberg, 1984), at base they have generally retained conceptions of social control as a matter of unification, and liberation as the fragmentation of this unity. The most extreme version of this is expressed in poststructuralism, where any unity — in the social, in discourse, even in the subject — is condemned as an instance of domination. But these associations go back at least as far as the critiques of a homogenizing culture industry by the Frankfurt School, and are as current as the resistance-through-reading analyses of contemporary television theorists. Critical scholars may quarrel about how successfully dominant culture serves the project of unification — Adorno and Horkheimer argue that the culture industry molds subjectivity with mechanical standardization, creating a subject population ripe for Fascism, while John Fiske argues that ideological unification inevitably fails as different subcultural audiences create their own meanings from pop culture texts — but they agree that subjective and discursive unification is the path to social domination, and that this is the aim, if not the effect, of mass-produced culture.

I think these standard conceptions of control and resistance need to be re-examined, as do the media theories that conform to them. In fact, I suggest that mass-produced culture does contribute mightily to the maintenance of the social order in late capitalism, but that it does so more through social and semiotic fragmentation than by forging any sort of ideological unity among the subordinate.

The notion that culture is now characterized by a breakdown in signification is a common theme in analyses of 'postmodernity'.[1] In these versions of postmodernism, audiences are no longer seen to engage mass-produced culture on the level of ideology, myth, or even pragmatic information. Instead, cultural consumption is viewed as centering on a fascination with the spectacular surfaces of media forms, the play of ever proliferating and intermingling signs and images disconnected from their meanings. Thus, the media are no longer presented as a force for ideological unification. Unfortunately, however, this work has either sidestepped the issue of how mass-produced culture figures in capitalist social control, or it has pasted the same old concept of control on to the new vision of the media, leading to an endorsement of the blankness or semiotic chaos it finds in media products and their reception. In addition, while much of our mass-produced culture may indeed be fragmented or emptied of meaning, much of it is not. Meaning and ideology may no longer be fashionable but they are far from dead. Those theories of postmodern media that do not ignore these hermeneutic holdouts entirely have little to say about them. The questions of what sort of social or cultural relationship exists between different sorts of popular culture, and what the politics of this relationship might be (as opposed to merely the politics of this or that style) are largely left unanswered. In this essay, then, I want to take certain theories of postmodern culture as a starting point, make some key modifications, point the whole apparatus at the question of mass-produced culture and social control, and attempt to address those unanswered questions.

Implosion

The two theorists who have advanced the 'collapse of meaning' thesis most forcefully and prominently are Frederic Jameson and Jean Baudrillard. Both of them see this semiotic implosion as a general social or cultural condition. They both paint a generally depressing picture of postmodernity, but wind up with something positive to say about it on political grounds, although they both also suggest postmodern culture mitigates against any form of active social opposition.

Jameson (1984) argues that, from the Pop Art of Andy Warhol to such 'nostalgia' films as *American Graffiti* and *Body Heat*, the dominant mode of cultural production has fallen into a depthless, blank pastiche of the surfaces of previous forms. History has been effaced. Spatial order gives way in the delirious busyness of the contemporary landscape and the new architecture. The subject can no longer locate itself in time and space. Since the production of meaning requires the sign to connect the present to the past or the future, the disappearance of temporal structure in culture leads to a breakdown in the chain of signification: 'the breakdown of temporality suddenly releases this present of time from all the activities and the intentionalities that might focus it and make it a space of praxis' (Jameson, 1984: 73). Cultural activity becomes reconstituted as an aleatory, schizophrenic immersion in signs and images themselves, their referents having been severed. Political groups seeking to 'intervene in history' find themselves confronted with a 'form of image addiction which . . . effectively abolishes any practical sense of the future and of the collective project, thereby abandoning the thinking of future change to fantasies of sheer catastrophe and inexplicable cataclysm' (Jameson, 1984: 85).

Jameson traces the characteristics of postmodern culture back to the economic system. Postmodernism is 'the cultural logic of late capitalism'. The global spread and penetration of multinational capital, with its displacement of productive technology by reproductive technology (media, computers, etc.), has been so thorough that no geographical or critical distance from it can be established. The disorientation in culture reflects our inability to orient ourselves towards the centers of power that affect our lives. However, Jameson is determined to see large historical forces in a dialectic fashion. He attempts to inject a positive note into his otherwise disturbing analysis. This is the notion that by expressing the 'whole extraordinarily demoralizing and depressing original new global space' of late capitalism, postmodern culture embodies a 'moment of truth' in which the nature of this system 'has become most explicit, has moved the closest to the surface of consciousness' (Jameson, 1984: 88). For Jameson, this opens possibilities for 'a new radical cultural politics' of 'cognitive mapping' (1984: 89), which would 'endow the individual subject with some new heightened sense of its place in the global system', although he doesn't actually say how all the incoherence he has noted might be turned into a coherent social understanding.

Baudrillard (1980, 1983a, b) does not use the term postmodern, but his analysis of contemporary conditions is similar to Jameson's in many ways. For Baudrillard, the real has been replaced with a hyper-real: a series of simulations, models generated from other models, representations only of previous representations. Omnipresent media deliver an incessant stream of solicitous information. The individual has no defense, the exterior is forced into the interior, the bounds of subjectivity are torn away by the networks of information. But information no longer communicates; its mass overwhelms its meaning. Poles of opposition collapse in formal and operational abstraction and equivalence. Fascination with the code of transmission (the signifiers) replaces the construction of sense, stripping the communication of any message (the signified) the code might have carried. Meaning implodes, and thus the social implodes as well. The individual becomes a 'schizo', a mere surface or screen, passively reflecting the image of other surfaces transmitted by the information networks.

Such a vision may seem dark to many of us, and Baudrillard is often taken to be an extreme pessimist. But he holds fast to the notions that control equals unification, and that meaningful unification remains the intent of dominant culture, and this leads him to argue that postmodern blankness and the implosion of meaning represent forms of resistance to domination:

> the objective of information is always to circulate meaning, to subjugate the masses to meaning . . . The masses remain scandalously resistant to this imperative of rational communication . . . They intuit the terrorizing simplification behind the ideal hegemony of meaning and they react in their own way, by reducing all articulate discourse to a single irrational, groundless dimension, in which signs lose their meaning and subside into exhausted fascination. (Baudrillard, 1980: 142–3)

For Baudrillard, the indifference of the media audience is a form of resistance. He compares the resistance of the-masses-as-objects, 'infantilism, hyper-conformism, total dependence, passivity, idiocy', to the resistance of the-masses-as-subjects, 'disobedience, revolt, emancipation', (1980: 147), and concludes that in the face of the hegemony of meaning, only object resistance has much chance of success.

Lawrence Grossberg and Fred Pfeil have also discerned a loss of meaning and a play of surfaces in contemporary culture but, in contrast to the global visions of Jameson and Baudrillard, Grossberg and Pfeil locate the postmodern condition as centered within a particular subculture, and give more specific accounts of its origins and characteristics.

Grossberg (1988) analyzes postmodernism in the context of contemporary American youth culture. He argues that young people are caught between the demands of subjectivity ('boredom') and commodification ('terror'). They react to this situation with the irony, detachment, ambivalence and irreverence embodied in slogans such as 'If you're on the Titanic, go first class', and 'Life's a bitch, and then you die'. They attempt to avoid both terror and boredom by refusing to look behind the surface. The only form of authenticity lies in acknowledging that everything is faked. When young people engage in traditional forms of behavior, they do so without investing themselves in them. 'Everything can be taken seriously and simultaneously made into a joke' (Grossberg, 1988: 139). Grossberg explains the apparent conservatism of youth evidenced in their support for Reagan as a preference for the less boring candidate, the one entirely and obviously defined as a media image, a celebrity, a shimmering surface with nothing hidden below. Youth did not endorse the meanings or values to which Reagan subscribes; all such political depth represents the sort of demands youth is trying to escape and thus no longer acknowledges. Grossberg suggests that youth's postmodern 'affective structure' is not necessarily conservative — that while it has been articulated to conservative politics, it might also be rearticulated for more progressive ends. He doesn't know how this could be done, exactly, but he urges us to look for the means of accomplishing it.

Like Grossberg, Pfeil (1985: 264) considers postmodernism 'as a cultural-aesthetic set of pleasures and practices created by and for a particular social group at a determinate moment in its collective history'. However, for Pfeil this group is not youth but the 'professional-managerial class' (PMC) of the baby boom, people who were between twenty-five and thirty-five in 1980. Like the other theorists discussed above, Pfeil argues that postmodern culture is characterized by a general evacuation of meaningful content. In this absence, cultural appreciation becomes a matter of *deja lu*, the always-already-read — texts composed of a bricolage of quotation from the pop culture past are apprehended with a pleasure of estranged recognition, approached with manic swings from exhilaration to contempt directed to the textual sources as cultural objects, not towards any internal meanings they may once have had. Fictional characters and presentational performers have become 'de-individualized': presenting a self-conscious collection of media stereotypes and cliches or offering an effacement and dispersal of individual characteristics in place of any unique 'personhood'. Pfeil has an interesting analysis of the social influences leading to the rise of postmodern culture, which I will turn to later in the essay. When he turns to political evaluations, Pfeil, like Grossberg, does not view postmodernism as necessarily reactionary. Behind the detachment and disinvestment of the PMCs he detects a dissatisfaction with existing conditions, a 'desire for home' and a repressed dream of collectivity which might be rearticulated with progressive politics.

To one degree or another, these theories all suggest that the media, and capitalist culture generally, exhibit the exact opposite sort of tendencies from those usually attributed to them: the deconstruction of sense and cultural collectivity rather than the molding of them to a unified dominant model. And though the theorists may try to find some way to put a positive spin on the postmodern practices they perceive, none of them seem able to suggest any concrete ideas about how postmodern culture might be brought to aid a progressive challenge to dominant social structures. This suggests that these political evaluations may be more than a bit off the mark.

Ideology and postmodernity as forms of control

Let us compare an ideological, unifying culture and a superficial, fragmentary culture from the perspective of a Machiavellian late-capitalist prince.

A form of social control based on disorientation to social relations — in the sense of either confusion or detachment — offers several advantages over a form of control based on orienting the masses to social relations in any particular way. Ideology is not self-evident; like any meaningful sign system it must be decoded. Thus, ideological subjects must possess fairly sophisticated decoding skills. They must have the desire and ability to work through the rhetorical construction of arguments, to draw semiotic connections, to look beneath the surfaces of signs and establish hermeneutic depth. In order to support these skills, the dominant system must foster in its subjects some forms of rationality and cultural literacy. It must also foster some form of social literacy, as the language of ideology is necessarily political. Ideology assumes an attention to social affairs, and an understanding of them in some form as well. In short, ideological control is problematic because it must address the relations of dominance in order to support them, and it must promote mental and cultural abilities which can also be turned around and used to generate analysis, critique and oppositional strategy. In order to be effective, ideological control must rigidly police the employment of its techniques. However, such a restriction is extremely difficult to maintain. A primary function of public education is to prepare the population for ideological control by developing the cultural skills necessary to perceive and partake in ideology, yet limiting them and channeling them towards the desired ends. As evidence that this function fails on a regular basis we need only look at our own critical activities. We were allowed to develop cultural and intellectual abilities in the hope that we would employ them to participate in the prevailing ideological systems. Instead we have turned them, at least on occasion, against those systems. Ideological control always faces this threat.

In contrast, control through postmodern fragmentation presents fewer liabilities. The form of cultural literacy necessary to appreciate deindividualization and *deja lu* requires only a recognition of familiarity of the image as an image. Postmodern culture asks for no connection to be made between the text and the world outside the media. Being self-enclosed, it avoids the issue of social relations entirely. Its language, if it has one, is apolitical. Time that might otherwise be occupied by subjects attempting to understand their position in the social system is taken up by fascination with depthless image fragments. The tools of rationality are neither demanded nor promoted by spectacle. If culture lapses into schizophrenia and fascination, any resistive subgroups that do manage to congeal within the general soup of postmodern fragmentation will be unable to orient themselves toward the social system in a manner conducive to any effective form of oppositional action.

But what of Baudrillard's object form of resistance? Even if the masses do undertake a purposive rejection of meaning, which is questionable, I don't think this would present great cause for worry to the wise capitalist prince. What difference does it make if people refuse to participate in the system of cultural meanings? If they refused to participate in the economy, acting as infants or idiots on the job — if they stopped going to work or stopped buying things — that would be a problem. But Baudrillard's disengaged audience is still an audience, still required to consume cultural products (which play an ever larger and more profitable role in the capitalist economy) in order to achieve a-semic fascination or to have an opportunity to display their idiot-infantile indifference to the message. In fact, the captains of the cultural industry have never really known nor cared what goes on when people use their products. The only form of feedback they seek from the audience is a measure of relative size. Once the industry knows that the product has been purchased or the program is being watched, its interest in the audience's reactions stops. If the masses were to demonstrate their cultural indifference by refusing to consume, this resistance might actually be registered by the industry. However, as long as the ratings and the receipts stay respectable, if indeed the masses are thumbing their noses at authority through an indifference to meaning, the gesture is empty because the authorities are not aware of it.

Capitalism, control and history

One problem with unity-as-control concepts is that they fail to mesh with the historical trajectory of capitalism, which has been marked by a continuing centralization of power accompanied by a dispersal of power effects, diversification in enterprise and an elevation of form over content. The parallel movements of concentration and diversification are not contradictory. On the contrary, the latter provides the basis on which the former is constituted.

We can see one example of this in the history of the American mass media. At the turn of the nineteenth century, journalism was dominated by the partisan press. There were many newspapers in operation, each filled almost exclusively with hotly contested politics, each addressed to a particular political faction and thus with relatively limited circulation. Newspapers as a product did not play an important role in the economy. They were not produced by capitalists in order to accumulate profit, but by middle-class merchants supporting themselves through patronage from the various political interests they served.

With the advent of the penny press, journalism was drawn into the center of the capitalist economy. Newspapers began to show the potential for generating significant profit on their own. The control of the press moved from the middle-class entrepreneur to the finance capitalist. In order to generate mass appeal, the press turned away from the specialized politics of the partisan papers. Political matter was replaced by sensational-ized crime stories. Graphics began to play an important role; it mattered how a paper looked as well as what it said. Yet, the greatest change in newspaper form wrought by the penny press was an explosion in the range of material it contained. The penny papers were composed of a variety of departments addressed to different segments of the population — the religion page, the women's page, the sports page. Content immediately expanded beyond various aspects of news to include comics, horoscopes, advice columns and other entertainment features. The centralization of the journalism industry was constructed upon this diversity. The mass papers drove the many factional papers out of business, and journalism began its inexorable march toward monopoly. Throughout the twentieth century, media producers have continued to maintain or expand the diversity of their products while control of production has become ever more centralized. Media companies have merged to create communications conglomerates, which in turn have been swallowed by larger ultra-diversified multinationals attracted by the culture industry's consistently high rate of profit.

An even more telling history, and one that addresses the issue of control directly, is provided by Richard Edwards's (1979) study of transformations in the capitalist workplace. Edwards defines workplace control as the ability to obtain desired behavior, to effectively convert labor power into labor. The entrepreneurial capitalism of the nineteenth century was characterized by what Edwards calls simple control: the direct personal authority of the boss. Firms operated on a relatively small scale — concentrated in one geographic location, dedicated to a single form of production — and were generally controlled by a single individual or family. The capitalist knew all of his employees personally, and had direct knowledge of the requirements of their jobs. Thus, he could guide their work directly. Whether the boss inspired contempt or loyalty, workers had a meaningful relationship with him. The source of authority and control was also plainly evident in the boss's often idiosyncratic commands.

Capital expansion produced a crisis for this form of control. The sites of work spread beyond the immediate access of the owner; the boss no longer knew all of his workers, could no longer see what they were all doing. Moreover, with technological development and specialization, the boss lost much of his knowledge of the work processes under his command. Initially, capital responded by instituting what Edwards calls hierarchical control, modeled on a military chain of command. Here authority was delegated to a series of 'sub-bosses'. Each foreman maintained a personal relationship with the workers under him, and exercised punishment, reward and other work directives in the same autocratic manner as the boss. The nature of hierarchical power was 'naked and clearly visible', and without the ameliorating paternalistic effects of the workers' personal involvement with the big boss, hierarchical control revealed the oppressive nature of capitalist relations and provided a natural focus for resistance. The great labor disruptions around the turn of the century, from the Pullman strike to the steel strike, evidenced the failure of hierarchical control: 'the system that was supposed to control workers became one of the chief burdens motivating them to fight back' (Edwards, 1979: 65).

Capitalism addressed these failures of control with a variety of experiments, from worker welfare programs to scientific management. Though these experiments were largely unsuccessful, they revealed useful techniques that would be employed in the improved control systems to come later. Welfarism showed the benefits of adding minor incentives for workers within the overall control structure. Taylorism showed the benefits of separating conception from execution, fetishizing work by removing its purpose from the domain of the worker, leaving only the empty shell of its formal requirements. 'Plans of representation' demonstrated that grievance procedures reinforce management prerogative rather than threatening it, and if workers' complaints are handled on an individual basis, they are kept from addressing their concerns in a collective manner.

The first successful alternative to hierarchical control appeared with assembly line production. This is an example of what Edwards calls technical control. The task to be performed is defined by the position on the line, and the worker must perform it each time a product arrives. The foreman monitors the work, but has no personal responsibility for directing it. 'Instead of control appearing to flow from boss to workers, control emerges from the much more impersonal "technology" ' (Edwards, 1979: 120). Technical control tied workers to their stations, making them isolated and immobile. In addition to this atomization, it produced a form of homogenization in the workforce as well, tying workers to 'a common pace and pattern of work set by the productive technology' (Edwards, 1979: 127).

However, while technical control solved the problem of translating labor power into labor for each individual job, it displaced this conflict on to a plantwide level. Thus, the smokestack industries where technical control is practiced have historically been subject to strikes and go-slows, which, though nowhere as threatening as the great labor conflicts of the past, nevertheless remain a significant thorn in the side of capital.

Moreover, technical control proved impractical as the economy moved away from large-scale manufacturing into high-tech and information products under the auspices of giant, diversified corporations. This led to the development of what Edwards calls bureaucratic control, exercised through individualized work rules and the 'impersonal force' of company policy, which is now the primary means of control in the workplace. Bureaucratic control integrates the lessons of previous control forms and the struggles they inspired. Instead of demanding a problematic homogenization, it creates a stratification of the workforce through 'carefully articulated job descriptions' which 'establish each job as a distinct slot' (Edwards, 1979: 137). The separation of conception and execution is maintained without the discipline of the line or the time–motion man. Workers labor without direct supervision; the rules define the task and

ensure that the required result will be reached. The formal structure of
rules and policy takes precedence over the actual content of work.
Bureaucratic control builds allegiance to its rules in the form of incentives,
'through the mechanism of rewarding behavior relevant to the control
system, rather than simply to the work itself' (Edwards, 1979: 148).

With direct personal power and technical necessity removed, the
relations of production disappear into the policy structure.

> Above all else, bureaucratic control institutionalized the exercise of capitalist
> power, making power appear to emanate from the formal organization itself.
> Hierarchical relations were transformed from relations between (unequally
> powerful) people to relations between job holders or relations between jobs
> themselves, abstracted from the specific people or the concrete work tasks
> involved. (Edwards, 1979: 145)

Bureaucratic control has not eliminated workers' opposition, but its
stratified structure channels discontent into expressions by individuals and
small groups that pose little threat to the firm. Similarly, for Edwards the
larger effect of contemporary control strategies is the splintering of the
working class into distinct 'fractions'.

> During American capitalism's first century it inherited and recruited a highly
> heterogeneous labor force, but it reshaped its wage laborers into an increasingly
> homogeneous class. In the twentieth century, the economic system has attracted
> groups as divergent as before, but capitalist development has tended to
> institutionalize, instead of abolish, the distinctions among them. (Edwards,
> 1979: 163)

Edwards concludes that these distinctions have served capital well. 'The
inability of working class-based political movements to overcome these
divisions has doomed all efforts at serious structural reform' (1979: 184).

Edwards's analysis has several implications for media theory. He shows
that attempts to establish a common ground of control inevitably open a
common ground of opposition. Thus, the dominant have good reason to
avoid providing any common ground to their subordinates, and control has
been more successful when they have done so. Control is also more
effective when it obscures the contents and purposes of activity, focusing
on its formal surface, and when it grants limited forms of autonomy and
incorporates limited rewards — Edwards calls them 'bribes' — for the
subordinates who behave as desired.

Bureaucratic culture

If capitalism no longer produces unity and meaningful understandings of
social relations in the culture of the workplace, why should it do so in the

cultures of leisure? In fact, popular culture fits the larger trajectory of control perfectly, displaying the benefits of fragmentation and superficiality well before they are adopted in the workplace. Unfortunately, media studies keep addressing control models capitalism has already discarded. For example, resistance-through-reading theorists posit a 'dominant ideology' reminiscent of simple control as the intent of cultural production (see Fiske 1986a, b). The pop culture text is theorized as attempting to resolve contradictions in line with the prevailing ideology, but subcultural audiences create their own meanings, which are necessarily resistive since they contradict the dominant discourse. These scholars conduct ethnographies to show the variety of subcultural readings, and that no unification of meaning exists among the audience. However, this is not necessarily a sign of progressive politics. Edwards would certainly agree that there is cultural diversity among capital's subordinates. The question is, does this indicate successful local resistances or only fragmentation of capital's address to its subjects, a series of carefully articulated cultural job descriptions? The Frankfurt critique and the apparatus theories in film studies see culture operating as a form of technical control, an example of the ultra-rationalization Habermas once labeled 'technological fascism'. However, popular culture has never operated with the uniformity of an industrial plant, never demanded specific activities on a regulated timetable. It has always offered a variety of texts and a variety of ways to use them, and placed access to them at the discretion of the reader.

Moreover, popular culture has always provided some sort of rewards for its participants. The reception theorists recognize that popular pleasures do not necessarily entail identification with a paternalistic social authority. However, since the creation of this identification is still taken as the intent of the system, they argue that pleasures that diverge from it must necessarily be resistive. From the perspective of bureaucratic control, however, these textual rewards may only be the bribes that ensure the subordinate's adherence to the behavioral goals of the system by providing a small measure of subjective autonomy.

The fragmentation and formalism of bureaucratic control clearly find one cultural equivalent in postmodern popular culture. The job description defines work in superficial, formal terms, and requires no personal investment on the part of worker or supervisor. Postmodern culture displaces content for a depthless fascination with form, and its consumers too remain detached and disinvested. Bureaucratic control is the fetishization of work. Labor power, like any commodity, finds its content displaced by its function in the system. Similarly, postmodernism is the fetishization of culture. Meaning falls before the profit motive. The surface is all that is left.

Pfeil ties the social conditions that helped foster a postmodern esthetic in now upwardly-mobile baby-boomers to developments in corporate society generally, and to bureaucratic work specifically. In the 1950s, corporate power responded to the housing needs of its employees with suburban development. Suburbanization fragmented traditional cultural structures. 'By snapping the nuclear family out and away from wider networks of neighborhood, kin and clan' (Pfeil, 1985: 266) it paved the way for 'the commodification of daily life on a newly expanded scale' (Pfeil, 1985: 267). The suburb contained no site for a traditional public sphere, which had been fragmented at the hands of the market. 'For most of us, in fact, television was all the public sphere we had' (Pfeil, 1985: 271). The increasing entrance of women into the workforce and the emphasis on 'scientific' childrearing eroded the construction of gender identities, which in turn contributed to 'a partial dissolution, decentering and devaluation of the autonomous ego' (Pfeil, 1985: 268). These developments are the source of the deindividualized postmodern style that 'mimes the ceaseless process of the consumerized self's construction, fragmentation, and dissolution at the hands of a relentless invasive world of products' (1985: 278). Pfeil relates the postmodern evacuation of sense directly to the PMC position in bureaucratic production:

> Divorced from both the site and the experience of material production, separated by virtue of the mystified opacity of our own professional codes from the real systemic function of the reproductive functions we serve, what appears around us in our lives as administrators, social service workers, teachers etc., is apt to look like a welter of random codes to be administered and observed . . . If in the public world signification is always a ruse or a shuck, in the world of the professions an auto-referential result at best, on the cultural terrain the PMC prepares for its own delectation the draining-off of sense and referentiality will become an aesthetic principle. (Pfeil, 1985: 284–5)

However, postmodern implosion is not the *only* cultural reflection of capital's bureaucratic 'logic'. Many contemporary popular texts are clearly *not* postmodern. They still articulate meaningful ideologies. Yet, this does not mean they have escaped the influence of late capitalism. Rather, ideology has followed the corporate path into stratification, specialization and individualized address.

The matrix of domination

Capitalism is not responsible for every aspect or instance of domination or control in capitalist societies. Patriarchy and racism existed well before capitalism appeared on the stage of history. In addition to these broad manifestations of oppressive power, society also contains a variety of local forms of authority at different levels, vested in the family or in other personal relationships, in geographic communities, ethnic communities, class norms, etc. These other centers of power and control are generally articulated to capital in some way, but they cannot be subsumed under it.

The genius of capitalism is its simplicity of motive. As long as profit can be accumulated and maximized, other considerations are secondary. This gives capital great flexibility, allowing it to form alliances of convenience with other centers of power. As in politics, the presence of such an alliance does not mean the parties involved are consistent with each other or totally repress their own desires on the other's territory. The waning of specific forms of dominance need not signal liberation; relief from one form of control may be due to its usurpation by another equally as heinous. Cultural conservatism, the traditional authoritarian family so beloved of the American religious right, has been a good friend to capitalism over the years, and vice versa. But as it becomes increasingly profitable to bring women into the workplace (at 60 cents on the dollar of equivalent male labor cost), it also makes sense to let them stay there by aborting unwanted pregnancies. In any event, Mom isn't back in the kitchen baking that nurturing apple pie. As an economic system, increasingly focused on the production of information and entertainment, finds huge profits in the spectacular, sensual, hedonist and nihilist popular culture (Freddy Krueger slasher movies, Prince 'jerk-off' records), the kids are no longer satisfied by that boring, wholesome pie, either. Thus the standards and practices of cultural conservatism become usurped by its erstwhile ally. The politicians still give lip service to the old values, but do precious little about it. The small acts of censorship leveled at the scourges of sex and violence are almost wholly symbolic (as opposed to the censorship of political opposition, which still has real teeth). Despite a major public brouhaha, and the presence of the wives of several influential senators on the side of the prosecution, the Parents Music Resource Center's campaign against pop music filth has had virtually no effect on the industry, except possibly increasing the popularity of stigmatized bands like Slayer, Megadeth and Motley Crue. The senate hearing held on the issue found the legislators following each condemnation of sex/drugs/rock'n'roll with promises that they had no intention of creating legislation to impinge on the rights of free expression and free enterprise. When values struggle with dollars, put your cash on the cash every time.

In general, the various forms of allied social power are negotiated into a hierarchy with capital at the top. However, in any specific instance positions in this hierarchy may be redistributed and realigned. Capital may prevail in large-scale clashes, but cultural conservatism is probably still on top in the home of a fundamentalist Christian minister. At different social locations then, we see different manifestations of control.

We might define a cultural practice as oppositional if it resists a primary form of power in effect at the site where it occurs. Since these sites differ, opposition would always be context dependent. Thus, we might say that attending a George Michael concert would be an act of opposition in Santiago, an act of complicity in Minneapolis, and rather ambiguous in Moscow (where society now seems to be teetering between repressive state socialism and aimless neo-capitalist consumptionism). However, this sort of labeling is too easy and misleading. Opposition is not a universal category, not only in terms of any specific text, but in terms of any specific location of reading. These sites are almost always a complex intersection of different and often contradictory forces of dominance, some operating locally, some globally, some somewhere in the middle.

It is possible to be oppositional locally without being oppositional globally. Kids can resist the authority of their own moms and dads without challenging the power of the patriarchal family as a whole. Opposition to one global form of power may support another. For example, in *The Hearts of Men* Barbara Ehrenreich (1983) shows how the male revolt against the bourgeois family in the 1950s fed both patriarchy and a narcissistic consumer culture, yet at the same time embodied 'a blow against the system of social control that operates to make men unquestioning and obedient employees'. Thus opposition to the locally inscribed capitalist power of the workplace provides backhanded support not only to the continued exploitation of women but also to the more general capitalist urge toward consumption.

The complex intersections of power make it difficult for subjects to recognize exactly what forces of dominance are operating on them, and which forces are responsible for particular subjections. This confusion is one way in which capital's alliances with other forms of dominance works to its advantage. It sits high enough above its cohorts that its role is seldom perceived, and there are plenty of fall guys around to take the blame for its misdeeds. But there is another way in which these alliances serve capital. The inflection with various local forms of authority aids capitalism in fragmenting its discourse, creating differentiated ideological 'job descriptions' and thus instituting a cultural equivalent to the stratification of bureaucratic control.

Capitalism accommodates different cultural roles for different groups of people to play, and different sets of myths or different cultural pleasures to go along with them. It does not now present, nor has it ever presented, anything like a single, unified dominant ideology. It tells different stories in different places. Presidential candidates often present contradictory positions to different sets of voters. In the Northeast Bush is for ecology; in Texas he is for the energy industry. In Mississippi Dukakis rattles sabers; in Oregon he is a pacifist. These statements are exaggerated reflections of a more general condition. Capitalist culture offers different discourses to each faction of race, class, ethnicity, religious conviction, geographic section, etc. This is not to say that capitalism created these divisions, or their discourses. As these subgroups have desired to assert their identities through culture, capitalism has been happy to oblige them, as long as it can nudge those identities into articulating with its basic economic requirements.

Of struggles and social systems

British cultural studies regularly celebrate the presence of contestation in popular culture. The system is taken to desire total control of the subordinate, in subjectivity as well as behavior. In the face of the dominant's desire to become Big Brother, all social and cultural struggle is valorized. However, if we replace the Orwellian image with a model of fragmented and multifaceted power, struggle becomes problematic, and its liberatory value cannot be automatically assumed.

Edwards shows that struggle is never absent from the workplace; work is always contested terrain. Successful control comes from channeling struggle into non-threatening paths. In fact, he argues that worker struggles contributed to the development of more effective control systems by displaying the weaknesses of previous models and indicating areas where worker desires could be incorporated into the system with minimum disturbance in production or authority.

This is true in cultural struggles outside the workplace as well. Capitalism can easily suffer those struggles that fail to address the social relations of profit accumulation. It is even in its interest to encourage them. They draw attention and energy away from the prevailing economic structure and its effects. In allowing these struggles, capital also gives its subjects a sort of reward or bribe in the form of limited autonomy. As we engage in various forms of local contestation, we feel better about our social position. When cultural struggle does produce popular discourses that might challenge capital's position, capital becomes alerted to its weaknesses and is able to identify the next target for incorporation (although the motivating force behind incorporation is generally an attempt to exploit markets for new cultural products, rather than any Machiavellian political intent). Over the long term, many of our struggles may merely be part of the ritual of domination. They give us a chance to play in the great sport of self-determination, and so we keep showing up for the games, even though it's all fixed and we lose every time.

If struggle has always been present, if capital can never extinguish it completely, then simply finding it is no big deal. Domination does not demand the absence of contestation or difference, only an unequal balance of power leading to all but predetermined outcomes of ineffectiveness or irrelevance. We must examine the consequences of particular struggles, and value them only to the degree that the continuing bases of social domination are effectively threatened.

Where did we go wrong?

If capitalism exercises its power in a fragmented series of different local effects, staged in a variety of alliances with other forms of power which still maintain some independent control effects of their own, why have Left media theorists repeatedly painted a picture of it as being, or at least desiring to be a single, central Big Brother? I believe we have misidentified capitalist control mechanisms by confusing the operations of capitalism with the operations of other realms of authority.

Capitalism is, after all, a relatively recent historical phenomenon. The final displacement of aristocratic state authority by private capital, and capital's consolidation of that power within large corporate structures are even more recent. We do not approach questions of dominance and resistance with a blank slate. We inherit a long tradition of received understandings about what dominance means and what resistance means, embedded in philosophy, literature and folklore. Most of these understandings were developed in societies with relatively simple structures of power — alliance between church and monarchy — and are, I think, appropriate to that form of social order and control. Before the rise of monopoly capital, social dominance was largely exercised through direct, unified control practices with an identifiable center (king, queen or pope). Power was not only employed to enforce economic roles across society, but cultural roles as well. Before the reformation there was one church, with one set of totalistic prescriptions for living the godly life. Before the bourgeois revolutions, the state addressed most of its subjects in the same manner, for beyond the aristocracy and a small bourgeoisie there was little differentiation of class or social role.

The dominant voices in Left media theory have belonged to Europeans, and the experience of Fascism plays a central role in this thought. However, I would argue that Fascism resulted from a crisis in the then still unstabilized global economy of capitalism, which led to a momentary accession of social systems operating very differently from the general tendencies of capital. The will to social and discursive unification under Fascism (and Stalinism) was very real indeed. Theories that posit massification as the desire of dominant cultural productions would make sense if history had presented us with a continuing supply of Hitlers. However, although a host of aspirants such as M. Le Pen keep auditioning for the role, capital is too well organized now, too many stabilizing mechanisms have been applied to the system. Certain social minorities may fall on hard times and become prey for Fascist hatemongers, as in recent cases in middle America where a resurgence in right-wing fanaticism was fueled by the farm crisis. Yet, overall the system is structured to continue providing the minimum comforts of consumption to the majority of the people most of the time. Even a stock market collapse rivaling the one that started the great depression does little to disturb the everyday life of the average citizen, and Wall Street is back to business as usual within a week or two. Yet, European thinkers, quite understandably, cannot shake the unspeakable horrors of the 1930s and 1940s from their memories. Fascist control remains the dominant presence in Continental theory, though actual Fascists have been reduced to bit parts in the Western political theater and can only take center stage in the undercapitalized, neo-colonial periphery.

In America, where national history started with the overthrow of kingly authority, and which remained untouched by direct experience of Fascism, the situation is necessarily different. Even today, libertarianism in one form or another remains the dominant strand of American political thought. Social and political issues relating to media are almost invariably framed in First Amendment terms. While this perspective is seldom taken up in the media theory of Leftist academics, where European influences generally rule, it is no stranger to the Left generally, as a review of the coverage of media issues in popular Left journals such as *Mother Jones, The Nation* or *The Progressive* will attest. Libertarian thought may now be employed in some quarters as a cynical ideological cover for creeping corporate power. Yet, the 'Founding Fathers' were sincere in their individualism. The American revolutionaries aimed to create a haven for autonomous individuality (except for slaves, of course), and as they looked at the world they inhabited, they saw that the only force of central organized power impinging on the rights of the individual was the state. So they created a government that placed unprecedented limits on that power, assuming that individuals would thus be left free to pursue their own destinies in their own fashion. Yet in so doing they could not foresee the changes that would be brought with industrialization. Jefferson imagined an agrarian democracy in perpetuity. He had no idea that the new form of government would provide an opening for the almost immediate succession of another form of power — more dispersed than monarchy but with no less effect on the lives of the average citizen — industrial capitalism. Mainstream American thought has still not caught up with industrialization, much less postindustrialization. Most Americans still cherish their individual liberty, yet encouraged by a variety of mutant forms of libertarianism, still locate the primary threat to individual autonomy in the state: taxes, busing, etc. Our historical consciousness still has most of us resisting an image of old King George rather than General Foods, General Motors and General Electric.

American oppositional thought, Leftist and otherwise, tends to display legacies to libertarian individualism in that it tends to view social authority as the pressure to conform. I suspect that for most American Leftists, a non-conformist self-understanding preceded the adoption of their political position; an alienation from prevailing institutions felt on a very personal level came before any analysis of its social and political origins. As a result, our images of liberation are ones of freaky diversity. Jesse Jackson supporters are presented as a wild heteroglot collection of political non-conformists, affronts to middle-American consensus. American images of resistance to authority are dominated by the romantic, individualistic rebel, the figure of the outsider: Kerouac, Kesey/MacMurphy, James Dean, Elvis and the Wild One. Popular Leftism here has often attempted to reconcile this individualism with a broader social consciousness, to articulate Marx through Lennon. The movement's foray into politics was based on the idea that if by getting all the outsiders together, an effective majority could be created. This was the motive force behind the McGovern campaign, and reappeared in the rhetoric of Jackson supporters in 1988.

The authority figures who appear in our mental dramas of resistance are paragons of conformity: country club Republicans, macho football coaches, small town moralists, Mom and Dad. Yet these all represent local force, and have little global authority. However useful their conformist programs are for capital, obviously none of them are necessary. As *Playboy* demonstrated, all of these conformities could be opposed from within the bosom of consumer capitalism. Even the Beats' disgust for the organization man, though necessarily anticorporate, got clawed back into the service of capitalism as ideological metaphor. If corporate managers understood themselves as organization men, culture presented them with a variety of images to say, 'that's a fine, useful and rewarding position in life'. But if this image of reassuring conformity troubled them, they could also imagine themselves as free market entrepreneurs, on-the-road individualists burning across the economic highway (see Gitlin, 1986). This is the postmodern ideology of non-conformism: free identity construction through consumption, be-what-you-want translated as buy-what-you-want.

What I believe media theory has done, then, is to overgeneralize the whole issue of control and opposition, to interpret capital in the terms appropriate to the more primal and familiar local forms of authority. There is something distinctly Oedipal about our paradigms of non-conformist rebellion, and indeed male voices have dominated our theory. Perhaps we have been unable to properly separate Marx from Freud, capitalism from parental authority (Dad, who wouldn't let us listen to the Stones or grow our hair or take the car out late Saturday night). Capitalism has generally benefited from Oedipal revolt, partly by defining it in terms of consumption, but more directly by employing it as motivation to enter the workplace. Before the 1960s, when college opened to the vast middle class instead of the select few, the only clear path out of the house for young men was to get a job as soon as possible. Work provided the means for independence from the family: a car, an apartment, spending cash. The boss was far less demanding than Mom and Dad, too. He only ruled life from 9 to 5, and his prescriptions for behavior were less totalistic — he didn't care who your friends were, and he wasn't always after you to clean up your room. Besides, you could always look for a new job, an option the family did not present. (In the age of mass post-secondary education, you get out of the house for job training at college, and corporate socialization in fraternities, instead of by going directly to work.)

Perhaps the route many American men followed to Leftism entailed an awareness that the job wasn't really that different from Dad's prescriptions after all, a valid recognition that work was just another usurpation of autonomy, which unfortunately led to an inaccurate assumption that both Dad and capitalism were manifestations of the same larger evil, both after the same results and both working in roughly the same way.

Individualistic rebellion is constantly validated in our culture; it is a staple of popular music, films and literature. Therefore, it offers an easy model for social and political opposition. Active experience in collective struggle, progressive unionism for example, teaches a different lesson: that some sort of unity is the only way to get things done. Yet few people, including few of those who enter the academy, have had access to this sort of experience, while images of romantic rebels are always ready at the doors of consciousness. Perhaps the recent American passion for Derrida, Lyotard and other thinkers who speak well only of difference and implicitly reject any collectivity as a terrorizing totality is merely another manifestation of the lone rebel motif. At any event, with the discrediting of the movement by its own erstwhile members, we seem to have lost the last model of collective opposition that was able to challenge individual rebellion in the public imagination. In 1968 we believed we had a chance to remake the world to the prescription of brotherhood, of people coming together and loving each other. That we can no longer resort to these terms without irony is a sign of how far we have come (or is that sunk?) in the last twenty years.

Paradoxically perhaps, when we were trying to get everybody together in the 1960s and early 1970s, the old control/unification equation of Continental theory held a certain intellectual and practical appeal. The collective project of the movement required the articulation of some common ground between its members. Certainly an analysis that posited a unified force of dominance attempting to enforce standardized forms of obedience presented a more powerful basis for this than any model of dispersed and differentiated control effects. By setting up an opposition of centralized bad guys and a heterogeneous oppressed, theory gained the rhetorical advantage of speaking in terms resonant with the long history of domination and resistance; it was easy to understand. By understanding control through the model of Fascism, the forces of domination were identified with a concrete, distasteful (and unified) villainy any righteous human being must oppose. There was just something so 'right on' about shouting 'Fascist!' at anyone who stood in the way of the movement. The academic descendents of this politics, including the subject positioning theory of *Screen* and the apparatus theory of Baudry, maintain this sort of Leninist clarity. They speak with clear moral implications and the urgency of outrage (albeit now to a very select audience). However, although there is a real short-term political power in such analyses, they necessarily fail in the long run since sooner or later empirical evidence contradicts them. Moreover, they can only lead, as they did twenty years ago, to strategies of opposition that are misinformed and thus ineffective.

Divide and conquer

Although the fascination and implosion presented in the apocalyptic visions of postmodernism appear to be operating in certain quarters or at certain times, there is also strong evidence of subcultures defining themselves through rich structures of meaning. Postmodernity certainly mitigates against the formation of active, local collectivities in many ways. Yet many such collectivities continue to exist, and certainly some of these do employ (stylistically) postmodern texts in their culture, investing them with some sort of meaning (however resistant the text may be to such treatment otherwise). Still, the evidence of superficiality and detachment is also strong enough to indicate that subcultural reading theory cannot be applied as a general explanation of how popular culture works either.

Are these tendencies necessarily contradictory? I don't think so. The project of capitalism is a very material one. It aims to accumulate the maximum amount of profit. Capitalism's needs in social control are also explicitly material — to make sure that people continue to work, to consume and to refrain from mounting any effective challenge to the system. Any combination of ideologies, or anti-ideologies that work towards these ends will serve just as well. It is to capital's interest if any challenges it might face remain local and isolated, held beneath the global, multinational scale at which capital operates. Thus it is to capital's interest to keep its subject population as fragmented as possible. In avoiding challenge, it is also to capital's interest if disinterest in the nature of social relations is fostered, and if the workings of the social system remain as obscure as possible. To the extent a cultural system can yield these results, and still provide motivations for production and consumption, it serves the maintenance of capitalist control.

I'm afraid the products of the existing culture industry fit this prescription all too well, yielding a relatively consistent 'divide and conquer' effect which takes the form of at least two basic mechanisms.

The first of these is social fragmentation through ideological diversification. Here people and their sign systems are divided from one another. The social — work, consumption, lifestyle, community — is invested with one meaning here, another there. These meanings — some of joy, some of bitterness — serve in some way to send the people off to perform their roles in the economy (or at least present no obstacle to their doing so). Culture produces sense, even political sense, but sense is non-commensurable from one reading position to the next. Social subgroups fail to understand one another. The subordinates of capital, divided along a variety of other lines, act at cross purposes in regard to the relations of its dominance (when they act at all). The tribes of capital are sent forth from the antenna towers of babel chattering in a host of different tongues. And so they are prevented from coordinating the creation of structures to challenge the ultimate master.

In order to theorize the internal workings of this mechanism, I think we need to perform a simple (but crucial) modification on the body of hegemony theory as presented by Gitlin: hegemony is rule by consent. Thus it is a collaboration between the dominant and the dominated. It does not coerce: it 'persuades, coaxes, rewards, chastises' (Gitlin, 1987: 241). It is 'the orchestration of the wills of the subordinates into harmony with the established order of power' (1987: 242). Power can only be guaranteed through orchestration because these wills cannot be shackled or extinguished; the hegemonic system allows space for their expression. Therefore, as a site of hegemonic practice, in popular culture:

> groups can declare themselves . . . consolidate their identities, and enact — on the symbolic level — their deepest aspirations, fears and conflicts. The genius of the culture industry, if that is the right word, lies in its ability to take account of popular aspirations, fears and conflicts, and to address them in ways that assimilate popular values into terms compatible with the hegemonic ideology. (Gitlin, 1987: 243)

This is all very fine up to the point where we get back to 'dominant ideology' again. Popular values are assimilated not to any particular justification of these relations, but to many different sorts of justifications. Consent is structured without consensus. It finds different conceptual bases at each subcultural site. A host of hegemonic ideologies coax different groups of people with different rewards, opportunities for different identifications.

The second mechanism is social fragmentation through semiotic implosion. Here sign systems themselves are divided from their social meanings. The non-commensurable sense of the first strategy is replaced by merely *non-sense*, the 'fascination' of Baudrillard's masses. This seems to be the real up and coming cultural method of capitalist control. Admittedly, disorientation and spectacular superficiality are hardly new. They have been with us since the dawn of modernization, and find their way into Marxist cultural theory at least as early as the work of Walter Benjamin. However, they were able to play only a minor role in control until the arrival of certain technological developments, most notably the development of inexpensive miniaturized electronics, which allowed media to establish a ubiquitous presence in the nooks and crannies of everyday life. The postmodernism of depthlessness and imploding signs described by Jameson and Baudrillard is not so much a characteristic of texts as a sensibility, a way of seeing. This sensibility seems to be growing with each generation. In terms of the now middle-aged baby-boomers, I think Pfeil is right in locating postmodern culture among the educated professionals. However, I also think Grossberg is right in arguing that for younger people the postmodern sensibility constitutes a much more widely shared mode of experience. Still, it is doubtful that anyone, even an MTV junky, actually lives as a postmodern 'schizo' all of the time. Yet as long as fascination fills just those cultural spaces where meaningful understandings of economic relations might otherwise go, capital is well served. And even if this displacement fails to occur all the time for some people, or occurs not at all for others, there is always mechanism number one. Opposition doesn't face one form of cultural control or the other; it gets double teamed.

The overall systemic function of popular culture within capitalism is to reconcile capital's subordinates to their position within the economy. It does not lead them to love their domination, or even necessarily to deny it. It merely provides enough rewards in the form of pleasure, escape or identification, and enough opportunity for limited autonomy through channeled or unfocused resistance, to make subordination bearable and to keep us coming back to the culture industry for more limited relief. Jaded detachment and withdrawal into surface pleasure is one form of reconciliation. The articulation and validation of struggle without change is another. The subordinate share the responsibility for the development of these positions with the culture industry. We have been active, not passive, in our popular culture. The question, though, is what has come of our actions?

Conclusion

The fact that cultural contestations are frequently recuperated or otherwise stacked in favor of capital is no reason to cease struggle altogether. It does suggest, though, that we cannot consider struggle in narrow terms. We must choose our struggles wisely, with an eye towards their systemic effects not just their local ones. As such we must also constantly look for ways to get around the rules of struggle capitalism has provided. We must learn to cheat the system, and to reappropriate the recuperated.

This will send us back to the terrain of popular culture. Nothing I have said here should be taken as a blanket condemnation of all popular art.

The problem is not in the specific works themselves, or in our readings of them, but in the larger cultural context in which these are enmeshed. We do not need to seek a high culture avant-garde alternative. We are not going to start the revolution by getting people to listen to Schoenberg. Nor do we necessarily need newer, better, more progessive pop texts. From Pete Seeger to punk rock to Pee Wee, I think we have plenty of models of popular practice with critical potential. The problem is to pry that potential out from the greater system of capitalist pop culture that subverts it with nauseating regularity. Admittedly, I have no idea how we can do this, short of seizing the dominant means of production — although I can't help thinking now and then that our cause would be at least slightly better off if we were all working to create and distribute films, videos, records and accessible commentary instead of writing academic essays.

I realize the analysis I have offered here makes things look rather bad. Well, I honestly think they *are* that bad. Pessimism is unfashionable these days, but I am not sure just who is the greater pessimist. It seems to me that in the wake of the alleged failure of 1960s politics, many of us have lost our belief that we can be agents of change. Thus, since we can no longer be optimistic about ourselves, we develop an overly optimistic view of existing conditions. In other words, too much of recent media scholarship seems to say, 'Okay, *we* can't change the world, but not to worry; the dominant system is so full of holes that things are going to get better anyway.' This stands Gramsci on his head; it is optimism of the intellect and pessimism of the will. I think we would do better to put him back on his feet. Look, the situation is dire. The question, as ever, is what are we going to do about it? Let the words of Joe Hill be our inspiration as we confront the cultural fragmentation of capitalism: 'Don't mourn. Organize.'

Note

1. Postmodern is *the* academic buzzword of our time. In search of scholarly 'hipness', a vast number of people have appropriated the term and attached it to vastly different objects and theoretical projects. It is impossible to give a definition of the term that encompasses all its uses or that even stakes out any meaningful common ground between them. There are many postmodernisms, and many of them suggest a very different view of popular culture from the authors mentioned here.

References

Baudrillard, J. (1980) 'The Implosion of Meaning in the Media and the Implosion of the Social in the Masses', pp. 137–48 in K. Woodward (ed.), *The Myths of*

Information: Technology and Postindustrial Culture. Madison, WI: Coda Press.
Baudrillard, J. (1983a) 'The Ecstasy of Communication', pp. 131–2 in H. Foster
    (ed.), *The Anti-Aesthetic.* Port Townsend, WA: The Bay Press.
Baudrillard, J. (1983b) *Simulations.* New York: Semiotext(e).
Edwards, R. (1979) *Contested Terrain.* New York: Basic Books.
Ehrenreich, B. (1983) *The Hearts of Men.* New York: Anchor Press.
Fiske, J. (1986a) 'Television: Polysemy and Popularity', *Critical Studies in Mass
    Communication* 3: 391–408.
Fiske, J. (1986b) 'Television and Popular Culture: Reflections on British and
    Australian Cultural Practice', *Critical Studies in Mass Communication* 3: 200–16.
Gitlin, T. (1986) 'We Build Excitement', pp. 136–61 in T. Gitlin (ed.), *Watching
    Television.* New York: Pantheon.
Gitlin, T. (1987) 'Television's Screens: Hegemony in Transition', in D. Lazere
    (ed.), *American Media and Mass Culture: Left Perspectives.* Berkeley: University
    of California Press.
Grossberg, L. (1984) 'Strategies of Marxist Cultural Interpretation', *Critical Studies
    in Mass Communication* 1: 392–421.
Grossberg, L. (1988) 'Rockin' with Reagan or The Mainstreaming of Postmodernity',
    Cultural Critique Fall: 123–49.
Jameson, F. (1984) 'Postmodernism, or The Cultural Logic of Late Capitalism',
    New Left Review 146: 53–92.
Pfeil, F. (1985) 'Makin' Flippy-Floppy: Postmodernism and the Baby-Boom PMC',
    in M. Davis et al. (eds), *The Year Left.* New York: Verso.

3

Post-Marxism: critical postmodernism and cultural studies

Kuan-Hsing Chen

Collapsing effects

Current debates on post-Marxism have centered around the works of Ernesto Laclau and Chantal Mouffe.[1] The sharp antagonism between different positions has not made the platform of debate a very productive one. Here, I would like to shift the ground of analysis by confronting another round of debate, this time more productive, yet largely ignored: when Marxist cultural studies declared war against postmodernism.[2] My strategy here is to frame this debate *within* the terrain of post-Marxism; conversely, it is only within the context of this debate that a wider post-Marxist spectrum can be established and diverse politico-theoretical concerns specified.

Before entering into the debate, let me point out that the version of postmodernism discussed here *is* different from what I shall call 'dominant' ones. Elsewhere, through the post-1968 works of Michel Foucault, Gilles Deleuze, Felix Guattari and Jean Baudrillard, a 'critical' postmodernism has been proposed (Chen, 1988). This critical postmodernism distances itself from a dominant 'aesthetic' criticism which privileges art works as its central site of analysis (Lyotard, 1984); it departs from a philosophical criticism which locates itself within the history of philosophy (Habermas, 1987); it supersedes a cultural criticism which centers on the elite sectors of cultural lives (Huyssen, 1986); it diverges from a social criticism which reduces the ('postmodern') social world to a reflection of the ('late capitalist') economic mode of production (Jameson, 1983, 1984); it differs from a 'moral' criticism which calls for a return to a ('post-pragmatist') ('bourgeois') social solidarity (Rorty, 1984); and it also breaks away from a

Media, Culture and Society (SAGE, London, Newbury Park and New Delhi), Vol. 13 (1991), 35–51

popular culture criticism which focuses on the unraveling of new cultural texts. Instead, what may be termed an alternative 'critical postmodernism' attempts to articulate the dynamics between history, theory and cultural politics, and to stress the critical location of mass media within the strategic field of postmodernity. Because cultural studies has taken issue with the theoretical works of Foucault, Deleuze and Guattari and Baudrillard (as central referent points of postmodernism), there seems to be a common ground for pursuing a critical dialogue. The 'identities' of both cultural studies and postmodernism can perhaps be more clearly elucidated through a converging of their 'differences'; their internal limits and problems will likewise be in sharper relief.

In order to avoid the 'sliding' tendency of postmodernism, which conflates levels of abstraction, this paper will proceed along three axes: history, cultural politics and mass media. These distinctions are strategic. As we proceed, it will become clear that one axis immediately implies, is entangled with and connected to others. Having worked through central issues involved in the debate and defended certain viable positions of postmodernism in response to cultural studies' challenges, I will then consider the possibility of negotiating a space 'in-between' in order to forge political alliances. Finally, I wish to pinpoint problematic assumptions of postmodernism, to urge the necessity of confronting long neglected issues, and to move beyond the limits of both postmodernism and cultural studies. In effect, the convergence of these two discursive domains will result in a 'cut 'n' mix' (Hebdige, 1987a), or more precisely, a 'collapsing effect', thereby constituting a new critical space, crossing over and eliminating the boundaries and identities of both. I shall call this critical zone 'postmodern cultural studies'. Moving toward a postmodern cultural studies within the space of post-Marxism is the central motive of this paper.

History: is there such a thing called postmodernity?

In the interview, 'On Postmodernism and Articulation', Hall (1986: 46) asks critical questions:

> Is postmodernism the word we give to the rearrangement, the new configuration, which many of the elements that went into the modernist project have now assumed? Or is it . . . a new kind of absolute rupture with the past, the beginning of a new global epoch altogether?

In response to Hall's question, I will argue that postmodernity denotes a 'rearrangement' and a 'new configuration' which have exceeded the boundaries of modernity. Although it is not an *absolute* rupture, one has to realize, with Gramsci (as Hall himself does), that no historical era is ever absolute; that 'Stone Age' elements remain, albeit entering new relations with other internal elements. In my view, what the term 'postmodernity' designates is precisely how the relations among internal elements in the current conditions of existence have been rearranged to the extent of constituting a new historical formation. Of course, to what extent it *is* and according to what 'criteria' one may define a new era, remain arguable. Nonetheless, the perplexities of contemporary culture have produced new structural transmutations which, as Hall (1986: 47) states, though with reservations, 'tend to outrun the critical and theoretical concepts generated in the early modernist period'. In agreement with Hall, I too doubt that 'there is any such absolutely novel and unified thing as *the* postmodern condition' (Hall, 1986: 47). If there is such a thing called a postmodern condition, it can only be plural, disunified, multiple and contradictory.

In this sense, both postmodernism and cultural studies emphasize *relative* continuity and rupture; both positions are against historical necessity and for historical contingency. Both oppose the linearity and unity of an evolutionary historicism. Both stress the plurality of origins and that of trajectories of movements. Both attempt to do 'ascending analysis', to write popular history, that is, to bring the repressed voices of history back into the historical agenda. And, most importantly, both see 'history' as the (discursively articulated) records or archives of war between the dominant and the dominated of various kinds.

The immediate markable differences between these two discourses is that postmodernism has begun to locate the courses of historical configurations, which are largely ignored on the side of cultural studies. Through different axes (relations of power, systems of representation, the flow of desire), postmodernism has attempted to chart the moving trajectories of new social formations. This is, however, not to deny that cultural studies' analysis is always historical in nature. Perhaps the divergence lies in a fundamental contention: Hall does not believe in the arrival of a new historical era, and thus there is no need to do such large-scale (re)analyses, which, however, may be seen as the starting point for postmodernism.

Hall (1986: 50) argues that: 'Postmodernism attempts to close off the past by saying that history is finished, therefore you needn't go back to it', and that it signals 'the end of the world. History stops with us and there is no place to go after this' (1986: 47). These charges against postmodernism are unfounded. The historical works of postmodernism precisely deal with reconstituting the past as a field of struggle. With Baudrillard (1987), one might argue that postmodernity denotes excursion into post-history in the sense that *that specific* Western monolithic thing called History is over and done with. As Iain Chambers (1986: 100) suggests: 'postmodernism . . . does suggest the end of *a* world: a world of Enlightened rationalism and its metaphysical and positivist variants . . . a world that is white, male and

Euro-centric'. And one might add: what is finished is the 'official', universal, unified, racist, sexist, imperialist History; from this point on, *that* History is finished. Thus, 'the end of History' means the beginning of histories: the history of women's struggle, the history of youth culture, the history of prisons, the history of madness, the history of the working class, the history of minorities and the history of the Third World.

In short, on the level of histories, post-Marxism has to continue this 'ascending' historical project, to write *in*, and from the point of view of minor discourses, to (re)inscribe forces of antagonism and resistance, to affirm differences while forging possible strategic alliances. More radically, post-Marxist cultural studies ought perhaps sometimes even to *become silent*, or alternatively, by using already occupied social positions, to open up spaces, so that minor discourses may speak (or not) and be heard.[3]

Cultural politics: what is politics anyway?

On the level of cultural politics, what postmodernism and cultural studies share most is the attempt to decenter or decentralize politics and recenter 'culture'. But this does not mean that politics has gone. Quite the contrary, in both positions, culture is pervasively politicized on every front and every ground, hence a cultural politics. Both discourses conceive of cultural practices as collective; cultural politics is empowering and endangering, oppositional and hegemonic; culture is neither the 'authentic' practice of the 'people' nor simply a means of 'manipulation' by capitalism, but the site of active local struggle, everyday and anywhere. Both positions recognize that contemporary power networks can and do no longer work solely through an imposition from 'above'; rather it operates 'on the ground' and can only establish its hegemonic dominance through linking with local struggles. Both positions are convinced that the current networks of power cannot be reconstructed without negotiating the space of the masses. Both sides realize that, to win the battle, one can no longer wait, one has to fight here and now.

The clash between the two positions is perhaps a matter of emphasis: cultural studies emphasizes that cultural politics operates through the domains of representation, signification and ideology,[4] while postmodernism underscores the terrains of the production of signs (as the real or the hyper-real), asignifying process and discursive and non-discursive practices — the space of the micropolitics of power (Foucault, 1979b), desire (Deleuze and Guattari, 1977) and the symbolic (Baudrillard, 1981).

Let me first respond to Hall's critique of what he sees as Foucault's overemphasis on the discursive, the latter's abandonment of the ideological and his notion of power. As Hall has argued, Foucault fails to realize the complexity of contemporary theories of ideology as these are reworked through Gramsci and Althusser. Abandoning the notion of the ideological, and displacing it with 'the discursive', Foucault runs the risk of 'neutralizing' the discursive, or to use Hall's (1986: 49) words, of 'let[ting] himself off the hook' of the ideological. For ideological forces, whether in the form of discursive or extradiscursive practices, are actively working in the concrete social field. These points are all well taken.

Yet, it is highly problematic for Hall (1986: 49) to say that, by 'abandoning the term' ideology, Foucault 'saves for himself "the political" with his insistence on power, but denies himself *a politics* because he has no idea of the "relations of force" '. First, Hall is perhaps right in claiming that Foucault does not have *a politics*, but he has many: the Foucaultian 'local struggles' are aimed at every corner of the social field. Second, according to my reading, if there is a definition of power in Foucault, it is nothing if not 'the relations of force'. As Foucault (1979b: 92) succinctly puts it: 'It seems to me that power must be understood in the first instance as the multiplicity of force relations immanent in the sphere in which they operate and which constitute their own organization.' Thus, Foucault's 'politics' is precisely to analyze the constellation of the relations of forces.

Hall (1986: 48) goes on to label Foucault's as a 'proto-anarchist position because his resistance must be summoned up from no-where', in the view of his 'evasion of the question' of ideology. In Foucault, Hall argues, 'Nobody knows where it [resistance] comes from. Fortunately it goes on being there, always guaranteed: insofar as there is power, there is resistance.' In fact, this attack reveals more of Hall's own problematical concept of power grounded as it is in traditional Marxist categories of power. For Foucault defines power as the *relation* of (confrontational) forces, always multiple and multidirectional. More importantly, resistance constitutes only partial forms of power relations. Resistance is in no way guaranteed to 'win', but it designates the forces against the dominant; in this sense, resistance does not come from 'no-where' but from everywhere. Whether resistance can be 'summoned up' to a larger alliance and more global type of struggle, which Hall apparently wants Foucault to address, is a different question. Thus, Hall's reading of Foucault's theory does not take it on its own terms. Second, embedded in Hall's assumption is the notion that power (that is to say domination) is in (binary) opposition to resistance, whereas Foucault has pointed out emphatically that power as such does not exist, what exists is always and specifically a power *relation* insofar as both resistance and domination are interconnected forms of power, among others; the opposition between them is never necessary but conditional and contingent (Foucault, 1979b: 94). In his reformulation of power, Foucault seeks precisely to avoid a dangerous entrapment: to place resistance in binary opposition to domination is to effect a reproduction of the dominant, of the binary logic set up by the 'strong' party; unless the resisting forces are strong enough to explode the logic itself, it will infinitely reproduce the original dominance. Thus, Hall's reading of Foucault is not so much incorrect as unproductive: it misses Foucault's formulation in accounting for the non-discursive (non-ideological) forms of power, and it fails to understand that, indeed, with Foucault, 'there are different regimes of truth in the social formation' (Hall, 1986: 48), of which the ideological is only one. In not recognizing these points, Hall has 'let himself off the hook' of having to theorize the ideological without the asignifying and non-representational dimensions. (One can perhaps understand Hall's 'binarism' as a strategic articulation of social antagonisms. But, the oppositions between women and men, working class and capitalists, blacks and white, or the third worlds and 'first' world, can no longer be understood as 'ontological' givens, but are rather articulated political effects of present social contradictions.)

If postmodernism has emphasized non-ideological domains, then this is precisely where cultural studies ought to come in. As Grossberg (1986: 72–3) has noted, ideological effects have to be connected to other types of effects, whereas overemphasis on the line of the ideological has made cultural studies unwilling to connect with other planes of effects. These 'other sorts of effects' are what Grossberg calls the affective dimension of life, what Baudrillard (1986) calls the other side of the real, what Foucault (1987) calls 'the outside', and Deleuze and Guattari (1987) call 'micropolitics'.

Although Fiske and Watts (1986) correctly insist on the urgency for a 'politics of pleasure', their Barthesian impulse fails to articulate useful analytical tools and fails to recognize Guattari's (1977) warnings that pleasure (*jouissance*) as an individuated effect lacks the possibility of collective politics. The 'rationalism' of cultural studies has been single-handedly supplemented by Grossberg's works on the 'affective economy'. In noticing a missing dimension in cultural studies, Grossberg (1984: 101) recognizes the importance of making a 'distinction between affect and pleasure'. Grossberg's 'affective economy' quite accurately points to a critical space which 'involves the enabling distribution of energies', or a plane of 'an asignifying effectivity' (Grossberg, 1986: 73). He further recognizes that 'like the ideological plane', the affective space 'has its own principles which constrain [and enable] the possibilities of struggle' (Grossberg, 1986: 73). Given his insertion of a much needed dimension into cultural studies, there are, nevertheless, problems in his formulation. His theorizing practices revolve *around* the space of the affective, describing the shapes of the terrain, making connections with other planes such as the ideological, the economic and the political. He has yet to pinpoint the working 'principles', or what I would call the *inner* logics of the affective. He is able to answer the questions 'where is this [affective] economy produced? And what are its effects?' (Grossberg, 1984: 103), yet does not address more immanent questions — how and through what process is the affective economy able to operate? And what are its internal dynamics? The affective economy becomes a shell without trajectories. Consequently, Grossberg is not able to historicize the affective structure. He is able to pinpoint the visible configurations of styles, of body, of youth, without theorizing the changes of more invisible inner currents. Do these inner currents always stay the same, even when styles or surrounding social conditions have become different?

Here, then, is what and where cultural studies can take off from postmodernism. Power as relations of forces, the immanent logics of desiring production and the effects of symbolic seduction and fascination may precisely articulate and historicize such inner mechanisms of the affective economy, and de-rationalize 'reason' as well as de-irrationalize 'emotion'. With Foucault (1980), one has to realize that just as domination is always present, resistance is always possible. With Deleuze and Guattari (1977), one has to learn there is always a danger of sliding from 'schizophrenia' to 'paranoia', from democracy to Fascism. With Baudrillard (1983a, 1988), one has to be sensitive to the changing historical conditions which shift the dominant (affective) logic of (hot) seduction to that of (cold) fascination, from interface confrontation to media absorption, from the mood of explosion (of a rock concert) to implosion (of MTV). Whether the economies of power, desire and the symbolic are 'correct' is perhaps a different question; these analytical tools offer an entering sluice for rethinking cultural politics. The weakness of micropolitical economy is that it remains abstract and its obscure languages produce the effect of an anti-elitist elitism: 'technical' terms cannot be understood *outside* the 'critical circle'. (But doesn't one badly need new languages to address historically neglected domains?) What postmodernism has to learn from cultural studies is to *localize* the inner logics of the affective, or to 'sociologize' the working logics within specific groups. Micropolitical struggle cannot afford to assume that similar effects exist in different social groups if postmodern politics is to preserve differences. In underlining the 'fluid' nature of micropolitics, postmodernism ought not abandon but rather ought to incorporate specific, local politics of gender, race and class.

To end this section, I would suggest that the ideological and the discursive, signifying and asignifying, representational and the affective, are not mutually exclusive categories. To avoid the political mistakes of 'either/or', a postmodern cultural studies has to recognize, on one level, the real effect of the discursive, the non-signifying and simulation, and on another level, the continual existence of ideological and signifying practices and representation. The questions become: where is the point of contact, what are the effects produced by one side on another? Do they cancel out or reinforce or remain indifferent to each other? These are the questions of cultural politics that post-Marxism must begin to address.

Mass media: the Baudrillard clash

The importance of mass media as a site for struggle for both postmodernism and cultural studies provides the final axis for my essay. The dispute resides mostly in the work of Baudrillard, notably on the questions of simulation, the status of the hyper-real and the masses. In what follows, I will use Baudrillard's work as a bargaining site to negotiate its validity and pinpoint its inadequacies.

The current 'Baudrillard clash' has triggered both antagonism and excitement. A common tendency of the responses is either a total rejection or an uncritical embracing. The strange thing is that neither side can entirely deny there is *something* at stake. What this something is, is still largely unclear. Hebdige (1987b: 70) thus expresses this 'ambivalence': 'I realize the pertinence of what he [Baudrillard] is saying. But I also have my suspicions that the kind of will motivating his work seems to be poisonous'. These very doubts define perhaps the possibility of negotiating a space, an in-between ground; beyond the logic of either/or, we can start to limit the levels and specificities, to slow down the speed, to mark out the critical zone where Baudrillard's movement goes too far, too fast.

The most debatable issue is Baudrillard's theory of simulacrum — the central area of cultural studies' contestation. Because of his 'inflation' of the simulation effect, Baudrillard has been accused with the following names and/or positions: he is an 'essentialist' (Hall, 1986: 46), a Frankfurt School follower with an even 'darker vision' (Chambers, 1986: 100); his work has produced 'cynicism/nihilism' and 'fatalism' (Hebdige, 1986: 92, 95); he is too 'pessimistic' (McRobbie, 1986: 110). The problem with such accusations is that it reinstates an 'essentialism' of the author and his text; whereas no attempt is made to actively appropriate the theory (not his), or whatever may be useful of it, for different, other usages.

Grossbergs's (1986: 74) critique does go beyond the naming game: 'Baudrillard's theory of the simulacrum . . . conflates the social formation with a particular set of effects, with the plane of simulation, rendering all of social reality the simple product of media causality.' This, then, is where Baudrillard's media imperialism unfolds. But that certainly does not mean that there is no such thing as the simulation effect. We should therefore limit his level of argument to one plane of effect, to de-essentialize his discourse, to recognize simulation as part of the real without reducing it to the *only* effect operating in the social world. As McRobbie (1986: 115) puts it, 'There *is* no going back. For populations transfixed on images which are themselves a reality', what we have to do is to theorize the 'images', 'texts' and 'signs' as themselves part of the real rather than as representations of the real. The incorporation of simulation into the real serves to avoid the unnecessary trap of truth and falsity, as well as the 'crisis of representation'. Only thus can cultural analysis come closer to the lives of the populace.

Let me come to the question of what Hall (1986: 49) calls postmodernism's assertion of 'the sheer facticity of thing: things *are just* on the surface'. The assertion that 'things are just on the surface', as a postmodernist tenet, has been profoundly misunderstood. Foucault's (1986) denial of hermeneutic depth is a rejection of the *essential* layer of an artifact (be it a historical event, or a cultural sign) which is seen as determining its final meaning; that is, there are always multiple layers or surfaces to be accounted for, none of which have the final say. Similarly, Baudrillard's (1988) notion of 'obscenity' points to the contemporary tendency in the media to render things visible, to strip away 'private' secrecy; but this does not mean *everything* is on the surface. Further, 'on the surface' does not mean visibility: desire, the symbolic and power are precisely not something that can be seen, but rather, that work, effectively, on the social and physical body. There are, therefore, two ways to read 'everything is on the surface': (1) since the collapse of 'the depth model', no privileged level, layer or surface can assume the final 'truth' any longer; (2) historically, what had been invisible depth, secrecy or interiority can now be 'brought to the surface'. Taking 'surface' thus, I would suggest that Foucault's (1979a) analysis of different surfaces of prison technology, Deleuze and Guattari's (1977) 'Body without Organs' (as the surfaces of inscription and circulation of capital and desire) and Baudrillard's (1983a) genealogical traces of the multiple trajectories of the simulation machines have all sought to address reality as produced within the relations amongst these surfaces after the historical collapse of 'the depth', or depth as the final determinant.

On the question of the subject, both positions hold that 'a unified, stable and self-determining subject' no longer exists (Grossberg, 1986: 72). Instead, cultural studies' multiple subject-positions and postmodernism's nomadic-schizo subject are always in fluid transformation, when moving from one context to another — 'The subject itself has become a site of struggle', as Grossberg (1986: 72) puts it. Nevertheless, cultural studies, in its concrete analyses, always privileges 'one' moment of subject positioning. For instance, influenced by film theory and traditional communication research, cultural studies will speak of the 'audience' (the spectator) in front of a TV program — the subject is positioned by the camera angle and inserted into a textually constructed context. Falling into a traditional model of communication, cultural studies fail to see that the 'moment' itself (e.g. watching TV) can always be multiplied; that is, an audience is not simply a reading subject, s/he can always 'work out', cook or fall asleep at the same time; and the textual context can also be plural. Further, when s/he reads 'intensely', the subject can flow into the hyperspatial apparatus and disappear from the 'local' context. To use the term 'audience' thus implies an extraction of particular instance out of a 'larger' social context: a bit like doing social science experimental research on a higher level of abstraction. (Yes, but how would or could one analyze otherwise than through abstracting and abstraction, whence the need perhaps not only to stop making sense, but to stop analyzing?) In effect, cultural studies' 'audience' research, its theory of encoding/decoding and its theory of preferred reading/actual reading largely reproduce the modernist communication model of transcendence. I do not dismiss this model for its modernism, but the model itself cannot adequately account for the complex flow of social forces and its various conditions of possibility. On the other hand, the postmodern schizo subject has recognized the fragmented and segmented flow without attempting to extract the privileged moment for analysis. In Baudrillard's works, the emphasis on spatial operation addresses the intertextual positionings of the subject; it always upholds multiple positions at each 'moment'. In fact, what postmodern cultural studies must analyze is not simply the location of the subject within the webs composed of multiple, intersected lines; it is also the unextractable *relations* (the lines on which partial subject-points are inscribed) which form the complex social networks.

Finally, I want to turn to the most critical issue: the masses. Deleuze and Guattari (1987), and Baudrillard (1983b) have attempted to theorize the masses as a spatial and functional concept, and as molecular flow, to displace 'empiricist' individuals and the composition of atomized units. Further, they stress the internal, non-separable linkage between the masses and the media to pinpoint certain working logics, strategies and effects within this hyperspace: absorption, neutralization, indifference, refusal or the black hole, and the critical implication of these effects in confrontation with dominant social powers. Admittedly, the postmodern reformulation remains abstract and does not clarify the 'differences' between social groups or spaces. But, this reformulation has gone beyond existing understandings of the masses (as a political imaginary, as cultural dupes or as an empty referent), and provides an entering point for further elaborations or challenges.

In attacking Baudrillard's notion of the masses, Fiske and Watts (1986: 106) make a moral claim: Baudrillard does not 'respect' social groups and 'lumps [these] dismissively under the term "the masses" '. If 'the people' or 'the popular' would make the analysis more 'respectable' and less 'dismissive', so be it. (Might not 'the people' and/or 'the popular' sound more respectful but be no less dismissive and homogenizing?) Hall's (1986: 52) argument is more specific: in Baudrillard, 'the masses and the mass media are nothing but a passive reflection of the historical, economic and political forces'. But I would argue that in Baudrillard, the masses are neither passive, nor active, nor a pure reflection, but functional. Hall (1986: 52) goes on to argue that 'postmodernism has yet to go through that point [the masses]; it has yet to actually think through and engage the question of the masses'. Deleuze and Guattari's 'molecular mass' and Baudrillard's 'critical' mass precisely address this crucial question. But when Baudrillard responds, as it were, to the call to think through, to theorize and to conceptualize the masses in micropolitical terms, Hall

(1986: 52) again charges him with 'renouncing' critical thought 'on behalf of the masses' and 'us[ing] "the masses" in the abstract to fuel or underpin [his] own intellectual positions'. The question at stake is, rather: is it illegitimate to talk *about*, to study, to theorize the people, the popular, the masses, because as soon as one talks about them, one runs the risk of 'representing' or speaking/writing 'on behalf of the masses'? In my view, to theorize the masses or to study the working class is different from speaking for them. (But ultimately, is it different enough? Might it not be a speaking *with*, a falling silent in order to listen to? Otherwise, how can one even begin to understand the particularities of popular forces?) Although Baudrillard's rhetoric does give rise to such a doubt and he should probably plead guilty to it, his formulations cannot, should not, so easily be dismissed.

In fact, both Hall and Baudrillard begin with Benjamin's observation of the masses as an emerging disruptive, historical force, as the subject of history. Hall however has not gone much beyond recognizing the power of the masses. On the other hand, Baudrillard is able to carry further the concept of the masses and elaborate 'its positivity'. Baudrillard's functional concept of the masses is non-existent in cultural studies; in the latter, the mass becomes either an imaginary (political) referent or a concrete individual. To conceptualize the masses as internal to the media and as moving spaces is a vantage point established by postmodernism. The problem, however, with conceptualizing the masses as a critical hyperspace does seem to do away with sociologism; it gives up sociological determination, although recognizes internal differences; but it cannot unite these differences into concrete struggles.

Following Hebdige (1986: 94), post-Marxism must pursue the politics of the 'popular': to produce what Foucault calls strategic analyses in order to grasp fully the detailed textures of popular desire, ideology and concerns. Post-Marxism must not only maintain structural analysis, both molar and molecular, of the relations within social networks, but also reclaim the insight of phenomenology, to 'experience' popular experiences, to forge strategic connection, to construct lines of flight.

For a political synchronizer

From the above, it seems that the (theoretical) differences and (political) contradictions between postmodernism and cultural studies are not as ineradicable as one might assume. It is always a difference in emphasis, and a concomitant neglect of certain domains. As a provisional conclusion, I would argue that it is cultural studies' refusal to 'abandon the terrain of marxism' (Grossberg, 1986: 70), or more precisely, the 'name' (as if it were a matter of essentials) of Marxism, that separates the two discursive formations. But when one looks closer, or from another angle, the 'post-Marxism' of cultural studies is not so different from the 'post-Marxism' of postmodernism. As Hall puts it,

> I am a 'post-marxist' only in the sense that I recognize the necessity to move beyond orthodox marxism, beyond the notion of marxism guaranteed by the laws of history. But I still operate somewhere within what I understand to be the *discursive limits* of a marxist position . . . So 'post' means, for me, going on thinking on the ground of a set of *established problems*, a problematic. It doesn't mean deserting that terrain but rather, using it as one's *reference point*. (Hall, 1986: 58; emphasis added)

If post-Marxism can be understood as (1) the movement 'beyond orthodox marxism', (2) as the attempt 'beyond the notion of marxism guaranteed by the laws of history', and (3) as the persistent usage of Marxism 'as one's reference point', then I do not see any *essential* difference, since these three problematics are precisely what postmodernism is engaged with. Perhaps the 'name' of Marxism does make a difference (to the extent that holding on to it claims and authorizes one's patri-lineage, affiliations and right to write and speak). However, (1) if both cultural studies and postmodernism agree on the necessity to fashion strategic alliances, or to 'advance along multiple fronts' (Hebdige, 1986: 94); (2) if the political concerns of both positions are similar if not the same (i.e. against domination, against capitalism, against racism, sexism and the exploitation of labor, in short, against the social status quo), no matter whether they share an *ultimate*, 'positive' goal (socialism? — a term which both positions no longer know how to define in its specificities); (3) if both positions try to stand *with* (rather than speak *for* or even *about*, and thereby impose on) the local oppressed groups, to open a space *for them to speak for themselves* (and withstand the will to encroach upon this space for the sake of better understanding them), to bring these 'minor' voices back into the present moment, as well as history; and (4) if both seek to intervene in existing social fields and engage in concrete struggles; then, cultural studies and critical postmodernism might begin to truly effect a collapse of academic disciplines and theoretical factions, and to constitute a new theoretical-political terrain (under the new name of post-Marxism?). (This is not to deny the differences within post-Marxism, but to activate these differences for productive usages.)

If our purpose is to herald a postmodern cultural studies which will move beyond the limits of both postmodernism and cultural studies, then 'it would be foolish to present a polar opposition between the Gramscian line(s) [of cultural studies] and the (heterogeneous) Posts [of postmodernisms] . . . there are clear cross-Channel links between the two sets of concerns and emphases' (Hebdige, 1986: 96). 'Toward' a postmodern cultural studies seeks then to effect a critical collage of postmodernism and cultural studies, to construct a 'political synchronizer' which will move toward a Marxism or post-Marxism or a post(modern)-Marxism of the 1990s. This is (and there is no better way of saying it)

a marxism that has survived, returning perhaps a little lighter on its feet, (staggering at first), a marxism more prone perhaps to listen, learn, adapt and to appreciate, for instance, that words like 'emergency' and 'struggle' don't just mean fight, conflict, war and death but birthing, the prospect of new life emerging: a struggling to the light. (Hebdige, 1986: 97)

Turning to 'the dark' side of the present is the ineluctable direction where 'the light' of a 'rearticulated' post-Marxism of the future may be seen.

A permanent (local) struggle

The irony, and perhaps the failure, of a critical postmodernism resides in its political double bind. On the one hand, it calls for a movement toward the local, the specific, the oppressed. On the other hand, it continuously operates at the level of the global, the abstract and the general. (Yes, this paper as well, sadly.) The local, the specific and the oppressed thus appear to be peripheral in the postmodern spectrum. It is perhaps at this final moment that a dismantling of hidden ideologies and problematic assumptions may begin.

The ideology of the new, or what Hall (1986: 47) calls the 'tyranny of the New', of the emergent, always runs the risk of diminishing potential political forces, no matter how archaic they might be. As Deleuze and Guattari (1977: 257) put it, 'archaisms have a perfectly current function . . . they represent social and potentially political forces'. The symptomatic assumption, that the formation of postmodernity (as a traversing configuration) has unequivocally taken place, whence the calling everything into question, is now to be challenged. Although it is possible to identify differences, changing formations and new constellations, this somewhat 'positivistic' strategy, which concentrates on identifying 'new' tendencies, fails to emphasize those problems which are as 'real', as 'bad' in both modernity and postmodernity, despite their having put on a new coat and entered into new relations. Totalitarian Fascism did not go with the end of the Second World War. In fact, it infiltrates our bodies, our minds, not simply in the world behind the (already torn down) 'iron curtain', but also in the so-called Western democratic countries. How does the USA support the totalitarian regimes throughout the world? Why do people support Ronald Reagan, Oliver North, George Bush, Maggie Thatcher? Moreover, although class relations in the 'West' become more and more complex, this does not mean that they no longer exist. The living conditions of Blacks and poor Whites are worse and worse: they have moved from a 'lower' class to an 'under' class (West, 1987). In the Third World countries, no one can deny that local class differences are an essential line of struggle. Poverty and the unequal distribution of wealth have intensified, explosively.

Hall (1986: 46) has indicated another problem inherent in postmodernism: 'the label "postmodernism", especially its American appropriation (and it *is* about how the world dreams itself to be "American") . . . is irrevocably Euro- or western-centric in its whole episteme'. Indeed, postmodernism has focused on America as the dominant (imaged and imagined) referent point of analysis, and has been thus in complicity with the American 'Empire', with hegemonic first world academic criticism and modes of analyses, despite 'critical encounters'; postmodernism ignores the rest of the world, despite the avowed suspicions of 'global' analysis.

Hall has also quite correctly asked: 'Is postmodernism a global or a "western" phenomenon?' (1986: 46). In my view, it is definitely a 'local', Western phenomenon. The attempt to globalize and the failure to localize postmodernism have taken Jameson into a 'critical' imperialism (Chen, 1989). A resistance to universality, however, is not equivalent to the contention that Western postmodernity has no connection with and produces no effects on 'non-Western' societies or vice versa. If 'late' capitalism is part of the 'postmodern project', can one eliminate its impact on the other 'half' of the globe (if one might still call this other half the 'socialist project') by arguing that it is a 'local' phenomenon? The fact is that the international structure of capitalism has escalated and has put most 'developing' countries in permanent poverty. From a local point of view somewhere between 'first' and 'third', it is within the geographical site of the 'underdeveloped' or 'developing' territories that the evils of capitalist exploitation are most nakedly revealed. The direct exploitation of the labor forces has moved from the West into the Third World countries.

Further, on political and cultural levels, does not Reagan's or Bush's 'postmodern' world policy *determine* the US's post-colonies', such as Taiwan's, cultural and political discrimination against Palestine and the Palestinians? To be sure, the cultural imperialism thesis is both valid and problematic. It is problematic if one understands the thesis in the sense that American imperialism is able to *mechanically* impose its ideological content on Third World countries without any resistance: watching *Dallas* would therefore amount to an unquestioning acceptance of bourgeois capitalist ideology. Historically, this is obviously an invalid argument. People in the Third World do watch *Dallas*, but in their specific ways, framed and in accordance to local history and politics. But, at the same time, that the 'imageries' (traces of American life) whereby ideological articulation is conducted are pervasively imperializing is unquestionable.

That is, it is not so much an ideological content but its form which seems to follow an American trend: TV culture, blue jeans, punk style or yuppie ways of life (Taiwan has translated, and sectors of the people live by, *The Yuppie Handbook*). I am not suggesting that 'quoting' American (and now, increasingly Japanese) emblems may not constitute oppositional forces in relation to local dominant culture. But at the same time one has to ask *why* that citation is American (or Japanese), not Nicaraguan. Thus, the thesis of cultural imperialism has to be transformed with an emphasis not only on the ideological but the simulation of ways of life, as a much more subtle form of articulation.

One simply cannot deny that struggle and resistance still go on throughout the world, no matter how archaic the form they might take, for no one has the right to deny the vitality of the local struggles of oppressed peoples (Hebdige, 1986: 73). Turning to the local and the oppressed is the political choice which post-Marxism must finally make. *A permanent (local) struggle* against the dominant conjoins (conjures up) and *collapses* the differences between the modern and the postmodern. It is here that postmodernism ends itself and a politically charged postmodern cultural studies of a post-Marxist sort has yet to begin.

Notes

Comments on earlier versions of this paper by Hanno Hardt, Larry Grossberg, Ien Ang, Jennifer Slack, Edward Chien, John Fiske and Ann Kaplan are gratefully acknowledged. I especially note and thank Naifei Ding for her voice from the outside and recurring, disruptive bits and pieces.

1. See Laclau (1977) and Laclau and Mouffe (1985). The major site of debate has taken place in *New Left Review*.

2. That this battle has largely been ignored might have things to do with the 'minor' site (the 'marginal' status of the journal) on which the debate was first initiated. In the *Journal of Communication Inquiry* 10(2), 1986, a special issue devoted to Stuart Hall, the battle was first initiated. In the interview with Hall and responding essays by Grossberg, Hebdige, Chambers, Fiske and Watts, McRobbie and Hardt, disrupting forces of postmodernism are sympathetically recognized, but hidden political dangers are critically contested by these practitioners of cultural criticism. My discussion will not be limited to these essays, but use them as a central line of organizing the debate.

3. It is perhaps only with the becoming silent of 'major' discourses (dominant and/or critical) that the 'minor noises' can be finally heard and listened. Whence the realization of this very project's complicity and affiliations, which 'authorize' its critique while at the same time defining its limited and limiting tactics.

4. Colin Sparks (1989) has lucidly traced the formation of cultural studies in the British social and intellectual history, which explains how these concerns became the focus of analysis.

References

Baudrillard, J. (1981) 'Beyond the Unconscious: The Symbolic', *Discourse* 3: 60–87.
Baudrillard, J. (1983a) *Simulation*. New York: Semiotext(e).
Baudrillard, J. (1983b) *In the Shadow of Silent Majorities*. New York: Semiotext(e).
Baudrillard, J. (1986) 'L'amerique comme fiction', *Art Press* 103: 40–2.
Baudrillard, J. (1987) 'The Year 2000 Has Already Happened', pp. 35–44 in A. Kroker and M. Kroker (eds), *Body Invaders: Panic Sex in America*. Montreal: The New World Perspectives.
Baudrillard, J. (1988) *The Ecstacy of Communication*. New York: Semiotext(e).
Chambers, I. (1986) 'Waiting on the End of the World?', *Journal of Communication Inquiry* 10(2): 99–103.
Chen, K. H. (1988) 'History, Theory and Cultural Politics: Towards a Minor Discourse of Mass-Media and Postmodernity', unpublished dissertation, University of Iowa.
Chen, K. H. (1989) 'Deterritorializing "Critical" Studies in "Mass" Communication', *Journal of Communication Inquiry* 13(2): 43–61.
Deleuze, G. and Guattari, F. (1977) *Anti-Oedipus: Capitalism and Schizophrenia*. New York: Viking Press.
Deleuze, G. and Guattari, F. (1987) *A Thousand Plateaus: Capitalism and Schizophrenia*. Minneapolis: University of Minnesota Press.
Fiske, J. and Watts, J. (1986) 'An Articulating Culture — Hall, Meaning and Power', *Journal of Communication Inquiry* 10(2): 104–7.
Foucault, M. (1979a) *Discipline and Punish: The Birth of the Prison*. New York: Vintage.
Foucault, M. (1979b) *History of Sexuality, Volume I: An Introduction*. London: Penguin.
Foucault, M. (1980) *Power/Knowledge*. New York: Pantheon.
Foucault, M. (1986) 'Nietzsche, Freud, Marx', *Critical Text* 3(2): 1–5.
Foucault, M. (1987) *Maurice Blanchot: The Thought from Outside*. New York: Zone Books.
Grossberg, L. (1984) ' "I'd Rather Feel Bad than not Feel Anything at All" (Rock and Roll: Pleasure and Power)', *Enclitic* 8: 94–111.
Grossberg, L. (1986) 'History, Politics and Postmodernism: Stuart Hall and Cultural Studies', *Journal of Communication Inquiry* 10(2): 61–77.
Guattari, F. (1977) 'Everybody Wants to be a Fascist', *Semiotext(e)* 2(3): 62–71.
Habermas, J. (1987) *The Philosophical Discourse of Modernity*. Cambridge, MA: The MIT Press.
Hall, S. (1986) 'On Postmodernism and Articulation: An Interview with Stuart Hall', *Journal of Communication Inquiry* 10(2): 45–60.
Hebdige, D. (1986) 'Postmodernism and "The Other Side" ', *Journal of Communication Inquiry* 10(2): 78–98.
Hebdige, D. (1987a) *Cut 'N' Mix: Culture, Identity and Caribbean Music*. London: Comedia.
Hebdige, D. (1987b) 'Hiding in the Light: Extended Club Mix with Dick Hebdige', *Art & Text* 26: 67–78.
Huyssen, A. (1986) *After the Great Divide: Modernism, Mass Culture, Postmodernism*. Bloomington: Indiana University Press.
Jameson, F. (1983) 'Postmodernism and Consumer Society', pp. 111–25 in H. Foster (ed.), *The Anti-Aesthetic*. Port Townsend: Bay Press.

Jameson, F. (1984) 'Postmodernism, or the Cultural Logic of Late Capitalism', *New Left Review* 146: 53–92.

Laclau, E. (1977) *Politics and Ideology in Marxist Theory*. London: Verso.

Laclau, E. and Mouffe, C. (1985) *Hegemony and Socialist Strategy*. London: Verson.

Lyotard, J. F. (1984) 'Philosophy and Painting in the Age of Their Experimentation: Contribution to an Idea of Postmodernity', *Camera Obscura* 12: 111–25.

McRobbie (1986) 'Postmodernism and Popular Culture', *Journal of Communication Inquiry* 10(2): 108–16.

Rorty, R. (1984) 'Habermas and Lyotard on Postmodernity', *Praxis International* 4: 32–44.

Sparks, C. (1989) 'Experience, Ideology and Articulation: Stuart Hall and the Development of Culture', *Journal of Communication Inquiry* 13(2): 79–87.

West, C (1987) 'Interview with Cornell West', *Flash Art* 133: 51–5.

4

Feminism and cultural studies

Sarah Franklin, Celia Lury and Jackie Stacey

Introduction

Both feminism and cultural studies have complicated and contradictory histories, inside and outside the academy. It would be impossible, as well as perhaps undesirable, to map out a comprehensive outline of these developments here, as if there were simply one single, linear or unified account. However, we feel it is important to highlight what we consider to be some of the key issues in these developments in order to consider the nature of their relationship. In the first section of this article we look at some parallels between feminism and cultural studies in terms of these histories; in the second, we look at the lack of overlap, and explore some more general questions about the feminist analysis of culture; and in the final section, we outline three areas of work that illustrate three kinds of overlap between feminism and cultural studies.

Inside and outside the academy — contested territories

Both women's studies and cultural studies have a strong link with radical politics outside the academy in common, having their academic agendas informed by, or linked to, the feminist movement and left politics respectively.[1] The interdisciplinary basis of each subject has produced consistent and important challenges to conventional academic boundaries and power structures. Thus, there has been a shared focus on the analysis of forms of power and oppression, and on the politics of the production of knowledge within the academy, as well as elsewhere in society. In addition,

Media, Culture and Society (SAGE, London, Newbury Park and New Delhi), Vol. 13 (1991), 171–192

both subjects have attempted to challenge some of the conventions of academic practice, such as introducing collective, rather than individual work, encouraging greater student participation in syllabus construction, and opening up spaces for connections to be made between personal experience and theoretical questions. These challenges have recently come under increasing pressure in the context of public spending cut-backs in Britain and the attempt under the Thatcher governments to transform educational practice politically in the name of 'enterprise'.

Feminism and women's studies

Despite the commonalities mentioned above, women's studies and cultural studies have developed unevenly. Women's studies has offered feminism an institutional base in further and adult education over the last ten years; there are now a number of undergraduate and postgraduate courses in women's studies, and most major publishers now have women's studies or gender studies lists, alongside the wide range of publications available from the feminist presses.[2] Many of these achievements have been hard-won, and feminists in all areas of education have struggled to get issues of gender inequality onto the syllabus and to keep them there. Struggling against tokenism, the 'add women and stir' approach, co-option, and marginalization, feminists have managed to establish a space within educational institutions from which to document, analyse and theorize the position of women in society.

Early interventions by feminists in the academy often involved highlighting the absence of attention to gender within existing theories and debates. As well as challenging existing academic knowledges, feminists have also introduced new issues into the academic arena. Many of these emerged from the women's movement in the 1970s and 1980s, where consciousness raising groups, political campaigns and national and local conferences were important in raising issues based on women's experiences, which were unfamiliar in mainstream political and academic contexts. Concerns such as male violence, sexuality and reproduction were introduced onto academic agendas by feminists convinced that the 'personal was political'. These topics, among others, became subjects of study in their own right in sociology, anthropology, history and literature, as well as within women's studies.

Alongside the documenting of women's oppression which occurred across a broad range of disciplines, feminists began to develop generalized theories to explain how and why women are oppressed. These theories have taken very different starting points and produced a highly complex and often competing set of perspectives on the subject of women's subordination. While it is problematic to summarize such a large area of scholarship, because of the dangers of reductionism and exclusion, a few examples are nonetheless illustrative of the developments in this area. Some feminists have drawn on already existing social theory to formulate generalized accounts of women's oppression; so, for example, feminists have extended existing Marxist theories of the exploitation of labour within capitalism to look at women's position in paid employment. These writers include Beechey (1987) Phizacklea (1983), and Dex (1985). Marxist theory has also been extended to examine areas conventionally outside its remit, such as the sexual division of labour within the household; so, for example, Seccombe (1974), James and Dalla Costa (1973) all contributed to the domestic labour debate. Other feminists, such as Ferguson (1989), Walby (1986; 1990), Lerner (1986) and O'Brien (1981), believe the basis of women's subordination to be located outside class relations, and have developed theories of patriarchy as a relatively separate system of exploitation. Among those who have attempted to introduce entirely new frameworks and concepts to analyse patriarchal society are MacKinnon (1982, 1987, 1989), Daly (1978) and Rich (1977, 1980). Finally, feminists who have emphasized the embeddedness of patriarchal social relations in a matrix of intersecting inequalities, such as racism, heterosexism, imperialism and class division, include Lorde (1984), Spelman (1990), Bunch (1988) and Hooks (1984, 1989).

The usefulness of the term 'patriarchy' in explanations of women's oppression has itself been debated within feminism (Rowbotham, 1981; Barrett, 1980; Beechey, 1987), and this, in turn, has encouraged a greater specificity in its use. One of the key issues in this debate has been the extent to which women are universally subordinated. Feminists working within anthropology (Ortner, 1974; Rosaldo, 1974; MacCormack, 1980; Strathern, 1980) and history (Leacock, 1981; Lerner, 1986; Riley, 1988; Davidoff and Hall, 1987) have been particularly significant in this debate about the commonality of women's subordination cross-culturally and trans-historically. The analysis of pre-capitalist societies has been a particularly important source of insight into the question of the extent to which gender inequality can be understood as a product of colonization, imperialism and capital accumulation (Mies, 1986; Leacock, 1981; Ortner and Whitehead, 1981).

Early feminist theory tended to emphasize the commonalities of women's oppression, in order to establish that male domination was systematic and affected all areas of women's lives. Feminists offered analyses of women's subordination, exploitation and objectification at all levels of society. This emphasis on commonality, however, often resulted in the neglect of differences between women. Differences based on ethnic identity, nationality, class and sexuality have been increasingly important within feminist work, leading both to the documentation of experiences (Bryan et al, 1985; Moraga and Anzaldua, 1981; Lorde, 1984; Walker,

1984), and to challenges to theories and concepts within feminism based on limited models of the category 'woman' (Carby, 1982; Parmar, 1982; Riley, 1988; Lugones and Spelman, 1983; Spelman, 1990; Ramazanoglu, 1989). These changes within feminist theory have been influenced by changes within the women's movement more generally, where differences between women have come to be seen as one of the strengths of the feminist movement, in terms of a diversity of both national and international politics (Cole, 1987; Bunch, 1988). These differences between women, however, have also been seen to call into question the collective 'we' of feminism (Ramazanoglu, 1989; Hooks, 1984, 1989; Cliff, 1983). The challenge remains, at both a theoretical and political level, for feminists to be able to hold onto certain commonalities in women's position in relation to oppressive social relations, without denying the very real differences between women and the resulting specificities in the forms of their oppression.

The questioning of the category 'woman' within feminist theory was not only a result of changes in the women's movement and challenges to the limits of its inclusions. It also drew its impetus from areas of academic theorizing which had a significant influence on feminist thought, namely, poststructuralism and postmodernism (Weedon, 1987; Fraser and Nicholson, 1988; Nicholson, 1990; Diamond and Quinby, 1988; Spivak, 1987). The general engagement with these theories of ideology, subjectivity, discourse and sexual difference, was seen by many feminists to offer a more complex understanding of the operations of patriarchal power and the reproduction of inequality. Indeed, the scepticism about the unity of identities, characteristic of these perspectives, produced a questioning of the possibility of a unified and meaningful category 'woman', the subject of so much recent feminist analysis. The influence of psychoanalytic theory in particular, which asserted the disruptive nature of the unconscious to any coherent, unified identity, undermined some of the foundational assumptions of feminist analysis. However, these influences remain relatively marginal within many women's studies courses and research projects, as well as being theoretical perspectives which many see as incompatible with feminism (for a discussion of this issue, see Wilson, 1981; Sayers, 1986; Brennan, 1989; Mitchell, 1975; Gallop, 1982; Rose, 1986). These are contested areas within feminist research, but what remains important is that feminist debates continue to produce more complex understandings of the different forms of women's subordination, patriarchal society and the conditions of its existence and reproduction.

Marxist theory, Left politics and cultural studies

Responding to changes in Marxist theory and Left politics, cultural studies has been a major site of developments within theories of cultural production, and more recently, cultural consumption. Like women's studies, cultural studies is not a unified body of work, set of practices or even an easily defined academic subject (Johnson, 1983). Rather, it has offered a place within higher education, and elsewhere in adult and further education, for traditional disciplines to be challenged, for the kinds of knowledges produced to be questioned and for power relations in educational practices to be transformed.

Cultural studies has been a particularly important site of developments within Marxist theory which attempt to leave behind the limits of economic determinism, and an over-emphasis on the mode of production as the key site of contradiction within society. This shift has taken place in Marxist theory generally, but cultural studies has been central in the development of analyses which take the cultural dimensions of power and inequality seriously. This is, in part, because cultural studies itself emerged from critical perspectives within several disciplines, including history, literature and sociology. These perspectives challenged the terms of previous theoretical assumptions within those subjects. For example, in the study of literature, Marxist cultural theorists challenged bourgeois notions of the literary, and the limited understandings of 'culture' prevalent in that academic subject. The study of popular cultural forms was introduced onto the syllabus alongside a re-evaluation of the literary canon (and indeed of the concept of the canon itself). Cultural studies has provided similar challenges to the academic analysis of history, the state, education and the media (Johnson et al., 1982; Hall et al., 1980) and, in conjunction with Marxist theorists in these fields, produced a substantial body of alternative knowledges and approaches.

Recent developments within cultural studies can be attributed to various influences. One of the most important of these has been the influence of critical theory, particularly the Frankfurt School, poststructuralism, psychoanalysis and postmodernism. Discourse theory, deriving from the work of Foucault, has been a significant strand in poststructuralist theory, challenging traditional understandings of the relationship between knowledge, power and politics. The notion of discourse provided an alternative to the concept of ideology which had been developed within Marxist-influenced cultural studies to explore the cultural aspects of the reproduction of inequality. Through an understanding of discourse as power–knowledge, dispersed in a network of micro-relations, this work criticized monolithic and totalizing notions of causality, determination and challenged assumptions of a linear, progressive history. It also proposed an understanding of the subject produced through the discourses of 'self'-knowledge, developed through the construction of social categories such as madness, discipline and sexuality.

The critical elaboration of psychoanalysis under the influence of poststructuralism, most notably by Jacques Lacan, and the subsequent emergence of what has come to be known as 'sexual difference theory', associated with journals such as *m/f* and *Screen*, has been another source of important theoretical influences on cultural studies. In particular, a concern with the importance of the unconscious in the formation of identity led to an acknowledgement of both the fragmented nature of subjectivity, and the difficulty of maintaining stable, unified identities. Taking the notion of the unconscious seriously meant that the previously unified subject of cultural analysis was called into question; instead social identities were seen to be complex and heterogeneous. In addition, questions about the role of pleasure, desire and fantasy began to be analysed more frequently as part of the process of cultural construction of subjects, identities and practices.

Most recently, the emergence of postmodernism as an influential critical perspective (Lyotard, 1984; Baudrillard, 1988; Jameson, 1984) has challenged the so-called foundationalist underpinnings which had informed previous theory within cultural studies. Postmodernism in this sense is associated with a set of questions about the state of knowledge in contemporary society. It poses a challenge both to conventional under-standings of the standpoint of the knowing subject (objectivity, neutrality, distance) and the traditional object of knowledge (a separate reality about which the truth can be discovered). These modernist, foundationalist or post-Enlightenment assumptions are challenged by postmodernism, which argues that they are essentialist, falsely universalist and ultimately unsustainable. Unlike poststructuralism, which also raised these issues, postmodernism is associated both with actual contemporary phenomena, such as architectural styles and other representational practices, and with broad changes in the organization of Western consumer culture. These changes are seen to include the breakdown of the historical distinction between high and popular culture, the disappearance of what is variously called the depth, content or referent of signification, and the increasing instability and complexity of contemporary cultural processes.

Another of the main influences transforming cultural studies through the 1980s has been the influence of feminism. *Women Take Issue* (Women's Studies Group, 1978) was an early example of feminist work within cultural studies, both using and attempting to transform Marxist theory. Looking at questions of cultural reproduction as well as production, *Women Take Issue* highlighted the need for cultural studies to engage with the 'personal' dimensions of culture in the political context of a feminist analysis. Since then, the effect of feminism on cultural studies has had an increasing significance. The shift, for example, from interest in issues concerning ideology and hegemony to those concerning identity and subjectivity can, in part, be attributed to feminist interventions, as well as to the influence of psychoanalysis and poststructuralism. Another area of increasing interest within some strands of cultural studies, which can be seen as evidence of the impact of feminism, is sexuality. However, while work on the construction of sexual identities (Mulvey, 1989; Heath, 1982), the analysis of narratives of romance (Modleski, 1982; Radway, 1987), cultural representations of AIDS (Watney, 1987), and studies of state regulation of sexual 'deviancy' (Weeks, 1981, 1985) address sexuality as well as gender, the way in which sexuality has been taken up has been selective, and often has not been integrated with feminist analyses such as those of the patriarchal institution of heterosexuality. Similarly, lesbian and gay issues are only very gradually beginning to be taken seriously within cultural studies.

Theories of ethnicity and analyses of racism have also made an important contribution to shaping developments within cultural studies. *Policing the Crisis* (Hall et al., 1978) stressed the role of racist representations of social problems such as crime, in the emergence of a law and order society in Britain in the early 1970s. Following this and other work on the construction and representations of ethnicity and national identity, *The Empire Strikes Back* (CCCS, 1982) criticized the pathologization of race within race relations and sociology, and the racism of some white feminist analyses. It also explored the importance of racist ideologies in both shaping aspects of state regulation in Britain, such as immigration law, and the construction of notions of Britishness and citizenship informing contemporary definitions of national identity. Another area in cultural studies that has been influenced by the study of ethnicity has been the analysis of subcultural practices (Hebdige, 1979). Earlier models of subculture were challenged and transformed to include an acknowledgement of both the history of ethnic inequality and racism, and the struggles for collective self-representation by black people. However, the *influence* of debates about, and struggles against, racism on cultural studies continues to be rather uneven.

Changes within left politics have also had an effect on the kinds of political questions taken seriously within cultural studies. What has been seen as a crisis in left politics has led to a rethinking of political strategies, allegiances and agendas by some on the Left. In certain circles, this has contributed to a broadening of agendas, and a desire for stronger political alliances with other radical forces such as the women's movement, black politics, the green movement, and lesbian and gay liberation.

These, then, are some of the principal influences in the development of cultural studies and feminism in the last decade or so. As this account makes clear, there are a number of points of overlap between feminism and cultural studies. Theoretically both are concerned with analysing the forms and operations of power and inequality, and take as an integral part of such operations the production of knowledge itself. To some extent, each has drawn on critical insights from discourse theory, poststructuralism, psychoanalysis, semiology and deconstructionism. Both have drawn on strands of critical theory which are seen to offer more sophisticated tools for analysing the reproduction of social inequality and relations of dominance and subordination at a cultural level. The analytic possibilities opened up by these approaches were seen to strengthen existing theories of power and resistance within both cultural studies and feminism. To some degree, then, overlaps in both areas have produced possible points of convergence between feminism and cultural studies.

The lack of overlap: feminism and cultural analysis

There are, however, also considerable divergences in interest which suggest a rather different ordering of priorities within feminism and cultural studies. Just as many feminists earlier posed critical· questions about concepts such as ideology and hegemony, drawing attention to the ways in which they and the traditions of thought which produced them, were gender-blind, there is now a caution about the use of concepts such as discourse, deconstruction and difference. In addition, although feminism has influenced cultural studies, there are limits to this influence which are important for what they reveal about the uneven interaction between the two fields. Perhaps one of the clearest indicators of the limits of this influence is provided by the lack of interest within cultural studies in the developments in feminist theories of gender inequality discussed earlier; for example, the models of culture employed within cultural studies have remained largely uninformed by feminist theories of patriarchy. This has produced a number of problems for feminists working in cultural studies.

Many of the reasons why the influence of feminism on cultural studies has been limited can be traced back to some of the more general understandings of culture employed within cultural studies. These include the models of culture derived from certain strands of Marxist thought. As discussed above, cultural studies was itself both central to, and in some senses a product of, a major set of shifts within Marxist perspectives away from the assumption of a mechanistic economic determinism. Indeed, the influence of feminism has been particularly significant within cultural studies around this issue. On the one hand, for example, the Althusserian framework offered greater attention to the cultural within (or, relative to other) Marxist frameworks, and has informed some of the most influential feminist work in cultural studies (Williamson, 1978; Barrett, 1980; Winship, 1987; Women's Studies Group, 1978). Yet on the other hand, the appropriation and development of these models within cultural studies did little to counter the marginalization of issues of importance to feminism.

Indeed, these theoretical frameworks, which are largely unable to account for sexuality, reproduction and violence, are characterized by quite fundamental conceptual limitations from some feminist points of

view. Within the Althusserian framework, for example, the social field is
seen to be composed of economic, political and ideological levels. But the
economic level, conceptualized in terms of the forces and relations of
production, is seen to determine all other levels in the last instance, and
thus retains a privileged significance in the construction of inequality. This
limited move away from economic determinism is inadequate for many
understandings of gender inequality. Some feminists, for example, have
disputed the Marxist conception of the economic, in so far as it is seen to be
based on the industrial mode of production associated with capitalism, and
to naturalize the sexual division of labour (Firestone, 1974; Delphy, 1984;
Mies, 1986). Other feminists (Daly, 1978; MacKinnon, 1987, 1989) have
suggested that not only is such an ordering of determination open to
question, but that the division of levels is unhelpful for an analysis of
gender inequality: how is sexuality, for example, to be understood in
relation to these discrete levels of power?

Another powerful model of culture which has been developed in cultural
studies has its origins in structuralism. This model has two principal
strands, deriving from social anthropology and linguistics. The first of these
was introduced into cultural studies through the work of Claude Lévi-
Strauss. This version of structuralism takes the exchange of women as the
original or founding cultural moment, thus creating an essentialist
tautology from a feminist point of view, and providing little hope of ever
changing patriarchal society. As has been pointed out, by constructing the
sexual division of labour and sexual difference as a priori constants,
structuralism reifies patriarchal dominance as a 'natural fact' (Rubin,
1975). The problem for feminists, therefore, is that this model of culture
takes for granted precisely what feminism is most concerned to explain.

The second broad strand of structuralist thought which has been
influential within cultural studies is based on the work of Ferdinand de
Saussure, who proposed a structural analysis of language as a system of
signs. This has since been extended in semiotic, poststructuralist and
'sexual difference' theories to the analysis of other cultural systems,
including, for example, fine art (Parker and Pollock, 1981), advertising
(Williamson, 1978), and film (Cowie, 1978). From this perspective, meaning
is understood to be produced through the play of difference, and is
relational (produced in relation to other signs) rather than referential
(produced by reference to objects existing in the world). The development
of these interpretive techniques, in which the analogy of language as a
system is extended to culture as a whole, marked a substantial break from
the positivist and empirical traditions which had limited much previous
cultural theory. However, while structuralism and poststructuralism have
been important for feminists in so far as they provided important critiques
of some kinds of reductionism and essentialism, and facilitated the analysis
of contradictory meanings and identities, their use has often obscured the

significance of power relations in the constitution of difference, such as patriarchal forms of domination and subordination.

However, one strand of poststructuralism, developed by feminists working within cultural studies, which has addressed the reproduction of such patriarchal relations, is that which draws upon psychoanalysis in order to provide an account of how difference is fixed as inequality through the acquisition of a gendered identity (Mitchell, 1975; Rose, 1986; Mulvey, 1989). This, in turn, has been challenged by others, who argue that sexual difference is so fundamental to the very terms of psychoanalytic thought (as in the strand of structuralism, which derives from Lévi-Strauss), that its use invariably contributes to the naturalization of gender inequality (Rubin, 1975).

The poststructuralist tendency in cultural studies outlined above has also been supplemented by the use of literary methods of analysis, such as deconstructionism (Derrida, 1981; Ricoeur, 1986; De Man, 1979), in which cultural processes are analysed as texts. The advantages for feminists of the bridge between literary analysis and social science constructed in the wake of 'the structuralist challenge' are clearly apparent. The ability, for example, to locate the production, criticism and consumption of literary texts in the context of the non-literary 'texts' of patriarchal social relations opened up an obvious space for more politicized 'readings' of both the literary canon and what had been excluded from it. Likewise, the emphasis on how meanings are 'encoded' into practices of cultural production and consumption opened up a whole range of radical re-readings of traditional subjects in both the humanities and the social sciences.

Nevertheless, this understanding of cultural processes as texts obscures the specificity and significance of different kinds of practices and results in a reductionism which raises problems for feminist analysis. Central issues for feminists, such as the control of women through their bodies, present problems for this textual analogy; some feminists would suggest that the female body cannot be considered simply as a text. Furthermore, such a method may contribute to the problem of objectification, whereby the female body becomes an object of scrutiny and investigation, devoid of subjectivity or personhood. Analysing gender within the model of culture 'as a language', then, presents specific problems for feminists who have highlighted the objectifying practices (or, the construction of woman as object) within language itself.

There have been other influential frameworks for the study of culture within cultural studies, including for example, the understanding of culture as 'ways of life' and 'ways of struggle' as developed in the work of Williams (1961, 1965, 1981), Thompson (1968, 1978), Hoggart (1958) and Seabrook (1985, 1988). These have sought to construct new understandings of culture based on working-class experiences and positions. However, while they have offered alternative models of culture to the dominant versions, based on bourgeois life and values, they have often excluded the gendered dimensions and specificities of working-class experience (Steedman, 1986).

Ethnographic work within cultural studies, drawing on perspectives from anthropology, has provided one of the main sources of exploration of 'lived cultures'. Working-class culture has been a particular focus of this work within cultural studies, where ethnographic material has been used as evidence of the relationship between dominant culture and subordinate groups. In particular, forms of resistance (Willis, 1978) and the formations of subcultures (Hebdige, 1979, 1988) have been explored in this context. These have also been challenged by feminists within cultural studies, not only for their gender specificity, but also for their lack of acknowledgement of the patriarchal elements of these forms of resistance (Griffin, 1985; McRobbie, 1980).

In this section, then, some of the important models of culture employed within cultural studies have been discussed in terms of the limits, as well as the possibilities, they pose for feminist analysis. The aim has been to show the way in which the frameworks outlined above pose substantial problems for feminists concerned with *patriarchal* culture, and limit the potential influence of feminism upon cultural studies, as well as of cultural studies upon feminism. Thus, while feminists have turned to disciplines such as cultural studies for frameworks to analyse the cultural dimensions of gender inequality, and while the work of feminists has been influential in both challenging and reworking these frameworks, there remain substantial difficulties in defining what might be meant by specifically feminist understandings of culture.

Ironically, this is true at a time when cultural issues are seen to be of growing importance to feminism. The power relations of pornography, abortion, male violence, technology and science have increasingly come to be seen not only in terms of social institutions and practices, but also in terms of symbolic meanings, the formation of identities and deeply-rooted belief systems. Even in those areas that appear to be most easily understood in conventional social and economic terms, such as paid work, feminists have begun to uncover the ways in which the construction of gender-appropriate identities and sub-cultures helps to organize, for example, the hierarchies in internal labour markets and the nature of workplace activities (Cockburn, 1983, 1985; Game and Pringle, 1984; Beechey, 1988; Phillips and Taylor, 1980). Indeed, cultural issues are so central to a wide variety of analyses of women's subordination that it might seem surprising that feminists have not developed general frameworks within which the significance of cultural processes might be more fully realized.

However, to the extent that feminism has long relied on an eclectic combination of frameworks and methods, often extracted from traditional disciplines and reworked to take account of gender, this may require less explanation. Moreover, the fact that some feminists have explicitly resisted overarching models and 'grand' theories, which belong to what has been seen as a masculine tradition, in part explains the lack of attention to a clearer definition of the elements of specifically feminist analyses of culture. Nevertheless, this lack of clarity about what is meant by cultural analysis in the context of feminism has led to some confusion in recent debates. This results both from the implicit or unacknowledged use of models of culture, and the explicit naming of a disparate set of analyses as 'cultural'.

One example of the confusion which results from the implicit use of different understandings of culture is provided by the current debate about pornography. Some feminists (Coward and WAVAW, 1987; Merck, 1987) see pornography as a process of signification or representation, ultimately irreducible to, and, to some extent, separate from, social and economic relations. They attempt to demonstrate the continuum between pornographic and other images of women circulating in this culture, arguing for the impossibility of drawing a fixed line between offensive and acceptable images. Pornographic images of women, then, are understood as the extreme articulation of the objectification of women *at the representational level*. The model of culture being drawn upon here is one which assumes that representations have a relative autonomy, and are a mediated articulation of social practices. Other feminists (Dworkin, 1981; Griffin, 1981; MacKinnon, 1979) propose an understanding of pornography not as a representational form of patriarchal culture, but as its exemplary moment of expression: pornography reveals to us the truth about what men really think about women. It is seen as an expression of male sexual violence and as an integral part of violent practices against women. Here, culture is seen to parallel directly the social, and is derivative of the misogyny deeply embedded in patriarchal society. Thus, an analysis of pornography forces us to face and to challenge the full extent of misogyny in this society. What is at stake, then, in the recent feminist discussions about whether it is possible to distinguish between pornography and erotica, or in disagreements about the role and relevance of censorship, are not only different understandings of pornography, but also implicit models of culture. However, this is rarely addressed in these debates.

Another important example of feminist work where the models of culture have not been foregrounded is the analysis of gender and objectification. Feminists who have emphasized the objectification of women in terms of commodity fetishism and the circulation of objects within capitalist relations of exchange often draw heavily on Marxist models of culture (Gaines, 1982). Another perspective criticizes the voyeuristic and fetishistic construction of woman in visual images, and uses a psychoanalytic account of the cultural construction of gendered identities to explain and challenge the patriarchal pleasures offered by such processes of objectification (Mulvey, 1989). A third approach develops an analysis of the forms of female objectification through the construction of female sexuality in patriarchal culture, and points towards a feminist methodology which could challenge such objectification (MacKinnon, 1979, 1982, 1987, 1989).

Finally, different understandings of cultural forces can also be seen as a means of distinguishing between recent feminist debates concerning the new reproductive technologies. Feminist concern over new reproductive technologies has centered around the perception that these technologies, and the institutions and knowledges in which they are located, constitute an extension of patriarchal control over the conception–gestation–birth process, and thus over women. Earlier arguments tended to posit a direct relationship between knowledge, technology and power. New reproductive technologies were seen to have both a colonizing and consolidating effect: further colonizing the domain of reproduction, and consolidating patriarchal power to define the reproductive process. Some argue that reproductive technologies are the locus of a refined patriarchal power base through which to extend control over women. 'The dominant mode of control of women is changing from the individual man through marriage to men as a social category through science and technology' (Corea et al., 1987:9). In such a claim, the constellation of knowledge, power and technology is seen as an overdetermined and tightly woven nexus. It is explicitly against claims of this kind, seen as determinist, that other arguments are put forward in which overarching theories are challenged by pointing to the destabilizing effects of new technologies at a cultural level. In the ways in which these new technologies challenge ideas about motherhood (Stanworth 1987), legitimacy (Smart, 1987) or choice (Birke, et al., 1990), the effects of the knowledge, power, technology constellation are seen to be more contradictory. Correspondingly, there is a reluctance by some feminists to invoke frames of reference which themselves consolidate particular constructions of knowledge or technology as essentially patriarchal, or construct women as simply subject to, and not acting subjects within, this domain. In such debates it is not only evident that there are different levels of importance attached to what might be called cultural forces, but also that there are differences about what is meant by culture and different models of how it operates.

As these debates make clear, attention to the cultural dimensions of gender inequality is not simply about arriving at a sharper understanding, or a more encompassing set of explanations. It is also about the strategies for change and transformation which are at the core of feminist politics. How one defines the power of pornography depends in large part on how one understands much more general processes involved in the cultural construction of meanings, images and identities. This, in turn, has direct implications for how to challenge pornography. Similarly, discussions about the question of whether the processes of objectification imply consent or coercion lead to very different strategies for change or resistance.

In addition to the problem of understandings of culture being present but submerged, as in the current debates over pornography or objectification, there is another set of questions that arise out of the explicit use of radically heterogeneous understandings of the 'cultural'. Again, bespeaking the divergent roots and resources of feminist scholarship across a wide range of disciplines, 'cultural criticism' has come to mean a very wide variety of things within feminism. The resulting confusion is perhaps most evident in the description of some American radical feminist work as 'cultural feminism'.[3] The proliferation of understandings of 'the cultural' further contributes to the need to define more clearly the assumptions underpinning frameworks in the analysis of culture, and raises the question of whether there are any commonalities which run through the various uses of 'cultural' as a modifier.

Some feminists working within women's studies have used more explicit models of culture drawn from the disciplines in which they are based. For example, feminist sociological theory tends to analyse the cultural as something distinct from the social, a differentiated sphere which is structured through specific institutions, such as the media, education and religion, and has drawn on a range of methods of analysis to conceptualize the specificity of the cultural in this sense. Alternatively, feminists working within anthropology, in which 'culture' is the traditional object of study, have drawn upon a diverse set of frameworks and methods for cultural analysis. These include detailed ethnographic accounts, cross-cultural comparisons, evolutionary and archaeological approaches, and linguistic studies. 'Culture' is also studied within other disciplines, such as psychology, linguistics, literary criticism and history, through frameworks which are formulated in various ways in relation to the primary object of study. Many of these approaches to the study of culture from the traditional disciplines have been 'borrowed' by feminists in order to investigate the cultural dimensions of gender relations.

The importance of theories of culture to feminism, then, arises from many different sources and for many different reasons. Be it due to the limits of existing models within cultural studies and conventional disciplines, the increasing importance of cultural issues within feminist theory and politics, or the confusion arising out of the use of divergent models of culture within feminist analysis, the need to clarify what might be meant by feminist analyses of culture becomes increasingly important. This concern arises from both the recognition of these problems, and the desire to provide a set of terms for an analysis of culture which addresses the specificity of patriarchal power and suggests ways in which to challenge it.

However, the question of what these terms might consist of is only just beginning to be asked. It might, for example, be possible to argue that a feminist cultural analysis would, given the intimate nature of women's subordination, be shaped by an interest in the construction of sexuality, the gendered body and the realm of subjectivity. Yet there are acknowledged problems with reinforcing links between the personal and the feminine which would require the issue of essentialism to be addressed. Debates about the implications of the conceptual distinctions between lived experience, the subjective and subjection, lie at the heart of many current debates within feminism, not the least of which is that concerning the strategic value of the category 'woman', and all of which are concerned to transform the significance of what it is to be a woman.

One of the primary aims of this article, in considering the relationship between feminism and cultural studies, is to consider the significance within feminist theory and politics of questions concerning the cultural dimensions of gender inequality and patriarchal power. We have suggested that there are two ways of exploring this significance: to investigate the role of culture in the reproduction of gender inequality, and to ask how an analysis of gender can contribute to an understanding of culture. However, it seems to us that while feminists have gradually built up a complex picture of the operations of patriarchal culture, there has been less of an attempt to systematize generalized theories of these power relations. We have tried to suggest some of the reasons for this, including both the limits to feminist influence within cultural studies, and the difficulties of asking what a specifically feminist cultural analysis would look like.

However, the diversity and heterogeneity of contemporary feminist analyses of culture would suggest that such a project, while focused on a common set of themes, is not, and is unlikely ever to be, unified. This is itself indicative of the strength and diversity of contemporary academic and political feminisms. This article has not sought to prescribe a definitive or comprehensive set of approaches. Rather, it has sought to suggest that there is some value in exploring the different kinds of overlap between feminism and cultural studies in particular areas of study. It is to three examples of these forms of overlap that we will finally turn.

Three kinds of overlap

We will explore briefly the overlap between feminism and cultural studies in three areas of study: popular representation, science and technology and, finally, Thatcherism and enterprise culture. Each of these demonstrates a different *kind* of overlap between feminism and cultural studies and highlights the specific configurations produced in different areas of analysis.

First, the analysis of cultural representations is an area of study in which both feminism and cultural studies have been well represented. This area includes work in which the overlap between the two different sets of approaches is well-established, due to the history of their shared focus on issues related to popular culture and the analysis of representation and identity. As noted above, this is possibly one of the areas within cultural studies where feminist work has had the greatest influence; indeed feminist cultural critics of popular film, television, magazines, as well as various lived forms of popular cultural practice have been central in the development of this area of scholarship (Coward, 1984; Williamson, 1978, 1986; Winship, 1987).

Feminism and cultural studies, then, have had similar concerns, and have witnessed similar changes in focus over the years in this area of shared interest. For example, there has been a shift in recent years towards questions of cultural consumption in both fields; feminist literary criticism is increasingly concerned with questions of readership, as cultural studies is with audiences. One influence on this shift from texts to contexts has been the increasing emphasis within feminism on recognizing differences between women and challenging the notion of *the female speculator* or *the female reader* assumed in much previous textual analysis. This, coupled with the increasing effect of the cultural studies' emphasis on audience activity and context in media analysis, has produced this overlapping interest in the processes of consumption and reception. Thus, cultural representation is an area of analysis which presents some of the most highly interconnected set of interests between feminism and cultural studies.

The second area of consideration, science and technology, represents a very different form of overlap, indeed more of a gap, between feminism and cultural studies. Here, rather than shared interests and approaches, there is little common ground between feminism and cultural studies. Whereas the analysis of science has become one of the most powerful trajectories within contemporary feminist scholarship and politics, it has rarely been the focus of sustained or critical investigation within cultural studies. Feminists have been concerned with challenging the ways in which medical, technological and scientific definitions of women's bodies, motherhood and pregnancy have increasingly been used to erode women's reproductive decision-making for many years, and yet the role of science remains a relatively unexplored aspect of cultural analysis within cultural studies. However, as Franklin and McNeil (1991) argue, the investigation of science in terms of epistemology, which has been a predominant strand within the feminist analysis of science, has reached something of a cul-de-sac. Moreover, they suggest that cultural studies approaches, which can investigate science and technology at a more everyday, commonsense level, can offer a number of possible ways forward in the continuing attempt to develop a feminist cultural politics around this increasingly important subject.

While the question of science and technology suggests the need for the introduction of cultural studies approaches into a set of debates which have been central to feminist research, our third example, Thatcherism and enterprise culture, suggests the need for the reverse, that is, the introduction of feminist approaches into an area which has been central to debates within cultural studies. Whereas the lack of overlap in the second example results from a somewhat curious silence within cultural studies around questions of science and technology, the discrepancy in this case results from an equally noteworthy lack of attention to the gendered dimensions of the sources of political and cultural change in contemporary British society.

Within cultural studies there has been considerable debate evaluating the significance and novelty of Thatcherism. Attention has been focused, for example, on its relationship to other forms of conservatism, and the role of the Left in providing, or failing to provide, a sufficiently popular alternative to the Thatcherite ethos. These debates about Thatcherism within cultural studies are part of a more general debate within Left politics and Marxist theory about how dominant culture reproduces itself and, in particular, the role of ideology in this process. Meanwhile, few feminists have undertaken to analyse Thatcherism in terms of gender, or in terms of patriarchal culture.[4] Yet during the last decade Thatcher governments have attemped to redefine notions of nationhood ('Britishness'), acceptable forms of active citizenship and the relationship between individualism and familialism. At the heart of many of these reformulations has been the construction of 'outsiders' and threats to the new British respectability, a project to which questions of gender, sexuality and ethnicity are all crucial (Franklin et al., 1991).

In these three examples, we have illustrated three different kinds of overlap between feminism and cultural studies. These in turn can be seen to offer opportunities to provide a number of different ways of approaching the question of how to develop feminist theories of culture. This important project can draw much that is of value from work within cultural studies. Yet, it must also take account of the shortcomings and limitations of the forms of cultural analysis on offer within cultural studies. In turn, as it has already done, feminist analysis will likely serve as both a resource and a stimulus to cultural studies, in their continuing shared project to challenge the existing conventions of producing and sharing knowledge and to combine theoretical debate with strategies for change.

Notes

The authors developed the ideas and arguments expressed here in a research group associated with the Department of Cultural Studies, University of Birmingham.

Another version of the arguments contained in this article appears in the introduction to *Off-Centre: Feminism and Cultural Studies* edited by Sarah Franklin, Celia Lury and Jackie Stacey (1991). We would like to thank Maureen NcNeil and Richard Johnson for their detailed comments on an earlier draft of this article.

1. While 'women's studies' and 'cultural studies' might seem to be more obviously analagous terms, we have chosen to use 'feminism' and 'cultural studies' in order to include developments in feminist theory and politics which have occurred outside the institutional boundaries of women's studies.

2. However, women's studies and cultural studies have rather different relationships to radical politics, given that women's studies emerged as a direct result of the women's movement. Cultural studies, on the other hand, has had a more tenuous and uneven relationship to Left politics.

3. The recent shift from women's studies to gender studies has produced considerable debate and controversy. Mary Evans offered a sceptical analysis of the political significance of this shift in her keynote paper at the Women's Studies Network Conference, Coventry Polytechnic, 18 March 1989.

4. The range of American radical feminist work labelled 'cultural feminist' is very broad, and thus the term is often confusing. It includes work which attempts to reclaim a 'woman-centred' culture, exemplified in the films of Barbara Hammer, as well as critiques of patriarchal culture and knowledge, such as those developed by Mary Daly.

Bibliography

Barrett, M. (1980) *Women's Oppression Today: Problems in Marxist Feminist Analysis*. London: Verso.

Baudrillard, J. (1988) *Selected Writings*. Cambridge: Polity Press.

Beechey, V. (1987) *Unequal Work*. London: Verso.

Beechey, V. (1988) 'Rethinking the Definition of Work: Gender and Work', in J. Jenson, E. Hagen and C. Reddy (eds), *Feminization of the Labour Force: Paradoxes and Promises*. Cambridge University Press.

Betterton, R. (ed.) (1987) *Looking On: Images of Femininity in the Visual Arts and Media*. London: Pandora.

Birke, L., S. Himmelweit and G. Vines (1990) *Tomorrow's Child: Reproductive Technology in the 90s*. London: Virago.

Brennan, T. (ed.) (1989) *Between Feminism and Psychoanalysis*. London: Routledge.

Bryan, B., S. Dadzie and S. Scafe (1985) *The Heart of the Race: Black Women's Lives in Britain*. London: Virago.

Bunch, C. (1988) 'Making Common Cause: Diversity and Coalitions', pp. 287–95 in C. McEwan and S. O'Sullivan (eds), *Out the Other Side: Contemporary Lesbian Writing*. London: Virago.

Carby, H. (1982) 'White Women Listen! Black Feminism and the Boundaries of Sisterhood', pp. 212–36 in CCCS, *The Empire Strikes Back: Race and Racism in 70s Britain*. London: Hutchinson.

CCCS (Centre for Contemporary Cultural Studies) Birmingham University (1982) *The Empire Strikes Back: Race and Racism in 70s Britain*. London: Hutchinson.

Cliff, M. (1983) *Claiming an Identity They Taught Us To Despise*. Watertown, MA: Persephone Press.

Cockburn, C. (1983) *Brothers: Male Dominance and Technological Change*. London: Pluto Press.

Cockburn, C. (1985) *Machinery of Dominance: Women, Men and Technical Know-how*. London: Pluto Press.

Cole, J. B. (ed.) (1987) *All American Women: Lines That Divide, Ties That Bind*. New York: Macmillan.

Corea, G. et al. (1987) 'Prologue', pp. 1–13 in P. Spallone and D. L. Steinberg (eds), *Made to Order: The Myth of Reproductive and Genetic Progress*. Oxford and New York: Pergamon Press.

Coward, R. (1984) *Female Desire*. London: Paladin.

Coward, R. and WAVAW (1987) 'What is Pornography? Two Opposing Feminist Viewpoints', pp. 175–82 in R. Betterton (ed.), *Looking On: Images of Femininity in the Visual Arts and Media*. London: Pandora.

Cowie, E. (1978) 'Woman As Sign', *m/f* 1: 49–63.

Daly, M. (1978) *Gyn/Ecology: The Metaethics of Radical Feminism*. London: Women's Press.

Davidoff, L. and C. Hall (1987) *Family Fortunes: Men and Women of the English Middleclass, 1780–1850*. London: Hutchinson.

De Man, P. (1979) *Allegories of Reading: Figural Language in Rousseau, Nietzsche, Rilke, and Proust*. New Haven, CT: Yale University Press.

Delphy, C. (1984) *Close to Home: A Materialist Analysis of Women's Oppression*. London: Hutchinson.

Derrida, J. (1981) *Writing and Difference*. London: Routledge.

Dex, S. (1985) *The Sexual Division of Work:* Brighton: Wheatsheaf.

Diamond, I. and L. Quinby (eds) (1988) *Feminism and Foucault: Reflections on Resistance*. Boston, MA: Northeastern.

Dworkin, A. (1981) *Pornography: Men Possessing Women*. London: Women's Press.

Ferguson, A. (1989) *Blood at the Root: Motherhood, Sexuality and Male Dominance*. London: Pandora.

Firestone, S. (1974) *The Dialectic of Sex: The Case for Feminist Revolution*. New York: Morrow.

Franklin, S., C. Lury and J. Stacey (eds) (1991) *Off-Centre: Feminism and Cultural Studies*. London: Unwin Hyman.

Franklin, S. and M. McNeil (1991) 'Science and Technology: Questions for Cultural Studies and for Feminism', in S. Franklin, C. Lury and J. Stacey (eds), *Off-Centre: Feminism and Cultural Studies*. London: Unwin Hyman.

Fraser, N. and L. Nicholson (1988) 'Social Criticism without Philosophy: An Encounter between Feminism and Postmodernism', *Theory, Culture and Society* 5 (2–3): 373–94.

Gaines, J. (1982) 'In the Service of Ideology: How Betty Grable's Legs Won the War', *Film Reader* 5: 47–59.

Gallop, J. (1982) *Feminism and Psychoanalysis: The Daughter's Seduction*. London: Macmillan.

Game, A. and R. Pringle (1984) *Gender at Work*. London: Pluto Press.

Griffin, C. (1985) *Typical Girls? Young Women from School to the Job Market*. London: Routledge & Kegan Paul.

Griffin, S. (1981) *Pornography and Silence*. London: Women's Press.

Hall, S. et al. (1978) *Policing the Crisis*. London: Hutchinson.

Hall, S. et al. (1980) *Culture, Media, Language*. London: Macmillan.

Heath, S. (1982) *The Sexual Fix*. London: Macmillan.

Hebdige, D. (1979) *Subculture: The Meaning of Style*. London: Methuen.

Hebdige, D. (1988) *Hiding In The Light: On Images and Things*. London: Routledge.

Hoggart, R. (1958) *The Uses of Literacy*. Harmondsworth: Penguin.

hooks, bell (1984) *Feminist Theory: From Margin to Center*. Boston, MA: South End Press.

hooks, bell (1989) *Talking Back: Thinking Feminist, Thinking Black*. Boston, MA: South End Press.

James, S. and M. Dalla Costa (1973) *The Power of Women and The Subversion of the Community*. Bristol: Falling Wall Press.

Jameson, F. (1984) 'Postmodernism, or the Cultural Logic of Late Capitalism', *New Left Review* 146: 55–92.

Johnson, R. (1983) 'What Is Cultural Studies Anyway?', Stencilled Paper No. 74, Centre for Contemporary Cultural Studies, University of Birmingham.

Johnson, R. et al. (1982) *Making Histories: Studies in History, Writing, Politics*. London: Hutchinson.

Leacock, E. (1981) *Myths of Male Dominance: Collected Articles on Women Cross-Culturally*. New York: Monthly Review Press.

Lerner, G. (1986) *The Creation of Patriarchy*. New York: Oxford University Press.

Lorde, A. (1984) *Sister/Outsider*. Trumansburg, NY: The Crossing Press.

Lugones, M. and E. V. Spelman (1983) 'Have We Got a Theory for You? Feminist Theory, Cultural Imperialism and the Demand for "The Woman's Voice"', *Women's Studies International Forum* 6: 573–82.

Lyotard, J. (1984) *The Postmodern Condition: A Report on Knowledge*. Minneapolis, MN: University of Minnesota Press.

MacCormack, C. (1980) 'Nature, Culture and Gender: A Critique', pp. 1–24 in C. MacCormack and M. Strathern (eds), *Nature, Culture and Gender*. Cambridge: Cambridge University Press.

MacKinnon, C. (1979) *The Sexual Harassment of Working Women: A Case of Sex Discrimination*. New Haven, CT: Yale University Press.

Mackinnon, C. (1982) 'Feminism, Marxism, Method and the State: An Agenda for Theory', *Signs* 7(3): 514–44.

MacKinnon, C. (1987) *Feminism Unmodified: Discourses on Life and Law*. Cambridge, MA: Harvard University Press.

MacKinnon, C. (1989) *Toward a Feminist Theory of the State*. Cambridge, MA: Harvard University Press.

McRobbie, A. (1980) 'Settling Accounts with Sub-cultures: A Feminist Critique', *Screen Education* 34: 37–49.

Merck, M. (1987) 'Pornography', pp. 151–61 in R. Betterton (ed.), *Looking On: Images of Femininity in the Visual Arts and Media*. London and New York: Pandora.

Mies, M. (1986) *Patriarchy and Accumulation on a World Scale: Women in the International Division of Labour*. London: Zed Books.

Mitchell, J. (1975) *Psychoanalysis and Feminism*. Harmondsworth: Penguin.

Mitchell, J. and J. Rose (eds) (1982) *Feminine Sexuality: Jacques Lacan and the Ecole Freudienne*. London: Macmillan.

Mitter, S. (1986) *Common Fate, Common Bond: Women in the Global Economy*. London: Pluto Press.

Modleski, T. (1982) *Loving with a Vengeance: Mass-produced Fantasies for Women*. London: Methuen.

Moraga, C. and G. Anzaldua (eds) (1981) *This Bridge Called My Back*. Watertown, MA: Persephone Press.

Mulvey, L. (1989) *Visual and Other Pleasures*. London: Macmillan.

Nicholson, L. J. (ed.) (1990) *Feminism/Postmodernism*. London: Routledge.

O'Brien, M. (1981) *The Politics of Reproduction*. London: Routledge & Kegan Paul.

Ortner, B. and H. Whitehead (eds) (1981) *Sexual Meanings: The Cultural Construction of Gender and Sexuality*. Cambridge: Cambridge University Press.

Ortner, Sherry (1974) 'Is Female to Male As Nature Is To Culture?', pp. 67–88 in M. Rosaldo and L. Lamphere (eds), *Woman, Culture and Society*. Stanford, CA: Stanford University Press.

Parker, R. and G. Pollock (1981) *Old Mistresses: Women, Art and Ideology*. London: Routledge and Kegan Paul.

Parmar, P. (1982) 'Gender, Race and Class: Asian Women in Resistance', pp. 236–76 in CCCS, *The Empire Strikes Back: Race and Racism in '70s Britain*. London: Hutchinson.

Phillips, A. and B. Taylor (1980) 'Sex and Skill: Notes towards a Feminist Economics', *Feminist Review* 6: 79–83.

Phizacklea, A. (1983) *One Way Ticket*. London: Routledge.

Radway, J. A. (1987) *Reading the Romance: Women, Patriarchy and Popular Literature*. London: Verso.

Ramazanoglu, C. (1989) *Feminism and the Contradictions of Oppression*. London: Routledge.

Reiter, R.R. (ed.) (1975) *Toward an Anthropology of Women*. New York: Monthly Review Press.

Rich, A. (1977) *Of Woman Born: Motherhood as Experience and Institution*. London: Virago.

Rich, A. (1980) 'Compulsory Heterosexuality and Lesbian Existence', *Signs: Journal of Women in Culture and Society* 5(4): 631–60.

Ricoeur, P. (1986) *Lectures on Ideology and Utopia*. New York: Columbia University Press.

Riley, D. (1988) *Am I That Name?: Feminism and the Category of 'Women' in History*. London: Macmillan.

Rosaldo, M.Z. (1974) 'Woman, Culture and Society: A Theoretical Overview', pp. 17–43 in M.Z. Rosaldo and L. Lamphere (eds) *Woman, Culture and Society*. Stanford, CA: Stanford University Press.

Rosaldo, M. and L. Lamphere (1974) (eds), *Woman, Culture and Society*. Stanford, CA: Stanford University Press.

Rose, J. (1986) *Sexuality in the Field of Vision*. London: Verso.

Rowbotham, S. (1981) 'The Trouble with "Patriarchy"', pp. 72–9 in Feminist Anthropology Collective (eds), *No Turning Back: Writings from the Women's Liberation Movement, 1975–80*. London: Women's Press.

Rubin, G. (1975) 'The Traffic in Women: Notes on the "Political Economy" of Sex', in R.R. Reiter (ed.), *Toward an Anthropology of Women*. New York: Monthly Review Press.

Sayers, J. (1986) *Sexual Contradictions: Psychology, Psychoanalysis, and Feminism*. London: Tavistock.

Seabrook, J. (1985) *Landscapes of Poverty*. Oxford: Blackwell.

Seabrook, J. (1988) *The Leisure Society*, Oxford: Blackwell.

Seccombe, W. (1974) 'The Housewife and Her Labour Under Capitalism', *New Left Review* 83: 3–24.

Smart, C. (1987) '"There Is Of Course the Distinction Dictated by Nature": Law and the Problem of Paternity', pp. 10–35 in M. Stanworth (ed.) *Reproductive Technologies: Gender, Motherhood and Medicine*. Oxford: Basil Blackwell.

Spallone, P. and D.L. Steinberg (eds) (1987) *Made to Order: The Myth of Reproductive and Genetic Progress*. Oxford and New York: Pergamon Press.

Spelman, E.V. (1990) *Inessential Woman: Problems of Exclusion in Feminist Thought*. London: Women's Press.

Spivak, G.C. (1987) *In Other Worlds: Essays in Cultural Politics*. London: Methuen.

Stanworth, M. (ed.) (1987) *Reproductive Technologies: Gender, Motherhood and Medicine*. Oxford: Basil Blackwell.

Steedman, C. (1986) *Landscape For a Good Woman: A Story of Two Lives*. London: Virago.

Strathern, M. (1980) 'No Nature, No Culture', pp. 174–219 in C. MacCormack and M. Strathern (eds), *Nature, Culture, Gender*. Cambridge: Cambridge University Press.

Thompson, E.P. (1968) *The Making of the English Working Class*. Harmondsworth: Penguin.

Thompson, E.P. (1978) *The Poverty of Theory and Other Essays*. London: Merlin Press.

Walby, S. (1986) *Patriarchy at Work: Patriarchal and Capitalist Relations in Employment*. Oxford: Polity Press.

Walby, S. (1990) *Theorizing Patriarchy*. Oxford: Blackwell.

Walker, A. (1984) *In Search Of Our Mother's Gardens: Womanist Prose*. London: Women's Press.

Watney, S. (1987) *Policing Desire, Pornography, Aids and the Media*. Minneapolis, MN: University of Minnesota Press.

Weedon, C. (1987) *Feminist Practice and Poststructuralist Theory*. Oxford: Blackwell.

Weeks, J. (1981) *Sex, Politics and Society: The Regulation of Sexuality Since 1880*. London: Longman.

Weeks, J. (1985) *Sexuality and its Discontents: Meanings, Myths and Modern Sexualities*. London: Routledge.

Williams, R. (1961) *Culture and Society, 1780–1950*. Harmondsworth: Penguin.

Williams, R. (1965) *The Long Revolution*. Harmondsworth: Penguin.

Williams, R. (1981) *Politics and Letters: Interviews with New Left Review*. London: Verso.

Williamson, J. (1978) *Decoding Advertisements: Ideology and Meaning in Advertising*. London: Marion Boyar.

Williamson, J. (1986) 'Woman Is an Island: Femininity and Colonization', pp. 99–118 in T. Modleski (ed.), *Studies in Entertainment: Critical Approaches to Mass Culture*. Bloomington and Indianapolis, IN: Indiana University Press.

Willis, P.E. (1977) *Learning to Labour: How Working Class Kids Get Working Class Jobs*. Aldershot: Saxon House.

Willis, P.E. (1978) *Profane Culture*. London: Routledge.

Wilson, E. (1981) 'Psychoanalysis: Psychic Law and Order', *Feminist Review* 8: 63–78.

Winship, J. (1987) *Inside Women's Magazines*. London: Pandora.

Women's Studies Group, Birmingham Centre for Contemporary Cultural Studies (1978) *Women Take Issue*. London: Hutchinson.

5

Media, ethnicity and identity

Thomas K. Fitzgerald

The media and place-defined identity

Although the media are generally assumed to be powerful shapers of culture and communication, Meyrowitz has argued that media contribute to social change today in ways largely overlooked. He sees the media as the 'missing link' between culture and personality (1986: 22). In this framework, 'information' combines the study of media environments with the study of face-to-face situations in somewhat the same way identity itself mediates between culture and communication.

How do the media unite or separate different people into similar or different informational worlds? What is the relationship between *social place and physical place* as influenced by the media?

Joshua Meyrowitz (1986) asked these questions and hypothesized that the electronic media — especially TV — have led to radical restructurings of social life and social performance, undermining the traditional relationship between physical setting and social situation. Electronic media are able to do this by merging formerly distinct social spheres, blurring the dividing line between private and public, and thus severing the traditional link between physical and social place (1986: 71). The result is a diffusion of group identities. Meyrowitz speaks of a *'placeless* culture'.

Using Goffman's metaphor of the drama, which pictured humans playing different roles for different audiences, Meyrowitz (1986: 28) borrowed the idea of 'back region' vs. 'front region' to illustrate the shifts from once private (backstage) behaviours to now media-exposed public (on-stage) behaviours. Groups whose *place* was formerly shaped by physical isolation (for example, American Indian 'reservation isolates')[1]

Media, Culture and Society (SAGE, London, Newbury Park and New Delhi), Vol. 13 (1991), 193–214

are no longer segregated from larger social groupings. Aspects of group identity that were once dependent on particular physical *places*, and the experiences available in them, then, have been permanently altered by the electronic media (Meyrowitz, 1986: 125). The concepts we use to define ourselves are influenced today by the media as symbolic *place*.

The theme of Meyrowitz's powerful book is that electronic media allow people to escape from traditional *place-defined groups* (1986: 57). Emphasis is not so much on physical setting as '*place*' but on information, or social knowledge, that people have about the behaviour of themselves and others (Meyrowitz, 1986: 37). 'Electronic media affect us', argued Meyrowitz, 'not primarily through their content, but by changing the "situational geography" of social life' (1986: 6).

Electronically mediated interactions are no doubt reshaping both social situations and social identities (Meyrowitz, 1986: 117). 'Geographic identity', or *identity of place*, has been subtly altered by electronic media, resulting in an homogenizing effect on group identities. No longer identifying as 'Samoans' from a specific island in Samoa, islanders migrating to New Zealand, for example, are more likely to refer to themselves simply as 'Pacific Islanders'. The fact of migration cannot fully account for this difference. The electronic media, to some extent, have changed the social rules of behaviour. The media, of course, are not the only causes of homogenization or necessarily the ultimate moulders of behavioural changes; but Meyrowitz sees the media as an important causal backdrop for such changes. The media have profoundly changed both social relationships and perceptions of self.

Wilson and Gutierrez (1985: 233) claim that the communication media formerly kept society together by building a common culture which fed people in different parts of the country a similar diet of news and entertainment. The media have begun to play a different role with the emphasis on marketing to separate audiences. While the communication media once built a mass audience by looking for commonalities, today they may actually reinforce differences between groups (Wilson and Gutierrez, 1985: 216). The mass media can no longer afford to exclude minorities. In responding to diversity, the authors see an end to 'mass' media influence. This conclusion may be too simplistically formulated, as both cultural homogenization and social diversification seem to be happening simultaneously. The influence of the media is still a present reality.

Ethnogenesis: the metaphor of identity construction

Few attempts have been made to look at the complex relationships between ethnicity and the cultural media. Sollors (1986) explores a seeming paradox: whereas more and more people of different backgrounds share an overlapping culture influenced by the media, there is a strong tendency for certain groups today to insist that they are at least symbolically distinct. This process of 'emerging ethnicity' has been called *ethnogenesis*, the development and public presentation of a self-conscious ethnic group. Investigating the connections between objective cultural differences and similarities and the ethnic portrayals of such cultural differences, Roosens (1989: 46) defined ethnogenesis as 'how people feel themselves to be a people and how they continue to maintain themselves as such', even in the face of contradictory historical evidence. What happens to 'objective culture' in ethnic interactions, and how is the media influencing human perception?

In short, people are becoming more culturally uniform, but some ethnic groups try at the same time to differentiate themselves by deliberate appeals to traditions (the 'survival of cultural baggage' metaphor) and reinterpretations of past history.[2] Many aspects of what is really going on are obscured by the use of concepts, such as 'culture', 'cultural uniqueness', and 'past', and are often perceived by outsiders as 'fake ethnic' claims. One thing is for certain, such cultural revivals are never truly a return to the past. The past is usually reconstituted to serve the group as they try to go forward (Roosens, 1989: 125). The children of immigrants, for example, cannot return to a 'former culture' that they never had. Any second- or third-generation culture is truly a 'cultural mutation', to use Roosens's terminological appraisal.

Although profoundly modified by media reality, the peculiarly modern tendency for certain groups to try to keep their cultural traditions (clinging to an ethnic identity) has created a huge gap between the 'rhetoric about culture' and the everyday realities of social change and adaptation. Carroll (1987: 136) maintains that social and cultural changes are not identical and that we may be committing a serious error when we confuse the two.

People today may create identities from very few cultural relics. Roosens (1989: 20) suggests, as a case in point, that naive Canadians are being forced by Indian arm-twisting to recognize a 'non-existent' Indian people. The example given is the Hurons, a people who recently have sought to recapture their ethnicity after being nearly obliterated culturally (1989: 32). The Hurons are described by Roosens (1989: 57) as a 'counterfeit culture', a deliberate attempt to construct a stereotypically 'Indian counterculture': they no longer know their own language and probably today would not be identified by an outsider as phenotypically Indian.

Polyethnic countries are no longer an exception but the rule, yet 'ethnic group' is often confused with 'culture' in daily usage as well as in scholarly discourse. Sollors (1986: 25) sheds some light on this confusion. Arguing that the attempt to maintain ethnic distinctiveness despite a good deal of cultural assimilation is ultimately a source of cultural vitality, he suggests that such 'defiant ethnic revivalism' nonetheless calls for a rethinking of theories of ethnicity and a clarification of terms that describe this process of self-definition.

Ethnicity, according to Sollors (1986: 25), is a fairly new term coined by W. Lloyd Warner in 1941. In many parts of the world, ethnicity became fashionable in the 1960s, in vogue by the 1970s. For most people, however, the term retains the connotation of minority status, lower class, or else migrancy (Sollors, 1986: 39). Unfortunately, the metaphors used to describe ethnic groups have often reinforced this negative imagery.

Derived from the Greek word *ethnikos*, the label originally meant 'heathen', not people in general, but outsiders or 'cultural strangers'. This contrastive feature is central to the notion of ethnicity, thus generally excluding dominant groups (hence, the commonsense question, 'Are Yankees ethnic, too?'). Defining people contrastively gave way in the mid-nineteenth century to the more familiar meaning of ethnic as 'peculiar to a race or nation'. Nonetheless, we still retain the idea of 'non-mainstream culture', as well as the religious connotation of 'heathen' (Sollors, 1986: 25). Writers have sometimes employed conflicting metaphorical images in trying to represent the changes that have occurred in interethnic communications.

Sollors (1986: 84), for example, suggests that the 'melting pot' metaphor, which has dominated the ethnic rhetoric for decades, represents an ethnic extension of the religious drama of redemption and rebirth, portraying ethnicity in the imagery of melting in contrast to the stubborn hardness of boundaries.[3] This metaphor of regeneration has been gradually replaced by a more instrumental, 'building metaphor', which suggests that identity is something self-constructed ('achieved' identity) and morally 'good'. The popularity of such a 'generative metaphor' is, according to Sollors (1986: 221), that it provides a kind of 'moral map' of what people take to be 'wholesome change'. Metaphors may help to create identities and identities may feed on metaphors, but common metaphorical language does not always indicate consensus of feeling or thought about identity, ethnicity and culture.

Ethnicity has thus been transformed from a social liability to a desirable identity to be achieved. There is, in fact, an almost voluntary ('multiple-choice') aspect of identity as a modern ethnic. Sollors (1986: 33) gives the example of two American-born brothers, one identifying as German-American, the other opting for a Franco-American identity. This perspective sees ethnicity as a dynamic metaphor emerging through potential negotiations of identities by groups or individuals in social contexts.

The new ethnicity — defiant cultural revivalism

What is the real substance of this ethnicity is the question that challenges scholars of identity.

When considering the 'new ethnicity' (as political pressure groups), distinctions can be drawn between motivation, knowledge and performance as three different aspects of role behaviour. It is easier to say that one favours participating in a certain ethnic life-style than actually doing so. Modern ethnic identifications work more by 'external symbols' (symbolic identities) than any actual cultural ability, knowledge or performance (Sollors, 1986: 35). The emotional significance of such attachments persists while the actual cultural content has dramatically changed. More attention is given today to the attitudinal level of identity (subjective aspects) than to overt behaviours (objective aspects), to private versus public areas of behavioural change, and to 'situational' contexts of changing identities.

Ethnic status today can be conspicuously devoid of solid cultural content. Consider Sollors's (1986: 35–6) provocative question about ethnicity in the United States: 'Are ethnics merely Americans who are separated from each other by the same culture?' The consensus is that the term 'ethnic' should be used sparingly and with caution since not all scholars can agree on the cultural basis of ethnic identities. A moral polarization is more common today, supported by simplistic metaphorical images of culture, ethnicity and identity. In this 'idealized antithesis', ethnocentrism becomes 'bad' and ethnic 'good'. Americans now value ethnicity regardless of what it is (Sollors, 1986: 179).

Sollors argues further that scholars themselves participate in the 'ethnicizing process' with their dualistic tendencies, and the media offer previously isolated outgroups new forms of recognition, participation and control (Meyrowitz, 1986: 181). Ethnic feelings and concerns are more documented and commented on by the media today. Certainly media play a major role in reshaping relationships, hence social and cultural identities.

Meyrowitz (1986: 135) sees the real sign of the times as our sense of rootlessness caused by a media-influenced 'placeless society'. 'Contrary to general belief', he expounds, 'the recently popular search for "roots" and "ethnic identity" may not be a sign of rising group identity in the traditional sense, but an indication of its decay'. There is still an enormous gap between everyday *social* realities and unsupported discourse about *culture*. Confusion of the constructs *culture* and *society* is part of the problem rendering sometimes overly simplistic solutions. Identity does not necessarily involve the maintenance of a separate culture, and social changes may not detract from ethnic self-awareness; in fact, such changes may actually enhance identity.

Ethnicity — colour, class and culture

There are, then, definite limits to ethnicity. Sollors (1986: 38) outlines how race in ethnic studies has been largely ignored because of the National Socialists' campaigns of 'genocide' in the name of 'race', which gave the word a bad name and supported the substitution of 'ethnic' for 'race'. Race has virtually disappeared from scholarly discourse following extended criticisms of its scientific basis in the 1940s and 1950s (more recently as a result of tendencies in Pop Culture, which consistently lump society and culture together, calling any group with *socially* perceived differences a *culture*).[4] Keefe et al. (1989: 6) claim that 'the role played by physical attributes in establishing markers of and variation in ethnicity would appear to deserve greater attention'. In what ways, for example, is ethnic identity and group formation dependent upon physical differences?

It has been predicted that by 2080, Whites in the United States will no longer be a majority (Wilson and Gutierrez, 1985: 18). At the same time, Blacks are an economically and socially diverse group, and a certain percentage risk becoming polarized into an 'underclass' (Wilson and Gutierrez, 1985: 25). With the United States more racially integrated than at any other time in history, the media and other institutions seem positively responsive to racial diversity. In fact, today it has been argued that the 'successful' image of American Blacks in the media may be as far removed from reality as negative portrayals in the recent past (Wilson and Gutierrez, 1985: 112).

Nonetheless, van Dijk (1987), using discourse analysis, tried very hard to make a case for the existence of racism in his analysis of out-of-context statements concerning ethnic interactions in the United States and Holland. In considering the research conclusion of a major American study (Schuman et al., 1985) that 'attitudes about general principles of racial equality and integration have steadily improved', van Dijk (1987: 224) invokes the nebulous notion of 'symbolic racism' when he finds insufficient support for *actual* racism.

His study, like a lot of research on so-called 'cultures' today, is a not-so-subtle academic polemic about racism without much concrete evidence. Granted that racism (substitute the word 'ethnicism') can be subtly combined with other forms of ethnocentrism, it seems unsatisfactory to lump them together under the umbrella term 'racism'. When van Dijk recognizes that ethnic attitudes are embedded in present socio-economic contexts, perhaps the result of perceived competition for scarce resources, he is on firmer grounds (1987: 228). To further erode his argument, he uses 'ethnic prejudice' ('the mental programme of racism') rather loosely (1987: 222). Recognizing differences does not automatically translate as implied 'inferiority'. It would be equally interesting to look at the possible 'prejudices' of minorities toward the majority.

In my own study (Fitzgerald, 1986) which involved contrasting attitudes of Polynesians and New Zealand Whites, I found that each group held certain stereotypes about the other. Sometimes these were fairly serious misunderstandings, more often simply amusing. Thus, when each was asked about the other group's presumed food habits, they both said

essentially the same thing: 'Bloody beer and fish and chips!' was the
inaccurate and cryptic response. A certain amount of mutual out-group
stereotyping may be inevitable when ethnically different groups live side by
side, but these perceptions often serve different functions (such as
strengthening in-group ties at the expense of an out-group) without
necessarily implying *racism*. It really boils down to which group makes the
major adjustments and in what situations. 'Symbolic racism' is invoked
when one can no longer find *real* racism?

Race, however, doesn't go away so easily. Race may be only one aspect
of ethnicity but, being an important aspect, it can't be swept under the
carpet of a broadly conceived ethnicity. The categorical separation of race
and ethnicity leads to false generalizations. As Sollors (1986: 38) argued,
we may end up with hypocrisy about our past as a result. Ethnicity often
involves *colour, class and culture*. Today we tend to give most of the weight
to *culture*.

We accept cultural differences but try to deny their racial and socio-
economic consequences. As information about ethnic minorities is formulated and transmitted through mass media, for example TV, Marcus and
Fischer (1986: 38) believe that the tendency to play down the 'socially
negative' is reinforced by the widespread diffusion of communication
technologies. Certainly class, or economic positioning, is a case in point.

Roosens (1989: 13) argues convincingly that self-affirmation ('ethnogenesis', or creating ethnicity), although not a uniform process in all parts
of the world, is related to the defence of social or economic interests. In
short, people change ethnic identities only if they can profit by doing so.
All people seek material survival, improved living conditions, and
enhanced personal status.

'Not all people act this way all of the time', claims Roosens (1989: 156),
'but most do most of the time'. Economics, then, play a crucial role in
present ethnic aspirations; and the media often give sympathetic support to
ethnic causes, even sometimes to misleading charges of 'ethnocide'. 'In all
case-studies', writes Roosens,

> ethnicity has to do with material goods, whether in a positive or negative way:
> the Hurons [Canada] maximize their ethnicity in order to obtain resources,
> whereas the Aymara [Bolivia] try to destroy their own cultural and ethnic traits
> for the same reason. The longing for material goods does not by itself procure
> ethnic identity and ethnicity. Ethnicity, however, is directly concerned with
> group formation, and this with power relations (1989: 158)

Ethnic groups, through media dialogues, become 'pressure groups with a
noble face' (1989: 14). Ethnic identity, then, is a powerful psychological
reality whether based on authentic culture or not.

An interesting paradox is that the most vocal champions of cultural
revivals are almost always the educated elites among such minorities. This

is paradoxical because the slogans of 'ethnogenesis' are formulated by the very people farthest removed from their traditional culture. Roosens (1989: 153) argues that a certain level of economic prosperity must first be obtained before the 'cultural' struggle of ethnic groups can achieve any lasting effect. This economic theory suggests that claims for 'revivals' based on reputed tradition rely on a substantial degree of economic security.

My study of the New Zealand Maori university graduate (Fitzgerald, 1977), suggested a similar conclusion. The most traditional, often physically isolated of the group, are often the ones least concerned with selfconscious identity and self-defined ethnicity. The same theory applies to the children of immigrant parents as later generations are usually economically more secure, thus having more political clout. As such, their demands are more likely to be accepted by members of the larger society.[5]

Sollors (1986: 29–30) argues that among ethnic groups in the United States, there is little cultural distinctiveness that can be historically authenticated. Labels, slogans and self-naming have become the important goals; 'romantic racialism'[6] (championed by what has been called the 'Aren't-Negroes-Wonderful' School) has replaced real racism; and, symbolically, the ethnic has taken the place of the 'truly chosen one'.[7] 'In America', continues Sollors (1986: 31), 'casting oneself as an outsider may in fact be considered a dominant cultural trait'.

'Vulgarized cultural relativism'

Certain general principles, if not totally understood, would seem to be almost universally agreed upon today: (1) People should have a right to their own 'culture' (without being very sure what that culture is); and (2) People have a right to maintain their own 'cultural' identity (whether this involves a separate culture or not). In short, regardless of historical circumstances, ethnic groups are claiming the 'right' to both a separate identity and a matching 'culture' of their own choosing. This presumption rests on the dubious assumption that cultures, in fact, can be discarded or created as a matter of human will. *Social* realities may be more complex than the *cultural* metaphors we use to describe them.

This philosophical shift in perspective has been traced to a 'vulgarized cultural relativism' for its ideological support (Roosens, 1989: 152). In its heyday, cultural relativism, a powerful doctrine of intellectual critique, was a strong liberal challenge to the neglect of human diversity (Marcus and Fischer, 1986: 20). A form of egalitarian humanism, the original position simply stated that other cultures (societies) should be viewed from their own perspectives, trying not to impose on them an outsider's values. Unfortunately, cultural relativism has come to be interpreted as 'the equal validity of all value systems', making moral judgements virtually impossible (Marcus and Fischer, 1986: 32).

Although we may wish that people determine the content of their own 'cultures' in an unrestrained manner, it is an error to confuse culture with society or, by extension, cultural change with social change.

Related to the elastic use of the culture concept, but more central to the concerns of this paper, is the widespread tendency to treat culture and identity as essentially the same entity, assuming that where you find one (identity) you necessarily find a supporting other (culture). This paper questions such an assumption.

It is suggested here that identity — in large part, due to media influences — loses its 'placed-defined' quality and, in form and function, begins to act independently of culture per se. The terms 'ethnic group' and 'culture' were more or less interchangeable in scientific discussions until the early 1970s, but the terms 'culture' and 'identity' are unfortunately still blurred in popular discourse. The confusion of the constructs involving *colour, class* and *culture* remains a thorny problem for social scientists.

People often gain a sense of 'alikeness' by being isolated together, sometimes only then becoming conscious of minority status because of feelings of 'exclusion'. Meyrowitz (1986: 132) claims that sharing special experiences creates a *paradox* as far as minority consciousness is concerned. While many such minorities loudly proclaim special identities — often based on putative 'cultures' — unconsciously they hope to shed at least part of their 'specialness' in becoming a part of a larger grouping (Meyrowitz, 1986: 133). Protesting too much ('defiant ethnic revivalism', to use Sollors's label), in fact, may suggest a widespread degree of cultural assimilation.[8]

Meyrowitz (1986) has warned that this paradoxical call for both recognition of differences and blindness to them should *not* be interpreted to mean that minorities espousing separate identities actually want to be in a separate culture isolated from fellow human beings. Group identity can be both positive (inclusive) and negative (exclusive) — hence, the familiar modern-day dialogue between *social* reality and *cultural* rhetoric (as 'unsupported or inflated' discourse).

People can be 'different' in various *social* ways while still sharing the *same culture*. The rhetoric of distinctiveness, as Carroll (1987: 145) has reminded us, may change without the culture itself altering very much. In other words, when an individual changes socially, the cultural premises (and the logic which gives order to the world) do not necessarily change. What is changed, Carroll argues, is the way of expressing the basic truths, not the truths themselves. Hence, she acknowledges the attempts of Black Americans to try and create an Afro-American 'culture', i.e. accentuate belonging to a different social group, but strongly suggests that Black Americans in Spain, Africa or travelling in France will still be seen as *Americans first* (1987: 142). To confuse social change with cultural change is an error with serious implications for intergroup communication.

The notion of *'cultural authenticity'* is surely grounded in the idea that ethnic identity requires validation in concrete culture or life-style differences; but, as Roosens (1989: 152) informs us, cultural identity need not presume the existence of an 'objective' cultural continuity. Though seemingly a paradox, it is possible today to find examples of *cultural identity without a culture*. Cultural absence, however, does not preclude identity persistence. In fact, in some cases change seems to accelerate identity formation.

The Lumbee of eastern North Carolina, a racially mixed group (Black, White and Indian), whose struggle to gain acceptance as 'Indians' was studied by Blu in 1980, and the current movement to have the term 'Afro-American culture' adopted by the larger culture are both social facts described by Keefe et al. (1989: 2) as reflections of a contemporary concern with ethnic identity as a political force rather than cultural authenticity. The new labels, for both groups, may be a way to avoid the more negative connotations of previous racial terminology. By defining itself, ethnically or otherwise, a group escapes classification by others. Ethnic identity, as one among many possible identities in a hierarchy of identities, remains a psychological reality to be reckoned with whether or not based on authentic culture.

Keefe et al. (1989: 33) have studied Appalachian and non-Appalachian students using three dimensions of ethnicity, structural, cultural and symbolic, and concluded that, although cultural ethnicity did not emerge in the study as very significant, symbolic and structural Appalachian ethnicity were still apparent. Parenthetically, they further suggest that, if such cultural differences do not exist from the past, it is expected that the group may well 'create' new ones in the future in order to support the idea of difference.

The thesis here is clear. While cultural differences are minimal in distinguishing Mountain people from newcomers, structural (class?) and symbolic ethnicity are used to construct (using the typically American instrumental 'building' metaphor of self-construction) what it means to be Appalachian: 'They "know" they exist but they cannot articulate many distinctive cultural traits beyond recalling stereotypes' (1989: 34).

The metaphor of 'cultural property'

Richard Handler (1989: 20) offers the metaphor of 'cultural property' to suggest how scholars have attempted to validate ethnic identities in the face of cultural erosion. 'Culture' becomes the 'property' which proves the existence of a group. This possessive metaphor marks the group's existence in a concrete way and, as well, provides it with a sense of worthiness.

Citing 'Ethnicity in the Museum' as an example of the metaphor of 'cultural property', Handler (1989: 23–4) examines the issue of slavery in

Colonial Williamsburg and its presentation in contemporary museum contexts. Blacks, always a significant component of the Colonial workforce, have been variously portrayed in museums over the years. In the 1950s, slavery was something not talked about. By the 1980s it was insisted that slaves had a culture which, argues Handler, presumably 'allowed them to lead lives worth living . . . even under cultural domination'. This insistence on an identity based on a distinctive culture presents Afro-American 'culture' to the public as unproblematic; thereby, the autonomous slave culture is 'mystified and romanticized' so that the real horrors of slavery are 'minimized by the representation of resourceful slaves using successful cultural resources' (Handler, 1989: 25).

Although Handler would certainly applaud the contemporary movement to try to include ethnic minorities in mainstream museums, he raises an intriguing hypothesis that deserves more attention. The display of ethnic culture in museums, Handler (1989: 19) suggests, 'reproduces an ideology of culture which homogenizes and domesticates rather than enhances cultural diversity'. In a sense, argues Handler, all such groups are being more or less identical (doing the same thing) in such self-conscious claims for uniqueness based on so-called authentic culture. The metaphor of 'cultural property' may function to prove minority existence but, more importantly, gives these same groups social recognition.

Due to media homogenization and support, then, ethnics are becoming more alike even while many such groups continue to identify as 'different' in certain expressive domains of their lives (a need for diversity in face of homogenizing media 'unity'). A paramount concern for formerly 'under-classed' groups is surely 'self-esteem', or the attempts to gain recognition and respect as values in and of themselves. Royce (1982) has hypothesized that people identify as 'ethnics' today because such groups offer extended-family functions in a time when family has diminished as a major force in people's lives. Ethnogenesis seems to be one path to this end. The influence of the media on achieving such reconstructed ideologies is enormous.

An interesting example of how the press has helped to create sympathies for a group's *identity symbols* is illustrated in the recent attempted sale (in London) of a preserved and tattooed head of a Maori warrior. The case squarely raised the thorny issue of human remains as 'cultural property', whether belonging to the Maori of New Zealand or to archaeological science. The 'Maori warrior' incident drew international media attention. Because of a sympathetic press, the head was eventually returned to New Zealand (Keefe, 1989: 4).

Besides seeking material goods, ethnic groups are clearly seeking recognition, respect and self-esteem. Roosens (1989: 159), however, reminds us that claims for material goods and resources are often intimately related to the process of gaining recognition and respect since our culture largely equates the two. Thus, some form of 'positive discrimination', he argues, may be a necessary way of recognizing certain groups as worthy members of society (e.g. Afro-Americans).

It would appear that the upsurge of ethnicity (ethnogenesis) is only related to the perceived socio-economic gains it allows individuals whose identities have been submerged or whose status has been denigrated in the past. In such a case, identity functions as a political assertion of pride in what the minority regards as its rightful heritage, in spite of any considerations of cultural authenticity.

Metaphors, media and social change — second-generation Cook Islanders in New Zealand

Ethnic identity, however, can be a good deal more than merely economic advantage-seeking. This was certainly the case in my study of second-generation Cook Islanders in New Zealand.

In 1985–6, on a Fulbright travel grant, I returned to New Zealand on my third research trip to investigate aspirations of second-generation Cook Islanders born and/or reared in New Zealand.[9] Ethnic pluralism is a familiar characteristic of modern societies, and New Zealand is no exception. Under conditions of rapid social change, there is often intensification of ethnic identity at the same time that culture per se is diminishing. The present study, then, was an attempt to raise some theoretical questions about identity as it relates to migration, generational position and media influence.

Scholars, such as Bonnemaison (1985: 30), make a strong argument for cultural identity in the Pacific as essentially a *geographic identity*, one which 'flows from memories and values attached to places'. *Place*, or geographic residence, has been a dominant *metaphor* for definition of self in the Pacific.[10] Certainly, an abiding anchor for many Pacific Island people, including migrants, has been a profound sense of land and place.

Bonnemaison's metaphor for this phenomenon is a tree rooted in the earth. Furthermore, he argues, there may not be authentic identity beyond places of memory. This line of reasoning raises questions about the maintenance of identity over time, especially as migration brings about shifts in place and subsequent shifts in the loci of identity. The critical issue for second-generation, New Zealand-born Cook Islanders is how to maintain identity over the generations.

Although identity for most Pacific Islanders is still forged in the relationship between person and place (island home), what about individuals who have only dim memories of the traditions their parents associate with the true homeland? As 50 per cent of those ethnically classified as Polynesians are today born in New Zealand, what are the implications for such children born or reared in one place (New Zealand) but who still identify with another (in this case, the Cook Islands, 1600 miles from New Zealand)?

Important related questions: what happens when individuals have neither the skills nor the understanding to uphold the traditions of the parent generation? For the New Zealand-born Cook Islanders, what is the *place* to which they feel the greatest attachment? What is the primary locus of their identity? What has been the effect, if any, of the electronic media on identity for this generation? In this case, should one speak of 'identity of place' or 'mis-placed' identity?

This study looked systematically at *aspirations* and strivings of second-generation, New Zealand-born Cook Islanders who lived in Wellington, New Zealand.[11] Methodology included the usual anthropological partici-pant observation as well as an extensive psychologically oriented interview schedule that probed for aspirations regarding language, marriage, church attendance, work habits, visits to the Cook Islands, community partici-pation, and even 'hopes and fears' for their children's futures. As the theoretical perspective conceptualized identity as personality adjustment within specific social contexts, individual choice became a significant factor. Earlier analyses, by contrast, have tended to slight cognitive and affective dimensions of identity. People do make conscious decisions about the importance of ethnic origins and the relevance of their cultural heritage. Thus, following Brim (1960), Turner (1987) and Pacanowsky and O'Donnell-Trujillo (1983), who view personality differences as primarily characteristics expressed in social roles, major explanatory variables were, not only *motivation* — the much over-used explanation for personality — but also *knowledge* of role demands and the *ability* to *perform* these roles. Aspirations of second-generation Cook Islanders, then, were examined considering these three factors: *motivation, knowledge* and *ability (performance)*.[12]

The data suggested that identity, for the New Zealand-born, was often situational, more often symbolic than 'real' (based on authentic culture); certainly, at minimum, bicultural if not multicultural; and choice was dependent on more than mere sentiment about place. Despite its limitations, I too used the contemporary 'building' metaphor of self, identity being seen as something potentially negotiated or created within specific social contexts. It is possible that such an instrumental metaphor is a peculiarly American way of looking at this complex reality.

First, 'place' was obviously complicated by the migration process itself. In New Zealand, though, there were attempts made by Cook Islanders to recreate substitute *places* — mini-Cook Island environments that symbolically bolstered and reinforced identity and affiliation with 'things Cook Island' (for example, *tere* [dance] parties, *uapou* [religious] celebra-tions, or hair-cutting ceremonies at the Cook Island community hall).

Thus, one did not completely lose 'memory. of place' because of several overlapping factors: a strong parental socialization, which included images of a nostalgic 'island paradise'; the Island Church's continuous reinforcement of symbolic links between New Zealand and the homeland; possible periodic visits to the Cook Islands; and finally renewed aspects of the 'expressive culture', including language, music and dance still 'alive' in the New Zealand context.

Research results suggest that identity, for this sample, takes on an optional, almost voluntary ('multiple-choice') quality, often more symbolic than 'real' if one considers ethnicity solely in terms of authentic cultural tradition. This conclusion is essentially the same debate over cultural content in ethnic identity discussed earlier. Interview questions, however, were aimed at measuring *actual* cultural participation (*cultural performance*). In communication parlance, good communication equals appropriate performance which involves more than mere motivation if identity is to have validation from outside the group (person validation or media validation). One essential question asks whether performance is compromised by generational status, migration, or media.

Identity becomes an individual's strategic choice in a multicultural context, a kind of 'situational selection'. Within certain obvious limits, a Cook Islander may select identification in a more or less self-conscious way. This model is in line with Roosens's (1989) notion of 'ethnogenesis', or the development and public presentation of a selfconscious ethnicity — perhaps a world-wide phenomenon attributable to media influences. Although 'ethnic identity' can stand for almost anything, covering an entire range of entities from 'symbolic identity' to radical 'cultural revivals', Cook Islanders in this sample did not manifest 'radical' cultural revivalism as described by Roosens (1989) for the Canadian Indians.

To return to the theoretical variables outlined above: the data suggested strong *motivation* to identify as some form of 'Cook Islander'. This motivation was not, however, primarily *culturally* inspired. The present research documents a case where ethnic identity is still alive in a modern, urban setting although identity, in this case, does not necessarily involve the maintenance of a separate culture. Ethnic identity can be distinguished from objective culture even though there are sometimes gaps between social realities and everyday discourse about 'culture'.

To the extent that identity was grounded in 'place' (Islands), the migrant was by circumstance dis-placed, and the New Zealand-born generation found its memories of the original place shifting and rapidly growing dimmer with time. Eventually the identity became 'mis-placed' when most day-by-day experiences were firmly New Zealand-based with symbolic identity focused on a largely imaginary island culture.

There was evidence that the New Zealand-born Cook Islanders are becoming assimilated into their country of birth, with some primary commitment to New Zealand, yet without totally repudiating all things Cook Island. When asked, 'What is Cook Island culture?', few were very articulate about its essence. Most, nonetheless, had strong and positive feelings about this 'culture'. Cook Island culture, it was felt, places a high regard on all human beings and human relationships, despite differences in social class, age or wealth. This was, at least, the cultural ideal.

For almost everyone, the essence of this 'Cook Island way' was the family, or kinship ethic. 'With the Cook Island family', explained one man, 'you never feel alone'. Coupled with this generous spirit was the notion of a people who are basically happy, friendly and outgoing, perhaps less intense than the Samoans, more casual than the Europeans, often characterized by a marked sense of humour. Being fundamentally a 'religious' people, it was felt that they could teach Europeans a bit about 'caring, friendliness, and showing one's emotions', in short, about 'being happy'. There are often discrepancies between public and private conceptions of what 'culture' should be like. This was especially true in the present study.

At the core of identity, then, lay *the issue of self-esteem* (self-affirmation providing feelings of pride in the group). This sense of self-esteem is often spoken of, in everyday discourse, as if it were a 'culture' element. There was observed, then, a strong sentiment (motivation) for affiliation with 'things Cook Island' (this being the closest 'emic' equivalent of the concept of 'culture' among these respondents). But, in the Cook Island scheme of things, *culture* was primarily identified with the extended *family*. Note that this observation is essentially Royce's (1982) discovery. People identify today as ethnics because such groups offer stable extended-family functions in an age of the declining family.

Identity surely is related to strivings for acceptance and 'belongingness'. This factor may account for the strong sentiment (motivation) for affiliation with 'things Cook Island'. The essence of the Cook Island way (culture) in the 1980s was, first and foremost, family, respect for the elders, a sense of community (albeit restricted) and a continuing link with an idealized island paradise.

Although the motivation to identify with 'things Cook Island' was not absent with this generation, knowledge of Cook Island culture, or actual participation in Cook Island activities in New Zealand (i.e. cultural domains such as language, food, dress, naming, ceremonies), was much less obvious — in fact, statistically weak in this sample. There was passing mention of the need to maintain or revive aspects of 'our culture and traditions', especially Cook Island Maori language; but there appeared to be little concrete knowledge of what these customs were and how they would be revived. Cultural erosion, then, was well documented by this study. Roosens's (1989) claim that the second generation, being a 'true cultural mutation', cannot return to a traditional culture that it never had in the first place is a claim that would not be challenged by this research.

Motivation to identify with a particular group or even fair knowledge about this 'culture' did not assure the ability to perform appropriate role behaviours in a New Zealand context. The second generation of Cook Islanders has had to choose new ways of life, linked not necessarily to the Island culture, but to their own semiology of place.

Performance of role behaviours was complicated by place being primarily, if not exclusively, New Zealand-based. Even with knowledge of the Cook Island heritage, there were relatively few 'places' in New Zealand to act out this knowledge (i.e. the more restricted contexts for cultural elaboration somewhat analogous to those of American Indians 'isolated on Indian reservations'). Certainly, for this generation, economic rewards are more often New Zealand-inspired. This fact would seem to lend full support to Roosens's hypothesis that ethnicity may be obtained only through sacrificing what the group calls its 'culture'. Economy surely has a lot to do with cultural choice. Economics were fundamentally important in this equation, but psychological (existential) factors may be of equal significance.

Ethnic identity is, at all times, a powerful psychological reality whether based on authentic culture or not. Identity is something which lies on a continuum marked by both negative and positive poles; this group recognized both the negative as well as the positive aspects of cultural retention and identity maintenance.

On the positive side, a major function of any ethnic identification is surely the anchoring of personality in smaller, more personal units as culture change renders role expectations more impersonal or problematic. Social changes, however, rather than detracting from ethnic self-awareness, often enhance identities. This was essentially the scenario for the first generation, thrust into a strange and unfamiliar environment as migrants. To some extent, the same may be true for these children of immigrants: not fully integrated into New Zealand society, yet sometimes too shy to venture out of the more restricted places of cultural security. This conclusion adds confirmation to Meyrowitz's (1986) brilliant observation that minorities espousing separate identities do not actually want to be in a separate culture. Identity, in this framework, functions as a kind of 'face saving' device until the group is psychologically ready to proceed along the path to integration or accommodation.[13]

It is well to remember that identity often combines self-interest (the economics of identity maintenance) with strong affective ties (the psychological, existential components of the identity structure). It is this *affective component* which is so often persistent, even when obvious changes in both culture and role behaviour have already occurred.

Identity can touch the very core of self, an existential quality metaphorically described by one scholar as 'the taproot to the unconscious'. For many Cook Islanders, then, the foundation of identification is less 'Culture with a large C', or even 'status politics' (the 'new ethnicity's' emphasis on economic and political gains). Rather, identity is more a fundamental sense of belongingness based squarely on kin relationships (family). Functionally speaking, identity for this group offers a kind of 'psychic shelter' in times of stress and rapid change.

Too much concern with culture, cultural revivalism, and exclusive identity may have negative implications for these locally-born children of immigrants in New Zealand. To insist on a cultural identity that only partly 'fits', as Lowenthal (1985: 318) has stated the case, may be 'a kind of patronizing colonialism dressed up as liberal social science', or even a kind of psychological compensation for economic inequalities. Such revivalism, rather than helping this generation solve its problems of identity, can only intensify identity conflicts. At least a certain portion of the sample studied elected to abandon ethnic attachments altogether as a rational choice of action.

Research that over-concentrates on the replication of island culture in New Zealand will by design tend to exclude individuals who have become assimilated into the larger New Zealand culture and who no longer identify with the Islands. One of the fascinating discoveries of the present study was the numerous examples of individuals who had already made such cultural shifts. About 16 per cent of the sample had no interest whatsoever in maintaining cultural affinities. They did not participate in ethnic associations, politics, or cultural events. A study of these 'lost' Islanders may be as crucial as studying only those who have remained within the cultural fold.

Although some groups no doubt find it more interesting to appear as 'cultures' rather than be regarded as an 'underclass' or a 'race', it may be insulting to suggest that they can't or shouldn't participate in the present world arena which has become instantly accessible through the electronic media (the 'natives' of Melanesia and South Africa, in fact, have sometimes accused anthropologists of adhering to a 'zoo theory': the accusation that scholars want to keep an area and its people underdeveloped so as to have 'pure cultures' to study!).

This generation of Cook Islanders has been marked by the disappearance of many island symbols of distinctiveness, and many had only dim memories of the traditions that their parents associated with the 'true' homeland. Any over-emphasis on cultural identity (based on authentic culture), may in fact be counterproductive. A good example would be language loyalties. What was the 'first' language for this generation? Language used in the home was predominantly (79 per cent) English; the 'mother tongue' for the majority of these Cook Island New Zealanders was clearly English. In New Zealand there were, in fact, special difficulties involving different dialects and a high rate of intermarriage. If the language (Cook Island Maori) were to be taught in the schools, for example, which version of the language would be chosen?

Two media outlets for Cook Island news in Wellington are the 'Pacific

Island News' on radio and *Tangata atu motu*, a television programme. These young people were asked if they listened to either regularly. The distinction between 'ability' to perform roles and 'knowledge' or 'motivation' to do so became even clearer. Only 10 per cent mentioned listening to either news event and then only 'occasionally'. The vast majority (90 per cent) did not. A typical reply was: 'No, can't understand it when in Maori language.' Ethnic consciousness, then, based on language loyalty is a short-sighted strategy unless it is certain that the next generation will be motivated to follow.

In a rapidly changing world, Pacific Islanders are concerned with who they are and where they are going. What did this research have to say about the future of identity for second-generation Cook Islanders in New Zealand? The majority of the New Zealand-born still preferred to identify as some type of 'Cook Islander'. To reiterate a major theme of this paper, *identity may have important functions that transcend culture as such.* It seems possible that Cook Islanders may not need any inflated Pacific Island 'culture' to establish their identity. With or without culture, identity persists.

Increasingly, however, this generation of Cook Islanders has been combining *places* — island and New Zealand — in dynamic ways. In so doing many have become 'hyphenated New Zealanders': 'Cook Island New Zealanders' or 'New Zealand Cook Islanders', depending on the emphasis. Certainly, many individuals in this sample have considered both the costs and benefits of 'cultural exclusiveness'. A substantial number have chosen between ethnic identification and national identity and have decided on the latter.

One neglected aspect of the ethnic equation, then, is the response of the dominant society. Identity persistence can be explained, to some extent, by a weak opposition from the largely European majority in New Zealand. The climate today is definitely more accepting of minority aspirations, and this acceptance is nowhere more apparent than in media coverage.

The communications media bear a special responsibility because they are potentially able to educate the general public about ethnic issues. Although they often treat the smaller ethnic minorities as fringe audiences, the media in New Zealand seem to be responding positively to racial/ethnic diversity. It is now the goal and policy of the New Zealand news media that, ideally, there should be integrated news coverage. The lack of opposition to 'cultural' aspirations, then, has been fundamental to the legitimization of ethnicity in New Zealand.

Furthermore, access to media and technology, with the power that is associated with this technology, prevents any real turning back for this generation. There is slim chance that the second or third generations can ever return permanently to the Cook Islands, homeland of their parents or grandparents. No matter how this generation may feel about its socio-economic position in New Zealand, there is effectively no going home again.

For one thing, the media have changed the locus of the former 'identities of place'. Merging social spheres and severing the traditional links between physical and social space, the media result has been, as Meyrowitz predicted, a diffusion of group identity yielding a more or less 'placeless culture'. Even individuals in the first generation are no longer likely to identify themselves in New Zealand as 'Rarotangans', or 'Aitutakians' (from one of the specific fifteen islands within the Cooks), but rather simply 'Pacific Islanders'. Those in the second generation carry the diffusion even further, identifying as 'New Zealand Cook Islanders' or 'Cook Island New Zealanders'. The electronic media have changed the social rules of behaviour. Neither generational position nor the fact of migration fully accounts for these differences between generations.

Roosens (1989) has argued that it is exceptional for people to lock themselves voluntarily into traditional cultures when there are economic incentives to participate in a larger technology. Economic factors were indeed important with second-generation Cook Islanders in New Zealand. Television, for example, has made the mass influence of material products significant in ways unheard of a few years ago. It is generally recognized that the young universally are attracted to Western material goods advertised through the media, for these products symbolize personal freedoms over restrictive parental controls. In addition, no generation today can totally ignore the work demands of a modern economy and remain successful within it. There are also limits — despite the present academic emphasis on 'romantic racialism' — to how far a power majority can be asked to adapt to the needs of an underclass minority (Roosens, 1989).

This study demonstrates that self-affirmation is related to social, economic *and* psychological interests. Although there are surely complexities in trying to organize bicultural — in this case, *multicultural* — education for children of immigrants, this research strongly suggests that a vibrant and peaceful ethnic identity is possible in a multicultural society. Ethnic identity would seem to have important psychological functions, hence should be nurtured, without falling into the trap of assuming there must be a corresponding, separate culture. The challenge is how to nurture a strong *national identity*, yet still recognize a variety of different interest groups, ethnic styles and the persistent need for minority identities which carry with them a degree of self-esteem, dignity and pride. This pattern of *recognizing 'cultural' identities without separate cultures* fits the official, though at present unrealized, goal of an emerging multiculturalism in New Zealand.

Notes

1. Cf. the 'geography of Indianness', when the reservation itself becomes a significant place for self-definition.

2. Cf. the predictions of unity *and* diversity in *Megatrends 1990* (Naisbitt and Aburdene, 1990).

3. Echoing this position is the amusing Ford Motor Company's English School Melting-pot ceremony for foreign-born employees (1916) who would undergo a ritualistic rebirth especially designed by their employers. During the graduation exercise, they were led down into a symbolic 'melting pot', emerging fully dressed in American clothes and carrying an American flag! (Sollors, 1986: 89–90).

4. In defiance of all anthropological common sense, today we speak of 'cultures' of men and women; youths and elderly; gays; corporations; media; the work place; Blacks and Whites; 'cognitive', 'symbolic', and even 'subjective' cultures.

Many anthropological studies perpetuate the trend started by Montegu (1972), i.e., substituting the term *ethnic group* for the more emotionally loaded label *race*; others followed with the substitution of *ethnic group* with the very elastic term *culture*, eventually resulting in confusion of the constructs of race, ethnicity and culture.

5. Some would argue that Hanson's law ('What the son wishes to forget, the grandson wishes to remember') proves that assimilation does not occur in a predictable way, but Herbert Gans (quoted in Sollors, 1986: 216) says that this so-called 'law' applies only to academics and intellectuals; in fact, he argues convincingly that the whole 'ethnic revivalism of the 1970s' may be mainly a revival limited to intellectuals. There is little empirical evidence for such a 'law'.

6. Consider the novel conclusion of a Canadian Indian writer that the historically documented custom of 'scalping' was, after all, not really an Indian practice but one which came from the Europeans (Roosens, 1989: 68).

7. Communication scholars who misuse the constructs of 'cognitive' or 'subjective' cultures to justify Black–White differences in *social behaviour* demonstrate the subjective, cognitive power of 'romantic racialism'. While communication patterns between Blacks and Whites are consistently observable, there is the real possibility that such differences are more attributable to *social position* than to either ethnicity or culture. Research that controls for social *class* differences (rather than labelling such differences *cultural*, '*ethnic*' or '*cognitive cultural styles*') is needed to validate the numerous ethnographically based communication studies that posit a 'Black culture' versus a 'White culture' as reality. See Hanna's (1986) suggestion that 'body in motion' behaviour for Black Americans has its roots in Africa and the experiences of slavery; Ting-Toomey's (1986) contention that Blacks retain a distinctive *subjective culture* of values and norms of interaction in the context of the White culture's influence; and Kochman's (1986) more serious claim that many communication problems between Blacks and Whites result from differences in their 'cultural frames of reference'. All such studies cry for empirical challenge, especially when the examples given in the literature are so patently *non-cultural*!

8. '[A]n Afro-American and the grandson of a Polish immigrant will be able to take more for granted between themselves than the former could with a Nigerian or the latter with a Warsaw worker' (Sollors, 1986: 14).

9. Much of this research summary is taken from my monograph, Fitzgerald, 1988.

10. 'Spatial identity' is similar to 'identity of place'. A specific example might be the 'geography of Indianness', where the *reservation* itself becomes a significant

place for self-definition: 'Despite the persistence of native traits, theirs is not the aboriginal culture, but a "reservation culture", a distinct and novel form, adapted to their peculiar mode of existence. It is the groups with these "reservation cultures" that constitute what is referred to as the "Indian problem". . .' (Wax et al., 1989: 2).

11. The Cook Islands are now independent although migrant Cook Islanders in New Zealand hold dual citizenship somewhat in the way Puerto-Ricans do in the United States. The second generation, caught between two countries, makes for an interesting social and political subject for anthropological investigation.

12. The fact that this model treats ethnic groups as categories of interaction examined in a framework of 'social role behaviour' in no way precludes analyses based on broader, structural variables which obviously set limits to personality. The present theoretical frame is extended by the addition of questions about media influence, à la Meyrowitz (1986).

13. Stone (1989) makes the point that family stories, though not always factual or true, are central to our individual identity, often 'nudging and pushing' immigrants (or children of immigrants) 'in the direction of assimilation'. She does not, however, see this process as 'bad'. Like identity itself, family stories are, metaphorically speaking, 'blueprints' of reality guiding the individual in times of stressful change, or social/personal dislocations.

References

Bonnemaison, J. (1985) 'The Tree and the Canoe: Roots and Mobility in Vanuatu Societies', pp. 30–62 in M. Chapman (ed.), *Mobility and Identity in the Island Pacific*. Special Issue, *Pacific Viewpoint* 26(1).

Brim, O., Jr. (1960) 'Personality as Role-learning', pp. 127–59 in I. Iscoe and H. Stevenson (eds), *Personality Development in Children*. Austin, TX: University of Texas Press.

Carroll, R. (1987) *Cultural Misunderstandings: The French–American Experience*. Chicago, IL and London: University of Chicago Press.

Fitzgerald, T. (1977) *Education and Identity: A Study of the New Zealand Maori Graduate*. Wellington: New Zealand Council for Educational Research.

Fitzgerald, T. (1986) 'Diet of Cook Islanders in New Zealand', pp. 67–86 in L. Manderson (ed.), *Shared Wealth and Symbol: Food, Culture and Society in Oceania and Southeast Asia*. London: Cambridge University Press.

Fitzgerald, T. (1988) *Aspirations and Identity of Second-Generation Cook Islanders in New Zealand*. Wellington: Department of Education.

Fitzgerald, T. (1989) 'Coconuts and Kiwis: Identity and Change Among Second-Generation Cook Islanders in New Zealand', *Ethnic Groups* 7: 259–81.

Handler, R. (1989) 'Ethnicity in the Museum: A Culture and Communication Discourse', pp. 18–26 in S. Keefe (ed.), *Negotiating Ethnicity*. Napa Bulletin, 8, National Association for the Practice of Anthropology.

Hanna, J. (1986) 'Interethnic Communication in Children's Own Dance, Play, and Protest', pp. 176–98 in Y. Kim (ed.), *Interethnic Communication*. Newbury Park, CA: Sage.

Keefe, S. (1989) 'Introduction', pp. 1–8 in S. Keefe (ed.), *Negotiating Ethnicity*. Napa Bulletin, 8, National Association for the Practice of Anthropology.

Keefe, S., G.R. Reck and U.M. Lange Reck (1989) 'Measuring Ethnicity and Its Political Consequences in a Southern Appalachian High School', pp. 21–38 in S.

Keefe (ed.), *Negotiating Ethnicity*. Napa Bulletin, 8, National Association for the Practice of Anthropology.

Kochman, T. (1986) 'Black Verbal Dueling Strategies in Interethnic Communication', pp. 136–57 in Y. Kim (ed.), *Interethnic Communication*. Newbury Park, CA: Sage.

Lowenthal, D. (1985) 'Mobility and Identity in the Island Pacific', pp. 316–26 in M. Chapman (ed.), *Mobility and Identity in the Island Pacific*. Special Issue, *Pacific Viewpoint* 26(1).

Marcus, G. and M. Fischer (1986) *Anthropology As Cultural Critique*. Chicago, IL and London: University of Chicago Press.

Meyrowitz, J. (1986) *No Sense of Place: The Impact of Electronic Media on Social Behavior*. New York and Oxford: Oxford University Press.

Montegu, A. (1972) *Statement on Race: An Annotated Elaboration and Exposition of Four Statements on Race*. New York: Oxford University Press.

Naisbitt, J. and P. Aburdene (1990) *Megatrends 2000: Ten New Directions for the 1990s*. New York: William Morrow.

Pacanowsky, M. and N. O'Donnell-Trujillo (1983) 'Organizational Communication As Cultural Performance', *Communication Monographs* 50: 126–47.

Roosens, E. (1989) *Creating Ethnicity: The Process of Ethnogenesis*. Newbury Park, CA: Sage.

Royce, A. (1982) *Ethnic Identity: Strategies of Diversity*. Bloomington, IN: Indiana University Press.

Schuman, H., C. Steeh and L. Bobo (1985) *Racial Attitudes in America*. Cambridge, MA: Harvard University Press.

Sollors, W. (1986) *Beyond Ethnicity: Consent and Descent in American Culture*. New York and Oxford: Oxford University Press.

Stone, E. (1989) *Black Sheep and Kissing Cousins: How Our Family Stories Shape Us*. New York: Penguin.

Ting-Toomey, S. (1986) 'Conflict Communication Styles in Black and White Subjective Cultures', pp. 75–88 in Y. Kim (ed.), *Interethnic Communication*. Newbury Park, CA: Sage.

Turner, J. (1987) *Rediscovering the Social Group: A Self-Categorizing Theory*. London: Basil Blackwell.

Van Dijk, T. (1987) *Communicating Racism: Ethnic Prejudice in Thought and Talk*. Newbury Park, CA: Sage.

Wax, M., R. Wax and R. Dumont Jr (eds) (1989) *Formal Education in an American Indian Community*. Prospect Heights, IL: Waveland Press.

Wilson, C. and F. Gutierrez (1985) *Minorities and Media: Diversity and the End of Mass Communication*. Newbury Park, CA: Sage.

PART TWO

THE AUDIENCE AND EVERYDAY LIFE

6

Texts, readers and contexts of reading

Shaun Moores

Mass communications research, in its varied and changing forms, has long been concerned with the relationship between media products and the audiences which consume them. Within different theoretical frameworks and modes of investigation, different understandings of this relationship have been produced. Historically, one important division was between those perspectives which asked 'what the media do to people' and others which considered 'what people do with the media' (Halloran, 1970). Although a tension of this sort has remained present in Media Studies over recent years, the terms of the debate have shifted.

A number of questions about the mass media and their audiences have been raised: How do media texts construct for their readers particular forms of knowledge and pleasure, making available particular identities and identifications? How do readers' differential social positionings and cultural competencies bear upon their interpretation or decoding of texts? How does the context of reading influence the ways in which the media are made sense of in everyday life? This article situates these questions in a series of developments which have taken place in media theory and research since the mid-1970s, attempting a broad overview of approaches to the study of audiences.

Screen: spectator–text relations

My point of departure will be work in film studies which drew on psychoanalysis, linguistics and Marxism to provide a theory of spectator-text relations in the cinema. Although such work primarily considered the structure of the text, it nevertheless had important implications for our

Media, Culture and Society (SAGE, London, Newbury Park and New Delhi), Vol. 12 (1990), 9–29.

understanding of audiences — investigating the relations of looking and knowing which texts construct for their readers. In Britain, this type of analysis was most closely associated with Stephen Heath, Colin MacCabe, Laura Mulvey and Peter Wollen, who were all contributors to the film journal, *Screen*. Their approach owed much to advances in French film theory, and in particular, to the writings of Christian Metz and the political critique of mainstream cinema which followed the events of May 1968 (see Harvey, 1978).

In his essay, 'Le Signifiant Imaginaire', translated and published in *Screen*, Metz (1975: 18–19) argued for a broadened conception of the cinematic institution, stating that it 'is not just the cinema industry, it is also the mental machinery — another industry . . . i.e. the social regulation of the spectator's metapsychology . . . . The institution is outside us and inside us, indistinctly collective and intimate.' Crucially, his formulation saw the cinema as an apparatus for the production of subjectivities. As MacCabe (1985: 6) has acknowledged, it was 'the attempt to link questions of signification to questions of subjectivity' which characterized *Screen*'s project during that period.

For *Screen*, as for Metz, psychoanalysis appeared the theoretical tradition best suited to the study of film spectatorship. Jacques Lacan's reading of Freud was concerned precisely with the interrelation of signification and subjectivity (Lacan, 1977). It offered a theory of the constitution of the human subject in and through language — a subject constructed and divided upon entry into the symbolic order of culture (for useful commentaries on Lacan, cf. Lemaire, 1977 and Coward and Ellis, 1977). British film theorists like MacCabe also referred to Emile Benveniste's writings on linguistic enunciation and Louis Althusser's famous essay on the state and ideology which were touchstones for the analysis of film as discourse and cinema as ideological apparatus (Benveniste, 1971; Althusser, 1971).

Central to *Screen*'s approach was the proposal that film does not simply capture a pre-given external reality. Images are not transparent windows on the world. Instead, film was seen to be structured according to distinctive narrative conventions and codes of representation. Images are productive rather than reflective — they produce ways of seeing the world and thereby organize consumption in certain ways. They construct the 'look' or 'gaze' of the spectator, binding her or him into the fiction and into a position of imaginary knowledge.

The concept of 'suture' was used to theorize this 'constant welding together' (Heath, 1976: 90) of text and spectator in the flow of the film narrative. Originally elaborated within Lacanian psychoanalysis to refer to 'the relation of the individual as subject to the chain of its discourse' (Heath, 1976: 98), the concept was taken up within film theory by Jean-Pierre Oudart (1977–78) in France and by Stephen Heath in Britain. In order to come to terms with these arguments about cinema, it is first necessary to outline some of the basic principles of Lacan's model of language and subjectivity.

Psychoanalysis made a significant break with earlier conceptions of subjectivity found in western philosophy. The Cartesian subject — a conscious, rational human agent at the centre of thought and action — was displaced and de-centred. In Lacanian theory, there is no pre-existent consciousness which finds expression in language, rather it is language which provides the possibility of subjectivity. The biological individual is constituted as a subject 'through its positioning in a meaning-system which is ontologically prior to it and more extensive than it' (Frosh, 1987: 130). According to Lacan, this process involves a fundamental misrecognition. Although we feel as though we are the source of meaning and the site of origin for our sense of self, identity is always constructed on the site of 'the Other' — language, representation.

The constitution of subjectivity thus entails a subjectification in which the subject is divided upon entry into language. There is necessarily a split between the subject of speech and the speaking subject — between subject positions in language and the speakers who occupy them. As Heath (1977–78: 55) has noted, 'the subject of the enounced and the subject of the enunciation never fully come together'. The Lacanian, Jacques-Alain Miller, introduced the concept of 'suture' to account for the momentary and incomplete stitchings of that gap or wound (Miller, 1977–78). It names the flickering play of absence and presence in which subjectivity is constantly produced and reproduced in linguistic utterances.

Perhaps the most common way of trying to represent a sense of coherent identity to ourselves and to others is by uttering 'I', but as a pronoun, it is a profoundly unstable and precarious sign because its referent is perpetually in flux. During a conversation, 'I' is continually changing places as 'it only ever refers to whoever happens to be using it at the time' (Rose, 1986: 54). This shifting sign serves as an illusory symbol of unity where there is only an unstable and precarious subjectivity. Indeed, Benveniste (1971: 226) asked:

> How could the same sign refer indifferently to any individual whatsoever and still at the same time identify him in his individuality? . . . Then, what does 'I' refer to? . . . The reality to which it refers is the reality of the discourse. It is in the instance of discourse in which 'I' designates the speaker that the speaker proclaims himself as the 'subject'. And so it is literally true that the basis of subjectivity is in the exercise of language.

The instance of discourse discussed here by Benveniste is a suturing of the subject of speech and the speaking subject — a temporary sewing up of 'the distances of the symbolic' (Heath, 1977–8: 55). Lacanian psychoanalysis points to the 'I' of an utterance as the index of suture.

To study film as discourse, for Heath and others, was to identify the textual strategies whereby subject positions are generated for the spectator. This is to ask how a ceaseless stitching of viewer and screen fiction is effected — how the reader is sewn into the text in an ongoing and constantly renewed process. Film is not only concerned with constructing a scene, but also, and at the same time, with putting the viewer in a place before it — 'in place, the spectator completes the image as its subject' (Heath, 1976: 99). While cinematic language has no direct equivalent of the personal pronouns, it was argued that we can still distinguish certain procedures for the production of subjectivity.

The shot/reverse shot formation is often cited as an example of cinematic suture. This involves a complex interplay of looks between camera, spectator and characters in the fiction. It is a linking of two shots 'in which the second shot shows the field from which the first shot is assumed to have been taken' (Silverman, 1983: 201). For instance, an exchange between characters is edited so that Shot 2 reveals the protagonist whose point-of-view had been displayed in Shot 1, and the image 'of a fictional character looking in Shot 2 usually proves sufficient to maintain the illusion that Shot 1 visually "belongs" to that character' (Silverman, 1983: 202). A structure of this kind serves to construct a subject position which is occupied by the spectator in the auditorium who 'stands in' for the protagonist by identifying with a viewpoint which is simultaneously that of the camera and a character in the fiction. The shot/reverse shot sequence was understood as a suturing device in which the reader is caught up in the text's enunciation, 'spoken' by the text.

As Laura Mulvey (1975) pointed out, the business of looking and being looked at in the cinema is strongly marked by gender difference. In the shot/reverse shot formation of the classic text, it is usually men who look at women. Mulvey argued that, 'In a world ordered by sexual imbalance, pleasure in looking has been split between active/male and passive/female' (1975: 11). Within the signifying practices of Hollywood, man is constituted as bearer of the look and woman as its object. This system of looks is one which matches a voyeuristic male gaze with the exhibitionism of the female displayed as spectacle. The camera, taking up the point-of-view of the male protagonist, produces a masculine subject position. That is not to say that it is only male spectators who occupy this place, but that the mode of cinematic address has 'coded the erotic into the language of the dominant patriarchal order' (Mulvey, 1975: 8).

Whereas Oudart tended to concentrate on the shot/reverse shot structure in his discussion of suture, Heath warned against too narrow a use of the concept and looked more generally at the relation between film and viewing subject. When considering the construction of looks in the cinema, the conventions of realist representation — in which film denies its own status as image — were seen as important because they place the spectator 'in an identification with the camera as the point of a sure and centrally embracing view' (Heath, 1976: 77). This cinematic strategy has its roots in the codes of Renaissance perspective, and through the development of devices such as depth-of-field, long takes and continuity editing (Bazin, 1967), the cinema has perfected a visual illusion in which the viewer is positioned as an all-perceiving subject gazing directly onto an objective reality. Such a relation is, of course, imaginary. The 'impression of reality' (Heath, 1976: 78) is the product of a signifying practice which erases its own discursive basis. MacCabe (1976: 17) proposed that 'it is necessary to consider the logic of that contradiction which produces a position for the viewer but denies that production'.

Metz (1975: 44–45) went some way towards identifying a logic when he wrote that

> the cinematic signifier does not work on its own account but is employed entirely to remove the traces of its own steps, to open immediately onto the transparency of a signified, of a story, which is in reality manufactured by it but which it pretends merely to 'illustrate', to transmit to us after the event, as if it had existed previously (= referential illusion) . . . . Hence what distinguishes fiction films is not the 'absence' of any specific work of the signifier; but its presence in the mode of denegation, and it is well known that this type of presence is one of the strongest there are.

Elsewhere, using a term borrowed from Benveniste's linguistics, Metz has called this narration without a narrator 'histoire' (Metz, 1982). It constitutes a meta-language which 'simply allows reality to appear . . . lets the identity of things shine through' (MacCabe, 1974: 8–9). For *Screen*, the key feature of the classic realist text was the illusion of transparency — the discursive production of 'obviousness' which, argued Althusser (1971), is exactly that mechanism by which individuals are hailed as subjects in ideology.

Against the ideological operations of realist film, *Screen* posed a different tradition — the avant-garde practices of Jean-Luc Godard's cinema (MacCabe, 1980; Wollen, 1982), and before it, the theatre of Bertolt Brecht (Brecht, 1964). In contrast with Hollywood, Godard and Brecht were concerned to foreground the machinery of representation. Their political art was deemed to be properly 'materialist' because it refused to efface the materiality of the signifier. This refusal, it was suggested, made for very different spectator–text relations which were characterized by alienation rather than identification — 'passionate detachment' (Mulvey, 1975: 18). MacCabe and others were attracted to such practices because they seemed to make possible 'the breaking of the imaginary relation between text and viewer' (MacCabe, 1976: 21). There

are, of course, considerable problems with this avant-garde enterprise, but
here is not the place to open up the heated debates about politics and
aesthetics in Marxist cultural theory.[1]

Before closing this section of the article, it should be noted that while
Screen was concerned principally with the analysis of film texts, there were
also occasional discussions of television as a signifying practice. Heath, in
an essay written with Gillian Skirrow (1977), did attempt to open up
questions about the specificity of television's mode of address and its
differences from cinematic discourse — although their analysis of a TV
documentary is typical of *Screen*'s more general approach at that time.
Heath and Skirrow stated that their work set out to examine 'the
positionings of the viewer as subject . . . the kinds of construction and
address of view and viewer' (1977: 9–10). The focus remained on the
structure of the text and on the production of a place for its reading
subject.

CCCS: inscribed readers and social subjects

By the end of the 1970s, a valuable critique of 'screen theory' had been
developed by members of the Media Group at the Centre for Contemporary Cultural Studies in Birmingham. This critique, built on the foundations
of Stuart Hall's earlier work on the encoding/decoding model, is found
most clearly in the writings of Charlotte Brunsdon and David Morley
(Brunsdon and Morley, 1978; Morley, 1980a; Morley, 1980b; Brunsdon,
1981; Morley, 1981). It was not, however, limited to the work of the
Birmingham group, for dissenting voices could already be heard from
within the pages of *Screen* itself (Willemen, 1978; Neale, 1977). At the root
of these objections was the assertion that 'screen theory' failed to
distinguish between the reader implied by or inscribed in the text and the
actual social subjects who interpret or decode texts.

As Brunsdon (1981: 32–37) put it:

> We can usefully analyse the 'you' or 'yous' that the text as discourse constructs,
> but we cannot assume that any individual audience member will necessarily
> occupy these positions. The relation of the audience to the text will not be
> determined solely by that text, but also by positionalities in relation to a whole
> range of other discourses . . . elaborated elewhere, already in circulation and
> brought to the (text) by the viewer.

While recognizing the text's construction of subject positions for the
spectator, Brunsdon and Morley pointed to readers as the possessors of
already-constituted cultural knowledges and competencies which are
drawn on at the moment of interpretation — 'the repertoire of discourses
at the disposal of different audiences' (Morley, 1980a: 171). It was argued

that in the work of MacCabe, Heath and others, the text is 'not so much "read" as simply "consumed/appropriated" straight, via the only possible positions available to the reader — those . . . inscribed by the text' (Morley, 1980a: 166–67). Against such a model of spectator-text relations, Morley came to put particular emphasis on viewers as active producers of meaning and on media consumption as the site of potentially differential readings.

To counter 'the single, hypostatised text-subject relation' (Morley, 1980b: 162) found in much of *Screen*'s analysis, the concept of 'inter-discourse' was introduced. Reading was not to be theorized as an abstract, isolated relationship between one text and its implied reader. There could be no reduction in which the reader is seen only as the occupant of a single textual positioning. In the encounter between text and subject, 'other discourses are always in play besides those of the particular text in focus — discourses . . . brought into play through "the subject's" placing in other practices — cultural, educational, institutional' (Morley, 1980a: 163). In the words of the former Director of the Centre for Contemporary Cultural Studies, Richard Johnson (1986: 299), 'The whole pressure of formalistic work is to isolate the text for closer scrutiny. But the real tendency of the reading moment . . . is the opposite of this . . . . The reality of reading . . . is inter-discursive.'

The Birmingham Centre's *Nationwide* project was an attempt to apply some of these theoretical perspectives in a specific analysis of television texts and audiences. In its later stages, Morley sought to chart differential interpretations of the programme made by viewing groups drawn from various occupational and educational backgrounds — and as an empirical investigation into the relation of texts and readers, the research remains an important landmark in modern media studies. A more detailed discussion of the project will follow, but this must be prefaced by some comments on Hall's early paper written in 1973, 'Encoding and Decoding in the Television Discourse', an abridged version of which was later published (Hall, 1980).

Hall had conceptualized the production and reception of the television message within a semiotic framework. Televisual communication was to be understood as a complex social construction of meaning.[2] At both ends of the communicative chain — the encoding and decoding moments — symbolic 'work' is being done. To grasp the relationship between these moments and thereby specify the nature of the work performed should, Hall suggested, be the task of media research.

Drawing on the insights of structural linguistics, he rejected notions about the 'transparency' of media representation in terms which were similar in many respects to those used by *Screen*: 'Discursive "knowledge" is the product not of the transparent representation of the "real" in language but of the articulation of language on real relations and conditions' (Hall, 1980: 131). Language, in the broadest sense, does not offer up a faithful reflection of the world. Signification is dependent upon the operation of a code — for example, conventions of selection and combination. In a television news broadcast, an event cannot be transmitted in a 'raw' form. It has to be made to mean and is therefore encoded in particular ways. But in Hall's model, the codes of encoding and decoding 'may not be perfectly symmetrical' (1980: 131). There will be differing 'relations of equivalence' between the two moments and the reasons for this potential asymmetry are twofold.

Firstly, television texts are all, to some extent, polysemic. There are always several possible readings of the text. Especially at the connotative level of signification — the realm of what Roland Barthes has called second-order or associative meanings — signs possess a fluidity which enables them to be articulated in multiple ways (Barthes, 1971; 1973). However, as Hall (1980: 134) warns, 'Polysemy must not . . . be confused with pluralism . . . there exists a pattern of "preferred readings".' The text is not open to be read in any way the viewer freely chooses, since 'encoding will have the effect of constructing some of the limits and parameters within which decodings will operate' (1980: 135).

In a similar fashion, the Soviet linguist, Valentin Volosinov (1973), has remarked on the 'multi-accentuality' of the sign. For Volosinov, there are no fixed meanings in language because the sign is continually the site of a class struggle — 'a little arena for the clash and criss-crossing of differently oriented social accents' (1973: 41). So signs such as, say, 'the nation' or 'the people' are not wholly closed around a singular meaning (Hall, 1982: 78). They constitute a sphere in which meaning is contested, although as Hall would say, the competing accentuations will be 'structured in dominance' (Hall, 1980: 134). Indeed, Volosinov (1973: 23) argued that the dominant social class will always seek to reproduce the conditions of its dominance by making certain meanings appear taken-for-granted and obvious — by trying 'to impart a supraclass, eternal character to the . . . sign, to . . . make the sign uni-accentual'.

The second, and related, reason for the possible non-correspondence of encoded and decoded meanings is the interrogative and expansive nature of reading practices. Umberto Eco (1972: 110) has said that the reader may 'decode the message in an aberrant way'. In an essay published in the CCCS's journal, *Working Papers in Cultural Studies*, Eco suggested that the determinations for such decodings were to be found in the reader's 'general framework of cultural references . . . his ideological, ethical, religious standpoints, his psychological attitudes, his tastes, his value systems, etc.' (1972: 115). This is not to propose a theory of selective perception, where individuals make random, private readings. There exist what Hall has called 'significant clusterings' (1980: 135). Audience decoding studies would have to map out the connections between these clustered readings and the social/discursive positionings of readers — to sketch the boundaries of various interpretive communities (cf. Morley 1975 for an early attempt to approach audiences as cultural subgroupings).

Making use of categories first outlined in the work of the sociologist, Frank Parkin (1971), Hall tentatively identified 'three hypothetical positions from which decodings of a televisual discourse may be constructed' (1980: 136). In the first, the viewer operates within the dominant code and reads the meaning which has been encoded 'full and straight'. The second position is one in which readers adopt a negotiated code which 'acknowledges the legitimacy of the hegemonic definitions . . . while, at a more restricted, situational level . . . operates with exceptions to the rule' (1980: 137). Here, the preferred reading is not fully accepted. In addition, Hall referred to a third, oppositional, position — decoding the message 'in a globally contrary way' (1980: 137–38). Although there remained the problem of precisely how these meaning systems are related to the socioeconomic positions of readers,[3] Hall's notes on differential decodings opened up a space for later research.

In *Everyday Television: 'Nationwide'* (1978), Brunsdon and Morley presented a textual analysis which marked the first stage of an encoding/ decoding study. An examination of the programme's visual and verbal discourses, the analysis considered the distinctive ways in which *Nationwide* addressed its viewers. They argued that the programme's preferred reading of events was 'articulated, above all, through the sphere of domesticity', pointing to 'its emphasis on the ordinary, everyday aspects of issues, on the effects of general issues and problems on particular individuals and families' (1978: 74). This 'common sense' mode of presentation revolved around a certain image of the audience as a nation of individuals, united in their regional diversity and bound together through a shared experience of domestic life. The text's ideological effectivity was seen in terms of its construction of subject positions for viewers — its production of an imaginary relation, a misrecognition.

But as Morley clearly demonstrated in the second stage of the project, published in 1980 as *The 'Nationwide' Audience*, the programme's preferred reading was not necessarily accepted by actual viewers who were never reducible to the subject positions inscribed in the text. Morley carried out field research 'to establish how the messages previously analysed have in fact been received and interpreted by sections of the media audience in different structural positions' (1980b: 23). The research took the form of twenty-nine interviews conducted in institutional settings, in which groups drawn from different levels of the education system and from various occupations discussed recorded programme extracts.

Working with the pattern of the dominant, negotiated and oppositional positions set out in Hall's essay, Morley sought to classify the differential group decodings — 'to see how the different subcultural structures and formations within the audience, and the sharing of different cultural codes and competencies amongst different groups and classes, "determine" the decoding of the message' (1980b: 15). Readings did not correspond directly to economic class position. Morley noted, for instance, that apprentices, shop stewards and black F.E. students 'all share a common class position, but their decodings are inflected in different directions by the influences of the discourses and institutions in which they are situated' (1980b: 137). This was not to suggest that the ideological/discursive level of the social formation is autonomous or free-floating, but that 'it is always a question of how social position plus particular discourse position produce specific readings; readings which are structured because the structure of access to different discourses is determined by social position' (1980b: 134).

The 'Nationwide' Audience still stands as a ground breaking study of audience decodings[4] and a challenge to the theory of text-reader relations advanced in *Screen*, although there were significant limitations to the work which Morley himself recognized. In the encoding/decoding model there seemed to be little room to account for readers' pleasures, or for the extent to which a variety of media genres are relevant to the concerns of viewers and comprehensible in the light of the reader's cultural capital. There also remained the problem of the context in which reading takes place. In the *Nationwide* decoding research, readers responded to the text as members of groups situated in the institutional environments of education or work. Would the same viewers have made sense of the programme differently if placed in the more usual reading context of the domestic household? As Morley (1980b: 27) admitted, 'The absence of this dimension in the study is to be regretted and one can only hope that further research might be able to take it up.'

Towards an ethnography of reading

In a critique of his own work on decoding, Morley (1981: 13) declared his interest in 'the development of what might be termed an "ethnography of reading" '. Such an approach would address precisely those limitations found in the *Nationwide* study, investigating the habits and tastes of different 'reading publics' and focusing in particular on the context of media consumption. It is with these questions that his later work on television audiences was concerned (Morley, 1986), but he was not alone in turning to the study of reading as a 'system of cultural behaviour'. Dorothy Hobson — also based at the CCCS — had already carried out audience research in an ethnographic tradition. She considered the significance of radio and television in the day-to-day lives and routines of housewives (Hobson, 1980). Her analysis was based on observations of women at home with young children, and on tape-recorded interviews with the women about their everyday use of mass media.

In accounting for the appeal of daytime radio in the lives of the housewives, she pointed to the specific context in which it is heard. Hobson argued that radio serves, in part, to combat the loneliness experienced by women as a result of their location in the domestic sphere. Despite its usual status as background sound, she saw daytime radio as an 'important means of negotiating or managing the tensions caused by the isolation in their lives' (1980: 109). Broadcasting also provides a series of punctuations in the working day of the housewife. Unlike the highly segmented temporal structures of industrial labour, housework is characterized by its 'structure-lessness'. Michele Mattelart (1986: 65) has referred to this as 'feminine time . . . interiorized and lived through as the time of banal everyday life, repetition and monotony'. According to Hobson's research, 'the time boundaries provided by radio are important in the women's own division of their time' (1980: 105). The regular daily features of programming, as well as constant time-checks, enable women to sequence their domestic activities while listening to the radio.

When looking at her interviewees' accounts of their television consumption, Hobson concluded that there is 'an active choice of programmes which are understood to constitute the "woman's world", coupled with a complete rejection of programmes presenting the "man's world" ' (1980: 109). Where Morley's decoding research had seen the audience as a number of cultural subgroupings defined primarily by class position, Hobson's work pointed in addition to the importance of understanding television viewing in the domestic context as gender-differentiated. The women in the study clearly distinguished 'two worlds' of television. News and current affairs, as well as much documentary and adventure fiction output — such as war films — were designated as masculine and avoided, if possible, by many of the women. The genres which they most readily related to were quiz shows — especially those with a domestic, familial theme — movies with a 'fantasy' content and, most notably, soap operas.

In a subsequent study of the audience for the British television soap opera, *Crossroads*, Hobson (1982: 105–36) returned to these issues of gender-differentiated readings and domestic contexts of consumption. Once again, the research involved an observation of audiences in the household setting — followed by a recorded discussion of the programme. A coincidental shift in the scheduling slot from 6.30 p.m. to 6.05 p.m. provided her with an excellent opportunity to see how women viewers made space in hectic tea-time routines to watch their favourite programme.

Describing one of the domestic viewing situations, Hobson wrote: 'the woman with whom I had gone to watch the programme was serving the evening meal, feeding her five- and three-year-old daughters and attempting to watch the programme on the black and white television situated on top of the freezer opposite the kitchen table' (1982: 112). As she made clear, a viewing context of this sort is a far cry from the darkened room in which an academic might usually conduct a textual analysis. For Hobson, television consumption was to be understood as 'part of the everyday life of viewers' (1982: 110). In much the same way, John Ellis has reminded us of the difference between the cinematic context, 'the relative privacy and anonymity of a darkened public space' (Ellis, 1982: 26), and the setting of the television in the home — 'a profoundly domestic phenomenon . . . another domestic object, often the place where family photos are put: the direction of the glance towards the personalities on the TV screen being supplemented by the presence of "loved ones" immediately above' (1982: 113). It was in the context of home and family that the women in Hobson's research had to arrange their viewing of *Crossroads*. Watching television was not a separate, solitary activity, rather it was woven into the routine duties and responsibilities of household management.

There was also a tendency for 'some women to feel almost guilty and apologetic that they watch the programme . . . they excuse themselves for liking something which is treated in such a derogatory way by critics and sometimes by their own husbands' (Hobson, 1982: 110).[5] Perhaps the rejection of soap opera by husbands might be explained by the genre's focus on personal and emotional matters. One of Hobson's viewers perceptively suggested that 'men are not supposed to show their emotions and so if they watch *Crossroads* . . . then they think it's just stupid and unrealistic because they are not brought up to accept emotional situations' (1982: 109). It is interesting to note that this speaker refers to men's frequent dismissal of soap opera as 'unrealistic', for as Ien Ang (1985) has argued, the popularity of the genre lies in its 'emotional realism' for many women viewers.

Similar work on the reading of popular television and literature was being done in the United States by feminist academics like Tania Modleski (1984) and Janice Radway (1987). Modleski considered the form and flow of daytime television in relation to the rhythms of women's work in the home, while Radway's research into women's consumption of romantic fiction looked not only at their interpretation of texts, but more generally at the importance of romance-reading as a social event performed in the context of family relations and domestic obligations.

'The housewife functions . . . by distraction', argued Modleski (1984: 100). Her domestic labour is split between a variety of repetitive but unstructured tasks, and she must also be ready to offer care and emotional support to a number of other individuals in the family. The flow of daytime programmes and commercials — and, most importantly, the formal properties of soap opera — work to reinforce 'the very principle of interruptability crucial to the proper functioning of women in the home' (Modleski, 1984: 100). Soap opera's multi-levelled, open-ended narrative structures demand a viewer who is able to identify with a range of characters. Such a cultural competence is brought to the text by many women viewers as a consequence of their social placing as housewives and mothers. In turn, the inscribed reader of soap opera 'is constituted as a sort of ideal mother: a person who possesses greater wisdom than all her children, whose sympathy is large enough to encompass the conflicting claims of her family (she identifies with them all), and who has no demands or claims of her own (she identifies with no one character exclusively)' (Modleski, 1984: 92). There may, on occasion, be a female character in the fiction who demonstrates these qualities — Miss Ellie in *Dallas*, for instance.

In an exploration of romance-reading practices, Radway was also concerned to situate women's reading in its domestic, familial context. However, if Modleski had located the pleasures of soap-opera narrative in its correspondence to the rhythms of women's everyday lives, Radway saw the appeal of romance-reading in its potential to transport them, albeit temporarily, from their domestic routines. Her study of a community of women romance-readers in the midwestern town of Smithton was originally intended as an inquiry into their interpretation of the literature, but during the course of the research there was a shift in focus. Radway explained that 'the Smithton women repeatedly answered my questions about the meaning of romances by talking about the meaning of romance-reading as a social event' (1987: 7). For the Smithton women, the very act of reading the romance was significant, because it enabled them to mark out a time and space of their own in a day which was otherwise devoted to the care of others.

Rosalind Coward (1984: 199) has written of fantasy as 'the "other place" of the mind . . . like a secret room or garden, to be visited in a spare moment', stating that 'women talk of looking forward to the moment of escape when they can enter the rich and creative world of their own minds, hidden from the rest of the world'. It is precisely this sort of experience which is pleasurably anticipated by the Smithton readers, for as one of the women said, 'when I am reading . . . my body is in the room but the rest of me is not' (Radway, 1987: 87). This led Radway to critically unpack the notion of 'escapism', traditionally used in a derogatory sense. She suggested that when contextualized within the day-to-day setting of home and family life, the will to be transported elsewhere through the medium of fantasy literature clearly makes sense. It makes possible an escape in two senses of the word, both of which were expressed by Radway's readers:

> On the one hand, they used the term literally to describe the act of denying the present, which they believe they accomplish each time they begin to read a book and are drawn into its story. On the other hand, they used the word in a more figurative fashion to give substance to the somewhat vague but none the less intense sense of relief they experience by identifying with a heroine whose life does not resemble their own in certain crucial respects. (1987: 90)

The second sense of the term defined here by Radway is important in answering why it is that these women seek their escape via the genre of romance and not through other types of literature. They see in the romance's heroine a character who — although she often suffers humiliation and rejection from the male object of her desire — is finally united with a man who shows himself to be capable of caring. Crucially, the readers identify with a woman who is, in the end, nurtured — for in their own day-to-day lives they are destined only to nurture others.

Morley's *Family Television* (1986) had many parallels with Radway's research on popular literature — a debt he acknowledged — especially in its call for questions of interpretation and questions of use to be posed together. To borrow Radway's phrasing, we might say that Morley's most recent book focused on the meaning of television viewing as a social event in a familial context. Other influences for the book came both from within media research and from some unexpected sources outside it. Hermann Bausinger's study of how the Meiers, a German family, interacted with the media and with each other over the course of a weekend convinced Morley of the importance of seeing media reception 'as an integral part of the way the everyday is conducted' (Bausinger, 1984: 349). Switching on the television set, for example, does not necessarily signify an interest in the programme being broadcast. It may well be an excuse not to talk to someone else in the room, or again, it could be an attempt to engineer a shared experience with others. In connection with this question, Morley also referred to work in the field of family psychology carried out by Irene Goodman and others (Morley, 1986: 22–30). Just as psychologists studying family life have often observed the interactive rituals which take place around the dining-table, so Goodman looked to the domestic uses of television as a way of comprehending the formulation and negotiation of rules within the family unit.

To uncover the rules and rituals of television viewing is also to investigate what Sean Cubitt (1984: 46) has called 'the politics of the living-room', for family relations are power relations. Questions of age difference — of generation — were not developed in Morley's work, but were explored in more detail in a subsequent collection of essays edited by Philip Simpson (1987), where parents discussed the place of television in relationships with their children. Morley's primary concern was with the ways in which gender relations within the household structure TV-viewing as a form of cultural behaviour.

Drawing on material from eighteen recorded interviews with families living in South London,[6] Morley identified a number of themes and consistencies with regard to gendered viewing practices. He began by pointing out that the domestic space itself has very different meanings for men and for women. For men, it is primarily a site of leisure, defined in relation to 'work time' which is spent outside the home. For women, such a separation is often not evident. Even if she is employed in work outside the home, the woman remains responsible for household duties while situated in the domestic context. Morley argued that this makes for different styles of viewing, with most women only able to participate in distracted consumption. Indeed, while the men interviewed by Morley expressed a preference for watching quietly and attentively, the women described their viewing as 'a fundamentally social activity, involving ongoing conversation, and usually the performance of at least one other domestic activity (ironing, etc.) at the same time' (1986: 150). Only at times when the rest of the family are absent can women indulge in the 'guilty pleasures' of a solo viewing, taking a break from domestic responsibilities. Morley cited the case of one woman who 'particularly enjoys watching early morning television at the weekends — because, as these are the only occasions when her husband and sons "sleep in", these are, by the same token, the only occasions when she can watch television attentively, without keeping half an eye on the needs of others' (1986: 160). In developing a theory of the domestic uses of television, it is important not to lose sight of instances like this, because as Ann Gray (1987: 51) has said, the domestic context 'is not singular and unchanging, but plural and open to different permutations'.

Amongst the other aspects of gender-differentiated uses of television investigated by Morley were programme preferences stated by men and women. Echoing Hobson's earlier findings on the 'two worlds' of television, he confirmed that men have — or at least claim to have — a greater interest in news, current affairs and documentaries than in the fictional output preferred by their wives and daughters. Particularly interesting was the way in which husbands typically dismissed 'feminine' genres for exactly the reasons women enjoy them. During a discussion of the American soap opera, *Dynasty*, Morley recorded the following exchange — Woman: 'That's what's nice about it. It's a dream world, isn't it?' / Man: 'It's a fantasy world . . . no, I can't get on with that' (Morley, 1986: 165). In this respect, Morley's study of television in family life could clearly be seen as a continuation of debates about gender and genre, again raising the issue of viewers' differential cultural competencies and reading pleasures.

Morley's current work confirms his commitment to ethnographic audience studies. In a joint paper with Roger Silverstone, presented at the 1988 International Television Studies Conference [published in abridged form in this issue. Ed.], a further investigation of television as a domestic technology is proposed. This would involve developing a more detailed account of its contemporary and historical position in the geography and routine of the private sphere, and of its relationship with other information and communication technologies in the home. It would also require an examination of the ways in which broadcasting mediates between private and public domains, reproducing the mundane nature of everyday domestic life and familiarizing the social world beyond (Moores, 1988;

Scannell, 1988). Such a project, they argued, 'reframes' mass communications research within a broader analysis of the time–space structuration
of day-to-day social life.

The 'reframing' advocated by Morley and Silverstone is not intended to
replace a concern with texts and readers, although they noted that 'the
text–reader model does now require some reworking' (1988: 27). In the
case of television, they pointed to two major qualifications which would
have to be built into the model. First, they signalled the variability of
television viewing as an activity. As part of domestic ritual, viewing may
involve a number of different levels of attention and engagement — and
ethnographic research has already shown that there will be changing
combinations of viewers in various household settings. Secondly, in
conducting analyses of television output it is important to recognize the
multiplicity of television's modes of address across different genres of
programming. Morley and Silverstone clearly feel that the text still
requires close analysis, but suggested that 'what is necessary is to examine
the varieties of viewing and attention which are paid to different types of
programmes at different parts of the day by different types of viewers'
(1988: 27). This calls for a survey of the rhetorical relations between
television texts and readers in specific temporal and spatial contexts.

Future directions

The extensive developments in theory and research charted here have
opened up a number of important lines of inquiry for future studies. This
brief conclusion considers some of the directions which new work might
take, and says a little about methods of investigation and objects of study. I
will suggest that three principal issues require our continued attention —
the interrelated questions of meaning, pleasure and taste.

Most of the work done on audiences over the last fifteen years has
centred around the concept of 'meaning production'. As we have seen,
there have been several key shifts in emphasis with different perspectives
choosing to focus on different moments in the process by which meanings
are constructed. At one point, texts are taken to be the primary site for
analysis — and at another, readers or the contexts in which readings are
made become the focus of research attention. The time has come to
consolidate our theoretical and methodological advances by refusing to see
texts, readers and contexts as separable elements and by bringing together
ethnographic studies with textual analyses. This is not an appeal for any
grand new synthesis but a realization that we need what Radway (1987: 5)
has called a 'multiply-focused approach' which can do justice to the study
of an interactive process. Indeed, her own work on romance-reading is
perhaps the most sophisticated example to date of research which

addresses the complex connections between textual and contextual determinations of meaning.

Radway's study provides a particularly valuable model because it also attends so closely to the social production of pleasures. Seemingly the most 'natural' aspect of reading, pleasure always needs to be understood as a cultural formation which is again the result of an interaction between textual features and contextual situations. This has implications for a political critique of mass communication because pleasures, like meanings, are the product of a process and can never simply be 'read off' from the text. So, as Radway asks: 'Does the romance's endless rediscovery of the virtues of a passive female sexuality merely stitch the reader ever more resolutely into the fabric of patriarchal culture? Or, alternatively, does the satisfaction a reader derives from the act of reading itself, an act she chooses, often in explicit defiance of others' opposition, lead to a new sense of strength and independence?' (1987: 14–15). In exploring the role played by the media in maintaining or challenging existing relations of power in society, we have to remember that the fields of pleasure and meaning are contradictory and contested, neither coincident with a dominant ideology nor the terrain of a spontaneous opposition. Media studies is currently well placed to map these contradictions and contestations. In a recent article, John B. Thompson (1988: 379) has suggested that it can offer a lead to social theorists working in other areas, encouraging them to 'adopt a more dynamic, contextual approach to the analysis of ideology'.

A third, and lesser trodden, route for audience studies is the investigation of questions of taste. Morley and Hobson have offered useful notes on television viewers' gendered programme preferences, and future work must continue to look at the ways in which particular genres appeal to particular audiences. We might also ask how television preferences connect up with distinctions made in other areas of cultural consumption. An extraordinarily suggestive contribution to the analysis of taste has been made by the French sociologist, Pierre Bourdieu (1984), and for anyone interested in the recent debates about audiences his work would repay careful reading. To ask about tastes and preferences is a necessary complement to what we more usually think of as ideological analysis. It is of no lesser political significance because, for Bourdieu, the social patterning of taste and the distribution of cultural capital is intimately related to the reproduction of social power. His research looked at the tastes of different classes and class fractions in French society, stretching across preferences for different sorts of food, clothes, music, art and home furnishings — as well as books, films and broadcasting output — and his approach rejects any narrow delimitation of the object of study. Bourdieu's concern is with the distinctions people make in putting together their cultural identities and life-styles, with how social subjects articulate their leisure worlds. To engage in further projects of this kind would threaten the boundaries of mass communications research — but once we build the bridge between text and inter-discursive context, the limits of our inquiry will inevitably become more blurred.

Notes

1. In a retrospective piece, MacCabe (1985: 11) himself now admits to problems with such a position, referring to 'criteria of value which denigrated forms of popular cinema in favour of a certain number of avant-garde texts . . . . For those . . . who had looked to film theory to break out of the high art enclave, it had led firmly back there, albeit in a highly politicised version.'

2. This approach marked a fundamental break with the dominant behavioural tradition of mass communications research. For an account of differences between the 'behavioural paradigm' and what Hall has called the 'critical paradigm' of contemporary Media Studies, see his essay, 'The Rediscovery of "Ideology": Return of the Repressed in Media Studies', in Michael Gurevitch et al. (eds) (1982).

3. This question was caught up with a wider debate about the relation between 'the economic' and 'the ideological' in Marxist theory. Morley (1980b: 16–19) criticized writers such as Paul Hirst (1976), who had argued that ideological/signifying practices were autonomous of economic determinations. He was equally critical, however, of Parkin's 'fairly unproblematic' linking of meaning systems to economic class positions (Morley, 1980a: 172).

4. Since *The 'Nationwide' Audience* was published, a number of studies have enquired further into audience decodings of TV news and documentary output. See, for example, Justin Wren-Lewis (1985), Kay Richardson and John Corner (1986), as well as recent European work on reception — Peter Dahlgren (1985; 1988) and Klaus Jensen (1986).

5. For numerous examples of derogatory comments made by newspaper critics, see Brunsdon's essay, 'Writing about Soap Opera', in Len Masterman (ed.) (1984).

6. There are, of course, problems in defining exactly what a 'family' is — television viewers no doubt live in a variety of household groupings. Morley acknowledged that his sample of respondents all belonged to 'one specific type of household — the traditional nuclear family, with both parents living together with their dependent children'. In addition, 'all the families were white', and the sample was 'dominated by families from a working-class or lower middle-class background' (1986: 11). Despite problems of funding, his pilot study might have made more of the differences between household contexts.

References

Althusser, L. (1971) *Lenin and Philosophy, and Other Essays*. London: Verso.
Ang, I. (1985) *Watching Dallas: Soap Opera and the Melodramatic Imagination*. London: Methuen.
Barthes, R. (1971) 'The Rhetoric of the Image', *Working Papers in Cultural Studies*, 1.
Barthes, R. (1973) *Mythologies*. London: Paladin.

Bausinger, H. (1984) 'Media, Technology and Daily Life', *Media , Culture and Society*, 6 (4).

Bazin, A. (1967) *What is Cinema?*, Vol. 1, H. Gray (ed.). USA: University of California Press.

Benveniste, E. (1971) *Problems in General Linguistics*. USA: University of Miami Press.

Bourdieu, P. (1984) *Distinction: A Social Critique of the Judgement of Taste*. London: Routledge and Kegan Paul.

Brecht, B. (1964) *Brecht on Theatre*, J. Willett (ed.). London: Methuen.

Brunsdon, C. (1981) '*Crossroads*: Notes on Soap Opera', *Screen*, 22 (4).

Brunsdon, C. (1984) 'Writing about Soap Opera', pp. 82–87 in L. Masterman (ed.) *Television Mythologies: Stars, Shows and Signs*. London: Comedia.

Brunsdon, C. and D. Morley (1978) *Everyday Television: 'Nationwide'*. London: BFI TV Mono.10.

Coward, R. (1984) *Female Desire: Women's Sexuality Today*. London: Paladin.

Coward, R. and J. Ellis (1977) *Language and Materialism: Developments in Semiology and the Theory of the Subject*. London: Routledge and Kegan Paul.

Cubitt, S. (1984) 'Top of the Pops: The Politics of the Living Room', pp. 46–48 in L. Masterman (ed.) *Television Mythologies*.

Dahlgren, P. (1985) 'The Modes of Reception: For a Hermeneutics of TV News', pp. 235–49 in P. Drummond and R. Paterson (eds) *Television in Transition*. London: BFI.

Dahlgren, P. (1988) 'What's the Meaning of This?: Viewers' Plural Sense-Making of TV News', *Media Culture and Society*, 10(3).

Eco, U. (1972) 'Towards a Semiotic Inquiry into the Television Message', *Working Papers in Cultural Studies*, 3.

Ellis, J. (1982) *Visible Fictions: Cinema, Television, Video*. London: RKP.

Frosh, S. (1987) *The Politics of Psychoanalysis: An Introduction to Freudian and Post-Freudian Theory*. London: Macmillan.

Gray, A. (1987) 'Behind Closed Doors: Video Recorders in the Home', pp. 38–54 in H. Baehr and G. Dyer (eds) *Boxed In: Women and Television*. London: Pandora.

Hall, S. (1980) 'Encoding/Decoding', pp. 128–38 in S. Hall et al. (eds) *Culture, Media, Language: Working Papers in Cultural Studies, 1972–79*. London: Hutchinson.

Hall, S. (1982) 'The Rediscovery of "Ideology": Return of the Repressed in Media Studies', pp. 56–90 in M. Gurevitch et al. (eds) *Culture, Society and the Media*. London: Methuen.

Halloran, J. (ed.) (1970) *The Effects of Television*. London: Panther.

Harvey, S. (1978) *May '68 and Film Culture*. London: BFI.

Heath, S. (1976) 'Narrative Space', *Screen*, 17 (3).

Heath, S,. (1977–78) 'Notes on Suture', *Screen*, 18 (4).

Heath, S. and G. Skirrow (1977) 'Television: A World in Action', *Screen*, 18 (2).

Hirst, P. (1976) 'Althusser's Theory of Ideology', *Economy and Society*, 5 (4).

Hobson, D. (1980) 'Housewives and the Mass Media', in S. Hall et al. (eds) *Culture, Media, Language*. London: Hutchinson.

Hobson, D. (1982) *Crossroads: The Drama of a Soap Opera*. London: Methuen.

Jensen, K. (1986) *Making Sense of the News: Towards a Theory and an Empirical Model of Reception for the Study of Mass Communication*. Denmark: Aarhus University Press.

Johnson, R. (1986) 'The Story So Far: And Further Transformations?', in D. Punter (ed.) *Introduction to Contemporary Cultural Studies*. London: Longman.

Lacan, J. (1977) *Ecrits: A Selection*. London: Tavistock.

Lemaire, A. (1977) *Jacques Lacan*. London: Routledge and Kegan Paul.

MacCabe, C. (1974) 'Realism and the Cinema: Notes on Some Brechtian Theses', *Screen*, 15 (2).

MacCabe, C. (1976) 'Theory and Film: Principles of Realism and Pleasure', *Screen*, 17 (3).

MacCabe, C. (1980) *Godard: Images, Sounds, Politics*. London: BFI.

MacCabe, C. (1985) *Theoretical Essays: Film, Linguistics, Literature*. Manchester: Manchester University Press.

Mattelart, M. (1986) 'Women and the Cultural Industries', pp. 63–81 in R. Collins et al. (eds) *Media, Culture and Society: A Critical Reader*. London: Sage.

Metz, C. (1975) 'The Imaginary Signifier', *Screen*, 16 (2).

Metz, C. (1982) *Psychoanalysis and Cinema*. London: Macmillan.

Miller, J-A. (1977–78) 'Suture (Elements of the Logic of the Signifier)', *Screen*, 18 (4).

Modleski, T. (1984) *Loving with a Vengeance: Mass-Produced Fantasies for Women*. London: Methuen.

Moores, S. (1988) ' "The Box on the Dresser": Memories of Early Radio and Everyday Life', *Media, Culture and Society*, 10 (1).

Morley, D. (1975) 'Reconceptualising the Media Audience', *CCCS Stencilled Paper*, 9. Birmingham: University of Birmingham.

Morley, D. (1980a) 'Texts, Readers, Subjects', pp. 163–73 in S. Hall et al. (eds) *Culture, Media, Language*. London: Hutchinson.

Morley, D. (1980b) *The 'Nationwide' Audience: Structure and Decoding*. London: BFI TV Mono.11.

Morley, D. (1981) 'The *Nationwide* Audience: A Critical Postscript', *Screen Education*, 39.

Morley, D. (1986) *Family Television: Cultural Power and Domestic Leisure*. London: Comedia.

Morley, D. and R. Silverstone (1988) 'Domestic Communication: Technologies and Meanings', International Television Studies Conference paper, University of London Institute of Education.

Mulvey, L. (1975) 'Visual Pleasure and Narrative Cinema', *Screen*, 16 (3).

Neale, S. (1977) 'Propaganda', *Screen*, 18 (3).

Oudart, J–P. (1977/8) 'Cinema and Suture', *Screen*, 18 (4).

Parkin, F. (1971) *Class Inequality and Political Order*. London: MacGibbon and Kee.

Radway, J. (1987) *Reading the Romance: Women, Patriarchy and Popular Literature*. London: Verso.

Richardson, K. and J. Corner (1986) 'Reading Reception: Mediation and Transparency in Viewers' Accounts of a TV Programme', *Media, Culture and Society*, 8(4).

Rose, J. (1986) *Sexuality in the Field of Vision*. London: Verso.

Scannell, P. (1988) 'Radio Times: The Temporal Arrangements of Broadcasting in the Modern World', pp. 15–31 in P. Drummond and R. Paterson (eds) *Television and Its Audience*. London: BFI.

Silverman, K. (1983) *The Subject of Semiotics*. USA: Oxford University Press.

Simpson, P. (ed.) (1987) *Parents Talking Television: Television in the Home*. London: Comedia.

Thompson, J.B. (1988) 'Mass Communication and Modern Culture: Contribution to a Critical Theory of Ideology', *Sociology*, 22 (3).

Volosinov, V. (1973) *Marxism and the Philosophy of Language*. USA: Seminar Press.

Willemen, P. (1978) 'Notes on Subjectivity: On Reading Edward Branigan's "Subjectivity Under Siege" ', *Screen*, 19 (1).

Wollen, P. (1982) *Readings and Writings: Semiotic Counter-Strategies*. London: Verso.

Wren-Lewis, J. (1985) 'Decoding Television News', pp. 205–34 in P. Drummond and R. Paterson (eds) *Television in Transition*. London: BFI.

7

Reading reception: mediation and transparency in viewers' reception of a TV programme

Kay Richardson and John Corner

This article is an attempt to address questions about the processes involved when viewers 'make sense' of the diverse visual and aural signs of a TV programme and then render that sense in a spoken account. In particular, we want to explore the manner in which modes of viewing, and talk about viewing, include or exclude recognition of non-fiction TV as motivated discourse despite its conventions of naturalistic representation.

We take as our specific recorded and transcribed data the interpretative accounts of a small number of Liverpool respondents who we invited to watch a BBC2 documentary programme (*A Fair Day's Fiddle*) about 'fiddling' by the unemployed on a Liverpool estate, originally screened on 13 March 1984. However, the general framing of our analysis and its guiding ideas owe a great deal to recent research and argument about how audiences interpret media output. A heightening of interest in this area, stimulated by currents of cross-disciplinary influence – most notably from developments in cultural studies and from linguistics, literary theory and micro-sociology – has produced a usefully interrelated, if small, body of notions and findings regarding the nature of media reception (see, for instance, Brunt and Jordin, 1984; Corner, 1984; Dahlgren, 1984; Eco, 1972; McHoul, 1982; Morley, 1980; Pateman, 1983; Suleiman and Crosman, 1980; Wren-Lewis 1983, 1984). Much of this work, like our own, asks not only 'what does this mean?' in respect of particular readers or viewers but also 'how does it come to mean

Media, Culture and Society (SAGE, London, Beverly Hills, Newbury Park and New Delhi), Vol. 8 (1986), 485–508

this?', a question leading the inquiry into an ethnographic consideration of specific interpretative resources, competencies and activities. And since the design of our own project was in large part informed by our sense of what in previous studies could be built on and what needed to be rethought, it might be useful here to consider briefly some aspects of media reception studies as we presently judge them to have developed.

Most recent inquiry in this area, whatever its discipline basis, has registered as a key point of departure for its arguments a dissatisfaction with those approaches to the study of communicational and cultural processes in which textual forms receive exclusive attention. The assumption, which text-centred studies have tended to encourage, that meanings somehow exist as inherent properties of textual signification and are thus available there for identification and plotting, provided that a sufficiently powerful or sensitive 'reading' can be brought to bear on them, is rejected. Along with it is rejected the idea that such a 'reading' could ever provide an adequate base for pronouncements about the character and strength of audience response or of probable 'ideological effects'. In its place, there is an attempt to take seriously, and to carry through into empirical investigation, the idea that meaning is the product of particular *interpretative conventions* (variously commonplace or esoteric) being applied to textual imagery and language, so that any study interested in the functions or uses of public communications output must try to take both these conventions and their modes of application into account.

In this way, the intensively textual and semantic perspective on media research promoted, for instance, by some varieties of semiotics, is replaced by a perspective closer to that of linguistic pragmatics. Through this, detailed study of textual form is undertaken within the terms of a broader investigation into the contingencies of text-reader relations and the very elements and practices constitutive of reading, hearing or viewing.

Given this shift of emphasis, however, questions of theory are quickly joined by related questions of method – what kind of data might be obtained about what has frequently been seen as the 'black box' realm of audience perceptual and cognitive processings? And what kind of scheme of hypothesis and inquiry could be used to ask questions of this data?

Here it is perhaps important to note how most of the discussion to which we refer has differed from a long-established and continuing strand of audience research in media sociology (see, for instance, McQuail, 1983, for an overview of this). For whereas in this latter area questions of significance-for-audience are often addressed in a very general way, without any close interest in the operation of particular significatory elements or phases (and sometimes without relation to any particular programme or even genre), the newer research makes the relationships between localized signifying elements and interpreted meanings a primary focus for exploration.

Certainly, the most influential single project in tracing signification-interpretation relationships remains David Morley's study of the responses of various groups of viewers to taped editions of the early evening BBC news magazine *Nationwide* (Morley, 1980). This much-discussed study was an attempt to develop an ethnography of 'decoding' which could chart differentiations in interpretative activity and, more ambitiously, could correlate these with the larger economic, social and cultural categories from which the groups (largely internally homogeneous in these respects) were drawn.

Morley's work has attracted a fair amount of both theoretical and methodological argument (see, for example, Corner, 1983, and Wren-Lewis, 1983) with perhaps some of the most trenchant criticisms coming from Morley himself in a post-script article (Morley, 1981). We shall refer to selected aspects of these arguments later, but for our present purposes, the two most pertinent problems which the 1980 study posed for future initiatives may be summarized as follows.

1. The need to get as near as possible to the actual (in a sense, 'lowest level') business of audience meaning-making from what is shown, said or printed. Without this connection (retrospectively rendered in respondents' accounts) between specific items and viewer understandings there is a danger that the analyst's questioning of respondents will 'cream off' general responses and attitudes without generating much indication as to how, or at what point, these were formed and developed through the viewing experience. What in the way of more specific references do emerge are likely to be weighted towards the more directly propositional elements of the programme's verbal discourses and therefore to 'mask' the significatory work of the visual track.

2. The need to give sustained attention to the features and details of respondents' talk as they develop their interpretative accounts within the overall setting of interview/discussion. Here, the relative strengths of group and of one-to-one settings is a matter for consideration. Our view is that, whilst both situations are clearly 'artificial' in a way that always has to be remembered when using the talk as data, there are special difficulties with group work which suggest that research of this kind

should involve a substantial element of one-to-one discussion, particularly in the early stages. These difficulties include problems of speaker identification; the variables of domination, inhibition and consensus introduced by group dynamics (and frequently productive of 'fragmentary' types of utterance whose subsequent use by the analyst as independent and complete statements would be most questionable) and also the quite severe limitations on the opportunities for using 'follow-up' questioning to elicit supplementary or clarificatory comment. Against these factors though, there does have to be set the advantage of facilitating a form of talk which at times will probably be openly argumentative, questioning and supportive (as being between declared 'non-experts') and which may thereby promote and clearly indicate changes in respondents' interpretations and attitudes in the course of the discussion.

It was with these two related problems centrally in mind that we designed our own pilot inquiry into interpretative activity.

Reception ethnography and respondent language

In the context of work on TV audiences, ethnography has been undertaken primarily with the aim of tracing connections between the social positions of viewers and their interpretations – accepting that 'social position in no way directly correlates with decodings' (Morley, 1980: 137) and therefore that one of the tasks of research is to discover precisely what links do exist. Our own present research is concerned with what we regard as the preliminary project of discovering more about the general character of interpretation itself and the manner in which social knowledge is used to resource it.

Since we were not aiming to develop a sociological argument in this pilot study, sampling was not an issue, although we chose respondents who were not too socially/culturally homogeneous (a mix of gender, class and occupation) expecting (correctly) that their accounts of the programme would be significantly different. We explored this differentiation by paying close attention to the language used in the interviews that followed each respondent's viewing of the programme. This involved concentrating upon the different 'framings' that respondents gave to their accounts; their perception of various programme items as a *mediation* and/or as a *transparent* representation of people, settings and circumstances. We chose the BBC documentary because its formal characteristics (discussed later) offered the possibility of tracking interpretations in relation to a number of different visual and verbal devices. It also seemed likely that its subject-matter might be such as to provoke quite a high level of engagement and a subsequent richness of initial account in our respondents (again, given our specific aims, we did not see such a choice as compromising the research design).

The interviews were one-to-one sessions of about an hour's duration conducted immediately after each viewing. We chose this method because of our interest in the specific details of the interpretative process, and our sequencing and manner of questioning often varied from one interview to the next in our attempt to avoid the kinds of answers that are elicited in questionnaire-based audience research. We wished to explore the subtleties of viewer understandings even if this had to be at the expense of direct comparability between the different accounts. What we were confronting in the readings were examples of a particular form of discourse – the discourse of interpretation.

An interview with a respondent about a television programme that he or she has been asked to watch under unusual circumstances results in discourse that is very complex in its weaving-together of auto-biography, political and social beliefs, affective responses, description of programme content and speculation about the processes of production, to name only the most prominent themes. The research involves the selective reading of these recordings, treating them as evidence of how the respondents made sense of the programme, what they understood themselves to be seeing and hearing as the viewing experience progressed. Yet it would be a mistake to approach the recordings with the attitude that interpretations can be recognized and pulled out of their discursive context without an understanding of the fabric of that context. In the first place there is the problem of recognition itself. When, for example, a respondent comments in terms of his or her own attitude to 'fiddling' it will not always be obvious whether this is being set alongside a perception of the programme's attitude to that topic, as either 'like' or 'unlike'. And in the second place, there is a risk of drawing the line between, on the one hand, the *interpretation* (regarded as the principal data) and, on the other, its *discursive context* at the wrong point.

This is a risk, for example, with the following comments (hypothetical examples based on the data):

1. The guy with the beard was a clever bloke.
2. They presented the guy with the beard as a clever bloke.
3. The guy with the beard came across as a clever bloke.

At one level these comments offer the same interpretation: that one of the contributors to the programme could be perceived as 'clever'. But the syntax suggests differences of interpretation that should be taken seriously. The first version is, in our terms, an evaluative *transparency reading*. It comments on the character of 'the guy with the beard' *as if* he had been *directly* perceived by the respondent, rather than perceived through the mediation of editing and form of presentation. The second version by contrast is a thorough-going *mediation reading*, with a problematic exophoric pronoun as the source for the perception of cleverness that results, a perception in which 'the guy with the beard' himself is merely the carrier of a meaning that has a quite different point of origin. The third version involves a 'hedge'.' 'They' are no longer the explicit source of the perception, but neither is 'he' necessarily. Either explanation of the perception is possible under this formulation.

Differences of this kind are at least as relevant to the study of interpretative variation as the points of similarity. Too commonsensical a view of what constitutes an 'interpretation' would miss the point entirely by missing the way that the attribution of 'cleverness' is framed. Hence the framing is not an ignorable part of 'the context' of the respondents' interpretations (a matter, merely, of 'how they said it' and not of 'what was said') but is itself part of the interpretation.

In the following discussion of the respondents' uptake on specific aspects of the programme, we have made use of a provisional reading typology, differentiating between 'transparency reading' and 'mediation reading' as a first step. It is important to note that we use these terms primarily to characterize the tendency of specific utterances within an interpretative account rather than to classify whole accounts as being either of one sort or the other. We also became aware that either type of reading could be *displaced* (i.e., hypothesized by the respondent as what 'someone else' might say about the programme, ranging from 'my mother' to 'people from Basingstoke' – in the latter case a displacement in which class consciousness may have had a part to play); that readings could be offered as 'givens' about the programme's meanings or as the result of inferences on the viewer's part; and that readings could involve the recognition of a *manipulative intent* on the part of the programme makers.

Many of the details of this rudimentary typology have yet to be worked through but it is clear that the categories are likely to combine and intersect with one another 'on the ground' in ways that make it unrealistic to expect any tight, formal set of distinctions to emerge. Also, in the course of watching programmes and talking about them viewers may re-frame as mediated what earlier, perhaps due to their immediacy of response to the people and issues depicted, they treated transparently. Nevertheless, as a broad guide to important features of respondents' interpretations the categories have proved useful. For the purposes of an initial classification of the kinds of status, forms of address and intentionality attributed to news and documentary material by viewer/ respondents, such a scheme is an alternative to those based more directly on assessing the level of agreement/disagreement with a programme's propositional content. Morley's enterprising employment of the three 'ideal type' reading positions proposed by Parkin (1971) – dominant, negotiated and oppositional in relation to the point of view 'preferred' in the text – is undoubtedly the most well-known and widely-referred to scheme of this latter kind, though Morley's valuable comments on its limitations seem to have received less attention (Morley, 1981). Parkin's categories are troublesome to use, as Morley discusses, partly because they are insufficiently discriminating (e.g. as between different forms of 'oppositional' reading – so different in fact that putting them together under this heading is an intuitively unsound generalization) and partly because the status of the 'preferred' reading is itself ambivalent, and can barely be understood in a way that is consistent with the idea that decodings *other than* those at least encompassing the preferred one can be equally legitimately derived from the same text.

However, Parkin's scheme was adopted to enable audience research to give attention to questions of ideological reproduction, conceived in terms of the degrees of hegemonic dominance exercised over public knowledge by media accounts. As we shall suggest later, in any more extensive reception survey following on from this pilot study the terms we have devised would need to be related to some equivalent set of concepts in order that similar questions of social cognition and power could be addressed.

Our interest in the 'discourse of interpretation' is also somewhat different in its theoretical terms from the recent and illuminating arguments of Wren-Lewis (1983) concerning the use of respondents' accounts in ethnographic research. Wren-Lewis is concerned that respondents' accounts are too often measured against meanings already 'discovered' in the material by the research – for example, the 'preferred readings' found in the various items of *Nationwide* (Brunsdon and Morley, 1978; Morley, 1980). This approach, argues Wren-Lewis, risks imposing a spurious structure upon the range of responses offered by respondents, and neglects the possibility of finding alternative coherent structures of a parallel kind in respondents' own accounts. It amounts to a refusal to explore each account of the programme on its own terms. The researchers' terms are imposed upon all of the data.

Whilst recognizing these dangers, for our purposes we were not happy with the degree of relativism suggested by Wren-Lewis's approach. We had some specific, though tentative, hypotheses about aspects of the programme's meaning and organization. We sought to explore these hypotheses by investigating the extent to which, and the terms upon which, those aspects featured in respondents' accounts. Rather than imposing our own interpretation upon those of the respondents, so that the complexity of the latter became invisible to us, we were obliged to come to terms with the complexity of respondents' accounts if we were to discover anything interesting about the interpretative consequences of those programme features that we had tentatively identified as significant.

The most interesting sections of the interviews we obtained are those in which the framing of the interpretation is important in relation to the substantive issues that the programme deals with, as in the following extract (edited transcript):

> I think the programme or the makers focused on that area so that people, the ordinary person watching the programme, you know, the first thing that would spring to their mind would be 'Well, if they're living like that, you know, how can they afford that if they're on the dole or even if they've got a job on the side.' And I think that they were pandering to that prejudice that the ordinary person...the man or the woman in the street would have that. I'm thinking of people, say, my mother for example would say something like that, she often does say things like that.

This description overall takes the form of what we would call a manipulative, displaced reading. The implication of the quote is that the respondent's mother, as an 'ordinary person' (the respondent does not identify himself as an ordinary person) is already predisposed to believe that the unemployed are doing rather well on social security and hence that she would perceive – as the programme intends that she should – things such as the amount of drinking and smoking that goes on, and that the homes shown in the programme are well-furnished by her standards. She would take these facts as evidence that her belief about life on the dole was justified. But she would not perceive that she is intended to draw this conclusion. The respondent, recognizing the intention, is not manipulated by it. But his mother doesn't recognize the intention and is therefore manipulated. In this case a displaced reading allows the respondent to hold in place a reading of the programme that he makes but has reason to objectify as part of his own more complex reading.

The programme

The fifty-minute programme used in this study, *A Fair Day's Fiddle*, was a BBC production for the documentary series *Brass Tacks*. This series, made at the Manchester TV centre and screened on BBC2 has a particular interest in issues affecting the North-West. The episode examined was shot in Netherley, Liverpool, and is broadly concerned with life on the dole in this area, with especial reference to 'fiddling' which in this context means, for example: stripping materials from derelict buildings, tampering with electricity meters, and working on the side. The programme also deals with the question of debt in these circumstances and what to do about it.

The programme concentrates upon subjects' own accounts of their circumstances, their activities, their motives and their rationalizations. The reporter's voice is almost totally absent from the programme and no reporter ever appears in shot. The reporter who introduces the programme says, *inter alia*, 'local people speak for themselves'. Officially, then, it is the intention of the programme *not* to make moral judgments on behaviour that, nevertheless, will undoubtedly be subject to ethical standards when viewed by the television audience. This official forbearance is reinforced by the episodic (rather than rhetorical) shape of the programme, suggesting 'sampling' – of different problems, to which 'fiddles' are an answer; of different opinions about 'fiddling' generally, all from within the area; of different 'fiddles'. The progress of the film is broken on two occasions by 'musical interludes' when the visual material (shots of the Netherley area, its streets and its housing) is accompanied by music (slow, synthesized rock) rather than talk.

Stylistically, different episodes and sections of episodes are presented in varying forms (a useful account of some of these forms is contained in Heath and Skirrow, 1977). Sometimes subjects speak 'on camera'. Eyelines suggest an out-of-frame reporter, but since the reporter is generally neither seen nor heard by viewers, the result is an impression of 'unsolicited testimony' – talk volunteered without prompting. In some cases the content of the talk thus delivered is very personal. One woman describes how she was told that since she was not paying for her seven-year-old child's funeral she would have to sit in the funeral car with the coffin on her lap. The combination of personal subject matter and delivery without (apparent) reportorial intervention gives a spurious directness to the relationship between the on-screen subject and the viewer. In some cases, reporters are present at events involving pairs and groups of local people. In such cases filming shows them 'talking amongst themselves' as well as addressing the out-of-frame reporter. The unsolicited testimony effect is not so great in these sequences. Another presentational form is that of dramatic episodes enacted by the subjects themselves (but undoubtedly *acted*: this is not conventional *verité* footage although at points the programme uses a *verité* style). We address ourselves more directly to this aspect of the programme, which raises questions about credibility and authenticity, in a further, forthcoming paper on our research (Corner and Richardson, 1986). Finally, the programme uses various contributors for voice-over sequences. Sometimes they voice over footage of themselves; sometimes over footage which is thematically related to what they are saying. In both cases much of the accompanying visual action can be seen as 'enacted', if not always to the same degree or in the same manner as the footage in the dramatic episodes.

Notwithstanding the emphasis that the programme places upon the views of Netherley people themselves, and the interpretative openness of a programme that eschews reportorial framing of the subjects, there is arguably a subtext to the programme that owes more to the operations of the programme makers than to the Netherley people. The subtext concerns the standard of living that can be supported on the dole. It seems to us that the programme is organized and works to encourage a perception of fiddling on the dole as efforts made to maintain a good or reasonable standard of living – as against encouraging the perception that it is only fiddling which allows the unemployed to survive. Several factors can be adduced in support of this interpretation. Picking up on an earlier comment by a contributor, a reporter is heard at one point to ask him if he is saying that local fiddling occurs because people want to live rather than exist. The contributor assents to this proposition. On the visual side there are things that we may or may not be meant to notice, like the fact that a lot of cigarette smoking is going on in this community, that going out for a drink is a normal part of (male) life on the estate, that the homes from which people speak their minds to camera seem well furnished and decorated. At one point, two mothers talk about buying toys for their children, mentioning prices up to two hundred pounds.

Respondent interpretations: Speaker Three

In this article, rather than selecting 'sample' material from across the very wide spread of comment which we collected on the various themes, sequences and features of the programme, we have chosen to focus on the responses we got to the contribution of one participant/speaker who appears on a number of occasions. Since this person's contributions were regarded by both ourselves and the majority of our respondents as a major feature of the documentary, we feel that this restriction of focus (representing no more than half an hour of recordings out of the thirteen hours collected) is justifiable in that the specific interpretations and assessments made here are quite central to the respondents' general sense of what the programme was about and how it worked.

The thematic continuities gained by restricting the citation of data in this way also allows us to point up economically those relationships between elements of interpretative discourse and respondent cognitions and framings which we are suggesting that an ethnography of reception needs to take into account.

Speaker Three is the third person to be heard on the sound-track, excluding the reporter who introduces the programme. His importance within the documentary is constituted by several features which we can classify conveniently as *structural*, *stylistic* and *thematic*.

Structurally, the principal feature is the way in which both Speaker Three's presence and his verbal contributions serve partly as a kind of link across a number of different scenes and phases within the programme. In one instance this involves the use of a short sequence of generalized reflection by him (with face in shot) to follow and 'gloss' an enactment and interview scene in which particularized, biographical comment has been given.

The relevant stylistic features are both visual and verbal. Visually, a distinctive characteristic is the use of generously timed 'display' shots, establishing his presence quite strongly and inviting the viewer to give a measure of steady attention to his appearance, behaviour and immediate environment (e.g. in rolling a cigarette, buying tobacco from a mobile shop, entering his house and eventually watching TV from his sofa). Gaps in his voice-over or in-shot speech during these sequences mean that only location-sound is heard. During one of these sequences, the one which is shot in his room, considerable use is made of extreme close-up and shifting camera angles.

Verbally, it is very noticeable to us and to respondents that, in contrast with that of every other participant, his style of speech is very measured and carefully paced, having something of the rhythm of public speaking. Such an impression is further reinforced by the rhetorical organization of his comments. This makes effective use of parallelisms, as can be observed in an example from his opening voice-over:

> Our fiddles have been forced on us.
> Our fiddles are not done for gain or for profits.
> Our fiddles are done because it's necessary;
> it's necessary for us to exist.

Finally, and following on from this, in its themes the speech of Speaker Three differs from that of other participants insofar as it consists in good part of general social propositions rather than of particularistic, experiential ones. No one else says things like, 'There are four classes in Great Britain...' or 'Jobs are a thing of the past...'.

It is clear that all three above groupings of features will be interrelated and perhaps mutually supportive in their consequences for any interpretative 'uptake' on Speaker Three. Below, we have organized comments so as to allow a relative emphasis upon, respectively, the visual, the verbal and then the explicitly evaluative dimensions of the responses that were made to us. Most hesitations and repetitions have been removed from these extracts and conventional punctuation is used as a guide for readers; the texts thus represent considered *interpretations* of the spoken material and do not provide access to characteristics of the data as speech. (?) is used for indistinct passages, (...) marks editorial ellipsis rather than incompletion on the speaker's part, and (Q) indicates the interviewer's question.

Section I: reading visual presentation and setting

1. I think it follows him back into the house and all the time I was aware of the sort of staging of things, you know, when he goes to the van in the first place there's obviously a camera you know behind the shop assistant and he's made this comment you know, for the benefit of the camera, and the camera follows him back to the house. And this was a technique that I think that was used quite a lot, you saw the

individual and then you saw them in the context of their own house, and from what they'd been saying you suddenly, you follow them into the house and they're talking about squalor and deprivation and poverty and having no money, and then suddenly you see a beautiful three piece suite, you know, colour TV in the corner, video underneath, all kinds of you know, nicely kept pot plants and you think to yourself you know, this isn't squalor. But you're led into that argument by the camera you know, this kind of incongruity between what's being said and how they're actually living came up time and time again from the, you know. Presumably it was intended you know to raise questions in the viewer's mind as to you know, 'Why?' – which is I think a criticism that I would make because I think in that sense it was unsympathetic to the people it was filming.

2. Yeah, the man who, he was on his own, always on his own, he'd never got a wife with him. I don't know whether he lived on his own. He was always on his own, and they showed him sort of outside with the flats behind him, rolling his own cigarette and looking very bleak, and things like that.

3. I suppose everyone felt what he said anyway because of the situation they were all in it was just that he was in the position where he wasn't going to shy away from the camera he was going to say it wasn't he you know . . . so he was the type of character who would push himself forward to say it that's why I remember him you know.

   (. . .)

   I thought it was a bit of a mess-up really I mean he was saying things, he was saying he couldn't afford anything but you looked at his house you know.

(Q) Well, let's turn away from what he said to what he looked like and how he appeared on the programme, can you remember much about that?

   Well, he looked like a thug.

(Q) Did he?

   Yes don't you think so? I thought he did. Like I say he's one of those I wouldn't want to have an argument with you know. He came over as a heavy character didn't he?

4. He's in an armchair, he's relaxed. He doesn't feel pressured. Mind you there's nothing for him to feel pressured about because he doesn't insinuate that he is doing anything fraudulent or illegal to any extent that you might pick up on that. He's not boasting, he's griping. I didn't like his interview at all. I don't agree with anything that he says for a start so my impression of him would be one-sided.

(Q) What, his own comments one-sided?

   My comments on what he said would be one-sided so it would turn me away from giving a clear view of what I saw of him.

5. But he looked, to me, him and his family looked quite well off you know. Leather jackets don't come cheap do they?

This selection of respondent comments indicates a number of aspects of interpretative accounting in which particular elements of visual depiction are variously registered within 'mediation' and/or 'transparency' framings and variously related to elements of knowledge, assumption and evaluation produced from elsewhere, including from what is being *said* in the programme.

The degree of overall 'match' which respondents interpret across all the elements perceived as significant may be subsequently rendered either in terms of the coherence, or otherwise of the programme's communicative design or (more transparently) in terms of the personal qualities and credibility of those people appearing and speaking within it.

Items 2 and 4 give readings of the depicted settings for the participant/ interviewee's speech. In item 2 the respondent's doubts about what can be inferred from what is seen ('I don't know whether he lived on his own...')'pose as a possibility a gap between actual circumstances and specific programme depictions. Further comments in 2 – the attribution of agency to the programme makers ('*they* showed him...') and an indication of the compositional and associational properties of the depiction (...'flats behind him'; 'bleak') – also serve to render the speaker's solitariness as primarily an 'effect' of the programme for this respondent.

In 4, visually derived information is used more confidently in 'present-tense' recollection to inform judgments about the speaker's state of mind and attitudes. Here, the speaker's behaviour is perceived as occurring, as it were, 'authentically' (and it thus becomes directly relatable to matters of character) rather than being viewed partly as a product of programme conventions. Nevertheless, this respondent also suggests that initial, fundamental disagreement with the speaker's comments has skewed or limited the perception of his appearance and behaviour or, at least, the capacity to give a 'fair' account of that perception.

In some contrast with this reading of the speaker's position as relaxed and unpressured, item 3 develops an account of the conditions of speaking in terms of the forwardness of the speaker in securing his opportunity to contribute. There are some indications that this reading of character-type draws on personal appearance and its suggestiveness ('thug'; 'a heavy character'). Given this emphasis it would be unusual for such an interpretation to reference any mediating conditions acting upon the depiction, but the respondent *is* worried by the discrepancy between what is said and the appearance of the speaker's house. Just how far this is finally perceived as a loss of coherence in the programme's organization or, alternatively, as a matter of speaker dishonesty, is not clear, though 'mess-up' does suggest the former.

A comparable registration of inconsistency occurs both in items 1 and 5. In 5 the comment turns, after approval of what was said, to the noting of potentially discrepant aspects of the visuals – the respondent gives the example of a leather jacket as an indicator of being well off. For the respondent, this appears to put a question mark against the propriety of the speaker making the comments that he does, if not against their truthfulness.

In 1 as in 3 it is the information provided by 'seeing' the house interior which pulls against interpretation of the speech. However, the respondent in 1, who offers a sustained mediation reading (his reference to 'staging' for instance) of a kind we found only in a very few of our recordings, differs from all the other readers of discrepancy quoted above in regarding the inconsistency not as some form of lapse but as a device routinely employed by the makers of the programme to 'raise questions in the viewer's mind'. This appears to involve the respondent in producing what we have earlier called a 'manipulative displaced' reading, since although he reports himself as making the intended reading ('. . . and you think to yourself you know . . .') he also registers the cueing of this activity ('you're led into that argument by the camera'). This recognition presumably neutralizes the effectiveness of the device unless, in the phases of perceived incongruity, the programme is understood by him to be explicitly polemical.

Clearly, the relationships between hearing and seeing as they interact to inform the interpretative process need to be 'shadowed' as closely as possible through respondent accounts if understanding of the conditions and the tensions of 'knowing through television' is to be advanced.

Section II: reading speech

6. No I think, the way it came over to me was, he really was speaking for everyone. He was sort of putting into words which, simple, straightforward, everyday language which everybody should be able to understand, he was saying it all for the other people in their own little particular moans or grouses or trying to get a message across. And the whole thing together was, he said it all for them. That's the way it came across.

7. (Q) Mm. Do you, he gets more time, just about, perhaps, than anyone else?

    He speaks better.

    (Q) And you think he speaks better, yeah.

Well, he's using the utmost of his ability to come across clearly and intelligently. Not intellectual, but intelligent social comments.

(Q) And do you think that's why he gets so much time?

Yes I do because I didn't find him an interesting factor in the film. I found him very boring. I thought he was uncompromising, and I wouldn't like him.

(Q) But he's clear.

But he's clear and he's concise and he's got an aim even though it might not be right he's got an aim, he's doing something about it whereas the rest are suffering. He's the only one who is actually doing something about it. In his own way.

8. I think I said that he was more politicized than the others. He talked, the individual families or people that they looked at talked subjectively, you know, about their own plight, but he talked about the problem objectively, he talked about the overall problem, and he talked about it in his own sort of, I don't know, sociological terms or whatever, he had his own sort of views on the system but he talked, as I say, he talked more objectively than others. That's one of the reasons why I've labelled him as the link, the link.

9. The way the actual unemployed chap was treated, he was given a lot of time. I think he must have been given a lot of open questions, which were then slanted because he seemed to be railing against things quite a lot, I mean specific things like advertisements, like the status of the unemployed, like the class system, and I'm not sure really whether he was slightly set up to that. He seemed to be given a lot of time to express his grievances, and I think he must've been prompted in some way to talk about these things, on purpose.

(Q) What would the purpose be, though, do you think, if he was given lee-way?

Well presumably, to given an open honest view of how they felt, as unemployed people.

In this section we're focusing on the responses that our interviewees made when asked to think about the way that Speaker Three spoke and his function in the programme. The view was widely shared that he was somehow different from other participants, or treated differently, although the terms in which this 'difference' was characterized varied between respondents, as the above quotations show.

Whereas 6 refers to 'simple, straightforward, everyday language', 8 says that Speaker Three uses sociological terms. Whereas 7 emphasizes that *he* was using *his* ability to come across clearly and intelligently, 9 thinks that he is not totally in control of his own performance. Whereas 8 finds him 'objective', 9 notices that he is 'railing' and expressing his grievances. Whereas for 6 there is continuity between Speaker Three and the other participants in the programme (and the rest of the community?), for 7 there is an important discontinuity; 'he's got an aim, he's doing something about it whereas the rest are suffering'. These contrasted beliefs are not necessarily incompatible and must not be taken to represent the limits of any respondent's thoughts on this subject. But there is an interest in these contrasts between what respondents choose to mention first, to foreground or to emphasise.

Quotes 6 and 7 can be taken as broadly representing transparency readings of Speaker Three's contribution to the programme. They take him to be the 'author' of how he comes across: 'he really was speaking for everyone'; 'he's using the utmost of his ability to come across clearly and intelligently' – though 7 moves through qualitatively different phases: a descriptive phase, an 'intentionalist' phase, and phases of judgment – 'very boring' – and inference – 'he's got an aim'. The main thrust of 8 is transparent also, and descriptive in its orientation. However, it ends with a characterization that hints at perception of mediation (mediation reading is common for this respondent), in using the term 'link', with its suggestion of structural relations between Speaker Three's contribution and other parts of the programme. But the term is used with equivocation. Item 8 is explicit that the interpretation is personal – 'I've labelled him the link.' In one sense the entire corpus consists of personal interpretations. But when this feature is foregrounded in relation to any particular comment the result is a contrast between that comment and others not so qualified.

Item 9 is alive to the possibility that Speaker Three is not in all respects the author of his performance, although it uses truncated passives so the controlling agent(s) of the production process is (are) never named, even by generalization (e.g. 'the makers'). At the beginning it is as if 9 is saying that those in charge wanted to have someone say these specific things. But when invited to consider why (for example, to show viewers how resentful the unemployed can be) the answer virtually retracts this possibility: 'to give an open honest view of how they felt, as unemployed people'. For under this characterization the implication is that the openness of the question sought only honesty, and therefore that the programme makers *weren't* after any particular content.

Section III: sympathies and evaluations

   10. I think the film could've been more interesting and still had his point of view come
       across, if he hadn't been interviewed alone. If they'd had somebody with an opposite

point of view. I think if they'd had somebody with an opposite or different approach to his point of view to put his back against the wall where he had to defend his point of view, then that would have held my interest more than him just being given the lead to down-trod everything he thought was against him.

11. (Respondent has been asked if Speaker Three is an important functioning element in the programme.)

I think so because you see perhaps that's what helps controversy, the fact that you've got this guy saying those things, and it's making you respond. I mean you're responding basically to him and you're thinking, you know, how annoying. And the whole question of the unemployed and both sides are beginning to come out in your own mind. And it goes from sympathy for the person whose child has died, to him showing the other side, sort of resenting the fact he's unemployed, and it swings both ways. And I think that's important in a documentary otherwise you're having your mind made up for you, if it's say it all had been all sort of pitying images and full of sadness, now that's wrong because that's forcing it really into a corner and making you think, well I should be thinking this about the unemployed.

12. I think he reinforces it more. He sort of, he makes more of a point, you know. He sums it up well I think, each thing he says, yeah. He's got it summed up properly. 'Cos I can relate to things he says, see. I can relate all of what he says, so I'm agreeing. I'm sort of, you know, noticing him more because he's the way I feel about a lot of things like, he's sort of similar opinions.

13. He came across as a very strong-minded person, I think. I don't think that would have brought so much sympathy. His opinions I think were a bit too strong for perhaps certain members of our society who might be watching the programme because he seemed to be filled with resentment. Now that's not a bad thing to show resentment but I think if you put too much resentment in a programme you're going to alienate certain other sections of the society who'd be watching a BBC programme.

14. Well he obviously had some grasp of what was going on, you know, the situation. Which a lot of people tend to do, you know, often people have more grasp of what's going on than people give them credit for, specially in documentaries.

15. (Respondent has been asked whether she can identify with Speaker Three or not: 'the other one' is another of the programme's prominent participants already mentioned by this respondent.)

Well, no I would be behind the other one. Do you know what I mean? I'd put, I would think, he's generalizing about the whole thing but he does seem resigned to the fact and he can sit there and he can say that there are no jobs 'cos he said, you know, 'These people that say there are jobs if they go out and look for them, well there aren't.' But I mean if he's a painter and decorator, well there are jobs, 'cos people are always painting and decorating, aren't they?

(Q) Yes

And if he went out and looked for them. But he seems to say 'well there's so many classes and I'm the bottom class because I'm on the dole' and that's it, and he does seem to. It wouldn't build up your sympathy for him I don't think. I mean, I couldn't speak for anybody else, but (?).

16. It seems to me from what you're saying about him that you almost see him as providing the sort of material that a reporter could have provided or doing the same job that a reporter could have done about generalization or some kind of explanation. Is that right?

No. I think people who would be critical of the documentary would see him in that role. But I mean I just saw him as one of the people of Netherley. I think that he was used in that way merely from the director's or producer's, people who made the thing, if they're going to not have any reporter talking over, you know, I think you've got to use somebody, you know from an idea of producing and putting a package together you've got to have some kind of link in it.

17. (Respondent has been asked if Speaker Three's linking contribution to the programme is effective.)

In terms of a television programme it's probably necessary. If he hadn't done it, you see, if he hadn't done it presumably the commentator would have been doing it, or would've been directing questions to the other people to try and bring this sort of thing out. Presumably, I don't make television programmes, I don't know. But otherwise the whole thing might have fallen down without him, you know, the sympathetic approach might well have fallen down, you know.

18. He just, he was like a focus for me, on the thing, he drew the whole thing together it generalized you know, it wasn't. Although he was personally affected by it all he could see through that, he could see what the whole system was doing and what his role was.

(Q) You think then that more than other people he was offering generalizations?

Yeah, I think so. Yes, well perhaps the girls from the CAB also summed it up as well. But I think the rest of them were sort of case, individual cases, each sort of having different problems and their own different ways of coping with it.

In this section we have picked quotations where respondents talk about attitudes to Speaker Three – their own and others' – with especial but not exclusive reference to his opinions. We're particularly interested in the connections which respondents make between their attitudes to Speaker Three and their understanding of the programme and his function within it.

The differences between respondents are again of interest. There are respondents who align with Speaker Three in their different ways, such as 12 and 14, and those who don't, like 10, 11/13 (the same respondent) and 15. There are comments in which affiliation/nonaffiliation is based upon similarity or difference of *opinion*, such as 12, 'I can relate to all of what he says so I'm agreeing', and comments where (dis)affiliation is related to the *attitude* that Speaker Three conveys, such as 11 in which his 'resentment' is found 'annoying' or 15 which is unsympathetic to Speaker Three because he seems resigned. In the case of 15 it is interesting that nonaffiliation here also involves a difference of opinion about the possibility of finding work. There are respondents who consciously register their alignment position as a personal one, as 12 does, and those who generalize it, as does 13 and as 17 seems to do in referring to 'the sympathetic approach' and Speaker Three's contribution to it. For another quotation which explicitly refers to possible effects upon interpretation of the respondents' alignment position, see 4 above. In the case of 4 it is respondent *nonalignment* which is held to be significant in principle, whereas in 12 it is respondent *alignment*. Notice also that the generalized alignment positions articulated in 13 and 17 are attributed to the design of the programme. It is not by accident, then, that Speaker Three is found to be sympathetic by 17 and unsympathetic by 13.

There is a contrast between 12 and 14 although both support Speaker Three's ideas. The difference concerns the degree of separation that each makes between his assessment of those ideas as correct and his perception of them as opinions. It should be said that no respondent takes Speaker Three's propositions about society simply as truths. They do take participants' biographical information as truths, and it is possible that the social propositions could have been taken as (programme-intended) truths had they been spoken by a conventional television presenter, a true narrator or link-man, instead of by a man who is undisguisedly a member of the community with which the programme is concerned (cf. 16, discussed below). The phrasing in 14, 'some grasp of what was going on', suggests independent knowledge of the same thing-that-was-going-on as is referred to by Speaker Three. There is a similar feature in 18 in the references to 'what the whole system was doing and what his role was'. In 12 the quotation begins in such a way as to suggest this kind of alignment; 'he sums it up well I think'. Possibly this 'it' is the same for the respondent as it is for Speaker Three. However, by the end of the quotation there has been a shift. In saying explicitly that Speaker Three has 'similar opinions' to his own, 12 effects more of a separation between those opinions and his own evaluation of them. It becomes a case of saying that those opinions are like his rather than a case of saying/implying that they are true, although this respondent has elsewhere taken that approach as well.

The interest of 11 lies in the use that it makes of the respondent's reaction to Speaker Three as 'annoying' in articulating an interpretation of the programme. In the first place that reaction is generalized, it is not offered as purely personal.

Having generalized it the respondent is in a position to see that reaction as something which the programme makers have worked for, with a particular programme-form in mind, 'it goes from sympathy for the person whose child has died, to him showing the other side of, sort of resenting the fact that he's unemployed, and it swings both ways'. Item 13 is spoken by the same respondent, a few moments earlier in the interview. She appears to have shifted from a displaced reading in which it is other people, not herself, who are going to be alienated when they hear Speaker Three's strong opinions (see below for discussion of Speaker Three as a provider of provocative ideas), to a reading which she herself subscribes to. Also, whilst in 13 the displayed resentment and the consequent reaction ('alienation') seem to be characterized almost as a mistake on the part of the programme, in 11 the same resentment and the reaction of annoyance have become design features. This indicates the necessity of not taking any single thing that a respondent might say as independently definitive and final and of focusing upon shifts and inconsistencies within each of the accounts.

Item 10 is of interest because of its objection to the dominance of Speaker Three (and thus of his views) within the programme. This is expressed in terms of a personal judgment of the programme as less interesting because of his dominance. However, it is perhaps significant that the ideas he expresses are ones that 10 objects to, and it is possible that behind this formulation lies an anxiety about the programme being unbalanced in its present form (note the phrasing, 'being given the lead to down-trod everything'). Her suggestion for its improvement, the provision of actual debate between Speaker Three and someone who opposes his views, sounds like a request for a more conventional, perhaps studio-based, documentary discussion programme. It is useful to examine 16 in relation to this possibility. In 16 the question posed (after the respondent has already described Speaker Three as offering generalizations and used the term 'the link' – see 8 above) invites the respondent to assent to the idea that Speaker Three is a substitute for a conventional presenter. This idea is explicitly rejected despite earlier comments along these lines, echoed again here:'he was used in that way'. After rejecting this proposition 16 continues: 'I think people who would be critical of the documentary would see him in that role.' This displaced reading could almost be a characterization of the kind of interpretation we have suggested for 10 above, where there *is* a criticism of the programme and it *is* related to the centrality/dominance of Speaker Three. Item 16 is anticipating that some people will think that Speaker Three is speaking 'for the programme' and will therefore be critical of the programme because his ideas are so obviously provocative in their content. If, on the other hand, Speaker Three is just 'one of the people of Netherley' his controversiality is less of a problem since the ideas of participants in documentary programmes are allowed to be controversial.

Concluding comments: respondent accounts and reception surveys

At a general level, our preliminary work on the reception and accounting activities of a small sample audience has confirmed the arguments of earlier studies regarding the variety of meanings and motives which programme material is perceived to have as a result of viewers construing it within different interpretative schemes. It is also clear that an important element of these schemes is personal experience, which may be strong enough to cause an immediate questioning of a programme's depicted realities.

However, our primary conclusions, in line with our investigative aims, concern the character of interpretative processing itself, and the kind of methodology most suited to researching it further. Here, we have focused on a number of variables concerning the sorts of stance and relationship adopted by viewers towards what is seen and heard, with the interpretation of specific visual and aural information and with the interaction between screened representations and what viewers previously knew, assumed or believed. Our use of the categories *transparent*, *mediated*, *displaced* and *manipulation* has served as a basic grid within which they can be plotted.

We believe that the methods which we have followed and the ideas which we have started to develop here will prove of value when applied in the context of larger-scale studies with viewer respondents selected from within a more precisely designed scheme of sampling.

Ideally, such an application would include both one-to-one and group discussion sessions. We have already made out a case for the former but we are aware of the highly unnatural intensity of such speech settings and would seek to advance our inquiry by also using pre-constituted groups (e.g., political, educational, in the workplace) and groups assembled through our own invitation. One of the objectives here would be to consider more closely than in one-to-one sessions the ways in which differing interpretations are negotiated and contested by viewers through their use both of textual and extra-textual evidence. In this respect, we broadly agree with Morley's comments on the extent to which every-day interpretations of media material are 'collectively constructed' through social interaction (Morley, 1980), though we believe that it is impossible to replicate the conditions for such a phased process within *any* discussion group setting. Moreover, the interpretations given in one-to-one sessions are not to be regarded as somehow 'desocialized' simply as a result of their being 'first accounts' expressed with only the researcher present. For it seems clear to us that when respondents talk about the programme material they do so by drawing upon the fram-ings, categories and attitudes formed by their routine participation in talk about television. It is doubtless the case that, in actual settings, first readings and accounts are then often subject to lengthy and complex processes of revision – via talk with others and exposure to further texts, for instance – but this does not remove at all from the social significance of those initial framings and understandings which research of the kind proposed seeks to tap.

A further sociological dimension of this kind of reception survey would involve not only the offering of 'thicker' descriptions of media uptake but also an attempt to trace correlations across a number of factors bearing on the function of television as a source of popular knowledge and of public definitions. These factors include substantive topic, television form and language, viewers' readings, interpretative resources employed in producing these readings, and socio-demographic data concerning the viewers sampled. As previous work in this area makes clear, it would be a mistake to expect a neat fit between any two factors in isolation and therefore material would need to be examined by reference to a number of hypothetical grids and categories. At the moment, with so little empirical work yet done in this area, too high a degree of methodo-logical anxiety might be both inhibiting and naïvely premature. In exploring the social character of media reception, a much more extensive literature of documentation and attempted analysis is the pressing requirement.

References

Brunsdon, C. and D. Morley (1978) *Everyday Television – Nationwide*. London: British Film Institute.

Brunt, R. and M. Jordin (1984) '"The Controversial Candidate": British Television's Coverage of the Chesterfield By-election'. Unpublished conference paper for the July 1984 International Television Studies Conference.

Corner, J. (1983) 'Textuality, Communication and Media Power', pp. 266–81 in H. Davis and P. Walton (eds), *Language, Image, Media*. London: Basil Blackwell.

Corner, J. (1984) 'Criticism as Sociology: Reading the Media', in J. Hawthorn (ed.), *Criticism and Critical Theory*. London: Edward Arnold.

Corner, J. and K. Richardson (1986) 'The Documentary Viewer and the Discourse of Interpretation', forthcoming in J. R. Corner (ed.), *Documentary in Britain*. London: Edward Arnold.

Dahlgren, P. (1984) 'The Modes of Reception: for a Hermeneutics of T.V. News', in P. Drummond and R. Paterson (eds), *Television in Transition*. London: British Film Institute.

Eco, U. (1972) 'Towards a Semiotic Enquiry into the Television Message', *Working Papers in Cultural Studies*, 3: 103–21. Birmingham: Centre for Contemporary Cultural Studies.

Heath, S. and G. Skirrow (1977) 'Television: a World in Action', *Screen*, 18 (2): 7–59.

McHoul, A. W. (1982) *Telling How Texts Talk*. London: Routledge & Kegan Paul.

McQuail, D. (1983) *Mass Communication Theory: an Introduction*. London: Sage Publications.

Morley, D. (1980) *The Nationwide Audience*. London: British Film Institute.

Morley, D. (1981) 'The Nationwide Audience: a Critical Postscript', *Screen Education*, 39: 3–14.

Parkin, F. (1971) *Class Inequality and Political Order*. London: MacGibbon and Kee. (Also Paladin, 1972.)

Pateman, T. (1983) 'How is Understanding an Advertisement Possible?', pp. 187–204 in H. Davis and P. Walton (eds), *Language, Image, Media*. London: Basil Blackwell.

Suleiman, S. and I. Crosman (eds) (1980) *The Reader in the Text*. Princeton: Princeton University Press.

Wren-Lewis, J. (1983) 'The Encoding/Decoding Model: Criticisms and Redevelopments for Research on Decoding', in *Media, Culture and Society*, 5 (2): 179–97.

Wren-Lewis, J. (1984) 'Decoding Television News', in P. Drummond and R. Paterson (eds), *Television in Transition*. London: British Film Institute.

8

Teenage girls reading *Jackie*[1]

Elizabeth Frazer

I wonder who takes all the pictures and who are the people?

In this article I present some empirical data — the transcripts of discussion among seven groups of girls about a photo-story from *Jackie* magazine, and about *Jackie* and other girls' magazines like it, generally. The data are used to underpin an argument about the use of the concept of 'ideology' in social theory and research. Critics complain that the theory of ideology is typically ill-specified and vague, and I discuss these criticisms. Where 'ideology' is more tightly specified, on the other hand, it predicts a certain sort of relationship between readers and the texts which are said to be bearers of ideological meaning and is taken as an explanation of people's beliefs or behaviour. A more or less passive reader is depicted: my data shows that, on the contrary, readers take a critical stand vis à vis texts. This theoretical discussion also underpins some remarks about social research method.

The research with girls about reading *Jackie* is part of a wider enquiry into the acquisition of a feminine gender and sexual identity, and about the role of 'ideology' in this process. In recent years social and cultural researchers have taken feminine heterosexuality as peculiarly 'ideological'. Girls seem to suffer from what we might call 'false consciousness' in sexual matters; the social organization of sexuality benefits men and boys and disbenefits women and girls; sexual meanings and definitions uphold the valorization of masculinity and the oppression of females; behaviour, values and

Media, Culture and Society (SAGE, London, Newbury Park, Beverly Hills and New Delhi), Vol. 9 (1987), 407–25

ideals which to radicals look highly artificial and political are widely perceived as 'natural', and so on (for example: Barrett, 1980; Griffin, 1985; Hebron, 1983; Lees, 1986; McRobbie, 1978a, 1978b; Sharpe, 1976; Wilson, 1978; Winship, 1978). Sociologists have studied sexist beliefs and attitudes. Cultural analysis has paid attention to texts which are said to be bearers of the ideology of feminine sexuality: pornography, romantic fiction, girls' and women's magazines, sex education materials. One text which has received a considerable amount of this sort of attention is *Jackie* (Griffin, 1982; Hebron, 1983; McRobbie, 1978b). However, I could not discover any research in which readers were asked about the magazine.

In my fieldwork I had prolonged and regular contact with seven groups of teenage girls. One was a racially mixed working-class group who regularly go to a youth project in Inner London. I have used conventional sociologists' occupational status criteria for determining class; typical parental occupations from among this group are kitchen assistant, factory worker, shop assistant, cleaner. On the other hand, for racial identity I have used the girls' own self-ascriptions; this group is mainly black British, but included two white girls and one Turkish. They attend a variety of schools (mixed, or single-sex comprehensives, or single-sex convents) and range in age from thirteen to seventeen. There were also two groups of fourth formers (fourteen-year-olds), and a group of upper sixth formers from an Oxfordshire single-sex comprehensive. The parental occupations of these girls included secretaries, plumber, police officer, nurse, master butcher, cabinet maker, night porter. They were more homogeneous racially — one fourth former was Afro-Caribbean, and one sixth former was a black African. There were also two groups of sixth formers (one upper, one lower), and a group of third formers (thirteen years) in an Oxfordshire headmistresses' conference public school for girls. The parental occupations of these girls included barrister, managing director, solicitor, stud manager, stockbroker, landowner, army officer. They were all white.

In the *Jackie* session I gave the girls a photocopy of the story to read, and then just asked them to talk about it.[2] They were not surprised to be asked to do this as we had talked a lot about TV, books, advertising and so on before, and they knew what my research was about. Discussion about the story generally lasted about twenty minutes. After this the talk drifted off, different ways, depending on the group. The comprehensive fourth years, and the public school upper sixth began to talk about problem pages, with interesting results which I discuss later in this article.

To begin with, though, I want to discuss some philosophical and conceptual problems with 'ideology'. These problems are invariably overlooked, or ignored, by social theorists and researchers, but they have serious implications for the use of 'ideology' as the powerful explanation of social phenomena that it is often taken to be.

Problems with 'ideology'

If ideology is one of the most ubiquitous concepts in social and political theory, it is nevertheless one of the most contested. There are many ways of charting or mapping out the complex and many-stranded history of its use (two recent and useful accounts are McLellan, 1986; K. Thompson, 1986; see also J.B. Thompson, 1984). In political theory it generally refers to a coherent body or system of ideas, typically about the public realm and man's place in it, whose origin and continuing existence are explicable by reference to the social position and interests of some social group. In social theory, which is the subject of this paper, there is most often an additional notion of the function of ideology, which is to maintain some system of unequal power relations. This notion of function is a complication, methodologically speaking; but even the 'political theory' conceptualization already contains epistemological and social-theoretical difficulties (which, however, are usually ignored in specific instances).

To begin with, the social origin of ideology is, in ordinary language contexts, taken to imply falsity (although of course, arguments about *why* people believe what they believe are quite irrelevant to the truth-value of those beliefs). Nevertheless, in much political and social theory, 'ideology' is set against something like 'science'; this obviously means we do have to have a means of judging what is true in the social realm if we are to recognize the non-ideological and this raises complex philosophical difficulties. Second, there is a problem with exactly specifying the content of a 'coherent set of ideas'. When researchers 'look' inside people's heads, they rarely find 'coherent' ideas, and it is normally taken that this is because people are only partially subject to ideology, or are subject to multiple, and conflicting, ideologies. (This is to ignore other methodological difficulties with the project of 'measuring attitudes' or discovering opinion or belief.) In any case, most theorists take it that ideology is not properly a category of 'the mental', but of 'the social', and therefore 'exists' in the public realm, in 'texts', taking that in its broadest sense.

But this, also, raises difficulties: *which* texts are to be taken to be representative of, for example, liberal ideology? In addition, theorists normally take it that 'ideology' is in fact analytically distinct from the ideas expressed in the texts themselves. It is that which determines those ideas, or constructs the meanings of the text; it is logically prior to the text itself. For theorists who still consider 'ideology' to be to do with 'belief', the same sort of argument applies — ideology is logically prior to the formation of the beliefs themselves. But it can easily be seen that this makes 'ideology' a very difficult thing to research.

Of course, that a concept is of an unobservable does not condemn it out of hand. Many perfectly respectable scientific concepts fall into this category, and they fulfil the necessary function of explaining what we *do* observe. 'Ideology', in this tradition explains 'false consciousness' or the fact that people seem to have contradictory beliefs about the social world; or the maintenance of the class system; or the meanings of keywords, or texts; or (crucially for the purposes of this article) the positioning of 'subjects' in an 'objective' social order. But, it is the argument of this paper that the concept of 'ideology' is overly theoretical, in the sense that it is explanatorily unnecessary. The legitimation of social orders, what texts mean — all of these things must be explained by social theorists; I argue that we can explain them with concepts which are more concrete than 'ideology'.

Paradoxically, I shall also go on to argue that the concept is too monolithic, and, as it stands, predicts that people will be more, or differently, affected by 'ideology' than evidence actually shows they are. For there is no doubt that the ordinary language notion of ideology carries with it an implication of 'normativity' and of efficacy — ideology makes people do things. Although it is rarely spelt out as such, researchers and theorists work with an implicit model as follows: .

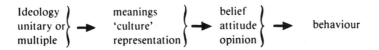

Texts as bearers of ideology

Much empirical research has focused on the third element in this chain, i.e. subjects' beliefs and attitudes. This work tends to take 'attitude' or 'opinion', or 'belief' to be measurable, and fixed. I believe that this in itself is an unwarrantable assumption. In this article, though, I want to concentrate on the work which attends to the second element — the meanings and representations of the culture which are encoded in texts of various sorts. Especially significant are semiotic, and other contents analyses of texts, which carry the implication that from the analysis we can infer the content of ideology, and predict or explain the beliefs and behaviour of readers.

Notable examples are the Glasgow Media Group's contents analyses of television news programmes; various reports on the television programmes children watch; Barthes's semiotic analyses of advertisements and so forth; the analysis of school text books by theorists of socialization; and, most pertinent for my present purposes, the several analyses of girls' and women's magazines, including *Jackie*.

All too often theorists commit the fallacy of reading 'the' meaning of a text and inferring the ideological effect the text 'must' have on the readers (other than the theorists themselves, of course!). We may oppose this strategy at two points. First, we may dispute that there is one valid and unitary meaning of a text. Second, we may care to check whether, even if we grant that there is one meaning, it does have this, or an ideological effect on the reader (see Richardson and Corner, 1986). In this article I am mainly concerned with the second of these two queries.

Some issues of method

When we had the discussions about the story I knew the girls in the groups fairly well, as I had had at least half a dozen intensive sessions with each, discussing topics loosely connected with 'femininity', and doing group work exercises, playing communication games and so on. They knew I was interested in what they watched, read and listened to, and that if possible I wanted to find out how these things affected them. A crucial part of my fieldwork methodology is feeding the analysis and concepts *I* use back into the groups, so in previous sessions we had discussed concepts like 'stereotypes', 'roles', 'alternative meanings' and so on. They were not, therefore, in the least bit surprised to be asked to read and discuss the photo-story. I gave them enough time to read it once from start to finish, and then said something like: 'OK, what do you think of that story then?'

Obviously, I have broken every golden rule about research method that has ever been enshrined in the hallowed pages of the research literature already. I will immediately be accused of eliciting a hopelessly biased account from the girls. My rebuttal is that I have certainly elicited a highly *structured and constructed* account, and I defy anyone to do different. In *any* research — for example a scheduled interview or a self-report questionnaire — the respondent is orienting herself to some assumed set of norms and her responses to individual questions are contextualized. When we interpret these responses therefore, we have to do our best to take cognizance of the context. If all we have is a table of ticked boxes to work with, it is tempting to accept a respondent's answers at face-value and ignore the fact that the constructed context may vary from respondent to respondent, thereby vitiating direct comparison of individual responses.

A good example to illustrate this difficulty is the kind of research that asks people to rank, say, occupations in some order of status: policeman, teacher, milkman, carworker. Although there is a world of difference between a Chief Constable and a beat police officer, the usual sort of questionnaire gives us no notion as to which of these two the respondent had in mind when she answered. It may be the case that people generally do, as a matter of fact, conjure up some uniform and stereotyped context to answer such a question (in this case, perhaps, in the UK, a picture of the traditional British bobby helping people across the street). If so we need some evidence of this, for one thing; and for another, it seems to me to be the more interesting research project to try and discover how and why this is so.

Such research, though, can't be done by questionnaires, but requires much more informal and in-depth probing. This probing often tends to uncover indeterminacy, shifts, or what some might be tempted to call downright contradiction in opinion. Many researchers are inclined to leave their findings at that, and explain the 'contradiction' by 'ideology'. This is unfair to the respondents. One example comes from Angela McRobbie's talks with girls in a

Birmingham youth club (McRobbie, 1977). At one point, these girls seem to say that women don't go out to paid work, but do domestic work and childcare at home. This is strikingly peculiar, coming from girls who are surrounded by female workers in shops, schools, factories and offices, most of whose own mothers did go out to work (elsewhere in the data it is quite clear that the girls do 'know' that women go out to paid work). If McRobbie had checked back with the girls themselves in more detail (and I'm sure that with hindsight she would agree with this [see McRobbie, 1982]), she could have discussed with them why, when their 'knowledge' comes into conflict with reality, it is reality which is rejected without comment.

This process of checking back would necessarily have involved a discussion of stereotypes, and as the girls came to acknowledge and understand the 'contradictions' and many levels of understanding which co-exist in one person they would have been understanding some of the concepts of social studies. This is why in my own work I am not at all interested in concealing the process of research from the subjects: I want to uncover any shifts, indeterminacies, and ambiguities in the girls' ways of talking. And it would be morally indefensible to do this, and then 'leave the field', leaving the girls painfully aware of their own incoherences, without taking any trouble to explore with them why these incoherences exist.

Obviously, all this means I was far from getting a 'naive reading' of the story from the girls. How one would go about eliciting a naive reading escapes me. As a youth worker I have countless times had the experience of seeing a young person looking at a poster, or picking up a magazine and reading an article, and I have seized the opportunity to talk: 'What do you think of that book/poster/ magazine/ TV programme?' The usual answer to this is something like 'It's OK', or 'all right', or even 'really good'. But this doesn't tell the youth worker, or the researcher, anything interesting at all. Therefore, in either role one is likely to persist, and say 'Why do you like it?', 'How does it make you feel?', or perhaps suggest some analysis like 'Don't you think it's important to have lots of anti-racist posters around?' If the young person hasn't by this time made it clear you are a bore, and walked off, she or he will have been pushed into a mode of thought and discourse we might call 'analytic' or 'self-conscious' or 'critical'. Some social theorists might say she is using a particular script, some that she is orienting to a particular set of roles or norms; whatever, she is a long way from a non-reflective and superficial reading. It seems to be generally assumed that *Jackie* and publications like it are read ordinarily in a superficial and lazy fashion, and judging by the number of 'It's OK's' my eager youth worker's questions have elicited in my time, I suppose I'm inclined to agree. But I see no way of discovering the *effect* of this sort of reading in the 'objective' way.

Reading *Jackie*

In fact, for what it's worth, my data lend credence to the hypothesis that *Jackie* is read lazily. Several of the girls didn't follow the story on one reading:

Zara	he's got a different jersey on, like different jersey, different trousers
Claire	well, it happens to be a different day, he changes
Zara	yes, but he meets her on that day doesn't he?
Dawn	he says, but I like you, I like that, your jealousy means you really care for me
Liz	that's Mike
Dawn	oh, is it? oh well...
(laughter)	

The discussion about the story generally lasted about twenty minutes — I worked quite hard to keep them on the subject (it is a very boring story) — and in the end the talk moved off, in the case of the comprehensive sixth formers into a general discussion on sexism, the double standard and gender stereotypes; in the case of the fourth formers into talk on books, magazines, and how what you read changes as you get older; and the public school third years got on to a very long discussion of class. Their reading of the story itself highlighted class issues too:

Claire	I like his jersey
(laughter)	
Sophie	I've been looking at his jumper
(laughter)	
Liz	d'you know boys who wear jumpers like that?
several	yes
Claire	I'd say most of Eton
...	
Liz	so you like the way he dresses, right?
Claire	I don't know what he's got on his feet though
(laughter)	

Claire	it's really annoying you know
Sophie	probably Adidas trainers or something
Claire	I wouldn't go out with him if he was wearing those
. . .	
Sophie	and then you know trousers that you know only come to about here then long white socks under
Claire	oh long *white* socks
. . .	
Liz	what, whether you'd like him or not?
Claire	well, it depends what kind of school he goes to, what kind of I mean that sounds really awful but I'm
Lucy	his classical background (laughs)
Claire	yes, no
Lucy	yes, but Latin and classical background
(laughter)	
. . .	
Claire	I don't like the jeans, I don' I don't like the way she dresses so I mean if he goes with people like her then I mean . . .

Above all, though, they read the story as a work of fiction:

Claire	it needs to be a bit dramatic though to get there
Liz	and there wasn't much drama in this one apart from would he or would he not turn up in the cafe
Claire	and that only took one picture in the thing so it wasn't particularly . . .
Lucy	and it was all a bit of an anti-climax in the end you know, it seems quite good at the beginning, but 'It's my nasty mind', I mean that's not much of a story . . .

(It was Claire who introduced this thought about the dramatic structure of the story, not me.)

Katherine	well there isn't a basic there isn't a sort of start and middle and end sort of things, there isn't a real story to it, she just thinks that was wrong and found out that it's wrong in the end but it wasn't really, I don't know there wasn't much to it
Liz	OK, what do you think of that story then?
Nannette	well, I thought it was a bit obvious that Ben lives next door to the cafe

Although there were other reactions which suggested that the reader was evaluating the characters as if they were real people:

Liz	OK, what d'you think of that story then?
Claire	I've read better ones
Lucy	I think she's quite vain, the girl's quite...

(Note that Claire is doing literary criticism from the first, while Lucy is not.)

Liz	right, what d'you think of that story then?
Helen	I don't know, she was just an insecure little person who had to keep shouting down these blokes and he found that attractive, there you go, that's it

Shifts from first- to second-order discourse occurred throughout the discussions, but on the whole, second-order talk is dominant; and the discussion tended to focus on why the story was or was not realistic when measured against the girls' own lives and experience. Much of their analysis considered the story as normative (or ideological), and evaluated the message promulgated:

Fiona	well, he might intend it to be sincere, but it's not true that you need the right bloke to make your life work, you need friends more than that
...	
Sharon	yeah, but if you read that now right, years ago and then you get to be fourteen and you haven't got a boyfriend then you're going to feel even worse from reading this

The comprehensive sixth formers didn't bother measuring the story against their own experience, as they assessed it from the beginning in the light of a pre-existing ideology of gender, of which they took the story to be a reflection as well as a reinforcement:

Liz	and why should she feel guilty?
Lucy	oh perhaps it's because she's expected to put up with it, no because she's expected to put up with it
Sam	it's OK for a man to have other girlfriends but
...	
Sam	oh yes well cos I'll tell you one thing that really gets me it's this bit that says 'you're jealous, that means you really care for me...'
several	oh yeah, oh, terrible...
Sally	you know I think girls' magazines have a lot to answer for in sort of building up self-confidence, because you don't get the same sort of thing with boys, I mean in these sorts of magazines all the emphasis is put on you know, you do something wrong you won't get a

	boyfriend, you've got to behave in a certain way to...
Sam	you've got to dress in a certain way
Helen	it's sort of like the girl who has to get the boy, it's not the boy who has to make an effort to get the girls sort of thing

The whole issue of why, if the 'ideology' is as powerful as the girls in this group argue, it has been possible for them to transcend or resist it was a live one between me and them, and was never satisfactorily resolved.

On the whole then, it seems that the girls I asked to read the photo-story do not coincide with the implied reader constructed by the text, who we can take to be a sympathetic confidante of Julie, the narrator and heroine. The pretence that Julie is a sixteen-year-old talking to a friend didn't come off at all with any of the teenage girls I talked to (including those who were closest to the fictional heroine in socio-economic status and age — the comprehensive school fourth years). This failure occurred first because, as we have seen, the girls were overwhelmingly reading the story as a fiction, with all that entails. Second, none of them identified with Julie's actions, thoughts, or attitudes. That is, these real readers were freer of the text than much theory implies.

However, there was one very significant exception — they could understand her being attracted to Ben because:

Lucy	he's sort of strong, silent
Sam	yeah, caring, yeah
several	yeah
Helen	big old beefy jumpers
Sam	that's it, it's the jumper more than anything and the little shirt coming out the top
Lorna	hands in pockets

We've already seen the attraction of the jumper to the public school girls! And:

Lucy	well, it's not that he's goodlooking, he's got you know
Sophie	he's quite a hunk
Claire	well he's not you know
Claire	wimpish or anything like that
. . .	
Lucy	he's so gentlemanly
Zara	yes
Claire	he's quite gentle

But one group thought he was a creep:

Jo	you wouldn't feel offended, you would feel that he's creepin a bit an he's it's not he's not, oh it doesn't show that he's creepin all the time but it's related in a way
Liz	mm
Alison	yeah but it's creepy the way he um...
Jo	in that picture there he's got his arms around her like y'know that shows...

This straightforward attraction to the hero, though, was understood as an ingredient of fantasy:

Jo	cos they're a bit like this you know fairy tales aren't they?
Alison	yes it's all like one of those dream things
Nannette	it all goes so well, it's always like he lives next door to the cafe, she goes walking a dog, her dog runs off
(laughter)	
Jo	all of a sudden there's the boy, exciting eh?
Alison	it's just a dream innit?

and the thirteen-year-old public school girls were just as clear about the role of fiction in constructing a fantasy life:

Liz	what would you get out of reading this kind of story week in week out?
Claire	boredom
Zara	I'd begin to know that the boy...
Claire	I'd know what's going to happen
Zara	you know because we're sort of I don't know, kind of shut up here we'd get to know more about I don't know outside life
Liz	sorry?
Zara	that sort of thing, well because we're
(laughter)	
Zara	not that, well I don't know because we're all prisonized here
Liz	yeah, cos you're shut up in school
Zara	you know we're all just shut up well we've got to get, I don't know in the towns and everything
Claire	cos we're not allowed to got to [nearest town] even
Liz	so, no
Lucy	so you can imagine yourself as the girl

(although it seems Zara might believe that 'life in the towns' is like Julie's life).

My preliminary analysis of the transcripts of these discussions, then, strongly suggests that a self-conscious and reflexive approach to texts is a natural approach for teenage girls. Further, they demonstrated a level of understanding, not only of the fiction, but of the genre of publications for girls of which *Jackie* is an example. They were even curious about the production of the text, which is entirely obscure in the magazine:

Claire   I wonder who takes all these pictures, and who are the people?

So far then, this empirical evidence suggests that the kinds of meanings which are encoded in texts and which we might want to call ideological, fail to get a grip on readers in the way the notion of ideology generally suggests. Ideology is undercut, that is, by these readers' reflexivity and reflectiveness.

However, I now want to move on to some further data which I believe suggest an alternative formulation to the concept of ideology. The sixth form public school girls and the fourth form comprehensive school girls all began to talk about problem pages during this discussion. They read problem pages, in all sorts of magazines; but they also all said that they were 'stupid', that the problems weren't 'real' problems, that the answers were pathetic and not helpful at all. When I asked them if they had problems, they replied 'Oh yes, but not like those ones'. Their problems, they said, were to do with issues like work, money and relationships with parents. So I asked them to write problems, serious ones, as if addressed to someone they trusted who might be really helpful. The problems they wrote were then passed on to someone else, anonymously, to reply to. I have pulled one of these problems and its reply at random from the pile:-

Dear Melanie, At my bus-stop I see a lush boy every morning. He knows me through one of my best friends' friends or ex-boyfriend. He smiles at me every time; I smile back but not much else seems to happen. The problem is I am very shy. Help me. Andy Ridgeway Fan.

Dear Andy Ridgeway Fan, Don't be shy, pluck up courage to say 'hello' to this boy; smile at him or even ask him how he is. Be patient, and remember, shyness doesn't get you anywhere.

This is absolutely typical of the fifteen or so 'problems' they came up with in this exercise. Other topics include wanting an old boyfriend back; fear of pregnancy; parents not letting you stay out late. That is, they varied in 'gravity'; but were all written in this, what can only be called typical problem page style.

Discourse registers

Here, I introduce the idea of a *discourse register* which I take roughly as an institutionalized, situationally specific, culturally familiar, public, way of talking. My data suggest that the notion of a 'discourse register' is invaluable in analysing talk — the talk of all the girls' groups I worked with is marked by frequent and sometimes quite dramatic shifts in register.

Other research has interpreted similar data as 'contradiction'. For example, Shirley Prendergast and Alan Prout interviewed fifteen-year-old girls about the subject of marriage and motherhood (Prendergast and Prout, 1980). They began by talking informally with the girls and elicited from a large proportion of them evidence of a body of 'knowledge' about the tedium, exhaustion, loneliness and depression which afflict mothers of young children. This knowledge was generally first-hand — that is, it was gained from sisters with young children, the experience of babysitting, being asked to help with primary childcare, and so forth. When, later in the interview, the girls were asked to agree or disagree with the statement: 'It is a good life for a mother at home with a young child', and give reasons for their opinion, and it was made clear that it was now *mothers in general* who were being discussed, they practically all *agreed*, and gave a variety of reasons which could all be characterized as in accordance with the sentimental notion or meaning of motherhood which Ann Oakley has argued is so powerful in this society (Oakley, 1979).

Prendergast and Prout characterize these two 'distinct bodies of knowledge' as 'illegitimate' and 'legitimate' respectively. The girls were aware of the 'contradiction' here, and uncertainly and tentatively negotiated means of simultaneously holding on to both. For example, some girls located the problem of motherhood in young mothers, and implied that if you wait until you're older everything will be OK; others came to terms with the negative image of motherhood by inserting into their assessments a series of conditional requirements, such as 'if you establish a routine...', or 'if you have a good husband...'. In Prendergast and Prout's analysis, illegitimate knowledge is not generalizable, while legitimate knowledge is: the sentimental stereotype is so powerful that when one's own experience comes into conflict with it, it is taken that the experience is invalid.

There are various problems with this. For example, the girls were interviewed alone. Prendergast and Prout comment that some of the girls indicated that the 'illegitimate knowledge' was *private* knowledge. For the girls I know who were talking frankly in groups this was not true — such 'knowledge' was shared among them, as it is among sociologists of the family, women in women's studies classes, consciousness-raising groups, and the like. Prendergast and Prout's girls are ready to discount their experience, and try to bring it into line with the perceived wider 'reality'. For the girls I talked to this wasn't the case either. Why should this be so?

I think it is that ways of talking, or 'knowledges', or 'discourse registers' will be dropped in contexts where they are not supported. The knowledge that Prendergast and Prout label 'illegitimate', in other words, is not illegitimate in all contexts.

Discourse registers both *constrain* what is sayable in any context, and *enable* saying. Prendergast and Prout's data support this proposition: in informal talk they could voice the unpleasantness of motherhood; in formal talk they could not (the girls were asked to agree or disagree with a statement — this is very like the kind of thing people are asked to do in school). What is said, and how it is said, are covariant. My data about *Jackie* problem pages illustrate the power of a discourse register to structure and shape what people can actually say in a particular context. In this session, the girls wanted to discuss *serious* problems; but it seemed that asking them to write the problems had the immediate effect of undercutting their gravity — they couldn't think 'writing problems' outside of the conventions of the problem page.

However, the register of the problem page is not monopolistic in the production of talk about problems. There is also, for example, the register of the small group discussion, informed by psycho-therapeutic theory. I had deliberately introduced this register into all the discussion groups, in order to achieve the intimate and frank atmosphere which I thought would benefit the girls and make the research a rewarding project for them, and would make the discussion of sexuality possible. In some sessions, there had been intense discussion about very personal matters, with a good deal of self-disclosure. The group rules had emphasized trust, and the importance of supporting other members. With one group a whole session was given over to intensive role-play about one girl's very difficult relationship with her parents, and the group discussed her and their behaviour in detail. My notes from that session are quite devoid of any of the stock responses ('Be patient'!) of the problem pages.

It does not seem appropriate to characterize the difference between these two contrasting sorts of discussion of 'problems' as *contradiction*. It is more apposite to say that the girls have available more than one way of discussing this topic, as Prendergast and Prout's girls had at their disposal more than one way of discussing the notion of motherhood.

There were some interesting differences between the groups which make clear that a structurally based analysis of what discourse registers are available to people is necessary. The girls from the youth club were very used to playing group-work games, and in the context of their girls' discussion group, self-disclosure, support and confidentiality came very naturally to them. The public school girls found these games the hardest, and in the first few sessions the sort of exercise where everybody completes the sentence: 'My greatest talent is . . .' made them feel embarrassed and mystified. However, it wasn't many sessions before they really came to enjoy such exercises (they organized our last sessions together, and we played some extremely advanced group-work games), and they quickly came to understand the conventions and rules of being in a girls' group very well. The transcripts of the sessions at the public school show very clearly the process of their grasping a new and alternative discourse register *in which different things can be said*.

It's very clear from the transcripts of the groups' discussions that all the girls have a multiplicity of discourse registers available to use. They could all, for example, switch in and out of the register of 'feminism' according to context, topic and mood. We have already seen that what is available to whom is socially variable — the youth club girls had the register of the discussion group; the public school girls had to learn it. This difference can be explained institutionally. Sometimes shifts made startling contrasts. For example:

Jane   I dislike the way boys treat girls in the sense that they've got
                the front to call them slags

Stella	when they're sleepin around more than you are
Jane	yeah and they think that they're hard if they go out and do something, like ... but if a girl does it she's stupid and things like that
Janine	if a girl wants to do the same job as a boy it's too hard

Compare this 'feminist' register with this:

| Janine | that's what gets me they beat up their kids and get about six months, especially the mothers right, cos you know in the [local newspaper] there was this woman she picks up her baby and hit his head on the banister and it was just born it was most probably three months and she was most probably still giving it milk still and it was hungry still so she picked it up right and she goes it was after feeding and she hit it across the banister and it died. You get soppy ones right who leave d'you know metal baths and you know in some parts of London they ain't got a bathroom she put the metal thing on the gas ring, and put the baby in it and left it in the boiling water, I think that it's bloody true, and d'you know cot deaths, I think that most of them are already... |
| Fetiye | most of them do that you know |

Shortly after this I intervened on the subject of cot death, and there was a shift to a quite different style of talk, a much more thoughtful and analytic style, with participants making much *shorter* contributions to the discussion. The discussion about boys was organized, or 'led' by me. The discussion about baby battering had been initiated by them, before the session proper started. In the one case a feminist discussion group register was appropriate and determined the 'tone' of what was said; in the other the register, and values, of the tabloid press was dominant.

Conclusion

The concept of ideology is unsatisfactory in two main ways, as I have argued. On the one hand real people don't seem to be 'in the grip of' ideology, as the theory (and especially much theory which is based on the analysis of texts) implies. On the other hand, 'ideology' is of altogether too ethereal a nature to be properly researched. Its existence is only and always inferred; we can never examine it directly.

However, I suggest that we take seriously the power of concrete conventions and registers of discourse to constrain and determine what is said and how it is said. Registers are material, and directly researchable. We can compare how real people speak with institutional discourse, for example the discourse of cultural artefacts like *Jackie*, the tabloid press, and with institutional practices like that of the 'discussion group'. We can pay attention to the forums in which people learn different registers, for example, girls in girls' groups learning the appropriate register; what registers are acceptable in school; the influence of popular culture. But we should not take it that people are unselfconscious about these registers, as do theories of ideology.

Notes

1. I gratefully acknowledge the work of Mary Talbot who was interested in the *Jackie* story from the viewpoint of a linguistician, and who has made detailed comments on the transcripts of the girls' discussion. However, the analysis put forward in this paper is entirely my own. Thanks also to Debbie Cameron, Tony Crowle, Alan Ryan, and members of the University of Liverpool Centre for Communications Studies for comments on versions of the paper.

2. The story is entitled 'It's My Nasty Mind'. Julie, the heroine, tells off her boyfriend, Mike, in no uncertain terms when he arrives late to meet her, accusing him of having been with another girl. He tells her that she has a 'nasty and suspicious mind', but that her jealousy proves she really cares. In response to this she says 'Goodbye Mike, if I never see you again it'll be too soon'. This altercation is overheard by Ben, who admires her spirit: 'That was a great performance', and takes her to a nearby cafe for a Knickerbocker Glory. When he leaves he says 'Next time you're giving some guy the big heave, let me know, I'd love to see you in action again'. Julie hangs around the cafe hoping to see Ben; when she does bump into him he repeats his admiration: 'Is some other guy about to get it in the neck?' Rather than admit that she wants to see him, Julie says that she is going to 'have a showdown' on the following evening and invites him to watch. She then has to find a boy to play the opposite part, but fails. When she arrives at the assignation she admits to Ben that she had treated Mike badly, and that she had made up the boyfriend: 'Do you think I'm dreadful? I don't think I'm a very nice kind of person' to which Ben says, among other things: 'You're insecure, and you've got a strong sense of justice' and 'You're too self critical' and he invites her to go out with him, and to go for another Knickerbocker Glory.

References

Barrett, Michèle (1980) *Women's Oppression Today — Problems in Marxist Feminist Analysis*. London: Verso/NLB.

DES (1983) *Popular TV and Schoolchildren* (the report of a group of teachers).

Glasgow University Media Group (1980) *More Bad News*. London: Routledge and Kegan Paul.

Griffin, Christine (1982) *Cultures of Femininity: Romance Revisited*. Birmingham: CCCS Occasional Paper.

Griffin, Christine (1985) *Typical Girls? Young Women from School to the Job Market*. London: Routledge and Kegan Paul.

Hebron, Sandra (1983) *'Jackie' and 'Woman's Own': Ideological Work and the Social Construction of Gender Identity*. Sheffield: City Polytechnic.

Lees, Sue (1986) *Losing Out: Sexuality and Adolescent Girls*. London: Hutchinson.

McLellan, David (1986) *Ideology*. Milton Keynes: Open University Press.

McRobbie, Angela (1977) 'Working Class Girls and the Culture of Femininity'. Unpub. thesis.

McRobbie, Angela (1978a) 'Working Class Girls and the Culture of Femininity', in CCCS Women's Studies Group, *Women Take Issue*. London: Hutchinson.

McRobbie, Angela (1978b) *'Jackie': An Ideology of Adolescent Femininity*. Birmingham: CCCS Occasional Paper.

McRobbie, Angela (1982) 'The Politics of Feminist Research: Between Talk, Text and Action', *Feminist Review*, 12.

Oakley, Ann (1979) *Becoming a Mother*. Oxford: Martin Robertson.

Prendergast, Shirley and Prout, Alan (1980) ' "What will I do...?" Teenage Girls and the Construction of Motherhood', *Sociological Review*, 28, 3.

Richardson, Kay and Corner, John (1986) 'Reading Reception: Mediation and Transparency in Viewers' Accounts of a TV Programme', *Media Culture and Society*, 8, 4.

Sharpe, Sue (1976) *'Just Like a Girl': How Girls Learn to be Women*. Harmondsworth: Penguin.

Thompson, John B. (1984) *Studies in the Theory of Ideology*. Cambridge: Polity Press.

Thompson, Kenneth (1986) *Beliefs and Ideology*. London: Tavistock.

Wilson, Dierdre (1978) 'Sexual Codes and Conduct — A Study of Teenage Girls', in Carol Smart and Barry Smart (eds) *Women, Sexuality and Social Control*. London: Routledge and Kegan Paul.

Winship, Janice (1978) 'A Woman's World: *Woman*, An Ideology of Femininity', in CCCS Women's Studies Group, *Women Take Issue*. London: Hutchinson.

9

What's the meaning of this? Viewers' plural sense-making of TV news

Peter Dahlgren

This article is divided into two parts. The first takes the form of a very brief 'history of ideas'. It treats some of the notions which have shaped the emerging focus on the problem of meaning — both in the media as well as among the audiences. The second part reports some preliminary findings which try to carry forward this research tradition. It emphasizes that the meanings people make of the media are expressed through an array of context-specific discourses, which occur not just at the site of viewing. This line of enquiry thus expands upon the theme of plurality of meaning within the media and the diverse nature of sense-making by audiences. These empirical observations, together with the notion of the plurality of sense-making, raise some important theoretical issues, not least for the conceptualization and status of ideology.

News programmes and the eclipse of the information model

Like it or not, television's prominence within the public sphere of Western societies continues to grow. National, regional and local news broadcasts, as well as current affairs and magazine-style programmes, have come to constitute an historically new 'tele-visual public sphere'. Also, news programmes on television seemingly enjoy more credibility than does the output from other,

Media, Culture and Society (SAGE, London, Newbury Park, Beverly Hills and New Delhi), Vol. 10 (1988), 285–301

more traditional, news media. Perspectives of course vary considerably on just how, and to what extent, the rise of television to this central position is altering the nature of politics, the social structure of knowledge and information, collective perceptions, and other social dynamics. For those who have not yet succumbed to a totally privatized perspective or to modish cynicism, there seem to be reasons for concern. However, nobody will deny the importance of TV's role in this regard. Even the dramatic developments in recent years in advanced information technologies do not alter the fact that, for the vast majority of citizens, television news — broadcast and/or cable-relayed — remains a prime source of information about the outside world.

This privileged status of television news is obviously not unproblematic, and one can observe over the years a variety of research responses to its role. In tracing this research, one finds that the programmes, as well as their audiences, have been approached in different ways, reflecting varying and even competing conceptualizations.

Without launching into a review of this massive literature, a basic point of departure for virtually all of the earliest research, and even much of today's, is a conception of TV news as 'information'. That is, the phenomenon of TV news is conceptualized within a framework which emphasizes the transmissions as the transfer of manifest factual content to the audience. Clearly there are obvious grounds for this — at a common sense level, TV news indeed has to do with 'information'. Thus, research questions within this tradition tend to cluster around such themes as content profiles, accuracy, impartiality, comprehension, and uses of the news.

It is worth noting that within the empirical and cognitive psychological traditions there has emerged a rather large and troublesome body of international literature which points out that viewers often have great difficulty comprehending and even recalling TV news items. Interestingly enough, this does not seem to have had any significant impact on TV journalists or producers. To the extent that one can detect changes in the audiovisual discourse (e.g. faster tempo) the trend seems to make informational comprehension all the more difficult. Yet public discussions about TV news are still premised on the informational model. While this can in part be accounted for by the institutional imperatives which shape TV news, it seems also to indicate the compelling nature of the notion of 'information' in our culture.

As an alternative to this information perspective there emerged, especially in the 1970s, studies which emphasized the ideological dimensions of the broadcasts. This critical research underscored among other things that factual information could be *systematically* selective and slanted. Of greater theoretical significance was the claim made here that the entire *structure of the audiovisual discourse* can (and normally does) have hegemonic import on the audience. Thus, this perspective posits that there is something more than just information which is conveyed in TV news and, more importantly, that these other 'messages' (ideology) are not necessarily apparent to the viewer. In other words, the real significance of the programmes is not to be found on the empirically manifest level but is latent, and must be ascertained by interpretive analysis.

The analysis of ideology continues, but in more recent years it has become clear that the critical work of the 1970s paved the way for a perspective not originally foreseen. For today we witness a growing concern with a problematic more fundamental than that of ideology, namely how TV news programmes produce and convey *meaning*, and what the parameters of that meaning might be. Here it is virtually a methodological given that meaning within an audiovisual text (from the standpoint of the researcher) is not identical with the manifest content, but dwells in a non-apparent realm of otherness.

Meaning moves to the fore

By 'meaning' I refer here to the processes of making sense of the world around us. It has to do with creating a general coherence in our lives, of establishing an order in which to anchor our existence. Also, it has to do with integrating into our world-view the continuous stream of new phenomena we encounter. For each of us the production of meaning can have a dimension which is very private and even idiosyncratic — we all have our own sphere of 'personal knowledge'. Yet the foundations of meaning are largely social. Collective interaction, intersubjectivity, cultural patterns and so forth are the basis for much of the sense-making we do in everyday life. Clearly TV news programmes, as well as other mass media, play a central role in the production and maintenance (and even subversion) of meaning. In our respective social microcosms media-derived meanings can contribute to a sense of belonging and community. This of course may actually enhance social relations of domination, in which case we would say that the meanings have ideological dimensions.

There are a number of strategies for the analysis of meaning in TV news stories. Research can focus on both trying to delimit the possible range of meanings available to an idealized or implied viewer within the audiovisual discourse; alternatively the meanings of the programmes can be probed from a broader cultural perspective. In both cases attention is paid to the manner in which sense is encoded and communicated by the news stories, and the overall programme format. The goal is also to flush out the implicit or hypothetical viewer's relationship, both to the world portrayed and as to TV news itself. The concern with TV news as a structured discourse — rather than as a collection of discreet informational facts — is paramount. Meaning is understood to be predicated upon the unified ensemble of elements which constitute the news programmes (or any other cultural production, for that matter).

To give it philosophical labels, one can view this as a shift from a Hegelian critique of domination to a Kantian concern with the epistemological dimensions and possibilities of TV news programmes and their audiences. This research direction does not necessarily disregard the issue of ideology or hegemony, but implies that we first need to ascertain how meaning is constructed in TV news, and what are its epistemic limits. This is necessary before we can evaluate whether that meaning is ideological, liberatory, or whatever, and also before we can begin to formulate what alternative programmes might look like.

The research on how meaning is generated in TV news programmes links up with studies which address the broader question of the epistemic nature of the medium itself. While McLuhan's somewhat impressionistic yet pioneering work is significant in the development of reflection on TV's epistemic dimensions, more recent efforts to specify the conditions, limits and possibilities of television have brought the issues into sharper relief. For example, from various points of departure, Lowe, 1982; Altheide, 1985; Meyrowitz, 1985; Postman, 1985; Gumpert and Cathcart, 1985, all address the question of the historical specificity of the medium's way of structuring our perceptions and knowledge of the world. The upshot of such work suggests that television as a medium is eminently ill-suited as a dispenser of information, which in a sense confirms, from a different angle of vision, some of the more empirical studies on programmes and audiences.

The epistemic character of the television medium itself, according to these authors, is not geared to conveying discreet messages, though all of them would say that certainly some messages and information do get conveyed. Rather, the real significance of television lies elsewhere, within the more fundamental domain of the organization of collective perception. For them, television is the key to understanding a historical transformation currently under way in the very manner in which we collectively produce meaning — literally, how we make sense.

Elsewhere (Dahlgren, 1985, 1986), I take up this theme specifically in regard to TV news programmes. I argue that, given the specific audiovisual structure of TV news and its production conventions, as well as the epistemic qualities of television, it is more instructive to treat TV news as a form of cultural discourse, rather than information. As such, the daily recurrence and readily recognizable features of the programmes serve to link the viewer and his/her everyday life to the larger world in a manner which is ritualistic, symbolic and ultimately mythic, rather than informational. Moreover, with the televisual experience, viewers' sense-making proceeds largely in ways which are essentially extra-rational. Such a view is by no means dismissive. On the contrary, it emphasizes the importance of TV news in a manner which perhaps exceeds the usual informational view.

One can travel some distance with these kinds of analyses, but ultimately the outer limits are reached. One can chart the range of possible and probable meanings within the televisual text but must at some point admit that the programmes retain a dimension which is equivocal and polysemic (Fiske, 1986). Further, one must also recognize that the meanings the programmes have for the viewers arise in the programme/audience interface. The implied viewer in the audiovisual discourse is not necessarily identical with the real-life viewer. Meaning is negotiated; it resides in the force-field between the givenness of the programmes and the sense-making of the viewers.

In the wake of the shift in programme studies from the analysis of information to the interpretation of meaning, it is not surprising that a new version of audience studies has also begun to appear; one which focuses on how viewers actively produce meaning from the transmissions within the context of their own everyday lives. Generally, within the realm of social analysis, the processes by which people make sense of the social world — and thereby in part create the social world — are increasingly moving to the fore of analytic concern. In the context of the media, this new direction in audience research has come to be called reception studies.

The turn towards reception: the active audience

Television reception studies are a relatively recent phenomenon; overwhelmingly they have thus far focused on soap operas and news/documentary programmes. In the latter category the major examples to date are by Morley (1980, 1983); Lewis (1985); Richardson and Corner (1986) and Jensen (1986). Jensen in particular traces in considerable detail the intellectual roots of reception studies within media studies and develops a conceptual model of reception. A variety of research strategies and techniques have been used in reception studies, but virtually all of them are based on recording in-depth individual or small group interviews before, during and/or after programme transmissions. Then follows the tedious task of transcribing the recorded material and making some sort of textual analysis of the spoken interaction. It can be tortuous work: Jensen, for example, interviewed 24 individual people and the average length of the interviews was about 45 minutes. This resulted in over 600 single-spaced pages of transcript to be analysed.

Among the basic points that Jensen and the other reception researchers make are that:

1. reception makes a difference — people do make different sense of the same programme;
2. the interpretations are socially patterned and do not merely express individual differences;
3. the sense people make of TV news is socially bounded — viewers do not just 'make up' interpretations in isolation from their social location, yet the relevant categories of social location seem to be on the order of 'subcultures' rather than the more traditional and broader notions of social class;
4. reception is constantly in question in the sense that it is an ongoing process whose results are largely 'until further notice' — meaning, in other words, never achieves final stability,

though the processes themselves may well take on the quality of the routine.

Reception research can be seen as a step towards analytically 'rehabilitating the audience', placing the active meaning production of viewers in the centre of research focus. Today it is in the vanguard of media studies. It should be said, however, that reception research at present finds itself involved in a form of balancing act. It wants to avoid treating the viewer as a 'cultural victim' (which the more traditional critique of ideology often did, at least implicitly) by emphasizing the active role of decoding or meaning production. At the same time it does not seem ready or willing to throw out the concept of ideology/hegemony and lapse into an idealism (that viewers make whatever sense they wish of TV news and it's OK). It would seem that this ambiguity will soon be receiving more attention.

As I try to pull together some of the research trends in this brief survey, it can be noted that the conception of the TV news text has moved from being treated essentially as closed and unproblematic to being viewed as polysemic; offering an array of possible readings. The viewer, in this research evolution, has graduated from being passive to active, in terms of creating his/her own meaning from the transmissions. I would also underscore the final point from the findings of the reception researchers, namely that meaning is a process characterized by an inherent instability. Meaning is protean and equivocal; it is difficult to grasp and pin down. A reception researcher tries to make an interpretation of the talk whereby a viewer expresses his/her own interpretation of TV news. And at some point the researcher must at least indirectly make his or her own interpretation of the transmissions and perhaps even try to make sense (reflexively) of divergences with the interviewee's interpretations . . . To analyse meaning is to take aim at a moving target.

Moreover, a point which many of us at times glibly make, but which we perhaps do not always take seriously: meaning is also situational. Context and its appropriate discourses play a large role in structuring and delimiting meaning. With this point in place, I wish to take the discussion in a more exploratory direction, to begin to probe what may lie beyond that which reception research has told us about viewer meaning production and what the implications of a next step might be. I try to find consolation for the tentative status of what follows by citing the closing words of Richardson and Corner (1986: 507) on reception: 'At the moment, with so little empirical work yet done in this area, too high a degree of methodological anxiety might be both inhibiting and naively premature.'

The great divide: official vs. personal talk

While meaning is a rather elusive feature for research to tackle, my emphasis of situation does not refer to the somewhat artificial circumstances under which reception research takes place. All the studies freely acknowledge this limitation, which is by no means unique to reception studies; it is a classic dilemma within social research. I do not set up a dichotomy of 'authentic' vs. 'artificial' meaning where the latter is an impure version or distortion generated by the research situation. Following the reasoning of the ethnomethodologists (e.g. Garfinkel, 1967; Handel, 1982; Benson and Hughes, 1983) I instead simply take the position that all talk through which people generate meaning is contextual, and that the contexts will inevitably somewhat colour the meaning. Thus, if there is a problem with reception research on this score, it is not that its setting produces accounts which diverge from what the respondents *really* mean, but that this research tends to structure one specific type of context which tends to foster, as well as preclude, certain sets of meaning.

In particular, I found when carrying out some modest reception research of my own that people tended to speak in a particular way when I asked them about TV news. They could express a variety of views, but I sensed that there was some kind of unifying quality to the forms of talk — the discourses — they felt appropriate to the situation, and which I generally found were difficult to get beyond. In fact, in a number of instances, once the interview was over, there was a decided shift in the respondent's entire demeanour and manner of speaking. However, I began to notice that it was not merely a question of research setting vs. non-research setting at work here, but rather something more fundamental. A change in the definition of the situation (i.e. from a research to a non-research setting) prompted a shift between what the late Erving Goffman (1974), with his interactionist sociology, called 'front stage–back stage' talk; or what I term official vs. personal discourse.

Official discourse (in the circumstances I am describing) seems to be generated by situations which people define somehow as 'public', in the sense that it mobilizes their role as citizen. Thus, in the research setting for example, they talk to me — a professional researcher — about news, information, democracy, the state, everyday life, etc., and apparently feel that they are 'on stage' in terms of their citizen role. Official discourse has an intensity and earnestness which is not matched by, say, the generally lax quality of TV news viewing which I have observed.

Sometimes, however, personal discourse manifests itself in the interviews; likewise, I began to notice that official discourse (about TV news) could also appear in other, non-research settings. These too had a 'public' quality about them: not that other people necessarily were present, but that the appropriate role for the respondent was one of a serious and dutiful citizen.

Thus, after a while, I abandoned the formal reception research in favour of more unobtrusive methods. I would merely make notes to myself of conversations and chats that I would have with people in a variety of settings: social gatherings like dinners and parties, on buses, trains and in stations, with neighbours, etc. I would try to steer the talk to TV news, but in a 'natural' way and without adopting the role of a researcher. I was not always successful and the interactions in which I did manage to elicit talk about TV news are far from representative. But they sufficed for me to develop a preliminary typology of talk about TV news. While it might have been fruitful to systematize the nature of the situations, I felt that this would be premature, given the somewhat sporadic nature of my investigations and the many possible ways in which situations could be defined. Instead, I chose to try to specify the discourses, which also seemed to display more regularity than the situations. Again, while a variety of views can be expressed within the same discourse, I suggest that each discourse delimits the possible range of meanings as well as fosters certain significations in regard to TV news.

Aside from the basic dichotomy of official/personal, I observed a number of other subcategories of talk. In what follows I present briefly the modes of discourse about TV news that I encountered. To repeat: it should be kept in mind that these are categories of forms of talk, not people. A person can (and often does) make use of more than one of these discourses.

Peter Dahlgren

For public consumption: modes of official discourse

As I mentioned, in this type of discourse the speaker is 'on' in
some sense, assuming a 'front stage' stance as a citizen engaged in
a form of public dialogue. I found three basic versions.

1. Incorporated discourse

This is the fundamental discourse of the dutiful citizen. One talks
about the newscasts with its own vocabulary: essentially the
dominant political discourse or some version of it. This takes TV
news on its own terms: as a (for the most part) factual rendering of
reality. At its outer reaches it can be politically critical, even
questioning the boundaries of the established political system.
This discourse represents a use, and perhaps an extension, of the
basic terms provided by TV news/the formal political system. All
references here are to people and things in the outside world/TV
news world; the discourse is not self-referential or reflexive.

2. Alternative decoding: rereading, solipsism

These are various forms of 'rereading', which derive from a
political interpretation of society significantly at variance with the
dominant view conveyed in the news. Usually, however, such
discourse does not comprise a full-blown alternative social theory.
Often it constitutes a general meta-commentary on themes of
morality, psychology, human nature and drives. To the extent that
history and social structure are absent from such discourse one
could say that it is a version of no. 1, i.e. incorporated. Solipsism:
in this version the talk has a decided, quasi-theoretic view of the
world, yet theses are posited with little regard to outside factual
evidence. Likewise, logic seems to play a minor role. One might
readily term such talk 'eccentric' or even 'crank', though it often
has an internal consistency of its own.

3. Media awareness/demystification

Such talk demonstrates awareness of televisual production elements; the speech stands upon a platform which treats the programme as a motivated discourse in its own right. This kind of talk renders the intentionality of the programme as a possible object of discussion. I can add that such talk can be characterized by both a critical–intellectual posture as well as one of a 'show-biz fan'. In the latter case the 'demystification' is actually somewhat populist, in the sense that there is a working assumption that *all* media phenomena, including news, are perceived as motivational — that they are engaged in 'impression management'.

Between you and me: modes of personal discourse

Here the talk is predicated on an understanding that the speakers are not in a setting in which their public role is required. There is a sense of 'well, now that we are alone, let me tell you what I *really* think . . .'. However, I wish to emphasize again that this is merely a reflection of an understanding of what is appropriate for a given situation, and I would not accord more or less authenticity to personal discourse than to its official counterpart. In this category I could witness four sub-versions.

1. Trivial/random personal association

This kind of talk links stories from the TV news programme to one's own realm of experience, but at a level of commonplace associations to a private sphere which is of little or no consequence for other people generally, let alone for the public sphere. Example: 'Oh, I have an uncle who lives in that town . . .' (where the news story takes place) or 'That reminds of the time when . . .'. Such discourse goes nowhere in terms of insight, new knowledge or understanding. The news becomes merely an occasion for private talk.

2. Modest practicality

In this discourse we have a personal version of the speech of the dutiful citizen. The discourse underscores the relevance of TV news for everyday life and lauds the personal benefits of 'keeping

up' with the programmes. While such talk will acknowledge the
limits of this practicality, it will still insist on the usefulness of TV
news for daily life. This insistence could readily withstand polite
probes and questioning (by me) aimed at highlighting the
extremely circumscribed nature of the news' utility in terms of
practical activity. Among the areas of interest most often
mentioned are economics, labour negotiations, and social welfare
legislation. Such talk seems to occur especially among people with
some practical relationship to the public sphere. Yet, interestingly,
the emphasis is on news as instrumental information, rather than
as a resource for a person's political role in society.

3. Political estrangement

This type of talk acknowledges apathy, lack of involvement, or
lack of information sufficient to partake of the TV news discourse.
Such talk may also be packaged as irony: a comic distance, or
gallows humour on the theme of the individual in relation to news
and democracy. An extreme version of this can be called cynicism,
where the discourse is an expression of a quasi-nihilistic perspective to the entire 'official' edifice. The personal discourse of
political estrangement at times intersects with the public discourse
of media demystification. This yields a particular form of sophisticated talk which pivots upon (and shuttles between) the 'front
stage–back stage' distinction.

4. Reflexivity: painful, pleasurable, embarrassing

To talk about the experience of viewing in relation to one's own
situation as well as to contextualize TV news in a larger societal
perspective which links the personal and the public is, of course,
rare. However, there are elements of reflexive discourse which do
appear not too infrequently. One version is predicated on the
pleasure of TV news: one likes to watch — TV news is simply an
enjoyable experience. This goes beyond the dutiful citizen
position, and actually conflicts with it, since the discourse of the
dutiful citizen gains its legitimacy precisely in the idea of social
obligation rather than pleasure. Sometimes this discourse will

reveal an awareness of this discrepancy and express a slight embarrassment about TV news being fun to watch.

Another, more profound form of reflexive discourse expresses the painful insight of powerlessness. It combines the discourse of alternative readings and media awareness to portray one's own situation. This is rare, but when it occurs it usually takes the form of manifest discomfiture, apparently in part based on the realization that there seem to be few contexts and ways in which this position can be communicated without at the same time eroding ones own normal social identity. This self-reflexive talk ties together and contextualizes TV news with both the public sphere and personal everyday life.

This discourse is genuinely troubling: it suggests that things don't work, we really are powerless in relation to the centres of political, economic and administrative command as well as to the media complex itself. The discursive discomfiture seems to arise from a feeling that there is no real legitimate official discourse through which to express this degree of alienation.

TV news and the dispersion of subjectivity

If reception research at the site of viewing mobilizes certain meaning production, I would argue that the experiences of viewing TV news also become lodged within viewers' consciousness such that they can be activated in different contexts and thus be given somewhat different meanings by the same person. This perspective is predicated on a model of dispersed subjectivity. Without subscribing to extreme Lacanian notions of a decentred subject who essentially only exists as a nexus of intersecting discourses, we are not always at one with ourselves: even if our identity (our conceptions of ourselves) is reasonably stable in the plurality of social microcosms we inhabit, our subjectivity is by no means consolidated or consistent. Our sense-making can be faithful to contexts, yet overall inconsistent with itself. On the theoretical level, I posit a modest and minimal notion of the unconscious as helping to facilitate this, and as the realm which makes actually possible such formal inconsistencies.

The discourses I have tried to identify naturally merge with one another in real-life talk, and here is one of my main points: that TV news for many of us facilitates a plurality of subjectivities which can become mobilized in different settings. This view of an enhanced spectrum of possible meaning production raises many questions, not least the feasibility of actually researching meaning at all. It may well be that our only methodological option is to seriously launch ourselves on the path of anthropological 'thick descriptions' of the interface of everyday life's many settings with the media environment.

Another consideration which this research direction raises is the problematic of ideology which, as I mentioned earlier, reception analysis has already begun to encounter. Clearly, domination and hegemony can work in many and subtle ways. It is my view that the analysis of ideology in the past has suffered in part because of simplistic assumptions regarding the fundamental processes of meaning production (signification) which have informed the analyses. The hermeneutic concern with sense-making, sometimes drawing inspiration from newer directions in anthropology, would seem to have much to offer in terms of conceptual tools. At the same time, such interpretive enquiry may soon run the risk of losing touch with the basic social and political features of the present historical situation — and thereby wander off into idealism. In other words, it could be productive to appropriate some of the ground gained from such hermeneutic efforts and apply them to a critical investigation of ideology.

We have now already arrived at a convenient meeting ground for the hermeneutic and critical perspective. The plurality of meanings which the more rigorous reception analysis has already demonstrated in the research settings it generates can now be even further expanded by taking into consideration the *other* possible contexts/discourses which may shape the sense we make of TV news. The critique of ideology has traditionally underscored the closure which characterizes ideologically laden cultural products. How do we reconcile this polysemic openness with the (by necessity) more narrow parameters involved in the critical concept of ideology?

One attempt to come to terms with this question is found in Fiske's (1986) important contribution. He emphasizes on the one hand the cracks and contradictions within the TV text and, on the other hand, the various subcultural groups who interpret the programmes. These groups, according to Fiske, manifest different relations to the centres of domination within the social order, and these relationships can account for the differences in the way in which programmes are decoded. Each group in essence refracts the ideological dimension through its own prisms and, by implication, would potentially resist ideology also from its own angles of vision.

While Fiske builds his argument (with a nice example) from popular entertainment programming rather than news broadcasts, I am sure that detailed analysis could find similar contradictions with the typical TV news transmissions. Also, it seems highly plausible that the decoding patterns of different subcultural groups could be shown to vary. However, I am not certain that it is really the actual contradictions in news programming which are so significant. Further, regarding the different sense-making of various subcultural groups, this implies a large sociological argument which, if it is to be empirically investigated, would require a massive research undertaking.

Thus, while Fiske's argument is quite compelling, it will no doubt be some time before we see any conclusive evidence on it. In the meantime I would offer another possible way of treating the issue of plural interpretations of TV news and the theme of ideology. This is admittedly more modest than Fiske's scheme, but may be fruitful nonetheless.

In another article (Dahlgren, 1987) I have tried to sketch in more detail some general considerations regarding meaning and ideology in the media. In that discussion I make use of an idea developed by John B. Thompson (1984) regarding the different ways in which ideology can operate. Among the mechanisms he identifies are reification, legitimation and dissimulation. The first two are obvious enough, but the concept of dissimulation is perhaps less familiar but of particular relevance here. Dissimulation refers to the processes whereby attention and reflection on social relations of domination are deflected or blocked. Usually in regard to ideology, this would suggest some forms of concealment or distortion. However, in the light of the kinds of viewer discourses on TV news which I have presented here, it would seem that dissimulation can also function via a dissipation of those meanings which are relevant for a political understanding of one's own situation in society. Thus, the very openness of the text (and here I would add: regardless of whether or not it contains contradictions) becomes a key to its success in obfuscation. The audiovisual discourse of TV news occludes social reality precisely in making available an array of possible meanings, none of which on their own terms invite or help the viewer to locate him/herself as a political subject in an historical setting.

To follow up this line of enquiry, the next step would be to return to TV news programming with a renewed analytic goal. One would try to specify those features which thus contribute to dissimulation within the audiovisual discourse and the dispersion of viewer subjectivity. Further it would also be important to elucidate the *interplay* of this openness with those elements which contribute to its (more traditional) closure.

Note

An earlier version of this paper was presented at the Research in Journalism colloquium at the Inter-University Centre, Dubrovnik, in May 1987. I would like to thank Colin Sparks for helpful comments.

References

Altheide, D. (1985) *Media Power*. Beverly Hills: Sage.
Benson, D. and J.A. Hughes (1983) *The Perspective of Ethnomethodology*. London: Longman.
Dahlgren, P. (1985) 'The Modes of Reception: for a Hermeneutics of TV News', in P. Drummond and R. Paterson (eds) *Television in Transition*, pp. 235–49. London: British Film Institute.
Dahlgren, P. (1986) 'Beyond Information: TV News as a Cultural Discourse', *Communications* 2: 125–36.
Dahlgren P. (1987) 'Ideology and Information in the Public Sphere', in J.D. Slack and F. Fejes (eds) *The Ideology of the Information Age*, pp. 24–46. Norwood: Ablex.
Fiske, J. (1986) 'Television: Polysemy and Popularity', *Critical Studies in Mass Communication* 4: 391–408.
Garfinkel, H. (1967) *Studies in Ethnomethodology*. Englewood Cliffs: Prentice-Hall.
Goffman, E. (1974) *Frame Analysis*. New York: Harpers.
Gumpert, G. and R. Cathcart (1985) 'Media Grammars, Generations and Media Gaps', *Critical Studies in Mass Communication* 1: 23–35.
Handel, W. (1982) *Ethnomethodology: How People Make Sense*. Englewood Cliffs: Prentice-Hall.
Jensen, K. (1986) *Making Sense of the News: Towards a Theory and an Empirical Model of Reception for the Study of Mass Communication*. Aarhus, Denmark: Aarhus University Press.

Lewis, J. (1985) 'Decoding TV news', in P. Drummond and R. Paterson (eds) *Television in Transition*, pp. 205–34. London: British Film Institute.

Lowe, D. (1982) *History of Bourgeois Perception*. Chicago: University of Chicago Press.

Meyrowitz, J. (1985) *No Sense of Place*. New York: Oxford University Press.

Morley, D. (1980) *The Nationwide Audience*. London: British Film Institute.

Morley, D. (1983) 'Cultural Transformations: the Politics of Resistance', in H. Davis and P. Walton (eds) *Language, Image, Media*, pp. 104–17. Oxford: Basil Blackwell.

Postman, N. (1985) *Amusing Ourselves to Death*. New York: Penguin.

Richardson, K. and J. Corner (1986) 'Reading Reception: Mediation and Transparency in Viewers' Accounts of a TV Programme', *Media, Culture and Society* 8(4): 485–508.

Thompson, J.B. (1984) *Studies in the Theory of Ideology*. Cambridge: Polity Press.

10

The politics of polysemy: television news, everyday consciousness and political action

Klaus Bruhn Jensen

Introduction

One of the most significant developments within media research during the past decade has been the revaluation of popular culture and its consumers. The position of recent qualitative research is that audiences have the ability to make their own sense out of the media and, further, that in the process of reception the media cater to a range of legitimate audience interests and pleasures (Ang, 1985; Jensen, 1987a; Lindlof, 1987; Lull, 1988; Morley, 1980; 1986; Radway, 1984). While this line of research has broken new ground from the theoretical and methodological perspectives, it also raises a number of fundamental issues which must be addressed from a political perspective. Academic research on the forms of culture appears to have reached a juncture at which the critical faculties and sensibilities of the mass audience are, in fact, celebrated. The accumulating evidence on decodings of media content can be taken to imply that audiences appropriate and transform meaning for their own ends. The further suggestion, however, that audiences may be resistant to the mass-mediated constructions of reality and thus presumably also to any ideological impact of mass communication needs to be critically examined. As argued by Schudson (1987: 66),

> The fact that audiences respond actively to the materials of mass culture is important to recognize and understand, but it is not a fact that should encourage us to accept mass culture as it stands or popular audiences as they now exist.

The concept of *polysemy* has been introduced to refer to the interpretive scope of media texts (Fiske, 1986; 1987). The argument is that several

Media, Culture and Society (SAGE, London, Newbury Park and New Delhi), Vol. 12 (1990), 57–77.

interpretations coexist as potentials in any one text, and may be actualized or decoded differently by different audiences, depending on their interpretive conventions and cultural backgrounds. It is polysemy which may, in part, account for the popularity of the same media text with rather different audiences. In political terms, it is the inherent polysemy which enables audiences to move beyond what may have been 'the preferred reading' (Hall, 1973) in order to construct their own reading. Such a reading may, in a wider perspective, be defined as an expression of opposition to the dominant forms of understanding implied by the media. According to this argument, then, polysemy is a political concept, and reception in itself may be conceived of as a political act.

Revising that position, this article argues that oppositional decodings are not in themselves a manifestation of political power in any specific or relevant sense. The wider ramifications of opposition at the textual level depend on the social and political uses to which the opposition may be put in contexts beyond the relative privacy of media reception. For analytical purposes, this means moving beyond the decoding of the individual text and focusing on the *genre*, its historical origins and designated social uses. A genre is both a conventional form of expression and a way of situating the audience in relation to a particular subject matter (Williams, 1977: 183), implying its relevance as political information, cultural event, pastime, and so on. In the case of news, we must ask whether the implied political relevance of the information is accepted or negated by readers and viewers and whether other forms of relevance are established. In particular, I want to argue that several such relevances coexist in the reception of television news, suggesting a contradictory or divided form of everyday consciousness. In fact, polysemy may be a characteristic of the *reception* of news, which bears witness to contradictions at the level of social structures. It is the polysemy of reception, rather than the polysemy of media texts, which must be explored in order to assess concretely the relative power of media and audiences.

News as political genre

The news audience is addressed as recipients of factual information about political life and economic matters. The specific relevance of this information for the audience, however, may be conceived in two different ways. On the one hand, the news text can be thought of as an *account* which reports particular political events and issues as a way of keeping the audience up to date as citizens and voters. In this respect, news works as an agent of representative democracy, documenting as well as legitimating this form of political process as a working reality.

On the other hand, news may be seen as a *resource* for the audience in a rather more participatory form of democracy. At least in an ideal sense, the information can become the basis of political activity and intervention, a notion which is familiar from the political revolutions of the western world (Habermas, 1962; Schiller, 1981; Schudson, 1978), surviving today in the rhetoric of political discourse. If audiences do not perceive news as a specific resource for political awareness and action, then the legitimacy of the political process and its institutions is arguably called into question.

The empirical point of departure is a qualitative interview study with American television viewers. The findings reported here begin to characterize the social and political relevance which viewers ascribe to the news genre, and the interview data also suggest the extent to which television news is an integral element of daily life in the home, a family resource. The methodology relies on depth interviewing and discourse analysis in order to explain the audience response as a process of making sense. In conclusion, the article considers the explanatory value of qualitative audience studies for a social theory of communication. It is the social implications of news texts which make them a central political genre, communicating in and about a particular historical context.

Methodology

A total of twelve news programmes and twenty-four interviews were recorded in a metropolitan area of the northeastern United States during three randomly selected weeks in the autumn of 1983. On a given night, a particular news programme was recorded, and on the following day the recording was shown to two respondents individually, who subsequently were interviewed individually. Since one aim of the analysis was to explore the profiles of public and commercial TV news as perceived by viewers, the newscasts represent an equal number of programmes from a network, a local commercial station, and a local public station. A further aim was to reassess the finding of research on news recall that different demographic groups approach news with different competences (Katz et al., 1977; Tichenor et al., 1970), by asking whether the social uses of news were perceived differently by specific audiences. The sample, drawn from a local university directory, represented two groups of twelve male full-time teaching and research staff and twelve males in various service or administrative positions; in order to focus the analysis, the gender variable was not considered. The data are available for further analysis at the University of Aarhus, Denmark (Jensen, 1986).

Whereas television may not be the main source of news for Americans in terms of information recalled (Robinson and Levy, 1986), it is nevertheless perceived as the most credible and comprehensive source (Roper, 1985). Moreover, television has become a cultural common denominator or forum (Newcomb and Hirsch, 1984) in which major social events and issues can be negotiated by the audience. While the respondents go into some detail about specific news stories, this article will focus not on their decoding of stories as accounts, but on their characterization of television news as a resource of everyday and political life. Taking the particular programme as a point of reference, each interview followed a semi-structured guide which was constructed on the assumption of both critical and mainstream research (Blumler, 1979; Holzer, 1973) that media may have at least three different relevances for recipients. First, media may be a source of information and a means of surveillance of the social context, suggesting a course of action, or at least a readiness for action. Second, media may be a source of social identity or self-legitimation, providing a sense of belonging to a community, (sub) culture or political order. Third, media may be a means of entertainment or diversion, offering relief for anxiety and escape from boredom.

Discourses of news reception

It is one central assumption of qualitative audience research that the reception of communication should be seen as *process* in which meaning is actively negotiated and constructed. While relatively open, this process is patterned by interpretive conventions and cultural practices related to the genre in question. The verbatim interview transcripts, totalling about 800 single-spaced pages, may be thought of as the discourses by which respondents construct their conceptions of the news genre. Specifically, the process of making sense can be traced in the linguistic details of the interview discourse. Linguistic discourse analysis has been shown to have a particular relevance for mass communication research (van Dijk, 1983; Jensen, 1987b), offering a systematic approach to the analysis of qualitative data which characterizes the meaning of linguistic elements in their discursive context. Thus, discourse analysis may avoid some constraints of formal content analysis while at the same time establishing some general linguistic structures in a relatively large interview material.

Whereas a variety of phonetic, grammatical and semantic features may be taken as keys to the analysis, it is the *pragmatic* level of linguistic description which is particularly relevant in the present context. Drawing on speech-act theory (Austin, 1962; Searle, 1969) and functional linguistics (Halliday, 1973), pragmatic analysis focuses on the *uses* of language, examining how people interact through language in everyday conversation and other social contexts, including mass communication (Crystal and Davy, 1969; Coulthard and Montgomery, 1981; Halliday, 1978; Leech, 1983). In reception interviews, it is especially important to establish the central arguments of the respondent, their relationship in the context of the whole interview as well as the substantiations and implicit assumptions which can be taken to support the arguments. In linguistic terms, the three major analytical categories are: coherence, presuppositions and implicit premises. Below, the interview data are reported, first of all, with reference to these linguistic categories, which are exemplified with specimen analyses. In the following sections, the audience uses of television news, as they emerge in the interview discourses, are categorized and interpreted further.

Coherence

Everyday talk produces more or less coherent textual universes, and the precise form of coherence (Arndt, 1979; van Dijk, 1977; Halliday and Hasan, 1976) may bear witness to what are arguably inconsistencies that have social implications. It is particularly relevant to examine the respondents' generalizations concerning their media use and the references to those examples which they introduce to support the generalizations. For example, asked whether he would be more inclined to watch the news if he were watching the programme immediately preceding it, an assistant professor of comparative literature says:

> No. I don't think so, because I have a real thing. When I was living at home my sister is one who just always has some appliance on, and I really, something deep in me, I really dislike that, so that, no, if I get up, and if the first story didn't catch me, or maybe even if I was done with that program I'd turn it off and not keep it on just because it had been on the hour before.

The respondent here begins to project an image of himself as a rational, goal-oriented viewer. The initial 'no' as well as the summarizing 'so that (no)' signal his generalized self-conception that he does not watch a television flow, but individual programmes, which he contrasts with his sister's media use. However, the two examples which are employed to substantiate this self-report are quite dissimilar. In some cases, it is hastily added, he may just turn off the set when a programme is over, but his initial suggestion in the first if-clause is that the appeal of the first news story may be the determining factor. Thus, it is implied that this professor may also watch television and its news programmes as a flow. Elsewhere the same respondent emphasizes that he will not turn to television as a major source of information, watching it only very 'occasionally' and 'selectively'. Still, the relevance of news-viewing as a *habit* emerges several times:

> . . . if I was there alone, you know, I would very often maybe turn it on while I make dinner or was eating dinner or something like that.

The implication may be that at least for this respondent news-viewing is, above all, a habit of everyday life with certain contextual uses.

Presuppositions

In some cases the respondents also advance concrete definitions of the news genre. Such definitions sometimes emerge in the presuppositions (Culler, 1981; Garner, 1971; Leech, 1974) of the interview discourse. A presupposition is what is taken for granted and not otherwise elaborated in the coherence of an argument. Presuppositions 'are what must be true in order that a proposition be either true or false' (Culler, 1981: 111). Talking about the time at which the news is broadcast, a printer finds it convenient:

> . . . it's a good time just to sit there while you're still kind of hyped up from the work, from the busy workday, and you get in and you see the news, and then you, after that you, whether you relax or you decide to go out, you did get that news in, right along with *the rest of the workday*. (emphasis added)

News-viewing is categorized as something belonging to the various daily duties of the workday. It is an activity which must be attended to before one can 'relax' or 'go out'. The fixed news times could, then, be seen as rather convenient because, as the same respondent says later on, 'there's the news right there before you get a chance to do anything else'. News-viewing has its place in the context of evening life and constitutes a habit within a daily routine. Compared to the literature professor above, however, this respondent emphasizes that news in particular allows him to perform a social *duty*. Being a news-viewer, he may exercise his responsibility as a citizen.

Implicit premises

In other cases, the premises on which an argument is based are not manifest in the interview discourse. Instead the premise may be implicit but deducible from the statement-in-context, or the very fact that the statement is made. Everyday conversation is permeated by such premises, and they are variously referred to as expectations (Leech, 1974) and pragmatic presuppositions (Culler, 1981). Conversation is made possible by the assumption that speaker and hearer will attempt to co-operate and, further, that the hearer can be expected to reconstruct the speaker's premises (Grice, 1975). From the analytical perspective, it is necessary to establish the implicit premises in order to grasp the points made by the respondents. For example, in the interview with the printer above, he was asked whether he would have liked to see some other pictures or news items in the programme he had just watched, but he finds nothing to criticize in this respect: 'If it didn't happen for that day, I can't really think of any outside thing that I would really wanna see.' Since the first clause is conditional, it does not in a narrow sense presuppose that nothing else happened on that day. Still, the clause makes the point that presumably whatever is in the news is what has happened. In addition, the clause appears to make the point that the news should concentrate on day-to-day occurrences, adding the notion of timeliness to the notion of news as something which has ostensibly happened. According to this argument, ultimately news is news, and hence it is difficult to imagine 'any outside thing' that should be included. The news may be conceived of as a naturalized element of everyday consciousness.

Summing up, we can say that the structures of coherence, presupposition and implicit premises are the linguistic devices by which the respondents reconstruct their conceptions of the news genre. It is true that the discourses do not derive from the natural viewing context and should be interpreted accordingly. However, since the object of analysis was not the recall of information under everyday circumstances, but rather the audience conception of the news genre as such, the interview data may be used for a preliminary categorization of the news as received.

The social uses of television news

The term 'uses' is employed to refer to that broad range of social, familial and individual relevances which viewers ascribe to news and other media genres. It goes beyond most formulations of uses-and-gratifications research (Blumler and Katz, 1974; Rosengren et al., 1985) by insisting that not just the origin but also the gratification of communicative needs through media use is a complex process which takes place in a particular social setting and cultural context. In his important new conception of media uses, Lull (1980) has shown how the immediate context of use in the family setting comes to shape the reception of mass communication. The characteristic contextual uses of different programme categories, however, as well as the wider political and cultural relevances of specific genres, have not so far been accounted for.

Contextual uses

Media are in many ways integrated elements of their context of use, not least in the family environment where they help to punctuate daily life (Hobson, 1982; Lindlof, 1987; Lull, 1988; Morley, 1986). The present interviews show that television news may play a special role in this respect, being scheduled at the juncture between the workday and the free time of evening. The respondents repeatedly note that news-viewing and cooking or eating are parallel activities that sometimes interfere with each other. As suggested by the literature professor above, however, the activities may be thoroughly integrated as elements of one routine. An ice-hockey coach who is only at home (and thus able to watch the news) for part of the year, describes this period as an occasion for being together with his wife as well as watching the news:

> . . . in the springtime, sometime, a lot of times we sit in the living-room. We have a nice table, then we just sit on the floor and eat dinner and then watch the news, but there will be times when we start talking about one of our own happenings that happened here in the course of the day, and before you know it you've missed 5 minutes or 6 minutes of the news.

At the same time, it comes out that family members do not have equal opportunity to watch the news, because the gendered roles and relations of power in the family also apply to media uses. This respondent for one is well aware that he is more likely to watch the news than is his wife:

> . . . we will be cooking dinner and I'm constantly [laughs], hold on a second, I'm gonna run in here and watch it, not while eating but while she may be making it. I'm the one who'll sneak away because she's more in charge of making the food. I help out and stuff.

News-viewing may, then, be seen as overdetermined by the roles and routines of family life; it is an integrated element of the evening context in the home. At the same time, news is labelled as a particularly important or privileged form of communication. Several respondents mention that they will make a special effort to be able to concentrate on the news. An assistant professor of astronomy describes how he will very often read a book while listening to the stereo and watching television with the sound turned off. He emphasizes, however, that he does not do this for news, which he categorizes as a contrast to 'run-of-the-mill television shows' or 'background'. Similarly, a professor of drama finds that he tries to schedule evening appointments after eight o'clock, so that he seems to 'organize my life around the news moments on television'.

It is further striking that the scheduling of news is accepted by the respondents as natural. There are no arguments, for example, that the evening news might be scheduled differently, fitting news to everyday life rather than vice versa. A professor of music who frequently travels across the country has noted that the daily rhythms associated with news times in different regions are very different, but asked whether he prefers what he finds in his home region, he says: 'Well, I'm just used to it, I don't know I have . . . [laughs]'.

Moreover, news is normally available several times during an evening from different channels, so that viewers have a choice of times. Particularly the stations affiliated with the Public Broadcasting System often broadcast their own news programme at a different time than the commercial stations and in a different format. While several respondents praise the news of the public station in the area as well as the *MacNeil–Lehrer* network programme for their depth and background, they nevertheless suggest that they will not specifically choose these programmes over the commercial news programmes. Some respondents mention that despite their preference in principle for in-depth news such as *The MacNeil–Lehrer Newshour*, they do in practice watch the news programmes of the commercial stations, which are broadcast simultaneously with the MacNeil–Lehrer programme. Other respondents explain that they may watch news from the public station in the area if they are already tuned to this channel. One professor of English literature describes the context in the following way:

> . . . I would be watching, oh, say, *Great Performances* or something like that between 9 and 10, and then at 10 o'clock that, that news programme, it would probably if, you know, if I were in a weakened moment [laughs], probably continue to hold my interest and I would watch it through . . .

In a similar vein, an accountant describes his viewing of the public news programme thus:

> . . . usually a movie or a sporting event goes from like 9 to 11, so if it's half-time or something of a football game I might turn over and watch it.

In both cases it comes out that television, including news programmes, tends to be watched as a flow (Williams, 1974; Ellis, 1982). Since the commercial channels dominate the spectrum of American television, they also tend to dominate the flow of viewing. While the news programmes from the public station are praised for their quality, not least by the professorial group of respondents, this quality may not motivate an actual choice. Still, the respondents insist that the quality of information is decisive: news presumably has a range of specific informational uses.

Informational uses

We may define the informational dimension of news, in preliminary terms, as factual knowledge of political issues and events which is relevant to viewers in a context of social action. The respondents support the relevance of television news in this respect with the arguments, first, that they may need the information in their roles as consumer, employee, and, above all, as citizen and voter, and second, that it is necessary to check this vital information, both over time and with reference to several media.

As far as the latter argument of checking is concerned, the respondents find it difficult to present any concrete examples of issues about which they might have to verify information. Instead, they support their argument with lists of general areas of news coverage as well as further lists of the news media that they read, watch or listen to as a matter of habit. Having argued that one should always rely on more than one source and, further, that he does do so for the day-to-day coverage of some issues, a security assistant exemplifies the issues thus:

> I don't know, maybe, there's always the political issues and the economic issues, and they run hand in hand usually, I guess, too, though. Social issues.

Furthermore, discussing whether, in fact, they ever get conflicting information from different news media, the respondents point to few concrete examples, and they do not focus on the conflicts or take them as the point of departure for consciously preferring one medium. This response serves to question the validity of the standard opinion polls on news media (Roper, 1985), which work from the assumption that audiences evaluate the news media with reference to such conflicts. A professor of English finds that rather than choosing one account, 'I'd just leave it until I got more evidence', and in response to whether he would, then, seek more evidence, he says:

> I would probably seek more evidence. You've got, it's kind of an interesting idea that, that two news, news sources, two, two medias who are in conflict in their reporting. It would be kind of interesting to see how, you know, how it works out, how it comes out.

After the initial generalization that he would 'probably' seek more evidence, the second sentence carries the implied premise that the issue is not just interesting but new to him. The interesting point is that at least this professor is only concerned about the quality of information in an abstract sense; in practice, he would not be likely to seek more evidence. The lexical choices are perhaps significant here, in that 'evidence' is something that one might 'get' just as a conflict is something which 'works out' and 'comes out', rather than something which is actively resolved. The further political implication is that the respondents' reference to several news sources is a way of proving competence as a political subject or, in other words, a democratic ideal rather than an actual form of media use. Asked what he would do about conflicting information, a professor of music spontaneously responds: '[laughs] You mean besides chuckle?'

These arguments raise the additional question of why, for what purpose, viewers might want to check their information and why, in practice, they do not. As the interviews turn to specific social uses of the information, the respondents suggest what appears to be a basic ambiguity of news reception. On the one hand, news is indeed categorized as an instrument or resource for political dialogue and action, at least ideally. On the other hand, the political uses of news which are brought up primarily have to do with a general form of political awareness between elections, or voting information, rather than any active participation in the political process. Talking about this ambiguity of news reception, the respondents express frustration or embarrassment. For example, an assistant professor of economics notes that the editorials of news broadcasts can be points of entry for the public into political debate, an opportunity which, however, does not materialize:

> . . . sometimes I see one of those and I think, I could make a much more balanced or, you know, what I think is a desirable view, point of view on that issue, but I don't do it. I mean, and it could be done, but I don't do it [laughs].

More fundamentally, the printer feels that in practice the opportunity for political participation has not materialized for him:

> Well, I can vote. As far as taking any further, I don't know. I guess the opportunity will have to arise. Being, you know, I feel I'm just the average person out here. . . . As a young person I always wanted to be in the, you know, the public view, I always, I don't know, my mother and, tried to push me to get into politics, and I, I did at one time wanna be a part of it, and I guess deep in the back of my mind I still want it too, even though I didn't pursue it, but, you know, it still affects me, and I, I'm very, I'm a very vocal person . . .

A discrepancy is manifest between the potential and actual relevance of news for the individual in politics. There is no institutionalized precedent or point of access for such social uses of news.

One additional use of news — in everyday conversation — is frequently mentioned. However, as the respondents characterize their conversations about news, their political relevance may be limited, being constrained in at least two different ways. First, the respondents indicate that they primarily engage in a brief exchange of comments, 'you say, hey, did you see such and such', or 'you say, how about so and so', rather than some form of sustained interaction. In this respect, news appears different from other genres, so that fictional genres such as soaps and other series may, in fact, be debated more intensively for the issues they raise than the explicitly political genre of news. This is because, secondly, news is delicately political, so that the respondents will refrain from discussion in several contexts, both at social occasions and at work, 'where your political opinions can affect you'. An engineer argues that he would hesitate to initiate a discussion about issues in the news, and he contrasts this with the relevance of news for forming one's own opinions:

. . . I watch the news. I just form my own opinion, just for myself. If someone happens to bring up the subject, then I'll, you know, I usually discuss it with somebody if they bring it up. I don't normally, you know, run around asking other people their opinion of the news.

In sum, a tension has emerged in the interview discourses between, on the one hand, the active and public uses which are associated with the news genre in a political perspective and, on the other hand, its more limited practical relevance for audiences in terms of 'keeping up' with issues for the purpose of conversation or voting in political elections. Interestingly, there is no manifest difference between the two groups of respondents as they formulate their uses of news. The interview discourses vacillate between two positions and point to a general contradiction in the social definition of news which amounts to a polysemy of reception. By reasserting the competence of viewer-citizens as political agents within a specific social order, news audiences may implicitly contribute not just to their own self-legitimation, but also to the legitimation of the social order as it currently exists. Such legitimating uses of news emerge as a central aspect of the news experience.

Legitimating uses

It is normally assumed that the media may have a 'personal identity' function (Blumler, 1979), providing a point of reference for self-reflection. The respondents specify that, at least in the case of news, the media address recipients' *social* identity and, further, that social identity is specifically associated with issues of political life. News-viewing, then, is less a matter of exploring one's personal identity in the abstract than of situating oneself in relation to a range of concrete political concerns. This may be one mechanism underlying the agenda-setting role of news which has been identified as a major form of impact by other research (McCombs and Shaw, 1977). The sense of checking one's information on current issues over time and with reference to several media may, further, be an important ingredient of the recipient's political self-image. According to a professor of communications: '. . . I think that's the democratic ideal, and I try to aspire to that [laughs] . . .'.

Elaborating on the political relevance of news to the individual, the respondents rely on the twin concepts of *control* and *distance*. The news may give its audience a sense of control over events in the world which would otherwise appear as distant. This is especially clear in the case of local political matters, which the respondents repeatedly refer to. The professor of communications thus contrasts local news with the 'far away' national and international news:

> Sometimes on the local level it's, if you can't do anything about it, at least it's more, it's closer to you, you know, and, you know, you feel like you can do something more about it maybe when it comes to voting or to some other activity.

The important implication is that in practice the local news may not be very different from other news in terms of what the viewer-citizen can control. Instead it is the *feeling* of control which is crucial, even if 'you can't do anything about it'. The sense of distance is underscored by other respondents when talking about the mechanisms of political influence. The printer says in this connection:

> . . . anything that would happen in the news that I would have to hear on the news I don't think I could control. If I could, maybe I would have known about it before it got on the news.

Political events, then, are characterized as distant from the concrete concerns of the audience, and the news is not conceived of as a mediator between the realms of politics and everyday life. Instead the news offers a generalized sense of community, of contact rather than control or influence. A computer operator notes that he is normally preoccupied with his own affairs and that the news provides an occasion to 'feel some sort of community with the rest of the people'. One important prerequisite for being part of a social or political community is having an awareness of a particular range of issues; in this context the respondents refer to issues ranging from housing to high-school achievement. News, thus, may work as a cultural forum (Newcomb and Hirsch, 1984), offering self-legitimation by enabling viewers to at least ask and be concerned about the same questions.

A news story may, in some cases, have very concrete implications for the viewer's sense of social identity and integration. A security assistant argues that economic information is relevant to his own life, and refers to a report of high unemployment figures as an example:

> . . . you may be less disgruntled and then keep your job as opposed to being unemployed, if you've got one [laughs]. If you're unemployed and you see those figures, I'd say it might be very depressing personally . . .

The implied premise is that an economic story may bring home to the viewer the pragmatic, class-based need to become integrated, subordinated, even pacified. Rather than assuming a general political viewpoint on the problems of employment and economy, the respondent appears compelled to focus on basic material issues from a personal perspective entrenched in the prevailing social order.

The concept of legitimation does not imply that the respondents unquestioningly accept the legitimacy of the television news medium itself. As indicated further below, there are several specific criticisms, for example, of the lack of depth or the 'glittering generalities' of local news, as one respondent puts it. As far as the genre or social institution of news is concerned, however, there is no argument or assumption that a reform of the news is necessary if it is to serve its purported political function. The recurring argument is that, in the context of everyday life, television is a convenient mechanism for keeping up with what is, in any event, crucial political information. When an assistant professor is asked repeatedly whether he would change anything in the programme he watched, he seems embarrassed since this is an issue on which he ought to have a critical stand but does not: 'I probably would, but I said that I haven't thought about it. I just haven't thought about it.' In the same context, the professor of communications criticizes the drama of news in the form of 'fires' and 'poor people who're suffering', but asked what one might do about it, he says:

> Oh, I might choose fires myself if my job depended upon it and, you know, in a commercial situation, because, you know, you, you don't work in a vacuum, you work in a system that's controlled by certain factors of economic and so forth . . .

The implied premise here is, first, that news must be dramatic in order to be successful and, second, that the 'system' of socioeconomic factors in which this is the case must be taken for granted. Similarly, the ice-hockey coach is willing to accept the fact that especially 'high-ranking' people are given access to the news as interviewees since they will 'sell the advertising and keep the television going'. While alternative social forms of communication might be conceivable or even preferable, the respondents rather point to the socioeconomic constraints on any change of the news, thus reasserting the limits of the political imagination.

Both groups of respondents give television news high marks for credibility. While survey evidence indicates that viewers with a relatively long education are more likely to also rely on print media and public television for their information (Comstock et al., 1978; Gans, 1979), television news may be seen generally as the most credible source of news (Roper, 1985). One professor of music finds that 'I do trust the newspapers and the TV to dig out the important facts.' It is perhaps more striking that the professors, who have been trained critically to gather information for research purposes, including the professor of communications, characterize television news pictures as direct representation, implying that they may be particularly credible. Thus, the communications professor:

> Sure, you like to see things, you like to see pictures of things that are happening and you think of it as sort of first-hand information . . .

It should, finally, be emphasized that the concept of legitimation does not imply that the respondents necessarily endorse the legitimacy of particular political positions. As shown by previous research on the decoding of news (Jensen, 1988; Lewis, 1985; Morley, 1980), there is a relatively great scope for selective and even oppositional interpretations of the individual news stories or *accounts*, dismissing dominant or preferred readings. It is in this respect that the news provides a forum for public issues to be articulated, and enables different audience groups to situate their particular concerns in a political perspective. When it comes to the social uses of information, however, these respondents suggest that the news genre is not conceived of as a resource by viewer-citizens in political practice.

Diversional uses

The legitimating and integrative uses of television news have led some researchers to argue that news is a political form of entertainment (Dahlmüller et al., 1973; Bogart, 1980), a spectacle which may divert the attention of the audience, not just from boredom or anxiety, but from major issues of social conflict and power. From a different position, gratifications research has assumed that, in principle, entertainment might be as relevant a use of the news genre as any other (McQuail et al., 1972; Levy, 1977; Palmgreen et al., 1980).

Revising these positions, this study argues that because news is defined socially as a political genre, it offers a specific scope for diversional uses. The respondents, to be sure, repeatedly note the importance of an appealing performance of news. An engineer who works in local radio draws the line between 'flash', which is excessive, and 'sparkle', which to him is a necessary element of the TV news mode of address. Other respondents point to the appeal of 'nice, trivial information', and the assistant professor of comparative literature suggests that diversion and pleasure may be integrated aspects of news-viewing; he describes his ideal news programme thus:

> . . . It would be more in the direction of something like *MacNeil–Lehrer* but with more pizzazz to it, with more visuals.

Various qualities of 'pizzazz' may, then, be an important additional or subsidiary gratification of news reception.

Diversional qualities are especially associated with two features of television news. First of all, the respondents emphasize that anchors must have both journalistic competence and personal appeal. A professor of drama, among others, talks at length about the stylistic qualities of the news teams at the various local stations, and a computer operator refers to one variety of happy talk, the banter of the anchorpeople (Altheide, 1976), which leads him to prefer a particular programme. Two local female anchors, named Natalie and Liz, are referred to by two respondents as Natalie Wood and Liz Taylor. And a chemistry professor who criticizes at length the 'self-conscious' effort of the female anchors to 'flirt with the camera' nevertheless likes to look at the 'pretty skirts' of the news teams. Recasting the anchors as glamorous objects, rather than subjects of a discourse on politics, the male respondents evidently derive a variety of visual pleasures from watching TV news.

Second, the respondents refer to the visuals of news events as an attraction in their own right. The images offer great variety, and may be used as an occasional diversion from house chores and other work. The diversional aspect of news may thus be important also for the contextual uses of television in the home during the early evening. Moreover, the visuals communicate a sense of experiential immediacy, which the respondents characterize with such adjectives as pleasing, enjoyable, easy, vivid and exciting. An accountant sums up the quality as a contrast to print: 'it's black and white compared to color'. The sense of immediacy sometimes blends into a sense of reality, particularly in the case of dramatic stories where the visuals tend to carry the narrative. Talking about a story of an airplane which had technical problems before landing, an administrative assistant remembers paying particular attention to the pictures:

> . . . I was looking at the airplane to see if there was any explosion. It turns out that there weren't. . . . I was a little bit curious, interested or curious to find out that it was actually broadcast that way. It could have been a near fatal catastrophe, and it was just, it would have been broadcast on national TV. That would, that caught my attention.

While the main argument here is that this kind of picture should not be broadcast, the underlying premise of the second but last sentence is that the story was aired *before* it was known whether it would result in a catastrophe. The implication of 'that way' in the preceding sentence is that this was live coverage, which ostensibly it was not. The 'mistake' suggests the holding power of the visual narrative.

Whereas the respondents thus refer to aesthetic, pleasurable aspects of the news experience, they nevertheless make a categorical distinction between news and entertainment. The news is distinguished from other, factual and fictional genres which have similar stylistic qualities or which, in certain respects, offer similar types of information, for example talk-shows and commercials. An associate professor of engineering notes that news is not 'just another' form of entertainment, rather 'it's the kind of entertainment that contains some information', and he contrasts it with '*The Dukes of Hazzard*, if you know what I mean'. A video engineer establishes the distinction in more absolute terms with reference to his own motives for watching the news: 'No, I'm not entertained, I'm informed. I watch to be informed and, like I say, there's really no entertainment there.' The implication is that the designated social uses of news and entertainment are different. If nothing else, the distinction between news and other genres may be seen as a social fact, which is established in reception, and which has consequences for the way in which audiences conceive of the information in everyday viewing.

Conclusion

Whereas a range of diversional and contextual uses are attributed to American television news, the respondents place a particular emphasis on the traditional political relevances of news. The interviews serve to identify a contradiction in the audience definition of 'political relevance'. Even though the concrete information of events and issues is characterized as, in principle, a resource for political participation and action, the respondents suggest that the central relevance of news be thought of in terms of *legitimation*. Television news provides a daily forum for the viewers' reassertion of their political competence within a representative form of democracy, but it is not conceived of as a point of departure for action in the institutions and organizations of political life. The contradictory nature of news reception bears witness, in a wider perspective, to a divided form of everyday consciousness which derives from contradictions at the macrolevel of social organization. On the one hand, the news media are potentially a tool for political influence and change; on the other hand, such social uses of news by the audience-public are not institutionalized and do not have a precedent in practical politics. It is a contradictory *social* definition of news which manifests itself at the level of media use and experience.

The interviews further suggest that, at least with respect to the social uses of news, the differences between socioeconomic groups may be negligible. While earlier research shows that there are major differences between such groups in terms of media consumption as well as their decoding of specific texts, it is plausible that viewer-citizens generally are constrained in their uses of news by the dominant social definition and institutional framework of politics. The reception of television news may, accordingly, be seen as an agent of *hegemony* which serves to reassert the limits of the political imagination. As the theoretical literature on hegemony argues (Gramsci, 1971; Sallach, 1974; Williams, 1977), even though the social production of meaning can be seen as a process in which the prevailing definition of reality may be challenged and revised, the outcome of that process is overdetermined by the historical and institutional frameworks of communication. The polysemy of media texts is only a political potential, and the oppositional decoding of media is not yet a manifestation of political power. As Marx notes, 'men make their own history, but they do not make it just as they please' (Feuer, 1959: 360). Similarly, people make their own sense of the media, but that sense is bounded by the social definition of genres.

The news genre may be considered a special modern form of knowledge (Park, 1940; Schudson, 1982), even the archetype of mass communication. Being shaped in a conflictual field of political and economic interests, its social nature and specific polysemy may be particularly apparent. Any genre, however, carries a social history, and its forms of reception bear witness to a particular range of uses for various audience groups (Bennett and Woollacott, 1987). It is the dynamics involving historical determination, genres of communication as well as interpretive conventions which reception studies have to account for in order to explain specifically how the audience-public contributes to the prevailing forms of culture.

Reception studies may, moreover, contribute to the articulation of the interests of the audience-public. Though the conclusions of the present study apply to American television news, it poses the general implication that neither the availability of political information nor a particular level of formal education will ensure substantive social uses of news. Beyond the availability of political information, an institutionalized system of public access to the means of communication is a constitutive element of any participatory political system, or any 'information society' to come. And beyond formal education, which focuses on print literacy, a broader form of media literacy is required. Since the political process is increasingly conducted through the mass media, popular participation depends on a new functional literacy comprising critical comprehension skills as well as concrete production skills (Masterman, 1985). Ultimately, it is the audience-public that must insist on the substantive uses of media, both within the political system and in other areas of social and cultural life, by transcending the ambiguous role of recipient. As they currently exist, the news media do not realize their potential, as suggested also by the two respondents in the sample who do not follow the news on a daily basis. In response to whether he does not, then, feel left out of society, a professor of physiology says:

> Well, let me ask you, what's the point of keeping up? [laughs]. I mean, you know, the reason for keeping up in many cases is so that you can carry on intelligent conversations about what's going on in the world and so on and, so it's nice to be able to talk to people about what's going on, but I'm not sure that, you know, that that's really critical. I think that it's important that those things which a person feels are important to him, that he should try to find out about them, but most of the things in news are not things that I think are important to me.

236   *Klaus Bruhn Jensen*

References

Altheide, D. (1976) *Creating Reality*. Beverly Hills: Sage.
Ang, I. (1985) *Watching Dallas*. London: Methuen.
Arndt, H. (1979) 'Some Neglected Types of Speech Function: The Principles of Functional Classification', pp. 31–47 in T. Pettersson (ed.) *Papers from the 5th Scandinavian Conference of Linguistics*. Stockholm: Almqvist & Wiksell.
Austin, J.L. (1962) *How to Do Things with Words*. London: Oxford University Press.
Bennett, T. and J. Woollacott (1987) *Bond and Beyond*. London: Methuen.
Blumler, J. (1979) 'The Role of Theory in Uses and Gratifications Studies', *Communication Research*, 6 (1): 9–36.
Blumler, J. and E. Katz (eds) (1974) *The Uses of Mass Communications*. Beverly Hills: Sage.
Bogart, Leo (1980) 'Television News as Entertainment', pp. 209–49 in P.H. Tannenbaum (ed.) *The Entertainment Functions of Television*. Hillsdale: Lawrence Erlbaum.
Comstock, G., S. Chaffee, N. Katzman, M. McCombs and D. Roberts (1978) *Television and Human Behavior*. New York: Columbia University Press.
Coulthard, M. and M. Montgomery (eds) (1981) *Studies in Discourse Analysis*. London: Routledge and Kegan Paul.
Crystal, D. and D. Davy (1969) *Investigating English Style*. London: Longman.
Culler, J. (1981) *The Pursuit of Signs*. Ithaca: Cornell University Press.
Dahlmüller, G., W. Hund and H. Kommer (1973) *Kritik des Fernsehens*. Darmstadt: Luchterhand.
Ellis, J. (1982) *Visible Fictions*. London: Routledge and Kegan Paul.
Feuer, L. (ed.) (1959) *Marx and Engels: Basic Writings*. London: Fontana.
Fiske, J. (1986) 'Television: Polysemy and Popularity', *Critical Studies in Mass Communication*, 3(4): 391–407.
Fiske, J. (1987). *Television Culture*. London: Methuen.
Gans, H.J. (1979) *Deciding What's News*. New York: Vintage.
Garner, R. (1971) ' "Presupposition" in Philosophy and Linguistics', pp. 22–42 in C. Fillmore and T. Langendoen (eds) *Studies in Linguistic Semantics*. New York: Holt, Rinehart, Winston.
Gramsci, A. (1971) *Selections from the Prison Notebooks*. New York: International Publishers.
Grice, H.P. (1975) 'Logic and Conversation', pp. 41–58 in P. Cole and J. Morgan (eds) *Syntax and Semantics*, Vol. 3. New York: Academic Press.
Habermas, J. (1962) *Strukturwandel der Öffentlichkeit*. Neuwied: Luchterhand.
Hall, S. (1973) 'Encoding and Decoding in the Television Discourse', stencilled occasional paper, CCCS, Birmingham.
Halliday, M. (1973) *Explorations in the Functions of Language*. London: Edward Arnold.
Halliday, M. (1978) *Language as Social Semiotic*. London: Longman.
Halliday, M. and R. Hasan (1976) *Cohesion in English*. London: Longman.
Hobson, D. (1982) *Crossroads: The Drama of a Soap Opera*. London: Methuen.
Holzer, H. (1973) *Kommunikationssoziologie*. Hamburg: Rowohlt.
Jensen, K.B. (1986) *Making Sense of the News*. Aarhus: Aarhus University Press.
Jensen, K.B. (1987a) 'Qualitative Audience Research: Toward an Integrative Approach to Reception', *Critical Studies in Mass Communication*, 4 (1): 21–36.
Jensen, K.B. (1987b) 'News as Ideology: Economic Statistics and Political Ritual in Television Network News', *Journal of Communication*, 37 (1): 8–27.

Jensen, K.B. (1988) 'News as Social Resource', *European Journal of Communication*, 3 (3): 275–301.

Katz, E., H. Adoni and P. Parness (1977) 'Remembering the News', *Journalism Quarterly*, 54 (2): 231–39.

Leech, G. (1974) *Semantics*. London: Pelican.

Leech, G. (1983) *Principles of Pragmatics*. London: Longman.

Levy, M. (1977) 'Experiencing Television News', *Journal of Communication*, 27 (4): 112–17.

Lewis, J. (1985) 'Decoding Television News', pp. 205–34 in P. Drummond and R. Paterson (eds) *Television in Transition*. London: BFI.

Lindlof, T. (ed.) (1987) *Natural Audiences*. Norwood, NJ: Ablex.

Lull, J. (1980) 'The Social Uses of Television', *Human Communication Research*, 6: 197–209.

Lull, J. (ed.) (1988) *World Families Watch Television*. Newbury Park: Sage.

McCombs, M. and D. Shaw (1977) *The Emergence of American Political Issue: The Agenda-Setting Function of the Press*. St Paul: West Publishing Company.

McQuail, D., J. Blumler and J. Brown (1972) 'The Television Audience: A Revised Perspective', pp. 135–65 in D. McQuail (ed.) *Sociology of Mass Communications*. London: Penguin.

Masterman, L. (1985) *Teaching the Media*. London: Comedia.

Morley, D. (1980) *The 'Nationwide' Audience*. London: BFI.

Morley, D. (1986) *Family Television*. London: Comedia.

Newcomb, H. and P. Hirsch (1984) 'Television as a Cultural Forum: Implications for Research', pp. 58–73 in W. Rowland and B. Watkins (eds) *Interpreting Television*. Beverly Hills: Sage.

Palmgreen, P., L. Wenner and J. Rayburn (1980) 'Relations between Gratifications Sought and Obtained: A Study of Television News', *Communication Research*, 7 (2): 161–92.

Park, R. (1940) 'News as a Form of Knowledge', *American Journal of Sociology*, 45: 669–86.

Radway, J. (1984) *Reading the Romance*. Chapel Hill: University of North Carolina Press.

Robinson, J. and M. Levy (1986) 'Interpersonal Communication and News Comprehension', *Public Opinion Quarterly*, 50: 160–75.

Roper, Inc. (1985) *Public Attitudes toward Television and Other Mass Media in a Time of Change*. New York: Roper.

Rosengren, K., L. Wenner and P. Palmgreen (eds) (1985) *Media Gratifications Research: Current Perspectives*. Beverly Hills: Sage.

Sallach, D. (1974) 'Class Domination and Ideological Hegemony', pp. 161–73 in G. Tuchman (ed.) *The TV Establishment*. Englewood Cliffs, NJ: Prentice-Hall.

Schiller, D. (1981) *Objectivity and the News*. Philadelphia, PA: University of Pennsylvania Press.

Schudson, M. (1978) *Discovering the News*. New York: Basic Books.

Schudson, M. (1982) 'The Politics of Narrative: The Emergence of News Conventions in Print and Television', *Daedalus*, Autumn 1982: 97–112.

Schudson, M. (1987) 'The New Validation of Popular Culture: Sense and Sentimentality in Academia', *Critical Studies in Mass Communication*, 4 (1): 51–68.

Searle, J. (1969) *Speech Acts*. London: Cambridge University Press.

Tichenor, P., G. Donohue and C. Olien (1970) 'Mass Media and the Differential Growth in Knowledge', *Public Opinion Quarterly*, 34 (2): 158–70.

van Dijk, T. (1977) *Text and Context*. London: Longman.

van Dijk, T. (1983) 'Discourse Analysis: Its Development and Application to the Structure of News', *Journal of Communication*, 33 (1): 20–43.

Williams, R. (1974) *Television: Technology and Cultural Form*. Glasgow: Fontana.

Williams, R. (1977) *Marxism and Literature*. London: Oxford University Press.

11

Women as audience: the experience of unwaged women of the performing arts

Susan Kippax

There are differences in the ways in which women and men talk about their experiences of, and participation in, the arts. This article takes as its starting point the experiences of women as audience members of opera, ballet, film, music, theatre and so on. It examines the ways in which these women's experiences of the arts are produced within their social relations and how these experiences, in turn, reproduce these relations.

It is argued that women's experience of the arts is produced in a set of contradictions. As well as the contradictions embodied in 'men's work' and 'women's work', there are contradictions in the world of the arts. To put it rather baldly, the arts are seen as feminine. Most boys and young men are actively discouraged from expressing an interest in the arts; they are turned to more 'manly' interests. Women rather than men are encouraged to become skilled in the appreciation of the arts (Kippax et al., 1986). Indeed, as Veblen (1899: 68–101) notes, with the demise of the leisured classes, women become the amateur presenters and performers of the arts while men busy themselves with more 'weighty' material matters.

Women are trained, while young, to play the piano, to embroider, to sketch, and in general, appreciate the arts. These talents enable them to adorn the homes of future husbands and thus, indirectly, display *his* artistic sensibilities. The acquisition of these talents also

Media, Culture and Society (SAGE, London, Newbury Park, Beverly Hills and New Delhi), Vol. 10 (1988), 5–21

keeps women suitably (in the eyes of men) amused and occupied. At the same time, however, women are excluded from the arts; they are not the celebrated composers, directors, or producers (Wolff, 1981: 42–3). Further, many of the 'crafts' at which they are encouraged and allowed to excel are not defined as art.

The individual processing of these contradictory meanings — in terms of which women appropriate the arts — is positioned in the arena of the dominant culture; one that is both essentially male and ruling class. An examination of these individual negotiations of the contradictions, particularly as they are related to attempts by women to wrest meaning from their lives and construct their identities, gives one an understanding of women's experience of the arts and their arts practices.

Participation in the arts, even as audience, is closely linked to identity. Bourdieu (1984) argues that the arts serve as marks of distinction. Williams (1981: 128–9), too, notes that artistic practices 'can serve social purposes of the deepest kind: not as food, or as shelter, or as tools, but as "recognitions" (new and confirming marks) of people and kinds of people . . . so deep a human interest — in the renewed and renewable means of recognition, self-recognition and identity — can be practised over a very wide range'. A more individualistic approach is taken by Kelly (1983), who argues that styles of leisure are stages on which we present our identities.

This article will focus on how women gain meaning from a subset of the arts — the high arts — in relation to how they fashion themselves into existing structures and thereby construct their selves. My conversations with women and men, selected because they were subscribers to the arts, focused on the ways in which, through their everyday lives, they build their identities. Thus I have concentrated on the personal responses of audience members to the art forms rather than on the art forms themselves and the meanings embedded in and carried by them. I have not neglected the art forms and, in one important sense, they are not separable from audience responses to them.

The method I employed was based on case histories.[1] These were collected via open-ended and unstructured interview schedules. The interviews were conducted rather like conversations, where the main aim was to get the audience members to talk about the arts, their enjoyment of them, how they became interested and the part the arts play in their lives.

From these interviews or conversations, which usually lasted about an hour or an hour and a half, individual case histories were constructed. These histories were looked at both individually and collectively, and similarities and differences were sought between and within various sub-sets of the sample — based on age, sex, occupation and so on. The concepts which emerged from the collective analysis were reflected back onto the individual case histories which were then theorized in the light of these reflections.[2] The ways in which each person constructs his or her identity, as noted before, are particularly important. The understandings which are subjectively significant to the person in the construction of identity provide the basis for the theorizing.

I shall use a small number of case histories, as well as excerpts drawn from these and other interviews, in order to explore and illustrate two major themes which are important to an understanding of women's experience of the arts. These two themes are:

1. The place of the arts in women's everyday lives; the relationships between the arts and family, work and social life.
2. The pleasure and enjoyment women gain from the arts.

In my discussion I shall place these themes or patterns, as they emerge from the case histories, within the context of the collective analysis. Case study material drawn from both men and women will be presented, in order to point up the particular impact of women's work on female responses to the arts.

The first pattern concerns the place of the arts in people's lives. There are four major variations on this theme.

The first is the 'cultural worker' variation. In this variation the individual places the arts in a central and fully integrated position in his or her world. Family, work and leisure are all of a piece, and the arts are seen as fitting into each aspect of life; there is little, if any, separation of work and leisure, the arts are part and parcel of both, as well as being part of one's family and social life.

This variation is extremely common amongst academics, teachers, writers, researchers, architects — the professional classes both women and men. For example, there is Edgar, an architect and Margaret, a teacher.

Edgar is in his early forties and is married. His wife is a film editor. They have two children. He subscribes to Musica Viva,[3] the ABC Recital Series,[4] and the Australian Opera.[5] He also subscribes to the Sydney Film Festival[6] and goes to another 'twenty or thirty movies each year'; he is a regular theatre-goer although not a subscriber, he subscribes to the Sydney Dance Company[7] and is a regular art gallery attender. His interests in the arts dominate his leisure, which is successfully integrated with his work; he is a member of the National Trust and is involved both at work and at play in conservation issues. Most of his friends are architects, and many of them have worked on or been closely associated with theatre design and production. He shares his interests with his wife, particularly his interest in film which has been influenced by her expertise. He encourages his children's interests in the arts and both children have music lessons. There is little separation of family, work, leisure and social life.

His aesthetic concerns were developed when a child and music and opera played an important part in his parents' lives. These early interests are extended, elaborated and transformed by his training as an architect, his work and his wife's work. His artistic interests are reshaped and we see a refinement of his music tastes to recital and chamber music. The latter interest 'grew out of the other forms of music and I think I started attending Musica Viva concerts when I was at university'. As an architecture student and architect he acquired an interest in the visual arts and in theatre design. His response to opera, his favourite art, has also been informed by his training. 'I think it [opera] is the most potent form of entertainment because it combines music, theatre and design. They are all the things that I like separately, and when they all come together . . .'.

Margaret is about the same age as Edgar. She is a teacher of English literature and has a higher degree in theatre history. She, too, is married — to an engineer with whom she shares many of her interests. Margaret subscribes to the theatre, the Sydney Theatre Company[8] and the Nimrod,[9] and goes to performances outside these two subscription series. She also subscribes to the Australian Opera, Musica Viva, and the Sydney Symphony Orchestral Concert[10] series. She enjoys talking, her friends are important in this regard, and she 'never stops reading'. As well as being a participant in the arts she is also a guardian of them, and sits on the higher education board which decides, among other things, on school curricula.

Two things in her life define her: her work and her arts interests. Of the latter she says:

> I think it is an intrinsic part of my life and I suppose that, for me, leisure is, involves doing things, it is so active, it is not passive, it is not lying around half asleep in the sun . . . I go [to concerts and to the theatre] because I like to go and want to go because it gives me pleasure and I find it stimulating and I find it moving and whatever. . . . I go simply because it is part of my existence and I think it is inconceivable for me to imagine life without doing those things.

Her response to her work is similar:

> I think work stimulates you. The more you do the more you can do, in a sense. It has to be involved work, you can't, to work on a switchboard or to work in a factory I think would be, it would not be what I would think of as being work, that would just be a grind. Work is important to me because it is interesting and because it is stimulating and because I am involved in it in lots of ways both intellectually and physically and emotionally and so on.

For both these people, and for many other professionals, their work, the arts, their family and social life, are all integrated and bound together; they all feed into and off each other. This pattern is found in men and women, in married and unmarried people, and in the young and the old. It is, however, rarely found amongst those who work in the commercial sphere. Bourdieu (1984: 11–96) identified this particular pattern in his study in France and distinguished cultural workers from others in terms of their accumulation of cultural and academic capital.

A second variation is the separation of the arts, which are seen as part of leisure, from work but not from the activities surrounding family and friends. It is a pattern that few professionals fit, and it is most common amongst those who earn their living in the commercial sphere — the business executives, or more generally, the management classes, both men and women. Bourdieu (1984: 11–96) also identified them in his study, and distinguishes them from the professional classes as being relatively low in cultural capital but possessing more economic capital. The people in this study who fitted this category often described themselves and their lives as 'balanced'; they saw a complementary relationship existing between their separate worlds of work and leisure.

Simon provides a clear picture of this separation. He is a director of a large company, his wife is not in waged work and they have two children. Leisure, for Simon, is 'something completely different from work' and something he shares with his family. He and his wife subscribe to the Australian Opera and Musica Viva, and they go to the theatre occasionally. Simon also goes regularly to the movies and always takes his children. The children, too, are included in the outdoor activities which are an important part of Simon's leisure and a part that is shared with friends. Simon's description of these two aspects of his life is that the family comes first and a balance is achieved between work and leisure — 'that's the secret'.

These two patterns suggest that work informs the arts practices of audience members. The professionals, particularly the cultural workers, prefer art forms which are intellectual in nature, such as chamber music. There is a direct relationship between work practices and arts practices: teachers of English literature bring their special knowledge into play when they go to the theatre, architects their feel for form, design and colour, and philosophers speak of bringing their analytic skills to bear on their appreciation of the arts.

Those in the management classes, the industrialists and business executives, identify more strongly than the professionals with theatre and opera. Although these people separate the world of work from the arts, the material success and glamour sought and often found in their work is celebrated in opera and some forms of theatre. Those in business define themselves in terms of tangible goods in contrast to the professionals who define themselves in terms of intellectual achievements.

There is a striking similarity between these data of audience membership collected in Sydney, Australia, Bourdieu's French data and the audience membership of the earliest classical concerts in Vienna, Paris and London. Weber (1975: 34–57) reports on these concert audiences: The rising mercantile class and the upper middle class business men had a taste for what Weber calls 'Rossini-type operatic' music and virtuosic instrumentalists, whereas the music of the classic German tradition was listened to by the nobility and the liberal professionals. 'Most business families ... had a self-confident, ostentatious life style and valued cultural pursuits of the same order. They looked to the famous virtuosi for an exaggerated picture of the success and glamour they saw in themselves' (Weber, 1975: 34). Of the nobility and liberal professionals, he said: 'They styled themselves connoisseurs, members of the learned elite who could appreciate the high culture of music' (Weber, 1975: 57)

The third but relatively uncommon variation on the theme was provided by people who separate the arts from their social and/or family life and integrate it firmly into their work lives. It is common among people who, because of divorce or other reasons, have constructed their identities within the realm of work and have tied their interest in the arts to their work. This pattern is found amongst both men and women. Michael is a doctor engaged in medical research. He is divorced and has two major interests in his life — music and medicine. He works six days a week and spends much of his time in the evening on his medical research while listening to classical music on the radio. Michael is a subscriber to Musica Viva and he goes regularly to the opera; he is not interested in film, theatre or ballet. His only other interest is cricket. When speaking of his work and music, Michael says: 'after many years I have probably about got it to just about where I want it . . . I am probably leading the life I want to lead'. Another doctor, a single man, Martin, with extremely similar interests to Michael, combines music festivals with medical conferences whenever possible. 'I look on my work as a holiday . . . just don't bother to take leave . . . no point going away to be bored.' This pattern is far more common amongst professionals than amongst those who work in the commercial sphere, and may be seen as a minor variation of the first pattern discussed above.

More interesting in the context of this article are the descriptions of women's lives being rebuilt around waged work. This work is often recently acquired and in many cases coincides with the attainment of independence in their children. In these cases, as with the two doctors described above, the arts are integrated as far as possible into the world of work rather than into either family or social worlds.

Sarah is fifty-three years old and recently separated from her husband. She has two adolescent children and an ageing father at home. She has a part-time job as a yoga teacher. Sarah's subscriptions to Musica Viva and the Australian Ballet are not of long standing; these interests were set aside at marriage and she is turning to them again. She shares them with her female friends, many of whom she has met through her work. They are not shared with her family. 'I decided if I was ever going to do any of those things and enjoy doing the things I like doing, music, ballet, and things like that, I would have to go out and do them myself . . . not sit around and wait for him to take me.'

This thought is echoed by Sally who, although still married, is carving out for herself an existence, an identity, outside her family life. She works as a teacher and has recently taken out subscriptions to Musica Viva, the Australian Opera, and the Sydney Theatre

Company. She goes alone but discusses what she sees and hears with her work colleagues. It is these outings which keep her sane:

> but honestly I really think the most important thing is at least once a week, and I think this is a very modest request, once a week, apart from being with people you have to be with for reasons of duty or responsibility or necessity, you should be able to once a week be with people whose company you simply enjoy and I think if I could do that once a week I would probably survive as a human being.

The relationship between the world of work and the arts is fairly tenuous for these two women. Sarah's job is part-time and Sally's professional world is not centre stage. But they and other women like them are attempting to build links between their work and the arts in order to redefine themselves. There is no doubting the importance of the arts for their lives. This pattern points the way to the fourth variation.

As in the case of Sally and Sarah, this fourth variation is one in which the arts play a central role. But in this case the role is kept completely separate from all other activities. The fourth variation severs the link between the arts, on the one hand, and the world of work and family, on the other. It is almost a universal pattern amongst unwaged women. There are no men who share any of its characteristics.

What is the relationship between domestic work and the arts? Why do these women's lives appear fragmented? Mary's case history suggests some answers. Mary is twenty-seven years old. She is an arts graduate and is married to a doctor who is studying for postgraduate qualifications and membership. The have a one-year-old child, their first.

Mary is no longer in waged work: 'I never got to the stage where I had developed a career'. Her work now involves caring for her young child and her husband. A great deal of her time revolves around these two people. Most of her current friends she met through her husband, and most of her social activities involve either her husband or are fashioned around child care. She goes for walks, to the beach, plays tennis with friends who also have young children, she goes to art galleries, and she likes having people around for dinner: 'it seems the easiest way to see them and not hassle about baby sitters'.

Since the birth of her child she has altered, either dropped or cut back on many of her previous activities. She has stopped playing golf; her subscription to the theatre has lapsed; she has stopped playing the flute; and her film-going has been reduced from 'about twice a week' to the Sydney Film Festival and 'about six other movies a year'. She has, however, maintained her subscription to Musica Viva and she occasionally gets to the theatre and the odd opera. She watches a lot of movies on television, and records and books have become important sources of pleasure to her.

Thus the two arts practices that she maintains during this period of cut-back are those associated with classical music (going to Musica Viva concerts, systematically adding to her record collection, listening to records, reading about music, and so on) and film (going to movies and watching old movies on television). It is interesting to note that the two practices that are maintained are sustained and reinforced by activities that are relatively easily incorporated into her everyday home-based world.

These two activities have become increasingly important to her and to her sense of self, and because of their importance they have been separated, by Mary, from the rest of her life; there is a psychological separation of the world associated with the arts and her world as wife, mother and housekeeper. The music and the film give her a psychological space outside the domestic sphere. Her arts practices enable her to construct a self, an identity, which is different from her public identity of wife and mother, an identity which is defined in terms of her relation to others.

When I asked Mary what it was about music and film that was important to her she replied:

> to go and immerse myself in a concert or to go to a movie or something is all mine. . . . It is just mine, it's completely selfish, it's all mine . . . and what I get out of it is what I can, it is my input and I build on my own character and memories of everything through that and I always feel that it is self-improvement.

In this world which is hers (and it is not something she shares to any great extent with her husband) she gains an identity, a sense of self, in which she can recognize herself as an intelligent and autonomous being.

> I mean that is what I miss most about work -- I miss my world where I am known only as me. . . . I am not a doctor's wife and I am not [my child's] mother . . . my leisure time enhances what I am.

Mary feels excluded from the world of work, which she recognizes as one way to gain public recognition. And she is ambivalent about her role as mother:

> by the time I became pregnant with her, which was a bit of a shock anyway, I hadn't created my niche and I am finding at the moment if I could go back to . . . and the fact that I didn't get to a position where I could negotiate . . . say, I never got to the promised managerial position . . . it all just comes down to another drudge job and what is the point of sacrificing her [my child] for that, and I am pretty happy, I am very happy. It is rather nice that I can pursue my interests while I am giving her a good upbringing. I think it would be lovely to go back and actually have something (a position or career). I suppose just about anybody can caretake.

So Mary ties her identity, or at least one important aspect of it, to the arts and arts practices. It is through the arts and her skilling herself in the arts, which she does assiduously, that she hopes to develop and construct an identity outside the domestic sphere. Thus she is systematically adding to her record collection, training her ear, reading up on composers, and so on.

> I have come a long way from the Four Seasons, let's put it that way, and I feel like I have gone from beginner music and I'm now in the intermediate . . . I am probably more than in intermediate.

She has appropriated the dominant (and male) view of the world, defining success and worth in terms of a career and devaluing motherhood. She reaches towards some characteristics of this success — intelligence, knowledge and confidence, through audience practices and associated activities. But she realizes this success, this worth, as an individual, privately. There is no collective realization nor public display — points to which I shall return below.

Her husband is one of the successful ones — a doctor. It is with him, in one sense, that Mary works through the contradictions in her life and she does this by competing with him. Sometimes she wins. For example when speaking of her involvement in film, she says:

> I think I am good enough now that I can actually notice the editing and all sorts of things that he [my husband] wouldn't have pin-pointed. . . . I get really excited about finding out that I can and I'm getting better and better at it.

Sometimes she loses:

and I have got a garbage mind for trivia so . . . I just love spotting the odd bits, so . . . and that's why I love old movies as well . . . I am the kind of person people like having around when the old movies come up.

Other women have travelled along the same path that Mary has begun. Some of them have attempted to resolve the contradictions in their lives by becoming unpaid or amateur cultural workers. They define themselves by appropriating the dominant structures. One such woman is Jean. In some ways she and Mary are very similar; they are both well educated and both have been trained and skilled in the arts. Jean learnt the piano as a child, Mary the piano and flute. Both are married to doctors but neither inherited vast accumulations of economic or cultural capital. Neither has ever had a career. They are, of course, different from one another and one of the important differences is age: Mary is in her twenties and has a young child; Jean is in her fifties and her children have grown up and left home.

Jean subscribes to the opera, ballet, theatre, and has three classical music subscriptions — Musica Viva, the Sydney Symphony Orchestral Concert Series, and the Philharmonia Society.[11] She also goes to the occasional jazz concert. She reads, plays bridge and is involved in debating. She takes a very active role in community work. She knits, sews, makes pots, cooks and goes to craft summer schools. And she plays tennis, she swims and she jogs. Her leisure, these activities, are her life.

I am very involved in many aspects in every way. I think that to be involved in *one* way, you are not living, you are not feeling, because you are not stretching yourself to find out what your feelings and abilities are . . . it's harder for me, I've got no profession.

She, like Mary, regrets not having a career and mingled with this regret is a sense of guilt. She compares herself to a butterfly: 'I probably do too much and get it all mixed up in my head'. She lacks confidence in her own abilities and skills, and feels that she has not been able to develop the self-discipline needed to fully appreciate the arts.

Like all the unwaged women to whom I spoke, Jean sees a career (not a job) as the typical and most direct way of accruing worth. As this path is closed to these women, they instead appropriate the arts. The arts and their involvement in them become extremely important to their self-definition; their definition of themselves as intelligent and successful human beings. But the worthiness they acquire is only a *self*-recognized worthiness, and one that is accepted in a timid and unconfident manner. Their definition of themselves as intelligent and successful is not a publicly recognized identity; rather it is one that is essentially private.

The expressive aspects of activities such as going to concerts, theatre, or opera or listening to music or watching movies are, for these women, public only in the most obvious sense of the word. The actions may take place in a public space but the mark of distinction, the worth that is accrued, remains anonymous. In this sense it remains a self-awarded, a personal rather than a public, distinction. For as Harré (1979: 5) notes, the expressive order involves the transformation of something personal into something public: 'It is from the *ex*pression of oneself in public performances and the qualities of such performances that other people form an *im*pression or series of impressions through their interpretation of the action.' Being there, in the cinema or concert hall, does not allow a full expression of oneself as a movie or music buff; nor does it enable others to form an impression of one as knowledgeable of or sensitive to a particular production or piece of theatre. There is little chance to make public one's response, except interpersonally to a husband or a friend, and there is little chance of discussion or debate.

The domestic world of unwaged women is unlike the hospital common room where doctors discuss the pros or cons of last night's performance of a Schubert quartet. Similarly, it is quite different from a space in which it would be considered appropriate for an academic dissection of Pinter's latest play. Women in unwaged work are caught in the private realm and there is no space for public display — no room and no space where artistic interests can be built on, tested out, fed, or elaborated as is the case for many workers, particularly cultural workers.

In negotiating the contradictions, women in unwaged work may become amateur cultural workers. Mary and Jean are two such women. Other women may, when their sense of responsibility permits them — for example, when their children leave home — integrate their arts practices into the newly adopted world of work in an attempt to provide a context for them. Sarah and Sally are doing this.

None of the women to whom I spoke resolved the contradiction by re-defining what counts as the arts. In attempting to gain distinction and accrue honour[12] women reproduce the social structures and relations which constrain and exclude them. They search for their sense of self and identity within the male domain.

Not only does this make it difficult for women to express their knowledge and expertise, and so enhance their public standing and social recognition, but it is difficult for them to express their enjoyment of the arts. The pleasure often associated with the arts, particularly music, is tied to the emotions. But for many women the emotions or their expression are suspect, especially if that expression is believed to be separate from some underlying rational response to the arts. Women's emotional responses are not easily articulated because women can only test out their ideas, experiences and responses to the arts in the male domain. And for unwaged women, as we have seen, this domain is closed.

Mary expresses this lack of confidence in the following way:

> I go with them. . . . I go all sparkle-eyed and say wasn't that wonderful and they will say, yes, that was quite pleasant would you like a gin and tonic and so I'm a bit taken aback that they haven't been enthralled. . . . I quite enjoy going by myself because sometimes I don't particularly want someone to say 'wasn't that nice'.

She reports going to a Musica Viva concert with a friend, a pianist:

> and I was absolutely amazed when at the end of a fabulous concert I said 'wasn't that brilliant' and she said 'yes, it was very restful' and I said 'restful!'. She loved going out to get away from the baby and she just loved feeling rested where I went for excitement. . . . It was just so odd I really disliked going with her.

Mary's experience is disconfirmed by her friends and she needs confirmation. She doesn't trust her own responses.

Mary's response is echoed by many other women. Sybil is 38, married, and has two children of school age. Her husband is often away from home for long periods of time because of work commitments. She describes her life as very full and demanding:

> it was like this last year, it was such a vile hectic year. . . . I suppose I haven't had time to do leisure things because the garbage has to be put out, the child has to have her lunch to take to school, or you have to feed someone an evening meal, or you must wash that particular garment or they won't have anything to wear tomorrow and they have to have it. They are the things that have to be done, they are more important.

So the arts become an escape: 'I think mainly it is the relaxation from stress, and then there can be excitement in it and that, that is entering with the music. It is different than a normal life, isn't it?' Sarah, whom we met above, also, speaks of relaxation. She describes her life as 'not very still . . . so Musica Viva and ballet are like something, are something to get out of this rat race and it is something like an oasis, a fantastic relaxation and [it] brings you back to sanity again'.

The responses of men and waged women, especially professional men and women, are confident and firmly tied to the world of work. For many of them, pleasure is achieved in informed and intelligent participation. Theatre, music, film, ballet and opera are discussed with reference to the meanings that particular performances or compositions carry. Distinctions are drawn between the 'greats' and the 'not so greats'. Professional men and women are confident of their responses to the arts and their responses are continually reinforced and confirmed in their everyday public worlds. So Margaret, the teacher and student of English literature, speaks confidently of this and that production. Although she says she is worried about her lack of formal training in music, she is confident in her experience of it: 'So I am a musical illiterate, I can't read music'. But: 'I think I have got a fair amount of ordinary knowledge about it and I am pretty receptive and responsive'. Simon, the business executive, speaks of his enjoyment of music deriving from 'logic and order . . . some emotion as well, of course'.

Unwaged women belittle their own knowledge and their own skills. Their response to the arts is separated from these areas of expertise because in many cases this expertise is acquired alone in the private realm; reading, listening to records, watching movies on television, and thinking. Their responses, which are tied to their individual needs, are untested. These women have a sense that there are readings of the arts other than their own, and that these readings are rationally informed. They are suspicious of their own private readings and this suspicion carries over to their own responses which are, as they are for most people, emotional. Mary illustrates this:

> I really enjoy [movies], I mean I can come out of a movie and feel that I have seen something that is important to my life. . . . I just feel that it is visually, I don't mean the story line or message or something, I just feel that it has enriched my visual or my mental kind of aspect.

She also speaks of music as 'feeding my soul. . . . My appreciation of music is really important to my psyche . . . an enrichment that can't go away'. It is as though the very emotionality of Mary's response makes it at one and the same time extremely important to her and suspect. Her emotions are not rational; they are feminine.

Compare Mary's response with that of Edgar, the architect. His response is full of confidence because he has had some say in the production of the arts and the discourse that surrounds them:

> there is some kind of shared human experience, if you like, which is transcended from the everyday, human shared experience which deals with emotions which are larger than life but nonetheless still accessible.

The emotions are painted in a way he understands, and his training has given him a language for expressing his understandings. The emotions and the way they are portrayed by the arts are accessible to him because each work of art is a collective representation of his world.

Thus unwaged women are doubly excluded. The arts themselves have been scripted and produced by others and for others. Women's experiences and feelings are not easily accessed, although, as Jean illustrates, it is not impossible. When explaining why she preferred to hear her music live, Jean said: 'I know all the other people in the audience are experiencing the same feelings as I am'. There is a common or collective sense of humanity.

As well, women's experiences *as women* are denied. The art forms which derive from the domestic realm are not seen as part of the arts, they have a different name to distinguish them — 'crafts'. As Judy Chicago (1977) argues, the things that are important in many women's lives are not considered the stuff of art or they are written in a way that shuts women out. Certainly as Wolff (1981: 40–5) and others[13] have documented, the social organization of artistic production over the centuries has excluded women from participation. This organization, I argue, has not only excluded women from the production of art but has repercussions for women as audience. Women are rendered unsure of their response to the arts. They are unsure even in an area where they are stereotypically well-versed — the emotions.

In summary, this article has used the differences in the responses of men and women to the arts to reach an understanding of women as audience. It is argued that women are forced into the personal sphere in the arts as in other areas of life and meaning. They are psychologically excluded from the social realm and their access to it is made extremely difficult. They remain in the personal realm at the intersection of the individual and the private.

There is a double alienation. Women are alienated from the public sphere, particularly those women in unwaged work. Women are also alienated from any collective realization. Paradoxically they seek distinction in an arena from which they are excluded. The art forms in which they are often skilled, and of which they have a keen appreciation, are not in the main produced by them or for them. As Vygotsky (1971: vii) notes:

> Art 'works' with human feelings and a work of art informs [incarnates] this work. . . . Sensations, emotions, and passions are part of the context of a work of art, but they are transformed in it. The significance of this transformation (metamorphosis) is its transcendence of individual feelings and the generalization to the social plane.

The enforced individualness of women's responses make this transcendence difficult.

The arts which are held up to women as the pinnacle of human achievement are, at the same time, perhaps by definition, withheld from them. This article describes women's attempts to negotiate this contradiction. De Beauvoir (1972: 713–24) believes the contradiction can be resolved and will be resolved when women win possession of themselves.

Notes

1. In the entire research project over 190 interviews were conducted. Most of the men and women interviewed were subscribers to classical music (chamber and symphony), opera, classical ballet, theatre or film (film festival). Seventy students from school, technical college and university were also interviewed. These students were selected for interview because they had some interest in the arts, as shown by their responses to a survey conducted prior to the interviews.

2. The method which evolved over the course of the study was guided by the work of R. Harré and P.F. Secord, *The Explanation of Social Behaviour* (Blackwell, Oxford, 1972); particularly their suggestion to collect accounts: B.G. Glaser and A.L. Strauss, *The Discovery of Grounded Theory: Strategies for Qualitative Research*. (Aldine, New York, 1967); and Frigga Haug, 'Memory-work' (Macquarie University, Sydney, 1985).

3. An Australian entrepreneurial organization which arranges the tours of visiting chamber music ensembles.

4. The Australian Broadcasting Corporation, which amongst other things arranges the tours of visiting musical celebrities for recital and concert performances.

5. The national opera company.

6. The annual Sydney Film Festival.

7. One of the two main ballet companies in Sydney.

8. One of the major Sydney theatre companies.

9. Another major Sydney theatre company.

10. The Sydney-based orchestra funded by the Australian Broadcasting Corporation.

11. A Sydney-based choral society.

12. R. Harré, (1979), pp. 19–26. Harré argues (p. 21) that in the expressive aspects of our social activities we make a public showing of skills, attitudes, emotions and feelings, and that these 'showings' provide evidence upon which others draw conclusions as to the kind of person we are.

13. See, for example, Rozsika Parker and Griselde Pollock, *Old Mistresses: Women, Art and Ideology*. (Routledge & Kegan Paul, London, 1981), pp. 50–81.

References

Bourdieu, Pierre (1984) *Distinction: A Social Critique of the Judgement of Taste*, translated by Richard Nice, London: Routledge & Kegan Paul.

Chicago, Judy (1977) *Through the Flower: My Struggle as a Woman Artist*. New York: Anchor Books, Doubleday.

De Beauvoir, Simone (1972). *The Second Sex*. Harmondsworth: Penguin Books.

Harré, Rom (1979) *Social Being*. Oxford: Blackwell.

Kelly, John R. (1983) *Leisure Identities and Interactions*. London: George Allen & Unwin.

Kippax, Susan, Koenig, Susan and Dowsett, Gary (1986) *Potential Arts Audiences: Attitudes and Practices*. Sydney: Australia Council.

Veblen, Thorsten (1899) *The Theory of the Leisure Class*. New York: Macmillan.

Vygotsky, Lev (1971) *The Psychology of Art*. Cambridge, Mass: MIT Press.

Weber, William (1975) *Music and the Middle Class: The Social Structure of Concert Life in London, Paris, and Vienna*. London: Croom Helm,

Williams, Raymond (1981) *Culture*. Glasgow: Fontana.

Wolff, Janet (1981) *The Social Production of Art*. London: Macmillan.

PART THREE
THE MEDIA AND PUBLIC LIFE

12

The alternative public realm: the organization of the 1980s anti-nuclear press in West Germany and Britain

John D.H. Downing

The coincidence of political turmoil in the 1960s and 1970s in industrially advanced societies with the increasing availability of small-scale media technologies, led both to an explosion of alternative media projects (Downing, 1984; Kogawa, 1985; Lowe, 1983; Mattelart and Siegelaub, 1983), and, more slowly, to attempts to reconceptualize the functions of these projects. Implicitly and often explicitly a major movement was under way to create models of media operation transcending the typical behaviour both of capitalist media conglomerates and of soviet-style 'transmission-belt' media. Debates about these new models focused on aesthetics (layout, language, 'non-political' themes), on internal organization (self-managed structures, finance), and on the interaction between media and oppositional political movements — all these dimensions being intimately inter-related in practice.

Debates on alternative media were especially lively in West Germany and Italy from the mid-1970s. In the former they quite often centred on the concept of an 'alternative public realm'. Here I propose first to present and comment on this concept, and then to review its utility in analysing one major example of alternative media, namely anti-nuclear movement media in West Germany, with some comparative observations on their British and other counterparts. By 'anti-nuclear' I mean the opposition both to

Media, Culture and Society (SAGE, London, Newbury Park, Beverly Hills and New Delhi), Vol. 10 (1988), 163–181

nuclear energy and to nuclear war (the two spheres being intimately connected).

The concept 'alternative public realm'

In English these three words lie awkwardly next to each other, each more or less clear in itself, but somewhere between the flat and the obscure in collective signification. Let us begin by clarifying the term 'public realm', and subsequently review the sense of 'alternative'.

'Public realm', sometimes with 'public sphere' or 'public domain' as substitutes, has generally been the term used to translate the polysemic German word 'Öffentlichkeit', whose fundamental sense is 'open', 'public', 'common', as against 'private', 'secret', 'restricted'. It is a term which can be used to refer to public debate in or out of parliament, publicity, a public action, the processes of formation of public opinion. As Habermas notes at the outset of his study of changes in the structure of public exchange (1962: 11): 'The use of "öffentlich" and "Öffentlichkeit" discloses a multiplicity of competing senses. They arise from different historical phases, and in their fused application to the relations of industrially advanced welfare state bourgeois society, assume an opaque connotation.' In his study Habermas located the development of the concept in social and constitutional changes in England, France and Germany during the centuries of capitalist transformation, and in the arguments of political philosophers from Hobbes to de Tocqueville. He summarized the constitutional changes thus:

> The basic laws guarantee: the *spheres* of public and private (the kernel of the latter being the sphere of intimate social relations); the *institutions* and *instruments* of the public on the one hand (press, parties) and the basis for private autonomy on the other (family and property); finally the *functions* of private people — political as citizens, economic as commodity-owners. (Habermas, 1962: 96, *emphases in original*)

These constitutional protections offered a measure of autonomy from interference by state or church with the emergent bourgeoisie, and thus created the conditions under which a public realm of debate could operate effectively, with direct implications for government decision making.

Habermas noted that both the constitutional and the philosophical formulations of this new public realm were derived in significant measure from its emergent forms of social organization. In England the typical early form of public realm was in the myriad coffee-houses and tea-houses of London from the end of the seventeenth century, with their innumerable pamphleteers and essayists (69–78). In France the Paris *salons* and clubs fulfilled a similar role, whereas in Germany the public sphere was typically actualized in readers' societies for the perusal and discussion of newspapers and periodicals (78–85).

In his use of the term 'public realm', therefore, Habermas specified the emergent organization of the conditions of democratic — not merely parliamentary — debate and the role of media within that context. He concluded however that the role of public debate in the formation of public opinion and policy was currently being eroded by the one-way vertical communication flows characterizing the atomized societies of the late twentieth century (Chs 22–25).

It does seem that notwithstanding the persistence of the rhetoric of 'public opinion', the realm of public exchange has been experiencing an increasing shrinkage (Elliott, 1986; Garnham, 1986). We might compare R.P. Woolf's complementary metaphor in his essay 'Beyond Tolerance' (1969: 54) of the 'plateau' as the restricted forum within which perspectives must circulate in order to be taken seriously within contemporary public media debate, and extend it to suggest that the cliffs of the plateau have grown more sheer, the mists of secrecy more dense (Demac, 1984; Downing, 1986). *Nowhere has this trend been more evident than in military and nuclear matters* (Aubrey, 1982; Gowing, 1978; Hertsgaard, 1983; Hilgartner et al., 1982; Jungk, 1979; Kemp, 1985; Williams, 1980).

Within West Germany itself, however, the ferment and turbulence of the 1960s and 1970s, and the numerous political movements of those decades (Huber, 1980; Guggenberger, 1980), pushed the attention of many political activists towards what could be *achieved* by mass communication projects and alternative media. Such groups were intent on pushing beyond a reaction of passive dismay at the seemingly inexorable encroachment of the power structure into the processes of public opinion formation (in Habermas' formulation, the 'refeudalization' of society, later to be termed the 'colonization of the life-world').

Many texts on alternative media were highly practical and specific in nature, as a list of some of the titles indicates: *Pages from Below, Counterpress, Airwave Squatters, What You Always Really Wanted to Know about Free Radio but Never Dared to Ask, The Alternative Press: Controversies, Polemics, Documents, Alternative Public Realm: Free Spaces for Information and Communication*. Influential in a more theoretical direction were Brecht's (1983) fragmentary but insightful meditations on the democratic potential of radio, and Enzensberger's much-translated 1969 *Kursbuch* article, 'Constituents for a Theory of Media' (1974), which urged the Left's attention to the possibilities of radio, photocopiers and other electronic media.

An influential and more theoretical text, however, was a work written on the bourgeois and proletarian public realms, *Public Realm and Experience*, by Oskar Negt and Alexander Kluge (1972). Some fundamental elements of their thesis were as follows. They sought to define a series of problems and possibilities for the working class and for dissident members of the intelligentsia allied with that class, in the effort to construct a future socialist society (16): 'to set out a framework for discussion which would open up the analytical concepts of political economy downwards into the real life experiences of human beings'. The text's fundamental problematic was that of classical Marxism: how does a class 'in' itself as an economic reality become a class acting consciously 'for' itself? The authors sought a partial answer in the development of a 'counter' public realm which would enable 'the commodity of labour-power to "speak" and to develop awareness', and thus to avoid being reduced simply to the status of object in the production process (111). They instanced trade unions as the most basic institution developed to meet this need. Their longer-term objective was the construction not simply of a counter-sphere, but of an autonomous proletarian public realm in which the dissonant experience and knowledge (*Erfahrung*) of the working class could be freely voiced, exchanged, debated, developed. In turn this new public realm could be expanded to a point at which it might supplant the processes and structures of the bourgeois public realm.

Underlying this discussion is their concept of working-class experience, hemmed in from self-expression. There is a presumption implicit in their analysis which would seem to have it that there is a kind of 'real' consciousness of this experience always struggling to well up from the proletariat. It is as though the bourgeois public realm were a cork, holding in the contents of a bottle under pressure. Lukács' 'false consciousness' problematic (1971) is not explicitly cited, except in an appendix, but seems to be lurking in the crevices. There is little question that many realities of working-class life and aspirations are excluded from major media (Downing, 1980), but a major conceptual leap exists between this recognition and the assertion of the proletariat's pristine *Erfahrung*, a leap which is theological rather than analytical. My sceptical stance does not deny exploitation, repression, political exclusion of wage-labour, but it does insist that the diverse sources and strands in working-class political awareness and its formation must be given their proper weight in analysis — a complexity which other elements in Negt and Kluge's discussion quite often illuminate. But if this 'bottled-up' image significantly distorts the actual situation, then the radical societal transformation their argument envisages can hardly be engendered so directly as their text seems to assume, via the development of an alternative or proletarian public realm. The entire process may be much more drawn out and problematic.

In general, their discussion of the working class is an uneasy amalgam of classical Marxism, observations drawn from empirical sociology, and Frankfurt School Marxist-Freudian analysis of proletarian culture and modes of life. The intelligentsia is conceived as divided into pro-bourgeois and pro-proletarian ideological tendencies (Negt and Kluge, 1972: 150–62), in an equally schematic manner.

Nonetheless, despite these conceptual simplifications, their emphasis on the centrality of exchange and debate within the process of seeking alternatives to capitalism (and sovietism) is of permanent relevance. Both Gramsci and Foucault in their different ways, not to mention Althusser, tended to underscore the prior structuring of communicative exchange by the power structure, thus implicitly downplaying the possibility of autonomous communication — though Gramsci predictably saw workers' councils, and later the revolutionary party, as the basic instrument of an emerging counter-hegemony. Negt and Kluge, however, held a less party-centric definition of the institutions of an alternative public realm. Even though they included the revolutionary party as one such institution, they also vigorously attacked the sectarianism and other flaws in their view commonly characterizing parties of the left (111–15, 293–4, 341–55), which they argued simply reproduced the features of the official public realm in a new guise.

The possibilities for societal change engendered by the exchange of debate in the capillaries of society are a facet of the processes of political communication neglected in much of the literature on hegemony, information, discourse and legitimation, which tends to convey a one-way, frozen pattern of communicative domination. The untidiness of the legitimation process, and especially the necessity to sustain hegemony through a reconstitutive process of debate and exchange are given much more weight within the problematic of the public realm/alternative public realm — and some would argue (Forester, 1985), within the problematic of Habermas' more recent work — than within these other conceptual frameworks. Negt and Kluge's argument ends up, however, rather awkwardly straddling a schematic Lukácsian false consciousness problematic, and a seemingly Gadamerian emphasis on the process of discovery through exchange.

Thus despite the vagueness of the term 'public realm' in English, its German source-word expresses not only a variety of ideas and processes, but particularly conveys the sense of activity, movement and exchange, meanings altogether missing from the usual connotations of 'public realm' or 'public sphere'. In English the term indicates a set of boundary-lines, a space; in German, the activities, the kinesis, within that space. The closest equivalent in English would be 'public forum' or 'public stage', but both of these connote a specific publication or occasion, not the sum of such opportunities.

Elsewhere (Downing, 1984) I have discussed both the purposes and conditions of successful operation of alternative media in creating an alternative public realm, though without employing that terminology. The examples varied by country, political system, purpose and organization. Nonetheless they had certain functions in common in most cases, notably the struggle to overcome political atomization in its numerous forms and to create an autonomous sphere in which experiences, critiques and alternatives could be freely developed. In turn, in a secular, sceptical eschatology, this sphere could be taken to prefigure an imaginable social democracy (if the term may be recuperated from its historical specificity). I would propose that Negt and Kluge's concept of a proletarian public realm should be reformulated along these lines, based on the actual experiences of organizing such media on a self-managed, democratic basis — itself a major alternative to the media hierarchies of the official public realm. This reformulation especially emphasizes the plain truth that the various alternative movements of the latter part of the twentieth century know much more clearly what they do not want (nuclear holocaust, nuclear pollution, militaristic budgets, capitalism, sovietism) than what they propose to put in their place. Since these movements eschew 'the transcendent correctness which Leninism implies' (Rowbotham et al., 1979: 47) as a latter-day form of authoritarian religion, only the development of debate within an alternative public realm offers any realistic chance of visualizing or constructing credible alternatives. Nor is this an exercise in utopian speculation, as anti-nuclear movement media demonstrate. Alternatives to nuclear war or the generation of nuclear waste are hardly issues which can be deferred, or left to a small set of hyperthyroid activists — or fatalistically to the nuclear powers.

In conclusion, it is appropriate to register the strange failure of analysts of the 'alternative public realm' to link the history of popular culture with this alternative domain. Popular culture is yet another polysemic, not to say often confused, concept, but it often denotes the production of alternative cultures from within the ranks of the general public (Burke, 1986; Eisenstein, 1986). The oppositional character of these alternatives, their level of development, the extent to which they have a symbiotic relationship with official, ruling class culture, their contemporary relation to 'mass culture', are all subjects for debate, but it can be recognized nonetheless that 'popular culture' broadly indicates the existence and productivity of an alternative public realm, stretching back many centuries, and characterizing class-divided societies. The public realm itself, as analysed by Habermas, began life as an alternative public realm. In focusing on anti-nuclear media, therefore, so far from merely squinting at a subculture, we are examining one major current instance of the dynamics of political and cultural change.

West German anti-nuclear media

West German anti-nuclear movements have had the most substantial impact, by several criteria, of any such European movements in the 1970s and 1980s. The Dutch peace movement drew proportionately even more demonstrators, and the British unilateralist movement had a longer history of militant action, but in West Germany the enduring issue was nuclear power, which always survived the fluctuating activity of the peace movement, while being linked to it for the duration of the latter's active phase. In France, due to the extraordinary party consensus in favour of the *force de frappe* and nuclear power, anti-nuclear opposition was largely marginalized. In Italy, after a late start, political ecology and peace politics began to gather momentum from 1982, as witness large demonstrations and the appearance of important reviews such as *La nuova ecologia* and *Papir*. But the German case is particularly absorbing, presenting a scenario apparently analogous to the renowned vigour of the Social Democratic movement before 1914, but sharply contrasted both in focus and in its de-centred, anti-authoritarian organizational moulds. The emergence of the Green Party in 1979–80 on to the national stage stood as one major expression of the confluence of these varying trends.

A full analysis of the reasons for this phenomenon is impossible here, but nonetheless two elements in the situation deserve brief comment. One has already been noted, namely the focus on nuclear power. The contrast with Britain is instructive. There the number of reactors built has been small, and environmental issues have often been adopted — with what effectiveness is another question — by the Labour Party, which contrasts with the SPD's early dismissal of their import (Rüdig and Lowe, 1986). The fundamental issue in Britain has been nuclear war, with the Labour Party's adoption of unilateralism into its platform acting as a spur to mobilization (Taylor, 1983; George and Marcus, 1984). Nuclear power, however, is not an issue which admits of political management in the same way as nuclear war (via disarmament talks or other political events). The enduring problem of the disposal of nuclear waste is an especially potent index of the issue's 'longevity'.

Within West Germany this logic expressed itself with particular force. Commitment to the countryside is especially entrenched in German culture, and the two rural sites chosen for nuclear waste reprocessing — first Gorleben in the north, later Wackersdorf in the south — succeeded in attracting many previously apolitical or conservative citizens in those regions and elsewhere into direct opposition. These however were only two highly publicized cases.

Already across the country by 1979 there were thousands of local civic initiatives groups (Bürgerinitiativen) concerned with environmental matters, in numbers which nearly equalled the membership of the parliamentary parties, i.e. around two million people (Mewes, 1983: 53–4).

In symbiosis with these initiatives was a social phenomenon referred to in West Germany as 'the alternative scene', 'die alternative Szene'. Its contours were familiar enough everywhere: bookstores, bars, coffee-shops, restaurants, food-stores, clothing shops, creches, therapy and medicine groups, fitness groups, micro-theatres, video-stores, musical groups, repairers, restorers, newspapers, magazines, illegal radio stations, cable TV slots, computer networks, squatters' groups, communes urban and rural, sometimes for all comers, sometimes especially for women, an ethnic group, gay people.

Much of this culture was what would be described as professional or artisanal, roughly 'middle class' as opposed to the designation 'proletarian'. Yet its political ambivalence was no more pronounced than in the popular culture of any other period. It was a zone of multiple disagreements, not a little self-delusion and potential careerism, but also of alertness to a variety of issues not quite permitted on to the plateau (Woolf, 1969) of the official public realm. It was also a zone of interaction for a considerable variety of purposes. Its foibles were often satirized (Hübsch, 1980; Baier, 1985), not least its intermittent pretensions to be somehow 'proletarian'. In the 1980s, however, it was a way of life, partial for most, total for some.

It should be stressed that whatever its flaws, this development had moved the Left from what used to be its highly ratiocinative, university character. As Negt and Kluge had observed in the early 1970s:

> It seems as though the left has a monopoly on rational discourse, the capacity for the concept, the analysis and the abstraction. The political right and its associated publications appear by contrast to have a monopoly on myths, dreams and images, i.e. to control the most important organisational means by which perspective, experience, desires, can satisfactorily reconcile themselves with each other. (Negt and Kluge, 1972: 293–4)

This tendentially middle-class public realm, then, has been the seedbed of many alternative media. A sociologically informed definition of this matrix is necessary in order to ground the concept 'alternative public realm' in West Germany, though that task cannot be pursued in any more detail here.

These then were the social and political sources of the ecology and peace movements, the latter mostly set into motion by the 1979 NATO decision to install Cruise and Pershing missiles. Both this history (Süss, 1986) and an attentive reading of opinion polls (Russett and DeLuca, 1983) combine to disprove the conservative contention that these political movements were pro-Moscow, or somehow controlled by Moscow (Vermaat, 1982).

West German anti-nuclear media: some case studies

These media fall into cross-cutting categories: a strictly anti-nuclear focus versus a general focus, and a party versus a movement basis. In terms of the media discussed here:

	General	Anti-nuclear
Movement	'Tageszeitung'	Atom
Party	The Greens' media	——

This subdivision is not watertight, however, as the Green Party exhibited many of the tendencies of a movement, and nuclear issues intertwine with such a wide range of others that the designation 'anti-nuclear' is in principle a very broad one.

The large numbers of all such media, mostly weeklies, monthlies and bi-monthlies, necessitates a selection. I have therefore taken key examples from each category, and will describe their character, their self-managed form of organization and their relationship to the anti-nuclear movement.

Die Tageszeitung (The Daily Newspaper) is a daily of the independent Marxist left which began publication in 1979 after three years of intensive debate among activists, mainly from Berlin and Frankfurt. Those involved were rooted in political currents of the 1960s and 1970s, including Marxists, feminists, ecologists, peace activists and others. They were agreed on three basic priorities: the urgent need for a paper which would not misrepresent the movements — compare the origins of *Libération* (Samuelson, 1978); that it should be national; and that it should represent the undogmatic left. By 1984 the paper was being printed in Berlin,

Frankfurt and Hanover, and had a second major editorial office in Hamburg, with small bureaus in Bochum, Bonn, Frankfurt, Cologne, Munich, Nuremberg and Stuttgart. In 1986 a Bremen edition was initiated. About a quarter of all sales were in Berlin, which despite the staff's efforts to ensure regional bases for the paper, tended to dominate editorially as well.

Energetic but sometimes inconclusive policy debates had frequently been a feature of the editorial collective, but during 1984–5 there came to be increasingly urgent debates inside the paper about its survival as a political voice. For a while the argument was that *die taz* (the paper's *Szene* name) should follow the example of *Libération* by making itself much less a paper of the left, and much more of a generalized young intellectuals' paper. This debate eventually subsided, but in September 1985, with its costs soaring and its financial survival under threat, the *taz* collective announced it had to raise subscriptions from 20,500 to 25,000 by the end of the year, or cease publication.

The response was remarkable: 29,000 subscriptions by the end of December 1985, and 32,000 by spring 1986. Interestingly, the response from journalists in major media was both helpful and energetic, with several articles in *Der Spiegel*, and visits from TV crews almost weekly. It seemed that those who worked full time in the official public realm were appreciative users of *die taz* as a welcome departure from the 'pack'. This was not an isolated instance: witness the similar sequence of events around Rome's *Il Manifesto* in 1983 (Downing, 1984: 246–8).

With the sudden onrush of funds, the paper took on more staff, expanded its format to twenty pages on weekdays and twenty-four on Saturdays, and began the Bremen edition. There were now four–five pages of national and six–seven pages of international news in each issue, an economics page and a cultural section. Yet no rigorous decisions concerning costs had been undertaken, and thus by 1987 the financial problem had essentially reproduced itself at a higher level of operation. The Bremen edition had lost a considerable amount of money, but was not the only financial haemorrhage. From March 1987, finances were stabilized through the offer of support loans at competitive interest rates and an advertising rate increase, based on a survey showing many readers to be quite affluent (moreso than the *tazler*). The Bremen edition's subsidy was reduced and, not least, national daily sales rose to 60,000.

Throughout this period *die taz* offered a consistent independent forum on the left for the exchange of views on a complete political spectrum, including nuclear and peace issues. The attention given in reporting to these latter varied in quantity and quality. For example in 1984 the paper had regular coverage of peace movement issues, including almost daily reports from the European Nuclear Disarmament movement conference in Perugia, but not of ecological issues, a situation directly derived from the specialisms of its staff at the time. By 1986, however, it had an ecology specialist once more, a top-flight investigative journalist, who provided excellent coverage both of the impact of Chernobyl on West Germany — largely unavailable through major media — and of the construction of a major toxic waste dump in the DDR, close to Hamburg, which was actively contracting to waste producers all over Europe. By then, however, its staff lacked a peace/disarmament specialist, although the superpower politics dimension of this issue, and the Green Party, were regularly covered.

Die Tageszeitung, however, was the only national daily to provide regular and critical coverage on nuclear issues. That alone gave it a major place inside the alternative public realm.

The reference to frequent policy debates inside the collective leads to a brief consideration of the internal editorial structure of the newspaper. Ultimate authority lay in a committee named Friends of the Alternative Daily Newspaper. Admission to its ranks was qualified on the basis of a history of political activism and a two-thirds vote of those present at a meeting. This was the body with powers to hire and fire. After three or four absences in a row, membership would be cancelled, although with quarterly meetings, this sanction was hardly a stringent one. Within the paper itself there was a staff of about 130. All staff were paid at the same rate, although from time to time this too came up for active discussion. A strenuous effort was made to ensure an equal gender balance inside the paper, although this policy was the fruit of lengthy protests by women staffers in the early years of the paper. Debates were conducted on policy by all parties, including administrative, graphics and layout, advertising and other non-journalistic staff.

Day-to-day editorial decisions were made by a group of six called the 'Co-ordination'. Since this group was in Berlin, it gave the staff there much more practical influence over policy than in the regional offices. Beyond this group, there were two individuals named as chief editors, but their tasks were purely to write systematic critiques of copy in the previous day's issue for discussion within the collective. Hiring and firing was not their direct responsibility, although in the former process their voice was an influential one.

The basic question of how effective such self-managed, discussion-based media can be is a large one. The experience of *die Tageszeitung* indicated that it can be fraught — indeed the term *Basisbürokratie* (grassroots bureaucracy) was coined in the West German alternative scene to denote the effective strangulation of action by interminable debate. Perhaps beyond inexperience and lack of funds, the insufficient ability to compromise, itself rooted in the utopian strain in socialist politics, tends to vitiate such projects. Rival utopias, rival mini-messiahs, supersensitivity to symbols, could all play their part in producing paralysis. Nonetheless, an eight-year history of a national daily newspaper, produced without political party funds or hierarchical authority, is its own demonstration of what is possible and effective in principle.

Atom, a bi-monthly magazine based in Göttingen, had had its genesis in the huge demonstrations against nuclear power plants in the winter of 1976–7. In its first year it printed between 2–3000 copies per issue, and by 1979 was bringing out 7500, with up to 10,000 for major events. In 1984 the numbers had fallen back to around 4000. By 1987 they had risen once more to 5–7000 copies an issue, with over 20,000 in the period after Chernobyl.

Until autumn 1984 it had been called *Atom Express*, but the new title marked its merger with another magazine entitled *atommüll-zeitung* (Nuclear Waste Newspaper), itself originally named *Gorleben Aktuell* (Dateline Gorleben). This latter had begun as a bulletin of the opposition to siting a nuclear waste reprocessing plant in Gorleben in the north-east, near the DDR. Its readership was much more likely to be rural and apolitical than that of *Atom Express*, which was largely based among the left in large northern cities. The merger combined these readerships and thereby provided a forum within which they could exchange views, offering considerable scope for the reinforcement of the anti-nuclear movement.

Atom was, self-evidently, a movement forum, albeit with a strictly anti-nuclear focus. Nuclear energy questions in West Germany were not its sole fare, however. Various issues carried articles on the peace movement during its most active phase, and on nuclear links between South Africa and the West, and between the Philippines under Marcos and the West. Its other contents were mostly a mixture of updates on nuclear news and movement activities, straightforwardly worded technical information on nuclear issues, and opinion exchange among activists. Hotly debated in this last section of the magazine during 1984–5, for instance, was the legitimacy of sabotage against physical installations as a tactic of anti-nuclear resistance.

The organization of *Atom* was much simpler than that of *die taz*. Based throughout its history in Göttingen, it was the most public project of the Göttingen Working Group Against Nuclear Energy, a leading university-based collective. (With the merger with *atommüllzeitung*, this base was extended.) The Working Group provided the magazine with many intellectual resources, although the publication's finances were self-sustaining from subscriptions and sales. The magazine's contents were also drawn from sources outside the working group. About a third were unsolicited, about another third were specifically commissioned, and the remainder was divided equally between strategy discussions and movement news and exchanges. *Atom* had excellent links with politically committed scientists and engineers around the country, and was able to call on them both to supply articles and to check out the material that sometimes arrived anonymously revealing some aspect of the nuclear industry. The checking process was to ensure that the revelation was not in actuality disinformation.

The staff consisted of about ten people, varying a little from year to year, with a couple more having a less direct involvement. Only one of these received a small stipend in order to co-ordinate production and distribution. The others were employed already. The editorial role of the working group was small. It was informed about upcoming publication plans, but had no veto power over material. The collective was fairly evenly balanced between men and women, and worked by consensus wherever possible, resorting to majority votes only on peripheral problems.

One important aspect of the history of the magazine, which acts as a salutory reminder that the concepts of 'public realm' and 'alternative public realm' may rapidly leave the conceptual level and become the subjects of power and control, was its harassment by the state. (It was not alone in this, as witness the constant banning of the Munich magazine *RadiAktiv* during 1986 and 1987 by the Bavarian *Land* government.) Two instances will suffice to make the point. One was the infiltration of the magazine by two undercover agents, whose identity was only uncovered after a year when their fictitious original addresses were noted. The second was a dawn police raid in March 1983, with about twelve policemen for each *Atom* member. They were initially charged under Article 129A of the Criminal Code, which deals with the very serious charge of 'advertising and support for a terrorist association'. (The ground cited was their publication of a letter from a group in which it announced that it had tried, and failed, to blow up a pylon.) After a major solidarity campaign in Western Europe, the charges were altered and fines of a thousand marks each were levied — far short of the heavy penalties provided for in Article 129A.

Reasoning, exchange, communication: these activities of the alternative public realm are not immune from the exercise of power on behalf of the official public realm. Casually as some observers may dismiss alternative media, their operation in many countries has nonetheless been of close concern to the power structure. The stronger the alternative sphere, the more this concern is likely to grow.

The Greens' media

This final section, dealing as it does with a multiplicity of publications, will be concerned mainly to convey the variety and scope involved. Fundamental to the Greens' origins and philosophy (Mewes, 1983) is their de-centred organization. Thus although the parliamentary Greens issued a weekly bulletin, *Die Grünen*, which reported on their activity in the federal parliament, and the Bonn office published a monthly magazine (*Grüner Basis-Dienst*/Green Grassroots Service), the core of the Greens' communicative work was local. Their pattern integrated well with the strongly regional character of German society. A list of some of their main monthly publications demonstrates this (see Table 1).

The writer has been unable to ascertain circulation figures for these publications, but their relative size probably gives an indication of the size of the *Land* Green party organization in question, and so also some sense of how widely they might be thought to circulate. As with *die Tageszeitung*, Berlin clearly dominated, followed in this instance by Hesse and Nordrheinwest-

TABLE 1
Some regional monthly publications of the Green Party 1981-5

Title	City	Year started	Size (approx. pp.)
GAL-rundbrief (The Greens/Alternative List roundletter)	Berlin	1981	96
Krokodil	Bremen	1983	8
Grüne Illustrierte Niedersachsen (Lower Saxony Green Illustrated)	Hanover	1983	32
Grünes Info	Bielefeld (Nordrhein-Westfalen)	1981	52
Grüne Rheinland-Pfälzer	Ludwigshafen (Rheinland Pfalz)	1983	24
Grüne Hessenzeitung (Green Hesse Newspaper)	Frankfurt	1981	76
Grüne Blätter (Green Pages/Leaves)	Stuttgart	1981	28
Grüne Zeiten (Green Times)	München	1981	36

falen. Some of these, like *Krokodil*, were in a very simple newspaper format, but most were more substantial magazines. By 1984 all were being printed on recycled paper.

Thematically all were fairly similar, dealing (beyond predictable issues of peace, nuclear energy, movement/party activity) with labour and unemployment, welfare, women's issues, local and regional elections, racism, international issues, welfare, media and animal protection, among other topics. The treatment was varied, taking the form of interviews, autobiographical statements, analytical articles and thinkpieces, usually with a good sprinkling of photographs and cartoons through the text. The language in most cases was straightforward, if not always striking. Each was edited by a collective, though the details of its organization in each case were not known to the writer. Contributors were drawn from the collective but also from many activists and readers, not necessarily members of the Green Party.

Collectively these constituted a major volume of communicative activity. They were joined, moreover, by still other monthly publications close to or actually part of the Green movement, such as *Stachel* (Thorn) in Berlin, *Kommune* in Frankfurt, *Konkret* in Hamburg and *Alternative Kommunalpolitik* in Bielefeld. With the exception of *Stachel*, the other three were heirs to the newspapers of three Maoist sects of the 1970s, which had formally or effectively moved into the area of Green politics in the early 1980s. Their pages were structured as a forum, not in the newspaper mode of the Marxist–Leninist sect. Their contents, although focusing heavily on nuclear issues, probably also touched on a wider range of political topics than the general run of Green publications. The difference seemed one of emphasis, rather than of substance.

Conclusions

It is evident that anti-nuclear movement media constituted a more vigorous alternative public realm in West Germany than other large Western European nations. (This article has, too, only focused on print media — there were important examples of film and radio anti-nuclear media as well.) In Britain, where there were but two national magazines (*Sanity* and the *END Journal*), and these centred almost exclusively on peace and disarmament topics — though a shift was becoming discernible by the end of 1986 in this respect — there was nothing comparable. This is not a judgement on the short-term political impact of the movements or their media in these countries. It could be seriously argued, however, that *over the longer term* an oppositional political culture was in the process of being much better nourished in West Germany than in Britain, and that this nourishment was not just a function of more widely circulating counter-information, but equally or even more so because of the experience of exchange inside a flourishing alternative public realm.

The utility of this concept, as was emphasized earlier, lies in its focus upon debate and exchange as the warp and weft of political change. Despite the rather arid flavour of the term as translated into English, it is to be hoped that this instance of popular oppositional culture, based on life-and-death nuclear issues, will serve to underscore the value of the term within debates on media and their cultural and political potential. Conceptualizing media simply as dominating agents of a kind of internal colonialism represents a crucial failure of perspective.

Note

I would like to acknowledge the assistance of a grant in the summer of 1984 from the Political Science panel of the PSC–CUNY Research Fund which enabled me to travel to Western Europe to conduct interviews with the staff of the main publications cited here. I should also like to thank especially Phil Hill, Reimar Paul and Stefan Schaaf for their assistance, both then and later.

References

Aubrey, C. (1982) *Nukespeak. The Media and the Bomb.* London: Comedia.

Baier, L. (1985) 'Die Gerührten und die Ungerührten', *Merkur*: 439–40.

Brecht, B. (1983) 'Radio as a Means of Communication', in A. Mattelart and S. Siegelaub (eds) *Communication and Class Struggle, Vol. 2, Liberation/ Socialism*, pp. 169–71. New York: International General.

Burke, P. (1986) 'Revolution in Popular Culture', in N. Porter and M. Teich (eds) *Revolution in History*. Cambridge: Cambridge University Press.

Demac, D. (1984) *Keeping America Uninformed*. New York: Pilgrim Press.

Downing, J. (1980) *The Media Machine*. London: Pluto Press.

Downing, J. (1984) *Radical Media: The Political Experience of Self-managed Communication*. Boston: South End Press.

Downing, J. (1986) 'Government Secrecy and the Media in Britain and the United States', in P. Golding et al. (eds) *Communicating Politics: Mass Communications and the Political Process*. Leicester and New York: Leicester University Press and Holmes & Meier.

Eisenstein, E. (1986) 'On Revolution and the Printed Word', in N. Porter and M. Teich (eds) *Revolution in History*. Cambridge: Cambridge University Press.

Elliott, P. (1986) 'Intellectuals, the "Information Society" and the Disappearance of the Public Sphere', in R. Collins et al. (eds) *Media, Culture and Society: A Critical Reader*, pp. 105–15. London: Sage.

Enzensberger, H.M. (1974) 'Constituents of a Theory of the Media', in H.M. Enzensberger *The Consciousness Industry*. New York: Seabury Press.

Forester, J. (ed.) (1985) *Critical Theory and Public Life*. Cambridge, Mass.: MIT Press.

Garnham, N. (1986) 'Intellectuals and the Public Sphere', in P. Golding et al. (eds) *Communicating Politics*. Leicester: Leicester University Press.

George, B. and Marcus, S. (1984) 'Unilateralism's Second Wave: the 1983 General Election and After', *Political Quarterly* 55(1).

Gowing, M. (1978) *Reflections on Atomic Energy History*. Cambridge: Cambridge University Press.

Guggenberger, B. (1980) *Bürgerinitiativen in der Parteiendemokratie*. Stuttgart: Kohlhammer.

Habermas, J. (1962) *Strukturwandel der Öffentlichkeit*. Berlin and Neuwied: Luchterhand. (Parts are translated in *New German Critique* 3, 1974, and in Mattelart and Siegelaub, 1983.)

Hertsgaard, M. (1983) *Nuclear Inc.* New York: Pantheon Books.

Hilgartner, S., R.C. Bell and R. O'Connor (1982) *Nukespeak: The Selling of Nuclear Technology in America.* New York: Penguin Books.

Huber, J. (1980) *Wer Soll Das Alles Andern?* Berlin: Rotbuch Verlag.

Hübsch, H. (1980) *Alternative Öffentlichkeit.* Frankfurt: Fischer.

Jungk, R. (1979) *The Nuclear State.* London: John Calder.

Kemp, R. (1985) 'Planning Public Sharing and the Politics of Discourse', in J. Forester (ed.) *Critical Theory and Public Life*, pp. 177–201. Cambridge, Mass.: MIT Press.

Kogawa, T. (1985) 'Free Radio in Japan', in D. Kahn and D. Neumaier (eds) *Cultures in Contention.* Seattle: Falling Comet Press.

Lowe, K. (1983) *Opening Eyes and Ears.* Geneva: World Council of Churches.

Lukács, G. (1971) *History and Class Consciousness.* London: Merlin Press.

Mattelart, A. and Siegelaub, S. (eds) (1983) *Communication and Class Struggle, Vol. 2, Liberation/Socialism.* New York: International General.

Mewes, H. (1983) 'The West German Green Party', *New German Critique* 28.

Negt, O. and Kluge, A. (1972) *Öffentlichkeit Und Erfahrung: zur Organisations-analyse von bürgerlichen und proletarischen Öffentlichkeit.* Frankfurt: Suhrkamp. (A section is translated in Mattelart and Siegelaub, 1983.)

Rowbotham, S. et al. (1979) *Beyond the Fragments.* London: Islington Community Press.

Rüdig, G. and Lowe, D. (1986) 'The "Withered Greening" of British Politics: a Study of the Ecology Party', *Political Studies* 34(4).

Samuelson, F.M. (1978) *Une Fois il'était libré.* Paris: Le Seuil.

Taylor, R. (1983) 'The British Peace Movement and Socialist Change', in R. Miliband and J. Saville (eds) *The Socialist Register 1983.* London: Merlin Press.

Vermaat, J. Emerson (1982) 'Moscow Fronts and the European Peace Movement', *Problems of Communism* (November/December).

Williams, R. (1980) *The Nuclear Power Decision: British Policies, 1953–78.* London: Croom Helm.

Woolf, R.P. (1969) 'Beyond Tolerance', in R.P. Woolf et al., *A Critique of Pure Tolerance.* London: Cape.

13

The popular press and political democracy

Colin Sparks

There is considerable contemporary concern in Britain about the state of the newspaper press. Although developments in this field have not been subject to the same sort of intense scrutiny that the rather more dramatic occurrences in the electronic media have attracted, there are nevertheless many voices expressing worries about what are seen as new trends. The most common charge is that a great part of the press has effectively severed its links with political life.

This is an important question, since it is the historic claim of the newspaper press to be one of the central guarantors of political democracy. The popular self-definition of the press as the 'Fourth Estate' points precisely in that direction. Both Macaulay in 1828, and Carlyle twelve years later, had political matters on their minds when they gave the term popular currency and both were certainly aware of its echoes of the most famous formulation about the Third Estate. It is worthwhile remembering that for Macaulay:

> The gallery in which the reporters sit has become a fourth estate of the realm. The publication of the debates, a practice which seemed full of danger to the great safeguards of public liberty, is now regarded by many persons as a safeguard tantamount, and more than tantamount, to all the rest together. (Macaulay, 1907: 71)

Recognition of the direct link between the press, liberty and the extension of political democracy did not necessarily imply approval. Carlyle was even more vigorous: 'Printing, which come necessarily out of Writing, I say often, is equivalent to Democracy', which he

Media, Culture and Society (SAGE, London, Newbury Park, Beverly Hills and New Delhi), Vol. 10 (1988), 209–223

did not regard as a very Good Thing (n.d.: 392). The plebeian proponents of press freedom were also the advocates of mass democracy, and the struggle over the 'taxes on knowledge' was for them one major part of the general struggle for the extension of the franchise. That concern continued. Forty years ago, a Royal Commission on the Press could confidently argue that: 'The Press may be judged, first, as the chief agency for instructing the public on the main issues of the day. The importance of this function needs no emphasis' (RCP, 1949: par.361, p.100) and go on to wax extremely lyrical about the 'democratic form of society' and the role of the press therein. Thirty years after that, the 1977 Royal Commission on the Press, while noting the 'entertainment' role of the press, still took the 'serious functions' as the acid test of press performance (RCP, 1977: par. 2.1, p. 8).

In much of the world the link between the press and politics remains a powerful and influential one: there are too many banned papers, jailed journalists and cowed editors for anyone to imagine that the link between at least some newspapers and political life is not a central concern to our rulers. In Britain, however, things are perceived differently. It is not so much that critics of the press are concerned with the political positions adopted by the press that interests us here: the support for one particular political party is such an obvious and pronounced aspect of the press that it hardly seems worthwhile adding to the mound of literature on that topic. Our interest is in the fact that in recent years the focus of criticism has shifted somewhat and is now concerned with the overall content of the press. This position is well summarized in the following:

> The trivialisation and the lowering of standards within the press has had three major detrimental effects on our democracy. These effects go well beyond legitimate concerns about bias in politics and touch the deepest nerves of our society.
>
> First of all, it has debased the level at which political and social debate is conducted and trivialised the most important issues of the day.
>
> The second effect derives from the fact that the vast majority of working people depend for their reading on the tabloids. It is that the tabloids are producing a gradual disenfranchisement of ordinary people from accuracy of fact, from the stimulation of debate and from discussion on the serious aspects of major issues of the day.
>
> The third way in which lower press standards are undermining democracy

> involves a specific charge. It is that the press has effectively ceased to be the people's "watchdog" over government . . .
>
> These three problems of trivialisation, disenfranchisement and reluctance to challenge the government of the day are issues which should cause serious concern to every single person who treasures our democracy. (Todd, 1987: 3–4)

Such a critique deserves taking seriously not only because it comes from the leader of what is still the largest organization of workers in Britain, and one which has been prepared to invest considerable sums of money in an ill-fated attempt, the *News on Sunday* project, to produce a popular alternative to the existing tabloid press, but also because it rightly locates the issue at the centre of political life. And although the case is here argued in terms of specificities of the British press, there are strong grounds for thinking that it may be of more general application.

Britain is a stable bourgeois democracy. It has been one in substance since 1929, and in final form since 1950, and therefore the adult lives of the vast majority of its citizens have been passed in such a political order. The population has an enormous experience of life in such a system and very few have any direct knowledge of any alternative, better or worse. There has been a fairly regular alternation of the political complexion of governments and there has not, as yet, been any serious threat to, or interruption of, that process. In that sense Britain is an example of a 'mature' bourgeois democracy in a way which it shares only with the USA among the major capitalist countries. In Europe, only Sweden has similar historical experiences. It therefore does not seem unreasonable to assume that the nature and functioning of the press in Britain illustrates the 'normal' functioning of the press in a society with this sort of social and political structure. One would, of course, expect differences arising from peculiar local traditions, circumstances and so forth, but in general the model prevailing here can be thought of as representative.

If the claim by Ron Todd is true, then it would seem to follow that the normal state of affairs in a bourgeois democracy is that the vast majority of the citizens are denied information which they need to function as political citizens and therefore, obviously, the claims of this form of political life to represent the 'will of the people' are clearly false. Put in more formal language, it is a condition of the existence of a 'public sphere' that 'access is guaranteed to all citizens' (Habermas, 1979: 198).

It is therefore a matter of some importance to ask whether the claim is in fact true.

Todd is not alone in his perception and, like others, he focuses on the polarization of the press into 'quality' and 'tabloid' components. Baistow is even more definite about the limits of the latter, writing that 'the drift towards the gutter and the subordination of news content to sensation, scandal, jazzy packaging and million-pound bingo in the scramble for sales have provided the most dramatic evidence of the tabloid revolutions' radical impact upon popular journalism' (Baistow, 1985: 57). The five 'quality' papers do indeed provide extensive information about the social, economic and political world, and it is undoubtedly the case that their readership is both very small in number, even taken together, and, relatively socially privileged. The majority of newspaper readers have to make do with the tabloid press, whose attention to political and economic life is both intermittent and abbreviated. On the face of it, then, Todd and his co-thinkers have a point.

There are, however, a number of objections which are worth considering. In the first place, it might be claimed that this is not a new development. In fact, Habermas, in the article quoted earlier, cited the press of the late eighteenth and early nineteenth centuries as the true organs of the 'public sphere' and argued that the commercialization of the press since around 1830 had been part of the 'refeudalization' of the public sphere, in which political life was increasingly conducted as a private matter between the state and powerful corporate actors. This is overstating the case to some extent since there seems to be no necessary reason why the motives of an owner should lead to exactly the type of press we have today: after all, if knowledge and free debate were the royal road to maximum profits then it would be a very foolish capitalist who filled a paper with anything else. More substantially, there is a long history of complaints that the press is becoming trivialized. Some of the early examples of content analysis were addressed to this question, recording a shift towards the 'trivial' in the US press of the 1890s (Krippendorf, 1980: 14). Closer to home, the journalist Jane Soames, writing of the British press in the mid-1930s, lamented that 'there is nothing to replace the lively uncensored comment upon public affairs which our great-grandfathers assumed to be essential to the formation of public opinion' (Soames, 1938: 108). Nearly thirty years later Raymond Williams, after a content analysis of the British press, wrote: 'the formulas seem to be hardening: "the masses" — crime, sex, sport, personalities, entertainment, pictures; "the minority" — traditional politics, traditional arts, briefings on popular trends' (Williams, 1968: 89–90).

It does seem likely that the processes which are the subject of contemporary criticism have been going on for rather longer than is often thought. One stage in the transformation of the press from an organ of political enlightenment into a compendium of interesting items was the emergence of the 'new journalism' of the 1880s (Lee, 1976: 117–30) and it took a major step forward with the drive towards mass circulation papers in the inter-war years (Curran and Seaton, 1981: 123:31). This has important consequences, in that it broadens the debate from outrage at a particular title or proprietor, but it does not really alter the main charge. It is useful to be reminded that the sort of apocalyptic denunciations directed at Rupert Murdoch by Peter Kellner (1987: 250–51) and *The Sun* by John Pilger (1987), in the name of some supposed recent golden age which he and his methods destroyed, are part of a much longer tendency. Indeed, it strengthens our concern with the 'normality' of the development since we would appear to be considering not a recent and therefore possibly temporary aberration but a long-term trend. We are not in a position to say that things are getting worse more quickly now than in the past, but we might note that Professor McQuail's attempt at a tripartite division of the press into 'quality', 'middle' and 'popular' does not seem to recommend itself to current critics (McQuail, 1977: 31). The evidence of opinion and research appears to be that the mass circulation press in a bourgeois democracy has only partially fulfilled the proclaimed aims of the press as an element of political life.

The second major objection is that, while it is true that the mass circulation press devotes relatively little attention to political life, the primary functions of constituting the 'public sphere' are now played by broadcasting, and in particular by television. This is one of the most powerful arguments mounted to defend the existence of publicly regulated broadcasting, since it is argued that these systems have a universal reach and that any fragmentation of these institutions and their audiences would result in the collapse of one of the few guarantors of the wide dissemination of political information, ideas and debate.

The first thing to say about this is that, in the form given above, it accepts the substance of the charge that the newspaper press is not an adequate mechanism for informing the citizen since, if it was, broadcasting would not have this vital role. The second point is that any truth that it may have looks like vanishing rather rapidly as the international restructuring of broadcasting continues. The third point is that even though television, and radio, do provide political and economic information at a time at which they are available to mass audiences, and although the priorities of reporting, the 'news-values', of TV news approximate rather more closely to the norms of the 'quality' rather than the 'popular' press, the amount of information they provide is extremely limited compared with that of the quality press. Consequently, anyone relying solely on the television news for political and economic information will be less equipped than a person reading the quality press, and will indeed have only a very limited account of the world. Finally, the evidence of recent research seems to suggest that the claim of TV news as the 'main source' is in fact untrue. Robinson and Levy:

> . . . described the barriers television faces in effectively transmitting news stories: too little airtime to tell most stories in sufficient depth; an easily distracted, often inattentive audience; the lack of viewer control over the pace of story presentation; the absence of clear separation between stories or story elements; inadequate historical perspectives or causal explanations to make the story meaningful; frequent inconsistencies between words and pictures; and the lack of redundancy to give more than one perspective. (Robinson and Levy, 1986: 232)

We do not need to share their belief that there either is or should be a 'meaning' to TV news which the audience fail to understand, or that there is some fixed quantity of 'information' which they should 'gain', in order to agree with their analysis of the problems associated with relying on TV news. The objection based on the replacement of the newspaper by broadcasting as a mechanism for enabling the citizen thus seems to be untenable.

The third major objection to this position is that the lack of political information in the popular press is an artefact of a particular and restricted definition of politics. On this account, if one broadens one's notion of politics from the traditional concern with the state and its works to include a much wider range of life experiences, then one would find that the popular press is indeed stuffed with politics. Thus Seaton and Pimlott locate the 'political' element of the media very widely and suggest that: 'It might be argued that non-political media coverage is politically more important in the long run than overtly political material because of the role of the media in establishing or modifying acceptable values' (Seaton and Pimlott, 1987: x). This is a persuasive argument, since it is impossible to deny that, for example, sports reporting is saturated with politics and does indeed loom very large in much of the popular press. We can, however, see the obvious difficulty with this position if we recast it in more formal terms. The argument is that the development of 'late capitalism' has indeed led to the atrophy of the classical public sphere, but that this has been replaced by a politicization of other areas of what was previously 'civil society', with the consequence that there has been the development of a number of different public spheres concerned with particular areas (Keane, 1984: 29). However correct it might be to argue that sport is deeply penetrated by chauvinism of various kinds, and however worthy it might be to attempt to constitute a public sphere in which this can be subjected to a rational critique, it is shockingly naive to imagine that such an activity is a substitute for, or even comparable with, the classical questions of state politics, for example war. Politics may be much more than struggle over the direction of the state, although in modern capitalism that is in itself a great deal, but it is also irreducibly centred upon that struggle. Any theory, then, which celebrates the politicization of the apolitical at the expense of the depoliticization of the political thus restricts itself to the horizons set for it by the existing order.

The final objection we must consider is very similar. In its journalistic form it expresses itself as 'giving the readers what they want'. In its more sophisticated form, this position argues that the common elements which constitute the mass taste have a positive value. The populist position argues that the readers are not passive dupes: they have the opportunity to purchase quality titles but make an active choice to buy the popular press. They do not passively consume the material they have chosen but discriminate within it and find in even the most unpromising material elements which speak to their concerns and experience (Holland, 1983).

We have no quarrel with this position in so far as it seeks to explain human behaviour. We wish only to point out that it is hardly an objection to the position on the nature of the popular press that we have outlined above. On the contrary, it provides an extremely forceful account of why that press is the way it is, and provides the starting point for a fuller analysis.

There is a well-developed account of the development of the British press, most clearly articulated by James Curran, which argues that in a society of commodity production with very sharp income stratification and relatively unrestricted advertising, there will be a tendency for the press to evolve into two forms. One will seek to reach a relatively small number of rich readers in order to maximize the specialized advertising revenue which forms a very large part of its total income. The other section of the press will seek to reach a very large audience and will depend more on cover price than general advertising for its income. We find this most persuasive and do not wish to challenge the overall analysis. However, it does not explain why the minority press should be relatively rich in political and economic material while the mass press should be relatively rich in scandals and so forth, particularly since Curran himself has shown in some detail that the reading tastes of the audience of the quality press are in many respects strikingly similar to those of the mass audience (Curran et al., 1980: 303–5). After all, there is no obvious and compelling reason of press economics as to why it should not be the other way around. The content of the popular press can only be explained by the dual action of the economics of the market and the nature of mass taste.

Clearly, there are objective limitations on mass consumption of the quality press. It is relatively expensive, sometimes hard to obtain and it demands quite a high level of cultural competence in order to consume it. However, these are secondary factors: despite low incomes and poor education a proportion of manual workers, for example, do read even the *Financial Times*. The vast majority do not because they do not choose to.

The implications of this analysis are very important, although they may discomfort some of its supporters. In an advanced and stable bourgeois democracy, the vast majority of citizens voluntarily choose not to be as well informed as possible about the political and economic life of the society that they allegedly control. Indeed, they choose a press which systematically prioritizes other matters over and above political life.

There are three possible responses to this fact. The first is to blame the producers — proprietors, editors, journalists or whoever. This is the response chosen by Todd. It seems to us wrong since it mistakes the moral irresponsibility of the agent for the underlying cause. The second is to blame the consumers. This is again an error since it assumes that there is some perfect standard, usually the preference of the writer, against which purchasers may be judged. The third is to accept the reality for what it is and enquire into its consequences.

If we take seriously the implications of the fact that the consumers choose this sort of newspaper because it speaks to them about things which matter to them then we are speaking more about social and political life in a stable bourgeois democracy than about the nature of the press. Whatever people might say to pollsters or politicians, their day-to-day practice demonstrates that they are much more interested in sport and entertainment and sexual scandal than in knowing about the world of politics. Since this practical judgement is based on a lifetime of experience it might be open to us to deplore it but we can hardly claim that it is based on ignorance. A much more satisfactory explanation for this state of affairs is that political and economic power in a stable bourgeois democracy is so far removed from the real lives of the mass of the population that they have no interest, in either sense, in monitoring its disposal. The infrequent rituals of elections apart, there exist few if any channels whereby any opinion that anyone might hold can be implemented or even heard. Football matches take place every week in winter and anyone who cares to pay for a ticket can go along and cheer. Consequently it should not come as a surprise to find that political life is most fully covered in just those periods when people get a say, however limited, in political life, whereas football matches get reported in detail with great regularity. If it is indeed the case that the amount of political and economic information available is decreasing in the mass press, then this would tend to confirm the hypothesis that as people have more and more experience of their place in the bourgeois democracy they display less and less interest in it. The reverse would also tend to hold good: those populations emerging from more repressive societies — fascist or Stalinist for example — would be expected to have a much greater degree of interest in the possibilities of political life since they have not yet learnt the tight limits of such activities. We might advance the proposition that the more stable and established a bourgeois democracy is the less interest the mass of the population will have in its workings and the more apolitical and 'trivial' the popular press will become.

In this perspective the anomaly to be explained is why quite large numbers of people still continue to choose newspapers which do provide substantial amounts of political and economic material. What is it that persuades a minority of people in Britain that it is more important to them to know about the US presidential contenders than about the sex life of pop stars? (Often, of course, there is some overlap . . .) In some cases this is undoubtedly because they wield substantial amounts of social, economic and political power and they need information on which to base their decisions. This group is a small number of people, as is the number of those who read these papers because they look forward to the day when bourgeois democracy is no longer a stable system. Others read these sorts of papers because they provide specialized information which is important to their working lives. But surely only a small proportion of the six and a half million people who read the quality press in Britain in 1985 were the ruling class, or revolutionary socialists, or wanting to change their white-collar jobs? The bulk of the daily readership of the quality press must consist of people who read papers of this kind because they believe it is important to them to know about the world. They believe this despite the experiences which have led the vast majority of their fellow citizens to reject such a belief and despite the fact that it is very difficult to see the concrete utility of any of this information. We might conclude that these people are very well educated but very credulous.

The fact that the market conditions and political realities of bourgeois democracy increasingly tend to persuade people to opt out of effective participation in the public sphere is further illuminated by the internationalization of the press. There is a well-known tendency towards the international ownership of the press and there are more recent tendencies, particularly in magazine publishing, towards the internationalization of operations. Both of these are important developments for study even if their impact is often grossly overestimated: the idea that the nationality of a press baron, and still more the nationality of the baron's holding company, might be of importance seems to us one of the sillier ideas about the press ever espoused. Our concern here is with the recent emergence of an 'international' press. By this we primarily mean those papers which now produce international editions. There is a fairly long tradition of this in magazine publishing, with the major US news magazines having long had an international scope, and the British based *Economist* has now joined them. There is also a long tradition of the 'expatriate' newspaper: the *International Herald Tribune* was 100 years old in 1987. There has, however, been a recent increase in the number of newspapers operating internationally, and arguably a change in their character. In the case of the *International Herald Tribune*, it is argued that the change began after the end of the Second World War with the dominance of the US in the life of 'the West' and a consequent increase in interest on the part of the world elite in the political and economic life of the USA (Vinocur, 1987).

The other two most obviously 'international' newspapers are the overseas editions of *The Wall Street Journal*, published in Europe and Asia, and the *Financial Times*, published in Europe and the USA. Both of these newspapers are the recent products of long-distance transmission and remote printing, as are the two Japanese-language and one Arabic newspapers which are published in Europe. In October 1987, the Maxwell Communications Corporation announced plans for a European newspaper. It is clear that, however problematic they may be at present, and however small their readership, these types of papers represent an important new development.

To consider only the English-language papers, we would distinguish them as examples of a different kind of newspaper because although they retain a considerable amount of material generated by their home papers, and significant elements of editorial control continue to reside in the home paper, the tendency in each of them is towards a more global sense of news. Although all the papers remain very dependent on the resources of their home news organizations, their editors expressed considerable concern with grappling with the unfamiliar problems of producing a newspaper whose readership was not constricted by the political and economic life of a national state (Cass, 1987; Keatly, 1987). The strategy of the papers is clear both objectively and subjectively: as the world financial market has become internationalized, with major interconnected centres in Tokyo, London and New York, so there has been a growth of the need for the international production of a newspaper aimed at serving that international market.

The readership of these newspapers is an international one: only about 10 percent of the readership of the European edition of the *Financial Times* are British expatriates, for example, and this proportion falls as the circulation rises. The readership of all three papers is also a very rich and powerful group. In the case of *The Wall Street Journal Europe*, taking the figures for 1985, 71.6 percent of subscribers were described as 'top management', and 52.9 percent worked for companies employing 1000 or more people. More than 90 percent were college educated. Their median employment income was $61,500. More than 20 percent earned more than $100,000 (*The Wall Street Journal*, 1985: 65–9). Of the European readership of the international edition of the *Financial Times*, in 1987, 71.4 percent of readers were board members and 80 percent earned more than £20,000 (approximately $32,000) per annum (FT, 1987). One in ten of the readers of the *International Herald Tribune* is a dollar millionaire. These people are well described by Nigel Harris:

> The elders of the world's tribes reveal the unification of the social system in the astonishing uniformity of their consumption patterns; or rather in the acceptance by all the world's rulers of the cultural style of the dominant section. Once the suit was the mark of Europe's tribes. But now even the Saudis increasingly don them abroad; they have long driven the same cars . . . At work the world of power is the same, the same desk in the same air-conditioned office, the same telephone to bark command, the same gadgets, the same potted plant and discreet secretary. At leisure, they bask on the same beaches, golf on the same links, and hob-nob in the same air-corridors . . . (Harris, 1983: 18)

We might add: and they read the same newspapers. The significance of this latter fact is obscured for those of us who speak a quaint, or perhaps cute, local dialect of the current dominant world language. It is revealed much more sharply and negatively if we consider the two Japanese international papers: these are perforce largely emigre papers due to the current low level of international diffusion of Japanese. The emerging world newspapers are in English, which is not the mother tongue of the majority of their readers.

Natural language has always been one of the key points of conflict in cultural and political nation-building. One of the claims to legitimacy of the existing press systems is that they are in principle available to all citizens since they are produced in the language of those citizens. This claim has always masked a certain hypocrisy and the marginalization of alternative tongues, but its acceptance at least in large part is obviously a condition for the press playing a role in the construction of a public sphere. Unless the information about political and economic life is in a language that the citizens can understand then it can hardly be public. The *Financial Times* is in principle available to the building labourer in Birmingham in a way that it is not to one in Kyoto, Dusseldorf or Madrid.

The emergence of an international press is a symptom that the national state is no longer the decisive arena of political life and a pointer to the emergence of an embryonic international public sphere. The class of people who inhabit that sphere not only wish to read the densest of available newspapers but are prepared to make the effort to do so in a language not their own. They do this because they need to run their daily lives. Those who, for whatever reason, have not mastered this symbolic system are excluded from that public sphere. Indeed, we can conceive of the theoretical possibility that advertisers might, in a particular national instance, find that they could reach their target audience of the rich and powerful more efficiently through the international press than the local quality papers, which would thus be without their economic grounding and would, left to the market, die. All that would then be left to the mass of the population would be a press effectively devoid of political and economic information and, if the international press happened to be in a language they had not mastered, they would be completely denied such information. The capitalist market would have destroyed the link between the capitalist press and capitalist democracy.

The provision of an international system of press-based information and opinion is thus dependent on an audience's desire for such material and corresponds to the development of real political and economic power which transcends the boundaries of the national state. Those who run the world economy have the information they need. Those who run the national economies and political systems have the information they need. Those who are forced to run by these interlocking systems have the private world as an attractive escape.

Two things follow from this. The first is purely conceptual. It is surely time to re-emphasize James Curran's point that we must stop thinking and writing about some unified category of the '*news paper*' (Curran et al., 1980: 305). Whatever they may have in common in their production, the two ends of the press spectrum are clearly different sorts of cultural commodities serving different sorts of markets and providing different sorts of satisfactions. We are unlikely to understand their social functions if we continue to use a blanket category designed for a quite different situation.

The second is more to do with politics. We have here argued that the nature of the modern popular 'press' is derived from structural features of capitalist democracy. It follows that all the legislative tinkering and noble alternative dreaming is doomed to failure so long as these social and political conditions persist. Subsidies could, no doubt, support a highly informative popular press, but it is most unlikely that they would persuade more people to be more interested in a political world with which they have no permanent link other than as subjects. The same structural realities, rather than the accidents of personality, are at the root of the failure of attempts to short-circuit the press system by borrowing its forms and to pursue worthy ends through: 'Responsible human interest stories (which) have integrity and can avoid the tabloids' tacky sentimentality . . . (and) can also provide sound information and background woven into the narrative' (NoS. n.d.: 10).

It does not follow from this that the outlook is one of Orwellian gloom. We have argued that the modern press is the product of the conditions of life in a stable capitalist democracy. The infrequent and ritualized political participation of such an order does not exhaust the possibilities for popular political life. Certainly, a ballot every few years is not the simple and unchanging definition of 'democracy': it would certainly be as unrecognizable as such to the men who gave us the term as their attitude to women, slaves and non-citizens would be unacceptable to us. It might also strike the honest observer that 'banana monarchy' is a likelier description of the future of Britain than 'stable capitalist democracy'. If modern press in Britain is the genuine product of the social and economic realities of the society, and of the working class's perception of its place within that society, then a change in those social and economic realities can lead both to a changed perception of the nature and scope of political life and to an irresistable demand for a different, more political, press.

References

Baistow, T. (1985) *Fourth Rate Estate*. London: Comedia.

Carlyle, T. (n.d.) 'On Heroes, Hero-Worship, and the Heroic in History', in *Sartor Resartus: Heroes and Hero Worship*. London: Dent (probably about 1900).

Curran, J. and Seaton, J. (1981) *Power Without Responsibility*. London: Fontana.

Curran, J., Douglas, A. and Whannel, G. (1980) 'The Political Economy of the Human Interest Story', in A. Smith (ed.) *Newspapers and Democracy*. Cambridge, Massachusetts: MIT Press.

FT (1987) *Information Pack*. London: The Financial Times.

Habermas, J. (1979) 'The Public Sphere' in A. Mattelart and S. Seigelaub (eds) *Communication and Class Struggle, Vol. I*. New York: International General.

Harris, N. (1983) *Of Bread and Guns*. London: Penguin.

Holland, P. (1983) 'The Page Three Girl Speaks to Women, Too', *Screen* 24(3) (May/June): 84–102.

Keane, J. (1984) *Public Life and Late Capitalism*. Cambridge: Cambridge University Press.

Kellner, P. (1987) 'Goodbye to *The Times*' in J. Seaton and B. Pimlott (eds) *The Media in British Politics*. Aldershot: Avebury.

Krippendorf, K. (1980) *Content Analysis*. London: Sage.

Lee, A.J. (1976) *The Origins of the Popular Press 1855–1914*. London: Croom Helm.

Macaulay, T.B. (1907) 'Hallam', in *Critical and Historical Essays, Vol. i*. London: Dent.

McQuail, D. (1977) *The Analysis of Newspaper Content*. Cmnd. 6810–4. London: HMSO.

NoS (n.d.) *New on Sunday: Final Report of the Feasibility Study*. London: News on Sunday (probably 1986).

Pilger, J. (1987) 'The Birth of a new *Sun*?' in *The New Statesman* 2, (January).

RCP (1949) *Report of the Royal Commission on the Press*. Cmnd. 7700. London: HMSO.

RCP (1977) *Final Report of the Royal Commission on the Press*. Cmnd. 6810. London: HMSO.

Robinson, J.P. and Levy, M.R. (1986) *The Main Source*. London: Sage.

Seaton, J. and Pimlott, B. (1987) 'Introduction', in J. Seaton and B. Pimlott (eds) *The Media in British Politics*. Aldershot: Avebury.

Soames, J. (1938) *The English Press*, 2nd edn. London: Lindsay Drummond.

Todd, R. (1987) *Henry Hetherington Lecture: The Media and the People*. London: TGWU.

Wall Street Journal (1985) *Worldwide Subscriber Study*. New York: Dow Jones.

Williams, T. (1968) *Communications*. London: Penguin.

Interviews cited in text

Cass, A. (1987) Editor *Financial Times: International Edition*.

Keatly, R. (1987) Editor *Wall Street Journal Europe*.

Vinocur, J. (1987) Editor *International Herald Tribune*.

14

From production to propaganda?

Philip Schlesinger

Daniel C. Hallin, *The 'Uncensored War': The Media and Vietnam.*
New York, Oxford: Oxford University Press, 1986.
Edward S. Herman and Noam Chomsky, *Manufacturing Consent:
The Political Economy of the Mass Media.* New York: Pantheon
Books, 1988.
David E. Morrison and Howard Tumber, *Journalists at War:
The Dynamics of News Reporting During the Falklands Conflict.*
London: Sage, 1988.
Justo Villafañé, Enrique Bustamante and Emilio Prado, *Fabricar
Noticias: las Rutinas Productivas en Radio y Televisión.* Barcelona:
Editorial Mitre, 1987.
Robin Erica Wagner-Pacifici, *The Moro Morality Play: Terrorism
as Social Drama.* Chicago and London: University of Chicago
Press, 1988.

I

The interrelation between sources and news media is a key issue
for the sociology of journalism. The study of media in Western
capitalist democracies is inextricably bound up with central social
institutions that seek to manage the flow of information. Hence,
the activities of the machinery of state and of the broader political
class have become a focal point of much research.

However, as I have argued elsewhere (Schlesinger, 1989), the

Media, Culture and Society (SAGE, London, Newbury Park and New Delhi),
Vol. 11 (1989), 283–306

sociology of sources tends to be media-centric: that is, it fails to focus upon the source–media relation from the standpoint of the *sources* themselves. Thus, in its Marxist-structuralist variant (Hall et al., 1978) official sources' access to the media is assumed to be guaranteed without further ado and as therefore affording them a 'primary defining' role. One effect of this standpoint is that the sociological question of how sources organize *media strategies* and compete with one another is completely neglected. 'Primary definition', which ought to be an empirically ascertainable outcome is held to be an a priori effect of privileged access. For their part, empirical studies, although more sensitive to the reality of active source competition (a game played on unequal terms), have for the most part remained trapped within methodological frameworks that preclude direct investigation of source strategies, as some have recognized (cf. Gans, 1979: 360, fn. 3; Ericson et al., 1987: 364).

How we conceive of the activity of sources directly relates to more general conceptions of the relative openness or closure of a given media system and therefore the operations of what Habermas has termed the 'public sphere'. In one form or another, this issue is central to a number of recent studies.

II

Critical sociological studies of journalistic practice in the Anglo-American tradition of the past couple of decades have been concerned with revealing the problematic nature of 'professional' claims to objectivity, impartiality and autonomy. That production routines are not value-free procedures for the construction of an unbiased depiction of reality is nowadays taken as axiomatic. The workings of political, economic and ideological constraints and their constitutive role in the very definition of professionalism are commonly cited as grounds for dismissing standard normative accounts of the free press.

Journalistic professionalism is closely tied up with the handling of sources: indeed, for practitioners one major aspect of being a good professional lies in making sound judgements between competing claims and in judging what are credible points of view. Professionalism functions as an all-purpose defence against outside attack — wherein, of course, lies the attraction of its deconstruction for critical scholarship.

The 'Anglo-Saxon' approach to news production routines has now for the first time been adopted by three of Spain's leading younger scholars, Justo Villafañé, Enrique Bustamante and Emilio Prado (1987) in a study of the output of two radio and two television stations. They have also broken new ground in Spain by for the first time undertaking several days' participant observation inside broadcasting organizations.

Fabricar Noticias (Making News) is particularly revealing for how it situates itself. The intellectual field is distinctive, namely a society that has but recently emerged from a long-standing dictatorship in which overt censorship was the norm. In this context, Villafañé et al. argue, defensive uses of the Anglo-Saxon type of professionalism was first of all liberative. However, with the development of post-Francoist democracy, professionalism — most notably in the national media, whether public or private — has clouded the real relations of political and economic dominance and needs 'demystification' since it covers up a routinized, homogenized manufacture of news that privileges the centres of power (1987: 146). Given Spanish journalism's new-found credibility (1987: 21) the authors want to draw attention to its limitations and to the lack of academic debate in Spain by comparison with Italy, France and Britain.

The intellectual landscape is extremely familiar, one in which ideology critique stands as the precondition for a journey to true democracy. But the irony is that such attacks upon professional ideology are never the property of the virtuous alone, but become open to general appropriation, as was so clearly recognized in Karl Mannheim's sociology of knowledge a good sixty years ago. Indeed, in Britain, in recent years, the arguments have been pushed on to an overtly political plane with far greater force and effect by the right than by the left, particularly in respect of the 'biases' and professional lapses of broadcasting, another handy bit of siege machinery with which to assail an already crumbling redoubt.

The authors' goal is not merely denunciatory. They quite explicitly adopt the empirical analysis of organizational structures, patterns of coverage, sources of information and selection criteria in order to redirect the argument away from cheap conspiracy theories and abstract functionalist conceptions of the media. The point of this is to demonstrate that *on the whole* the subordination of the media within the wider structures of power ensures that the system works perfectly well without any need for open intervention or censorship.

Underlying the detail of this account, however, is an implicit theory of change. One index, as noted above, is the shifting function of professionalism in the transition from dictatorship to democracy. Another lies in the key area of sources of information. The conclusion here, empirically supported, is not surprising. For Spanish broadcasters 'the principal reference point is institutional or official politics' (Villafañé et al., 1987: 62), sources which in Oscar Gandy's phrase offer an 'information subsidy' that is difficult to refuse. But this situation is the *outcome of a process*, a shift from relative openness after Franquismo to a new closure:

> a change of power with new actors opened up room for new sources, but once the period of uncertainty and readjustment had passed, the channels and sources of information seem to have arrived at an unprecedented centralisation and reduction in numbers, even taking account of the last decade of Franquismo'. (1987: 22)

In effect, the range of effective voices in the public sphere is an outcome of battles over information management in society in its broadest sense. Recognizing this, we obviously need to develop further our understanding of the conditions of success and failure in the development of information strategies by official and non-official sources.

III

Censorship is one such strategy of information management and a signal that structural constraints will not of their own accord do the necessary work: instead, interventive action is required.

War has been especially relevant to arguments about censorship, as it offers a context in which overt interference in media coverage may be seen as legitimate. A relevant distinction needs to be drawn between total war (e.g. the Second World War), an undeclared war (e.g. Vietnam) and a partial engagement (e.g. the Falklands/Malvinas conflict). During a total war the role of official censorship in liberal democratic regimes is generally accepted as a necessary evil in the national interest. But in undeclared wars or partial engagements different rules apply, for there is more scope to dispute what the national interest may be. The survival of the social order is not at stake, open opposition is not treasonous, and alternative versions of reality may legitimately be offered (although not always without attempts at delegitimation). In such contexts the case for censorship is harder to make and its effective implementation also more difficult.

However, as recent research into the role of the media during the Vietnam and Falklands conflicts reminds us, it is difficult to predict with certainty whether censorship will always be applied in armed struggles that fall short of total war. According to Daniel C. Hallin, the level of compliance by US media with official perspectives during the Vietnam war was generally so great that formal censorship was not actually needed. On the other hand, during the Falklands campaign, as David Morrison and Howard Tumber document in unprecedented detail, an apparatus of censorship was immediately activated — although not on the basis of a coherent information policy. If the British government learned the 'lessons of Vietnam' — spurious ones as Hallin shows — the US government in turn learned the lessons of the Falklands during its Grenada intervention in 1983.

Hallin attacks two central arguments. First, that relations between the US media and government were essentially conflictual (the standard Fourth Estate assumption); and secondly, the contention that the US media significantly contributed to the sapping of domestic morale and the turning of US public opinion against the war (a comforting nostrum routinely trotted out by counter-insurgency theorists and politicians bent upon tighter control of the media, which has long been used in Northern Ireland).

Underlying Hallin's approach is a structural assumption. Namely, that the development of the ethic of 'objectivity' in US journalism paralleled the rationalization of relations between news media and state, especially the Presidency. The professionalization and 'departisanship' of the press grants 'to political authorities certain positive rights of access to the news' and acceptance for the most part of 'the language, agenda, and perspectives of the political "establishment"' (1986: 8). The effect is to leave the media autonomous but deeply enmeshed in government, with an ideological commitment to what Hallin terms the 'national security consensus' that plays a hegemonic role in framing possible ways of addressing political issues. This consensus, so it is argued, was one in which South Vietnam was to be defended against Soviet-led expansionism as part of the grand struggle of democracy versus totalitarianism. In this optic (only now in the late 1980s coming under severe strain) a 'Western-backed regime' is faced by aggressive communist subversion. The background of colonialism and of a nationalist revolution based in rural class struggles was not a perspective that came through these filters.

The US media, it is held, are heavily reliant upon authoritative sources for their accounts of the world and for their political agenda, a view supported in substance by many other studies. The net effect, Hallin argues, at least in respect of coverage of the Vietnam war, is that the greatest diversity of opinion was expressed when there were serious divisions within the political class, in particular within successive administrations and military leaderships. The Cold War national security consensus underpinning reporting came under increasing pressure with the passage of time and the failure of the US war effort and political manoeuvrings to secure any lasting advantages in South Vietnam.

Thus, from 1961 to 1963 the Kennedy administration successfully managed the news in order to minimize public knowledge of the growing US role in Vietnam. However, the more combat troops were committed to support of the South Vietnamese regime the more difficult this policy was to sustain, because as the death count mounted this became news that could not be hidden. Outright suppression was impossible since war had not been declared, and censorship could not be instituted. In fact 'officials felt that censorship in the field would be of limited use in an undeclared war in which it could not be imposed in the United States as well' (Hallin, 1986: 128). Reporting began to reflect the views of those in the field as well as official views in Saigon. These were differences over military tactics rather than strategy, to be sure, but nevertheless this provided a basis for the emergence of differences. As Hallin notes, there were periodic upturns 'in journalistic and political activity when political divisions in the administration became acute' (1986: 54).

These problems could only become worse when in July 1965 the Johnson administration authorized a substantial rise in the commitment of combat troops. Hallin argues that, in effect, the conventions of 'objective' journalism followed by the *New York Times* when reporting the Gulf of Tonkin incident had turned it into 'essentially an instrument of state', explained by the use of official sources as authoritative voices. The focus on the President, the absence of wider interpretation and analysis and a stress upon immediacy combined to rob news reporting of perspective. However, as the process of 'escalation' began and dissenting voices rose in the administration, alternative views began to filter through the press. But you had to know how to read the various stories dispersed throughout the *New York Times* in order to gain some critical distance. The administration's information strategy was to pursue low-level, incremental announcements of the military build-up: the steps towards a major war were therefore difficult to discern.

Hallin turns his attention to television in the period 1965–73, observing that the medium 'came of age on the eve of Vietnam' (1986: 105). Unquestionably, in subsequent debate about the role of censorship the focus has been on the alleged sins of television, in particular its supposed role in demoralizing US public opinion. However, on the evidence, broadcasters' dependence on official sources coupled with an unquestioning commitment to Cold War ideology, ensured that broadly favourable coverage was secured right until the Tet offensive of 1968. Given its mass-market orientation and need to entertain, television news was heavily action oriented, offering a 'series of more or less timeless images of men — or, more precisely, of Americans — at war' (1986: 114). At war, moreover, in an analytical vacuum since the North Vietnamese and National Liberation Front were treated as terrorists lacking any political rationale.

After 1968, scepticism about the war began to be evident in US network television due to the changing political context: divisions in the administration, declining military morale, the spread of the anti-war movement into mainstream politics. This puts the familiar argument that television *led* the change in hearts and minds in its place. It is more that 'with officials divided and communication channels within the administration inoperative, the media became a forum for airing political differences rather than a tool of policy . . .' (1986: 187). But it is important to note the *limited* nature of this forum which 'remained open primarily to official Washington, despite the rise in political protest' (1986: 201). As Todd Gitlin (1980) has shown in his earlier, complementary study, radical anti-war protest was sidelined and delegitimized: dissent was only taken seriously by the mainstream media when it was respectable and reformist. However, even within the hegemonic frameworks of establishment-dominated news, change necessarily occurs and redefinition of the agenda emerges as the result of a process of renegotiation (Gitlin, 1980: 272–3). It is certainly not axiomatic that such redefinition is purely the result of debate *within* elites. The anti-war movement was important in raising issues that came on to the political agenda, albeit mediated and modified through respectable reformist critics. In recent years, one might point to similar processes occurring in the cases of both the anti-nuclear and the green movements. In both instances there has been a struggle to define the terms of reference. If such groups were of no consequence, the political elites would not actively try to delegitimize them and co-opt their ideas. Nor would so much effort be expended in trying to manage the overall ecology of information.

IV

We may distinguish two relevant levels of analysis. First, that of conflicts over the interpretation of given issues or events. And secondly — much more fundamental — that of conflicts over the very conditions for the functioning of a public sphere.

David Morrison and Howard Tumber's detailed analysis of the coverage of the Falklands campaign is located in the latter context, that of the wider 'battle for information' in Britain. For them, government attacks on the media during the Falklands campaign are part of a more far-reaching effort to loosen the liberal intelligentsia's 'grip on public symbolic life' by neo-conservatives eager to 'settle permanently the cultural landscape' in their own market-dominated image (1988: 350).

In contemporary Britain, such current tendencies towards closure include the current reshaping of official secrecy legislation and the impending marginalization of public service broadcasting as an effect of 'deregulation'. Both are important indices of how the underlying conditions for investigative journalism and a potential diversity of reporting addressed to a wide public are currently under threat.

Although Morrison and Tumber refuse the label of 'critical' research, preferring 'humanism' instead and insisting that they are looking at 'the journalist as person', their overall analysis does not differ significantly in import from the broadly Gramscian approaches already discussed. While much of their account deals with the experiences of the British journalists accompanying the Task Force to the south — and extremely vividly at that, letting them speak at often amusing, and generally revealing, length — there is an inescapable analytical need to place this narrative within the context of a system of information management. It becomes abundantly clear that the 'journalist as person' has hatreds, ambitions, idiosyncrasies and tricks of the trade all his own, but the strategies and tactics adopted for covering the war were nevertheless largely governed by rules and professional understandings which the authors cannot help but see as structuring and constraining.

The study is a welcome antidote to conspiracy theories and a heartening testament to the reassuring incompetence of our rulers, even at times of war. The state had no readily available information policy for the Falklands campaign. The picture that emerges from Morrison and Tumber's detailed reconstruction is of confusion throughout the campaign. There were conflicts inside the Ministry of Defence, inter-service rivalries and substantial differences in the understanding of public relations practice between the army and navy, unco-ordinated actions by civilian and military censors in the field, not to speak of a lack of clarity over the role of Number Ten in co-ordinating news management.

The confusion was apparent from the very start, when journalists were selected to accompany the Task Force. At first the selection of press correspondents was hived off to the Newspaper Publishers' Association by the MoD, which reflected the navy's reluctance to take lots of journalists on board. Faced with an outcry from the national press and Downing Street, eventually places were allocated to all the national dailies, the quality Sundays, the Press Association and regional press representatives, as well as the BBC and ITN — but no one from the foreign press. The media's representatives (with the exception of the redoubtable Max Hastings) were not in the least experienced in war correspondence. A similar lottery affected the choice of civilian MoD information officers (the 'minders') sent south. As the authors observe, with some understatement, the Ministry 'in terms of its information planning, was in disarray' (1988: 20). There were some old pamphlets on war correspondents' duties dating from the Suez campaign of 1956 — and even then not enough to go round.

Once aboard the Task Force, the journalists were given military ranks and were totally dependent upon the navy for equipment and communications. One consequence of the close involvement with the troops over the extended period of the campaign was a growing, and quite spontaneous, process of identification with the fighting man, a theme explored with insight by the authors. The public relations skills of the various senior officers varied and were a significant factor in shaping relations with the media. The army and marines, both tried and tested in Northern Ireland, were adept in their media strategies; the navy, on the whole, was not. The journalists at first believed the dispute with Argentina would be diplomatically resolved and as the going got rougher following the sinking first of the *General Belgrano* and then HMS *Sheffield* they, like the military, understandably experienced fear and anxiety — although these were not reported. There was, of course, great interest in British press coverage on the Task Force itself: the *Sun* was widely regarded with contempt for its gung-ho trivialization of war; the *Guardian* somehow never ever arrived on board (1988: 39–40).

Morrison and Tumber examine how the journalists both co-operated and competed. They co-operated in pressuring the MoD 'minders' and the navy to transmit as much news back to Britain as possible. They continually competed over access to the scarce communications facilities and for assignment to particular actions on the Falklands once the troops had landed. Much material sent back by the press correspondents was 'pooled', causing much bad feeling when some were felt to benefit at the expense of others. Morrison and Tumber observe that with different work norms this could have led to 'collective public service journalism', an insight whose broader implications they fail to discuss. But any potential collective action was dramatically contradicted by the atomistic ideology and practice of Fleet Street, the high point of which led to an attempt by one frustrated journalist at the war's conclusion to bayonet the successful Max Hastings. The broadcasters, for their part, were forced to co-operate, since ITN and the BBC shared a film crew. They could also project themselves as individual witnesses in what, on the whole, turned out to be a radio rather than television war.

There has been much speculation over the reasons for the slowness with which television film and stills came back from the Falklands once the Task Force had passed Ascension Island. The favourite hypothesis is obstruction by the military and the government. On their evidence, given the priority accorded military signals traffic and the technical difficulties caused by lack of suitable satellite systems, the authors have made a convincing case against the view that technological difficulties were just an excuse. After an extensive examination of the communications facilities available, Morrison and Tumber conclude:

> Although there was no deliberate conspiracy to prevent television pictures from appearing on screens at home, both the military and the Ministry of Defence were acutely anxious about the possible effect that any pictures might have on the morale of both the troops and their families. The general view among the military was that it was the nightly showing of television pictures from South East Asia which undermined popular support in America for the Vietnam war. (1988: 169)

The view was not, of course, ever put to the test, although Morrison and Tumber rightly discount it anyway. Nevertheless, a certain equivocation can be detected too: for as the authors also show, drawing on the evidence collected by the House of Commons' Select Committee on Defence, leading lights such as Sir Frank Cooper of the MoD, and John Nott, the Defence Secretary, did express their concern about the potential impact of pictures from the battle front and they certainly did not regret the technical obstacles that led to film being delayed for an average of two to three weeks. So while there was no 'conspiracy': 'It seems that, for the most part, operational reasons account for the delay in the BBC's or ITN's broadcasting material from correspondents. Some of the delay, however, was caused deliberately by the Ministry' (1988: 174).

However, the ministry was not united, nor was there a 'centralized system of control' or 'coordination between departments' more generally (1988: 190). There were disputes over policy at the top of the MoD public relations apparatus and a serious miscalculation in relations with defence correspondents when confidential briefings were for a time discontinued. There were disagreements between Number Ten and the MoD over news management, and conflicting pressures from civilian officials wanting to counter Argentine propaganda and military officers wanting to limit confirmation of operational losses. Unquestionably, there was censorship, but it was rather erratic, and in any case backed by self-censorship on grounds of 'taste' or morale-building by press and broadcasting.

Most controversial, probably, were the rows between Mrs

Thatcher's government and the BBC, and the use of 'disinformation'. On these questions, Morrison and Tumber add relatively little to what we already know from Robert Harris's incisive short account (1983). So far as disputes over media coverage go, the key points are these: that broadcasters could be seen as casting doubt on the British version of events by treating it in a detached manner (symptomized by the fury over *Newsnight*'s coverage; that current affairs television did attempt to explore alternatives to the dominant consensus by looking at political opposition to an armed conflict (in the case of the BBC's *Panorama*) and by making directly available the enemy's point of view (Thames TV's *TV Eye* interview with General Galtieri); that liberal dissent came under tremendous pressure, in the form of attacks by much of the press and Conservative MPs on the BBC, the *Guardian* and the *Daily Mirror* for treachery, although these media were defended by opposition and establishment figures including the Prince of Wales. It is noteworthy that these attacks on 'disloyal' media first began when concern inside the government began to rise over the potential political costs of a bloody campaign in the Falklands.

As for 'disinformation', it *was* put out on several occasions (most notoriously to mislead over the San Carlos landings [cf. Harris, 1983: 110–14]) and generally approved by the Defence Committee's subsequent report as being in the national interest. It did not take long for the manifest shortcomings of the Falklands information policy and censorship practices to be officially addressed and for preparations for the next media war to be set in hand. The blueprint for action next time around is spelled out in the report of the study group chaired by General Sir Hugh Beach (1983) which, *inter alia*, has considered the question of censorship in an era of proliferating media distribution systems, argued for the simplification of censorship, and for the development of an 'accreditation bargain' with war correspondents in the field in which facilities for coverage are offered in exchange for co-operation.

Whether the revamped MoD guidelines will be put into effective action *next* time is an open question. A rationalistic model of policy formation and delivery would leave us with few doubts on that score. But shortcomings of control even in the optimal conditions of the Falklands operation do not altogether exclude the fine Anglo-Saxon tradition of the cock-up.

V

Although slippage through the net of determinations is not entirely excluded from the 'propaganda model' recently elaborated by Edward S. Herman and Noam Chomsky, the general thrust of their approach is to stress the tendency toward virtual closure of the US national media system when reporting foreign affairs in the service of the powerful, whether the government in Washington or corporate capital with large financial stakes abroad. The assumptions upon which the model is based raise a number of theoretical questions which I shall address later.

Over the past decade Chomsky and Herman (and the latter together with Frank Brodhead) have published a series of substantial studies of the US mass media and their role in the foreign policy process. However, this work has received relatively little critical attention especially in the United States, a fact for which the authors have accounted by citing 'the selective policing of the flow of ideas by means of private structures and constrained access, while all the legal forms of freedom are in place' (Chomsky and Herman, 1979a: xvi). Critical attention outside the USA amongst communications specialists has also been patchy and slight, to say the least.

Certainly, the authors' message is an uncomfortable one for those who hold the United States to be a benign force on the world stage, for their central concern is to engage in a major exercise of ideology-critique and to expose successive American governments' role in supporting repression throughout what they have called the 'Pentagon-CIA Archipelago'. Those who know Chomsky's political writings will recognize the link to his earlier critique of the 'new mandarins', the technocratic exponents of intellectual irresponsibility and accomplices in the abuse of power. The echo of Solzhenitsyn's Gulag in the authors' designation of US support for 'Third World Fascism' offers a clear enough index of the goal of symbolic realignment in which they are engaged and also of the writers' self-conception as dissidents — subject to marginalization, though, rather than outright repression.

Manufacturing Consent builds upon and synthesizes all Chomsky and Herman's previous collaborative work on the media as well as including some new material. Thus there are case studies on Indo-China (Vietnam and Cambodia) that draw upon the controversial two volumes of *The Political Economy of Human Rights* (Chomsky and Herman, 1979a; 1979b). These books led to Chomsky and Herman being accused of apologizing for the Pol Pot regime. That controversy still crackles in the latter chapters of *Manufacturing Consent* and raises issues that go well beyond the scope of this essay. Nevertheless, from any dispassionate reading of this book it is clear that the authors are not arguing that the Pol Pot regime should be excused. Rather their point is that the equivalent death toll resulting from the impact of US policy prior to the Khmer Rouge's rise to power has been shamefully ignored.

The legitimization of rigged elections in Central America is a further theme, following an approach first developed in *Demonstration Elections* (Herman and Brodhead, 1984). And finally, there is a case study of the fabrication of the alleged KGB–Bulgarian plot to kill the Pope to which an earlier book *The Rise and Fall of the Bulgarian Connection* (Herman and Brodhead, 1986) has also been devoted. Prior to this latter book, in his volume *The* Real *Terror Network*, Herman (1982) had written a critique of the Reagan administration's use of 'international terrorism' as a foreign policy instrument and as a semantic category backed up ideologically by members of the 'terrorism studies' fraternity. Taken as a whole, this is unquestionably a significant output, leaving aside the numerous articles that have prepared the ground for the books cited above. Moreover, yet another book on *The 'Terrorism' Industry* is on the way. A lengthier evaluation than the present one is plainly overdue.

The starting point is a familiar one in critical research, namely, a critique of the normative assumption that the media are genuinely free and competitive coupled with the related argument that a dominant ideological framework is purveyed by the media. Herman and Chomsky go beyond other studies taking a 'political economy' approach, by inviting us to see the US media as analogous to those of a totalitarian system in which conformity is secured not by monopolistic control through a party–state bureaucracy but rather through the 'routes by which money and power are able to filter out the news fit to print, marginalize dissent, and allow the government and dominant interests to get their messages across to the public' (1988: 2). Clearly, this perspective assumes that powerful, unilinear media effects occur. But the problems of audience research are not addressed; the effects are 'read off' from the 'essential ingredients' of the propaganda model, which are identified as follows:

> (1) the size, concentrated ownership, owner wealth and profit orientation of the dominant mass media firms; (2) advertising as the primary income source of the mass media; (3) the reliance of the media on information provided by government, business and 'experts' funded and approved by these primary sources and agents of power; (4) 'flak' as a means of disciplining the media; and (5) 'anticommunism' as a national religion and control mechanism. These elements interact with and reinforce one another. The raw material of news must pass through successive filters, leaving only the cleaned residue fit to print. They fix the premises of discourse and interpretation, and the definition of what is newsworthy in the first place, and they explain the basis and operations of what amount to propaganda campaigns. (Herman and Chomsky, 1988: 2)

This is a highly deterministic vision of how the media operate coupled with a straightforwardly functionalist conception of ideology. The factors identified are held to have predictive force, although whether always in combination or not is not specified. If they do not always operate in combination, no *theoretical* grounds are given for the efficacy of one factor as against another at any given time. The first two refer to the level of economic determination in which the profit motive is the motor of explanation. The third concerns the differential structure of access to the media, the way in which economic and political resources may translate themselves into symbolic presence. The fourth relates to the exercise of political pressure as a means of control. Finally, the fifth points to the system-maintaining function of a dominant ideology present amongst media professionals.

Writing reflectively from within a political-economic perspective, Graham Murdock has pertinently remarked that one of its tasks is 'a more thoroughgoing analysis of the ways in which economic dynamics operate to structure both the range and forms of press presentations' (1980: 63). However, Herman and Chomsky's approach inclines them to dismiss this kind of concern as pluralistic: they do not deny that differences exist amongst media in the USA, however these 'remain faithfully within the system of presuppositions that constitute an elite consensus, a system so powerful as to be internalized largely without awareness' (1988: 302). The elite consensus, therefore, is seen as largely sealed off from external forces.

The propaganda model is quite consciously distinguished from the so-called 'newsroom gatekeeper models' which argue that

'Whatever the advantages of the powerful . . . the struggle goes
on, space exists and dissident light breaks through in unexpected
ways. The mass media are no monolith.' Such studies are seen as
too focused on the newsroom and media organization and as
'without any larger frame of analysis' (Herman, 1986: 173). One
might pertinently ask whether these strictures apply to any of the
books discussed so far. Although none sets out a model in the
same terms as Herman and Chomsky, none rests purely at the
level of an examination of journalistic practice. However, no
developed critique of the varied theoretical positions contained in
the tradition of production studies is offered: as I have argued
elsewhere (Schlesinger, 1989) it is certainly a mistake to assimilate
them to 'pluralism'. Moreover, they cannot be lumped together
under the 'gatekeeper' category, a term long rejected as both
sociologically inadequate and as implying a passivity alien to
journalism as a process of construction.

The 'propaganda model' is presented as predictive: given outcomes may be expected as the result of the working out of its
structural determinations. The authors have selected a number of
case studies to demonstrate this. They certainly make some telling
points, but they have done this in the past as well without
generalizing the use of propagandistic techniques to become the
defining characteristic of the media system itself. The main consequence of this move is to underline the similarities between the
functions of US and Soviet media in maintaining their respective
power structures (although Soviet media are not analysed in any
detail but only casually invoked from time to time as a point of
contrast). Much critical media research in capitalist democracies
rests in one way or another on a similar conception of ideological
hegemony secured by inequalities of economic, political and
cultural power. But this has not led scholars to elide relevant
differences. Certainly, one question that springs to mind is just
how *generalizable* the Herman–Chomsky model is to other
democratic capitalist societies. We shall return to this point later
on.

Turning now to the case studies: these begin by arguing that 'A
propaganda system will consistently portray people abused in
enemy states as *worthy* victims, whereas those treated with equal
or greater severity by its own government or clients will be
unworthy' (Herman and Chomsky, 1988: 37). This thesis is
followed through in some convincing detail by reference to the

massive media treatment of the murder of Father Jerzy Popieƚusko in Poland as compared with the equally politically motivated killing of Archbishop Oscar Romero in El Salvador. The latter death was of an awkward priest who denounced right-wing repression supported by the US government. Weighed in the scales, his murder, together with that of the four US religious women killed in El Salvador, and numerous other priests in Guatemala, counted for very little in terms of comprehensive, well-contextualized media coverage.

Another acid test of the alignment of mainstream media with the foreign policy imperatives of successive US administrations, the authors argue, is the coverage of elections in given Third World states. They consider three such examples in the period from 1982 to 1985 in which the cases considered fall into favoured states (El Salvador in 1982 and Guatemala between 1984 and 1985) and an unfavoured state (Nicaragua in 1984). Essentially, the argument here (as with the matter of victims) is about the application of double standards. If we apply the usual standards of liberal democracy (freedom of speech, assembly, press, organization of parties and associations, absence of coercion, etc.) we find that these were met best — although certainly not ideally, Herman and Chomsky accept — in the case of Nicaragua.

However, the dominant framework of interpretation emanating from the Reagan administration was hostile to the Sandinista regime as a Marxist intrusion in America's back yard. The authors argue that the US media constructed the story in these terms, and hence the favourable reports of many independent observers about the election's conduct were largely ignored and the Sandinistas presented as engaging in coercion. By contrast, the 'relevant structural conditions' of exclusion of opposition forces and use of state terror in Guatemala and El Salvador did not figure in mainstream reporting, which leads Herman and Chomsky to observe that

> the degree of subservience to state interests in the cases we have examined was extraordinary, given the absence of overt coercion. The 'filters' yield a propaganda result that a totalitarian state would be hard put to surpass . . . we may fairly say that the US mass media, despite their righteous self-image as opponents of something called terrorism, serve in fact as loyal agents of terrorism. (1988: 141–2).

This observation is very much in line with their earlier writing on the subject, in which they have consistently argued that the truly significant terrorism in the world is that of states in the western spheres of influence rather than that of the nationalist and other groups using violence for political ends. One celebrated incident, which occupies a further chapter, is coverage of the attempted killing of Pope John Paul II by the Turkish terrorist Mehmet Ali Agca. In the accounts of a Soviet plot that were widely popularized, this was laid at the door of the Bulgarian secret services acting as surrogates for the KGB.

Herman and Chomsky take the story to pieces, showing for instance, how Agca's origins in the Turkish fascist group the Grey Wolves was largely ignored, and how his story kept changing under the tutelage of the Italian secret services and investigating magistrate. It is plausibly argued that if there was a plot it came from the Right rather than the Left and fitted in with the needs of various groups, including CIA-linked cold warriors wanting to lay 'international terrorism' at the door of the Soviet Union. The broader study upon which this is based, *The Rise and Fall of the Bulgarian Connection* (Herman and Brodhead, 1986), is probably the best single instance of how the authors have extended conventional analysis of the media by generally offering a detailed analysis of the relevant historical context of a 'story' — which allows us to judge the scope of routine media reporting — as well as providing a close analysis of the dynamics of information strategies by sources: in this instance the privileged access enjoyed by several 'terrorism studies' experts such as Claire Sterling, Michael Ledeen and Paul Henze is very well documented. Elsewhere, valuable use is made of little-read source material on human rights abuses in a way that certainly does raise sharp questions about the shortcomings of conventional journalism.

Yet the more systematic sampling of the main media (notably the *New York Times, Time, Newsweek*, and CBS News) gives way to a less rigorous treatment in the two chapters dealing with the Indo-China wars. The one on Vietnam adds relatively little to the arguments offered by Dan Hallin (whose work is cited). Those who argue that media pessimism contributed to slumping morale and defeat will note that negative assessments of the USA's capacity to win the war were rife in administration and military quarters — only these views were kept quiet. What the authors do underline is the unthinkable status of the proposition that the US *invaded* Vietnam, the invisibility of the wider historical context, and the patriotic assumptions underlying most US journalism, which on the whole turned frequent atrocities into rare aberrations and led to administration briefings being swallowed wholesale — perhaps most notoriously over the Paris Peace Agreements in 1973.

So far as Laos and Cambodia are concerned, it is argued that 'Media failure to report the facts when they were readily available, in 1968, and to investigate further when they were undeniable, by late 1969, contributed to the successful deception of the public, and to the continuing destruction' (Herman and Chomsky, 1988: 259). An issue singled out for particular emphasis is the failure to assess the impact of US bombing in the period before the emergence of the Khmer Rouge. The thrust of this chapter is towards a settling of accounts with the failings of scholarship and with writers such as William Shawcross, who is seen as wilfully dishonest and an orchestrator of selective outrage minimizing US responsibility.

VI

The propaganda model raises a number of general theoretical questions only some of which can be dealt with in passing here.[1] First, there is the matter of comparability. The authors themselves note the specificity of the US media, pointing to the 'narrowness of articulated opinion and analysis' as compared with 'most other industrial democracies' (1988: 305–6). No systematic evidence is produced, although to judge from the text, which occasionally cites British and French quality newspapers, these are the implicit points of comparison. Second, despite their formal adherence to a powerful effects model which assumes that dominant agendas are reproduced in public opinion, the concluding chapter observes that the 'system is not all-powerful . . . Government and elite domination of the media have not succeeded in overcoming the Vietnam syndrome and public hostility to direct US involvement in the destabilization and overthrow of foreign governments' (1988: 306). This obviously ought to provoke some general doubts about the deterministic picture painted, but only in the very last two pages do these appear. In the case of Nicaragua:

1. These issues will be addressed in a forthcoming study of Crime, Law and Justice in the Media in Britain. This essay draws on the concerns of that work, funded by the Economic and Social Research Council (UK), reference number: E 625 0013, whose support the author gratefully acknowledges.

> The partial failures of the very well organized and extensive state propaganda effort, and simultaneous rise of an active grass-roots oppositional movement with very limited media access, was crucial in making an outright US invasion of Nicaragua unfeasible and driving the state underground to illegal operations that could be better concealed from the domestic population — with, in fact, considerable media complicity (Herman and Chomsky, 1988: 307)

This example cuts across the overall determinism. Herman and Chomsky also briefly note countervailing potentialities for broader access in the rise of cable and satellite communications, local non-profit radio and television stations and public radio and television. They advocate the incorporation of media reform into programmes of political action. Plainly, this recognition of the limitations of structural determinism is important and an antidote to political fatalism; but it occupies very little space indeed in the overall argument.

VII

In varying ways, and in quite distinct national and conjunctural contexts, the studies by Villafañé et al., Hallin, and Morrison and Tumber all suggest that the relative openness and closure of media systems is strongly dependent upon divisions within the political class. In the propaganda model internal contention amongst elites is regarded as trivial given the assumption of an 'elite consensus' that can be imposed upon the public as a whole. Yet what if there is no single elite capable of establishing a consensus amongst its members, but rather several competing factions of a political class without common terms of reference? And what if the public is not unitary but also fractured into major groupings, each of which has its own interpretative frameworks, or 'root paradigms' as Robin Wagner-Pacifici calls them?

Wagner-Pacifici's (1986) study considers the symbolic politics surrounding the Red Brigade's kidnapping of the Italian Christian Democratic Party's (DC) president, Aldo Moro, in March 1978. Where the propaganda model sees mass communication as simply functional for the reproduction of dominance, the 'social drama' framework investigates the *strategies* employed by various political actors and the media in the contest to achieve a dominant interpretation. One crucial difference of emphasis, then, lies in stressing the *processual* dimension of ideological struggle and in conceiving symbolic dominance as something to be achieved rather than as largely resolved by built-in structural advantages. The normative criterion of veridicality for judging media performance is displaced by an interest in their role as contributors to the ritual or (as Wagner-Pacifici prefers) theatrical process of conferring contested meanings upon a key political kidnapping and assassination.

The importance of the comparative dimension was raised earlier. Italian media are certainly closely tied into the country's political class and (where not state- or party-owned) largely in the hands of major capitalist corporations. Similar political-economic assumptions to those employed by Herman and Chomsky could therefore be made as a starting point. But this would not necessarily take us in the direction of a propaganda model, as Italian media arguably function more as vehicles for the representation of divergent political and economic interests than as articulators of an elite consensus with well-defined boundaries. Moreover, given the endemic lack of credibility enjoyed by the Italian state amongst large sectors of the population, it makes little sense to see the media as reproducers of a dominant agenda and conferers of legitimacy upon the social order. The Anglo-Saxon conceptions of professionalism and objectivity do not on the whole apply, nor are they widely thought to.

The Moro affair is particularly well suited to the kind of analysis Wagner-Pacifici develops. It is a celebrated story with a beginning, middle and end. Aldo Moro, the leading Christian Democrat figure in Italy, was kidnapped by the Red Brigades on 16 March 1978, just as he was departing to parliament to resolve a long-standing governmental crisis. Particularly contentious was the proposed opening towards the Italian Communist Party (PCI), at that time intent upon effecting the so-called 'historical compromise' with the DC, a move unquestionably opposed on the Right, but also on the far Left. Moro's five bodyguards were killed and he was held prisoner for fifty-five days during which he was 'tried' by the Red Brigades (BR). Finally, Moro was murdered and dumped in the boot of a car, parked with self-conscious symbolism midway between the Rome headquarters of the PCI and the DC. The 'social drama' was enacted during the days of captivity and after Moro's death when a major state funeral was, quite literally, staged — without the *corpus delicti*.

The organization of the core of Wagner-Pacifici's book follows the anthropologist Victor Turner's conceptualization of a 'social drama' which

> consists of a four-stage model, processing from the breach of some relationship regarded as crucial in the relevant social group . . . through a phase of rapidly mounting crisis in the direction of the group's major dichotomous cleavage, to the application of legal or ritual means of redress or reconciliation between the conflicting parties which compose the action set. The final stage is either the public and symbolic expression of reconciliation or else of irremediable schism. (Turner, 1974: 78–9, cited in Wagner-Pacifici, 1986: 8)

During the 'Breach' phase a variety of positions began to emerge. The Communists saw Moro's kidnapping as a fascist plot, whereas the Right saw the Red Brigades as an offshoot of the Communists. There were competing views as to the target: the state (dominated by the DC), the PCI (seeking governmental influence), the Turin trials of captured *brigatisti*. Wagner-Pacifici sees these different perceptions and their wider articulation by the media as part of a theatrical process working itself out in the political domain. As she remarks, Italy is a country in which the self-conscious styling of politics is important: the PCI (sometimes coercively) mobilized its membership on to the streets in demonstrations which unprecedentedly mingled its party banners with those of the DC to signify widespread social opposition to the BR. Not least, this mobilization pushed the Lockheed bribery scandal into the background, not unwelcome for a political class so widely tainted by it.

The 'Crisis' phase saw a staking out of positions in what the author calls 'the forest of symbolic politics'. The central axis of division concerned whether or not to negotiate with the BR for Moro's release. The DC and PCI (the latter more Catholic than the Pope in defence of the social order) were against; the Socialist Party (PSI) were for negotiation as were the far Left. Public appeals for Moro's life to be spared came from figures such as the Pope and the UN Secretary General. The political divisions were aired in public, with their attendant justifications. Moreover, Moro's letters pleading for a dialogue with the BR and the terrorists' own communiqués all surfaced in the media, and were open to varying interpretation. As Wagner-Pacifici observes: 'a series of issues and statuses were being collapsed, one onto the other. Negotiation was being presented as necessarily indicating recognition, and recognition was being presented as necessarily leading to the Red Brigades' legitimation' (1986: 159).

The 'Redress' phase demonstrated the problem of finding a

form of unitary and authoritative address in a pluralistic society. Wagner-Pacifici has identified six 'root paradigms' or symbolic referents used in debate during the Moro affair which represented 'a contest of mastery among the several protagonists of the Moro social drama' (1986: 202). Thus, for instance, the PCI appealed to the Resistance past as a legitimate context for the use of political violence, as opposed to the BR's use of it in the present. The DC used the defence of democracy (seen as its dominance within the state) as a way of refusing negotiations. The PSI and ultra-Left emphasized the sanctity of the life of the individual as against the abstract *raison d'état* espoused by the Right. Other invocations involved the proletariat and the party. In each case the objective was for the various parties to gain recognition as legitimate authorities in their own arenas of operation (1986: 203).

The last act, Moro's death, came in the phase of 'Reconciliation' or 'Schism'. Moro was 'tried' by his captors and found guilty. Prior to this, a great deal of public debate and interpretative effort was engaged in by all parties in respect of the politician's letters, released by the BR and published in the press. For those against negotiations, the letter-writer who urged compromise to save his own life was not the 'real Moro', but one drugged, sick, or infantilized by captivity. This prepared the ground, as Wagner-Pacifici comments, for his sacrifice on behalf of party and state. Nevertheless, the circle of reconciliation could not be closed: with due sense of spectacle, but also with tremendous irony, Moro's state funeral was one at which neither his family nor his body was present (1986: 238).

The complex intercutting of political strategies through the media was 'one of (albeit unequal) competition among several centres of symbolic discourse' (1986: 275). Wagner-Pacifici argues that the outcome

> spelled the victory of one construction of the social drama over all others. And with it came the victory of one view of the self (as sacrificial victim to the state), one view of power (unambiguously resting with the legitimate and undivided authorities who make all the decisions) and one view of change (change in the service of stasis). (1986: 276)

This kind of approach, with its stress upon symbolic process and strategy offers a counterpoint to the functionalist verities of ideological transmission postulated by the propaganda model, and opens up the complex relations between questions of production, distribution and reception. The legacy of the past two decades of debate over structure and action, economism and culturalism, the dominant ideology thesis, Marxism and pluralism inescapably informs all the books reviewed above. Will the parameters of our thinking still be the same in the next decade?

References

Beach, General Sir H. (Chairman) (1983) *The Protection of Military Information: Report of the Study Group on Censorship.* London: HMSO.

Chomsky, N. and E.S. Herman (1979a) *The Washington Connection and Third World Fascism. The Political Economy of Human Rights*, Vol. 1. Nottingham: Spokesman.

Chomsky, N. and E.S. Herman (1979b) *After the Cataclysm: Postwar Indochina and the Reconstruction of Imperial Ideology. The Political Economy of Human Rights*, Vol. 2. Nottingham: Spokesman.

Ericson, R.V., P.M. Baranek and J.B.L. Chan (1987) *Visualizing Deviance: A Study of News Organization.* Milton Keynes: Open University Press.

Gans, H.J. (1979) *Deciding What's News: A Study of CBS Evening News, NBS Nightly News, Newsweek and Time.* New York: Pantheon Books.

Gitlin, T. (1980) *The Whole World is Watching: Mass Media in the Making and Unmaking of the New Left.* Berkeley, Los Angeles, London: University of California Press.

Hall, S., C. Critcher, T. Jefferson, J. Clarke and B. Roberts (1978) *Policing the Crisis: Mugging, the State, and Law and Order.* London: Macmillan.

Harris, R. (1983) *Gotcha! The Media, the Government and the Falklands Crisis.* London: Faber and Faber.

Herman, E.S. (1982) *The* Real *Terror Network: Terrorism in Fact and Propaganda.* Boston: South End Press.

Herman, E.S. (1986) 'Gatekeeper versus Propaganda Models: A Critical American Perspective', pp. 171–95 in P. Golding, G. Murdock and P. Schlesinger (eds) *Communicating Politics: Mass Communications and the Political Process.* Leicester: Leicester University Press; New York: Holmes and Meier.

Herman, E.S. and F. Brodhead (1984) *Demonstration Elections: U.S.-staged Elections in the Dominican Republic, Vietnam, and El Salvador.* Boston: South End Press.

Herman, E.S. and F. Brodhead (1986) *The Rise and Fall of the Bulgarian Connection.* New York: Sheridan Square Publications.

Murdock, G. (1980) 'Class, Power and the Press: Problems of Conceptualisation and Evidence', pp. 37–70 in H. Christian (ed.) *The Sociology of Journalism and the Press.* (Sociological Review Monograph 29). University of Keele, October.

Schlesinger, P. (1989) 'Rethinking the Sociology of Journalism: Source Strategies and the Limits of Media Centrism', in M. Ferguson (ed.) *Public Communication: The New Imperatives.* London and Beverly Hills: Sage.

Turner, V. (1974) *Dramas, Fields, and Metaphors.* Ithaca, NY: Cornell University Press.

teach critical awareness of how these manipulations take place 'behind men's backs'.

In this article I wish to revalue broadcasting's social role against its devaluation in arguments that regard it primarily as a form of social control, or of cultural standardization or of ideological (mis)representation. To the contrary, I wish to argue for broadcasting in its present form, as a public good that has unobtrusively contributed to the democratization of everyday life, in public and private contexts, from its beginning through to today. I do not see how there can be any reasonable case for the present system other than along such lines. I will attempt to defend this proposition first by developing an account of broadcasting as a public good and then considering the wider implications of this account in relation to possible objections and criticisms. In doing this I have in mind the work of Jurgen Habermas, whose concepts of the public sphere, and of communicative rationality, have helped to clarify my understanding of broadcasting. Again, I will not initially attempt a commentary on Habermas's theoretical concerns other than to note here that, although I do not accept the particular theoretical lines of enquiry he pursues, the issues he addresses and the problems he poses seem to me to be fundamental for the study of modern societies and the contributory role of modern media.

Two things I do take from Habermas that underlie what follows: a historical approach to the formation of broadcasting's public sphere (cf. Garnham, 1986, for a recent discussion of the concept), and a concern with the rational character of communication in everyday actual contexts. I will offer a brief, historical account of the development of broadcasting in this country which focuses on it as a *public* service in two related ways: first, in terms of a content — programme output — which constitutes a new kind of public life through the relaying and creation of real-world events and occasions that are public in a minimal sense, viz. open and accessible to the public. Two kinds of such events are taken into account; on the one hand those that are external to broadcasting but which broadcasting redistributes, from their own locations, to its audiences (a coronation, a football match) and, on the other hand, those that are internal to broadcasting which it has created for its audiences in its studios (a political interview, a chat show, a game show). The continuing interplay of such events, outside and inside the studios, make up what I will refer to as the public life of broadcasting. My second, related concern is with the audiences, the new kind of *general* public, on whose behalf this public life is routinely accessed and produced.

I

I have argued elsewhere that there were two essential characteristics that have remained, from the beginning through to the present, as constitutive of public service broadcasting: the provision of a service of *mixed* programmes on *national* channels available to all (Scannell, 1989). The principle of universal availability has technical and economic components. The full establishment of broadcasting presupposes a society that has, for the great majority, risen above the level of necessity. To enjoy the services of broadcasting people need at the least a marginal surplus of disposable time and income. In Britain before the war radio sets were not cheap, and represented a major item of expenditure in households with only pennies to spare each week. Nevertheless, 75 percent of households had a radio set by 1939, and today when 100 percent of households have radios it is common for household members to have their own sets; 98 percent of households presently have at least one television set. Thus as commodities radio and TV sets (as distinct from video display units) have become things that every household possesses.

At the same time the broadcasting authorities (BBC and IBA) have seen it as a fundamental part of their commitment to public service to make their programmes, as far as is technically possible, available to anyone with a receiving apparatus anywhere in the United Kingdom. The BBC's television services now reach 99.1 percent of the population. To reach that extra one-tenth of 1 percent, 65 new transmitting stations were added to the distribution system (Peacock, 1986: 130n). Such an investment is the mark of public service broadcasting's disregard of strictly commercial considerations in relation to its audiences. Where those are primary, broadcasters will deliver a service only to the most profitable markets — which lie in densely populated urban areas that can deliver large audiences without difficulties. The markets for cable services are likely to prove even more selective. The affluent areas of major towns and cities will be wired up, while the poorer areas will be neglected. More sparsely populated, remoter regions will be ignored entirely.

If the universal distribution of its services is one basic marker of a broadcasting service constituted as a public good, the other is the supply of mixed programme services to its nationwide audiences, i.e. a wide range of different kinds of programmes delivered on a single channel. The mix today is familiar in the output of the four national television channels at present available to all in the UK: news, current affairs, and topical magazine programmes; chat shows, game shows and quizzes; drama of all kinds from soap operas and situation comedies to police series and single-authored plays; documentaries on a wide range of topics — social issues, history, science, wildlife; religious programmes; children's programmes; music from the current top forty to the classics, opera and ballet; a wide and varying supply of sporting events that includes all the major sports and many new ones (to television, that is) such as American football, basketball, bad-minton and indoor bowling.

All this is deeply known and taken for granted, bedded down into the very fabric of daily life for all of us. In the sum of its parts broadcasting has brought into being a culture in common to whole populations and a shared public life of a quite new kind. It exists as such today in national television services but not in radio. The original Reithian concept of mixed programming was embodied in the pre-war National Programme (Scannell and Cardiff, 1982). After the war a three-tiered radio service was introduced — the Light, the Home and the Third Programmes — which stratified audiences into three broad cultural taste publics, lowbrow, middlebrow and highbrow. Reith, who had long since left the BBC, rightly saw this as a fundamental betrayal of his founding concept of public service broadcasting. The worm in the promising bud of his vision for radio was music. For obvious reasons music has always constituted the bulk of output on radio, but it was impossible — in the long run — to provide a general musical service on a single national channel because there is not, and never has been, a common musical culture (Scannell, 1981). Music consists of different taste publics defined as much in terms of what they loathe as what they like. This is especially so in relation to 'serious' music and the avant-garde for whom the idea of music for all, and of all music as of equal value, is anathema. Thus, the history of radio, viewed in the long term, can be seen as its gradual fragmentation into different musical taste publics (Radios 1, 2 and 3) with talk bracketed out into specific talk channels (Radio 4).

This development, which took place earlier in the United States under harsher economic pressures, is not explicable simply in economic terms. But it is economic and political pressures for deregulation today that threaten to fragment television into multiple-channel options provided by cable and satellite services owned by media entrepreneurs and conglomerates. Such services will consist either of low-cost repeats of popular Anglo-American television programmes and feature films, or of generic programming in which all the material in a particular channel is of the same kind. This latter development is at present most advanced in American cable services — Home Box Office (newly released films), MTV (music videos), CNN (Cable Network News) along with pay-per-view channels that offer mainly sporting fixtures.

Generic programming fragments the general public that is still constituted in today's four national UK television channels into particular taste publics whom advertisers are increasingly keen to target. In so doing it destroys the principle of equality of access for all to entertainment, informational and cultural resources in a common public domain. The Peacock Report has redefined broadcasting as a private commodity rather than a public good, replacing the general interest by individual interests. Individual consumers, in the media universe of the next century, as envisaged by Peacock, will choose what they want and pay for what they get. But consumers are not all equal in their purchasing power. The privatization of information, culture and entertainment may well create a two-tiered society of those who are rich and poor in such resources. Such a development would undercut the fundamentally democratic principles upon which public service broadcasting rests.

II

It is important to see that that service, as we know it today, rests upon a right of access, asserted by the broadcasters on behalf of their audiences, to a wide range of political, religious, social, cultural, sporting events and to entertainments that previously were available only to small, self-selecting and more or less privileged particular publics. What was *public* life before broadcasting? In a general sense there were certain kinds of buildings and spaces in which people could meet, outside their homes, for relaxation, pleasure or self-improvement; public parks and libraries and public houses. More specifically there were public events that took place in particular places for particular publics. Thus, attendance at church, a theatre, a concert or variety hall, a cinema, a football match, a public lecture, a political rally, a civic or state ceremony, would seem to constitute the main kinds of events that were, by definition, public — that is, open to anyone who could get there and afford (where necessary) the price of entry.

In the 1920s the broadcasters had a sharp struggle to establish the right of the microphone to relay such events beyond their immediate location and audience to the fast-growing listening public. Concert and variety impresarios feared a fall-off at the box office, the Football Association worried about declining gates and the churches foresaw diminishing congregations. Such initial fears were, in most cases, quite quickly overcome. More patient and persistent diplomacy was required before the authorities would allow the microphone to relay major state ceremonies, especially those involving royalty. One important kind of access that the BBC pressed for very early on was the right to transmit, on a daily basis, the proceedings of the House of Commons. This was rejected by Baldwin in 1926 and was not allowed (for radio) until fifty years later. Only now, on an experimental basis, has permission been granted for the television cameras to enter the lower House.

Thus the particular publics who hitherto had enjoyed privileged access to such events now had grafted onto them a *general* public constituted in and by the general nature of the mixed programme service and its general, unrestricted availability. The fundamentally democratic thrust of broadcasting lay in the new kind of access to virtually the whole spectrum of public life that radio first, and later television, made available to all. By placing political, religious, civic, cultural events and entertainments in a common domain, public life was equalized in a way that had never before been possible. Moreover, whereas previously such events had been quite discrete and separate, they took on new meanings as they came in contact with each other in common national broadcast channels.

Consider the FA Cup Final, the Grand National or Wimbledon. All these existed before broadcasting, but whereas previously they existed only for their particular sporting publics they became, through radio and television, something more. Millions now heard or saw them who had little direct interest in the sports themselves. The events became, and have remained, punctual moments in a shared national life. Broadcasting created, in effect, a new national calendar of public events. Unobtrusively threaded through the continuing daily output was the cyclical reproduction, year in year out, of an orderly and regular progression of festivities, celebrations and remembrances that marked the unfolding of the broadcast year. The calendar not only organizes and coordinates social life, but gives it a renewable content, anticipatory pleasures, a horizon of expectations. The BBC calendar became the expressive register of a common, corporate public life that persists to this day.

III

Thus far I have considered a range of public events that existed before broadcasting, and which radio and television redistributed to far wider audiences than they had ever hitherto possessed. One consequence was that many of the performers in those events achieved, through broadcasting, fame on an unprecedented scale. Today the faces of royalty, of leading politicians, churchmen, entertainers and sportsmen and women circulate on a global scale. Broadcasting has created a public world of public persons who are routinely made available to whole populations. But at the same time it has brought private persons into the public domain, thereby extending and enriching its character. Private life has been profoundly resocialized by radio and television. They have brought into the public domain the experiences and pleasures of the majority in ways that had been denied in the dominant traditions of literature and the arts. Raymond Williams has drawn attention to the gradual broadening of the basis of representation in literature and drama since the sixteenth century. In Shakespeare's day only those of gentle blood were suitable subjects for tragedy or romance. Rude mechanicals were fit subjects only for knockabout farce. Since then, art and literature have increasingly dealt with the uneventful lives of the middling classes. By the end of the last century, working people had become subjects for art and literature, but usually as objects of compassion or as social problems, and always as described by middle-class authors for middle-class readers.

Broadcasting, because its service was addressed to the whole society, gradually came to represent the whole of society in its programmes. I do not wish to imply that this was simply or easily achieved then or now. Nor do I underestimate the difficulties of middle-class, white, male institutions in adequately representing those who are other than themselves. Nevertheless, it is important to acknowledge the ways in which radio and television have given voices to the voiceless and faces to the faceless, creating new communicative entitlements for excluded social groups. We are now familiar with documentary programmes on major social issues such as housing, unemployment or poverty, in which people who live in such conditions describe what they are like. Such techniques had actually to be discovered and when, before the war, listeners heard for the very first time an eye-witness account of slum conditions in Tyneside, or the unemployed themselves in 1934 describing how they tried to make ends meet on the dole, they created a sensation (Scannell, 1980).

The deceptively simple techniques of broadcast documentary programmes have given rise to much debate, and their surface naturalism has been criticized for occluding the possibility of exposing the causes that lie behind the personal testimonies of those that speak in them (Garnham, 1972). There are indeed limitations to these methods, to which I will return, but here I wish to note that, at the very least in enabling people to speak for themselves, the broadcasting institutions acknowledge their ability and their right to do so, as well as their right to be heard. All the techniques of documentary are designed to foreground the testimony of the speakers, to let them speak spontaneously and naturally, and to minimize the interventions and presence of the institutions of broadcasting. In the hierarchy of voices that speak in documentaries, the voices of ordinary persons, speaking as persons, tend to have a privileged status over the voices of experts, officials and commentators. Documentary techniques are grounded in consideration and respect for their subjects and their experiences.

But broadcasting has done a great deal more than to present ordinary people in programmes dealing with social issues and problems. It has discovered the pleasures of ordinariness, creating entertainment out of nothing more than ordinary people talking about themselves, playing games or doing silly things in front of live studio audiences. *That's Life!* such programmes say, and

Esther Rantzen celebrates it. The first programme series to celebrate ordinary life and experience was *Harry Hopeful*, produced in the BBC's Manchester studio before the war for a northern working-class audience (Bridson, 1972; Scannell, 1986). This was the first time ordinary people came to the microphone to talk about themselves and their lives, to sing a song or recite a dialect poem, or perform a knockabout double-act with Harry Hopeful before a live studio audience of relatives, friends and neighbours. The show was the first to take ordinary people and their ordinary experience and transform them into a public, shareable and enjoyable event. The sound of the studio audience singing, laughing and applauding powerfully enhanced the effect of public and communicable pleasures which the programmes generated. In multiple ways this principle has since been extended in radio and television: the essential components are a studio, a host or compere, ordinary people as performers and a live, studio audience. *Have A Go!, Jim'll Fix It, The Generation Game* and *Blind Date* are all in the tradition that invites ordinary people into the public domain for shared laughter and enjoyment.

IV

Broadcasting, then, brings public life into private life, and private life into public life, for pleasure and enjoyment as much as for information and education. The many voices that speak in this domain — the broadcasters themselves, public persons and private people — amount to a universe of discourse. The totality of output of mixed programmes in nationally networked channels adds up to a complete world. The repertoire appears exhaustive, and what lies outside its catchment — what is not broadcast — is not part of the 'normal' range of the needs and interests of the audience as expressed in the sum of its contents. To make this point is to underline the importance of trying to think of broadcast output as a totality, and always to register what it excludes as well as what it includes. The crucially sensitive 'boundary' topics for broadcasting have been political and moral: the state intervening to regulate the former and public opinion influencing the scope of the latter. Although today there are constraints on politics, sex and violence in terms of what can be said and shown, and how it can be said and shown, there is no doubt that broadcasting has in the sixty years of its life enormously extended the range of what can be talked about in its public domain.

Nothing is more interesting, and nothing more elusive, than the domain of the 'merely talkable about' and its historical development in broadcasting. When it started up in the 1920s, there was so much that could not be talked about in public, or at least not in front of women, children and servants. In a class-divided society like Britain one of the things that had, in the novel context of mass democracy, to be claimed and asserted, was the entitlement of all to have opinions, to have them heard and to hear those of others. Here is a woman from Sunderland, whose husband is out of work, talking on radio in 1934 of her feelings when she finds she is pregnant again:

> I know I've cried when I knew I had to have another baby, not for myself, but for what they have to be brought into — no work, no means, no jobs for them. But it means expense to avoid them. I know all about the avoidance part, but I haven't the means to carry it out. It costs money . . . I think we ought to have information from somewhere given to us. It's ignorance on some people's part; or, for people like myself who know, we haven't got the money. (The *Listener*, 16 May 1934, p. 812)

Mrs Pallis's passing reference to birth control in the course of her account of how she managed to feed a family of five on a dole of 16 shillings a week brought sackfuls of letters to the BBC complaining that the subject was mentioned on radio. There were pressures, in 1935, from some of the governors for the subject to be broached in talks programmes, but it was not allowed to be discussed on radio until the 1950s. Reith had met Marie Stopes, who wished to advance the cause of contraception on radio, but he regarded her as a fanatic. Corporation policy was expressed in a letter to the National Council for Civil Liberties in 1942: 'The subject of birth control . . . has never yet been discussed at the microphone in this country. Broadcasting is not, in the Corporation's view, a suitable medium for the discussion of this subject'. Birth control had only a fugitive presence as talkable about on pre-war radio.

In the decade after the war, as the BBC's television service gradually developed, previously excluded issues were taken up in new, dramatized forms of social documentation (Scannell, 1979; Bell, 1986). Careful studies reveal the ways in which such programmes, while introducing new and delicate issues such as birth control and divorce, contrived to resolve and close off their troublesome, disturbing implications (Booth, 1980). It was not until the late 1950s, under the impact of competition and a changing social and political climate, that broadcasting's universe of discourse began to open out and blossom. The introduction of a strictly limited competition for audiences between the BBC and ITV gave the BBC something other than its political masters to worry about. Deference to political authority was replaced by a more populist, democratic stance as the broadcasters asserted the public's right to know by making politicians answerable and accountable to the electorate for their conduct of the nation's affairs. In news interviews, studio discussions and debates, current affairs and topical magazine programmes, in documentaries and documentary dramas, a whole clutch of political and social issues came onto the agenda through the medium of television — became part of the public domain, matters of common knowledge and concern. In this way broadcasting came to fulfil — never without difficulty, always under pressure — its role as an independent public sphere, as a forum for open public discussion of matters of general concern.

If a moment can be selected to illustrate the transition to more open, democratic styles in broadcasting, it might well be found in the differences in the coverage by the BBC and ITV of the first televised State Opening of Parliament in 1958 (Dimbleby, 1977: 326–30). The Prime Minister, Harold Macmillan, in giving permission for this television 'first', had made it clear that it was to be treated as a state and not a political occasion. The BBC Outside Broadcasting Unit provided visual coverage of the event, but ITV took a feed from the BBC's cameras and provided their own commentary. The BBC's commentator was, naturally, Richard Dimbleby; ITV chose Robin Day. These were their commentaries on the closing stages of the ceremony as the Queen left the Great Hall of Westminster having delivered her speech from the throne:

Dimbleby: Later today, in the Commons, the debate and doubtless the argument over the Government's programme will begin. But for now, as Her Majesty returns to the Robing Rooms and thence to Buckingham Palace, she leaves behind in all of us, a memory of a State Occasion at its most magnificent.

Day: The Queen will go back to Buckingham Palace. The Crown will go back to the Tower of London. All the scarlet and ermine will go back to wherever they came from. And Parliament will go back to work.

Over the final shot of the empty throne, and as suitably solemn music was faded up, their last words were as follows:

> *Dimbleby*: The Throne remains, rich and shining, near yet remote; the symbol of this rare meeting of the Queen, the Lords and Commons — the Three Estates of Parliament. And so begins, with ceremony that springs from the very roots of our democratic history, the fourth session of the three hundredth Parliament of the Realm.

> *Day*: Everyone is wondering at Westminster what Government will write the next speech from this Throne. Before Her Majesty sits on it again there may be a General Election. That is when we have our say. And what Her Majesty reads from this Throne depends on what we put in the ballot box.

The differences, as Jonathan Dimbleby observes, are more than a matter of style. Since these are institutional voices they express differing institutional attitudes to the authority of the state and the force of tradition. The auratic discourse of Dimbleby puts them beyond all question, while the post-auratic discourse of Day serves precisely to bring them into question.

It was Robin Day who, with his colleagues at ITN, began for the first time to make those in authority answerable to the public through the television news interview. Interviewers now asked questions not to please politicians and let them say what they liked, but on behalf of the viewing public, and in their interests. Broadcasting thus came to align itself not with governments and parties but with the electorate. The direct, searching and penetrating kind of interview developed by Day and others, pursued, challenged, probed and, where necessary, clarified and reformulated what interviewees said (Heritage, 1983). It claimed an equal footing between broadcasters and politicians in order to create an equal footing between viewers and their elected representatives. The news interview became a more flexible, lively and influential instrument of journalistic enquiry. As such it helped to create a broadcast public forum with, for the first time, a real degree of political autonomy that was exercised on behalf of viewers and listeners.

But it would be a mistake to think of the public sphere in broadcasting as restricted to news and current affairs with documentary and 'serious' 'contemporary' drama thrown in for good measure. The transformation of the universe of discourse reached into all parts of output: in entertainment taboo subjects could now be joked about, and previously stigmatized situations and relationships could routinely serve as the basis for situation comedies. I do not wish to imply that the changes that took place from the mid-1950s to the 1970s, though fundamental, were irreversible. The extent of 'openness' in the system is something that varies according to the social, economic and political climate. The thresholds of tolerance are not fixed, and in the late 1980s the broadcasters are under greater political pressures from a radical right-wing government and from moral crusaders against violence and sex than at any time since the mid-1960s. It is notable, however, that the present government enhanced the public sphere of broadcasting at the beginning of the 1980s by authorizing Channel 4 to give special attention to the needs and interests of minority groups, and to commission a significant proportion of its programmes from independent producers.

V

I have discussed, so far, the public sphere in broadcasting in terms of the sayable and unsayable. But it has always been a question of how things are said, as well as what is said. Broadcasting's universe of discourse is as much a set of relationships as a content. What changed, crucially, in the 1950s were the style and manner of broadcasting. One thing that has forcibly struck me and my colleague, David Cardiff, in listening to recorded material from the 1930s, 1940s and 1950s, is the sheer awkwardness of the first faltering efforts to discover ways of, for instance, organizing a studio discussion, or a game show, or of interviewing a prime minister or the proverbial 'man in the street'. Linguistic analysis has yet to develop ways of accounting for communicative unease, though we can all in actual situations recognize embarrassed and embarrassing talk. So much, of course, is lost in transcription, and there are no conventions for rendering voice, intonation and all the stilted mannerisms that produce uncomfortable effects for contemporary ears. At the same time there are critical historio-graphical issues in attempting an historical study of communicative style. Would what sounds awkward today have sounded so to listeners forty years ago? The same question can be asked, of course, in relation to dialogue in movies from the period, and the answer must be probably, no. If what once seemed natural now seems unnatural this is because of changes in performative styles

— forms of talk — as much in real life as art over the years. There is no doubt that in drama, movies, radio and television today the performed talk — in most instances — is more seemingly relaxed, natural and spontaneous than forms of talk in life and art forty years ago. I regard this change in the communicative ethos of modern society as one that broadcasting has helped to bring about, and I see it as constitutive of the particular character and quality of the broadcast public sphere.

The problem of communicative manners and style, of how to address absent audiences in national channels, was acknowledged from the start. When the BBC became a public corporation in 1927 talk on radio was institutionalized as the responsibility of the Talks Department, and attention now turned to the art of radio talk. This concern arose in large part from a problem succinctly defined by David Cardiff as 'the domestication of public utterance' (Cardiff, 1980). The talk that prevailed in early broadcasting in Britain was monologue rather than dialogue, in which selected speakers spoke at length on predetermined scripted topics from the studio to absent listeners. It soon became clear to Hilda Matheson, the first Head of BBC Talks (1927–32), that the established traditions of public speaking were inappropriate for broadcasting. The voice and rhetoric of the sermon, lecture or political speech were all, in their own way, unsatisfactory. The 'holy voice' used by the clergy to read the lessons in church was a special voice set apart for religious purposes, more devout than the ordinary voice of everyday life (Matheson, 1933: 70–1). But the 'parsonical drone' was peculiarly unsuited to radio, and had a tendency to make listeners switch off immediately. Matheson noted the problems of another special voice — the declamatory 'poetic' voice used for acting or for public readings of poetry and literature. This voice, with its polished elocution and exquisite pronunciation, seemed mannered and affected to the listening ear. Again, the political voice and the rhetoric of the platform put the speaker at a disadvantage when used for broadcasting.

> The microphone [Matheson noted] has a curious knack of showing what is real and unreal, what is clear and what is woolly, what is fact and purpose and what is stock phrase, what is sincere and what is an appeal to the gallery, what is constructive and what is destructive. (Matheson, 1933: 99–100)

Matheson conducted a series of experiments with broadcast talks which led her to the view that it was useless to address the microphone as if it were a public meeting, or even to read it essays or leading articles. The person sitting at the other end expected the speaker to address him personally, simply, almost familiarly, as man to man. (Matheson, 1933: 75–6)

Broadcasting could not treat its audience as a crowd. It had to learn to speak to them as individuals. The quest of the Talks Department for an idiomatic, conversational style has been traced by David Cardiff, and needs no summary here. What I have tried to clarify is something still not properly understood, namely the dynamics of the communicative process in broadcasting and its basic social, relational features. The pivotal fact, it seeems to me, is that the broadcasters, while they control the discourse, do not control the communicative context. The settings in which listening and viewing take place are always beyond their control. When Reith proposed, in 1923, that the infant BBC should be allowed to relay live the marriage service of the Duke of York and Lady Elizabeth Bowes-Lyon, the Dean of Westminster refused for fear that men in public houses would listen with their hats on (Wolfe, 1984: 79).

Thus broadcasters do not have the authority and power over their audience which the institutional context, combined with real presence, bestows upon public speakers. Whereas the onus is upon the audience attending church, a political rally, a public lecture, a theatre or concert performance to affiliate to the situation and align their behaviour with performer(s) and setting, the situation in broadcasting is reversed. The communicators must affiliate to the situation of their audience, and align their communicative behaviour with those circumstances. The burden of responsibility is thus on the broadcasters to understand the conditions of reception, and to express that understanding in language intended to be recognized as oriented to those conditions.

In the first decade of its corporate life the BBC, in spite of the efforts of Hilda Matheson, tended to suppress the context in which listening took place and to ignore its implications. Concentrated, attentive listening was demanded from listeners who were brusquely informed that if they only listened with half an ear they had no right to criticize. The deliberate avoidance of continuity in and between programmes, and of fixed scheduling (apart from the news bulletins) were the major ways in which programme planners sought to discourage lazy, non-stop listening. Rather they were expected to consult *Radio Times*, select the programmes they wanted to hear, listen to them carefully and then switch off. Listeners were expected to try and overcome the inconvenient fact that they were listening at home with all its attendant distractions, and to behave as if they were at the theatre or concert hall, or at a public lecture. To get in the mood for listening to radio plays, the BBC's advice was to be in your favourite armchair five minutes before 'the curtain goes up', with the lights in the living room turned down in order to assist the imagination.

By the late 1930s, under a range of pressures, the broadcasters had discovered that the audience did not behave itself as it was supposed to do. Most people most of the time — no matter what their class, education, age or gender — tended to treat the radio as a cheerful noise in the background, as a companionable and sociable domestic resource which occasionally — in moments of national crisis, celebration or mourning — became compulsive listening. As the broadcasters came to acknowledge how people listened in their homes they began to adapt their service to those conditions. I have discussed elsewhere one fundamental way in which this was done, through programme planning based on listener research that provided evidence about who, in the national audience, was available for listening and at what times of the day. Broadcasting had to learn how to adjust its programmes to chime in with the day-to-day life and routines of the population (Scannell, 1988a).

This new understanding of how, where and when people listened first found expression in new patterns of programming and in new kinds of entertainment programmes. In the late 1930s greater care was taken to organize daily output on routine, regular lines. Popular programmes were increasingly scheduled in fixed time slots. *Monday Night at Seven*, the BBC Variety Department's first continuity show, was an early and successful attempt to produce a fireside entertainment that recurred at a known time and could be pleasurably anticipated as a predictable enjoyment in the week. By the late 1930s, programme planners were adjusting daily output to chime in with the time routines of ordinary daily life for the whole population. At the same time, in new forms of participatory entertainment — quizzes, parlour games and puzzles — the broadcasters found new communicative styles — more spontaneous, personal and relaxed. In an audio-cassette made for the Open University's *Popular Culture* course, David Cardiff has shown how this was achieved across a ten-year period from the late 1930s to the late 1940s (Cardiff, 1982).

For all the formidable difficulties it involves, it is possible to reconstruct historically, in all areas of output, the development of effective styles of address and performance that generated a sense of ease between institution and audiences. It was an uneven process that emerged in broadcast entertainment well ahead of cultural and informational programmes. In the sphere of news and politics the prevailing style until the late 1950s, and the impact of ITN, is suggested by the title of a political talks series called *Men in Authority*, produced in 1951 by Grace Wyndham Goldie (Goldie, 1977: 80). Serious talk on serious matters called for serious, impersonal and authoritative modes of address from accredited authorities (Cardiff, 1980). Work on early television documentary reveals the awkwardnesses of interview styles at a time when it seems that both interviewers and interviewees were nervous when talking to each other as strangers across class barriers in the unfamiliar public context created by the cameras (Corner, forthcoming). What seems to have happened thereafter, through the ubiquity of television, is that as everyone has been gathered into its public sphere, everyone has become familiar not simply with its modes of address but crucially with its performative styles. Communicative ease is partly a result of knowing how to behave appropriately in the appropriate broadcast context. It is also, reciprocally, the result of programme formats appropriate to the contexts of listening and viewing.

A seminal example of how the two came together, in early television, came in 1957 when the BBC — under the spur of competition — decided to break the so-called 'toddler's truce', the period between six and seven in the evening when there was no television, partly, it was said, to make it easier for parents to get their young children to bed. The BBC decided to fill this gap with a programme that chimed in with what viewers were likely to be doing at that time. Enquiries were made.

> They would be coming and going: women getting meals for teenagers who were going out and preparing supper for men who were coming in; men in the north would be having their tea; commuters in the south would be arriving home. There was no likelihood of an audience which would be ready to view steadily for half an hour at a time. What seemed necessary was a continuous programme held together by a permanent staff of compères, reporters and interviewers but consisting of separate items so that any viewer who happened to be around could dip into it knowing that he had lost nothing by not being able to watch from the beginning. (Goldie, 1977: 210)

The result was *Tonight*, the first major topical magazine programme to be presented five nights a week at the same time, and its successor through the 1970s, *Nationwide*.

Work on the conditions of reception for cinema has shown it to be a visually overwhelming experience that demands and gets from audiences a rapt attention in a state of high anxiety and expectation (Elsaesser, 1982). By contrast, listening to radio or watching television are distinctively underwhelming experiences. If cinema is a regime of wonder in which the conditions of viewing, forms of narrative and mode of visual presentation all combine to produce such an effect, broadcasting is the negation of that experience. Its pleasures are ordinary, specifically intended as such, adapted to the conditions of listening and viewing in mundane, daily domestic contexts. Cinema, and most other forms of public culture, religion and entertainment, stand apart from routine daily life. Broadcasting is deeply enmeshed in its very fabric. The usage of radio and television are interrelated, interactive with other activities and interests, and a means of maintaining sociable contacts between household members, as Bausinger has shown in his account of a typical German family's weekend (Bausinger, 1984). The characteristic look that television produces is the glance, and its output is designed to be understood by audiences who may be only half-watching, popping in and out of the room or even channel-zapping.

The communicative ethos of broadcasting, which I have tried to characterize both as a series of structuring temporal arrangements and as a communicative style, an orientation towards relaxed, natural and spontaneous modes of address and forms of talk, points up the specific quality of the public life that is continuously produced and reproduced through broadcasting. The world, in broadcasting, appears as ordinary, mundane, accessible, knowable, familiar, recognizable, intelligible, shareable and communicable for whole populations. It is talkable about by everyone. This world does not exist elsewhere. It is not a reflection, a mirror, of a reality outside and beyond. It is one fundamental, seen but unnoticed, constitutive component of contemporary reality for all.

I have tried to catch the multi-faceted realities of broadcasting in the following terms. First, for a new general public, a new access was won to previously restricted forms of entertainment and sport, and to exclusive political, cultural, religious events. As these entered into a common public domain new relationships and meanings were created between them. At the same time a new public culture of the studio was developed in which a wide variety of programme formats — from discussions and interviews to games and chat shows — created new forums for the debate of matters of general concern and new forms of shareable pleasure and play. The public life that is maintained by mixed programming in national channels may be thought of as a totality, a universe of discourse, whose boundaries had at first to be established and have, ever after, been a matter of dispute and struggle between broadcasters, the state and society. The universe of discourse inscribed in the totality of output is not merely a content, but a set of relationships, a communicative ethos, that registers the quality and manner of social intercourse between institutions and audiences and, beyond that, the expressive idioms of public and private life.

VI

One objection to this account might be that the audiences of radio and television are not genuine publics, and that it is a pseudo-public life that is constituted in broadcasting. Listeners and viewers watch and listen — it is said — as atomized, fragmented, isolated individuals, not as participant members accessible to each other in the moment of participation. Moreover there is no interaction between events and audiences; no *feedback*. Broadcasting is a one-way system of transmission, with no possibility of interaction that is the basis of any properly communicative situation. Here the metaphysics of presence reasserts itself again with the jargon of authenticity in support. Consider first the position of the 'authentic' publics in most public contexts: the audience at a concert or the theatre or a public lecture, the congregation in a church, the spectators at a sporting event, the members of a political meeting. In most of these cases, though the audiences are in each other's presence they are not communicatively present to each other. Indeed it would be quite mischievous to attempt to strike up a conversation with the person beside one in the pew, or during the lecture, the performance, the speech by the party leader. Such an effort at communication would violate the situational proprieties. On the other hand, it seems normal and natural while watching television — often with other people in the room — for there to be simultaneous comment and chat about the same event being watched 'in private'.

The reality is that the self-selecting publics in most public events accept — voluntarily and willingly as the price of admission and of being there — a whole range of quite unusual bodily and behavioural constraints: to kneel and stand in church, to applaud on cue at the rally or concert, to take notes at the lecture, and at all events to be silent and motionless for the most part. In most public events the nature of the communication is a one-way affair: there are the performers who perform and give voice and there are the live audiences to receive the performance and appreciate it. What live public events have is undoubtedly the 'aura' of presence, but aura is as low in communicative properties as it is high in ritual characteristics.

If the aura of presence glows more faintly for absent broadcast audiences they have far greater freedom in their behaviour while watching and listening. They can walk out on the event (a peculiarly difficult thing to do in church, for instance, or during a concert or play) and come back again, they can switch to some other channel, they can freely express their opinions about the merits or shortcomings of performer(s) and performance. In short, the absent listeners and viewers — the pseudo-public — have much wider behavioural and communicative options than the real and present publics whose behaviour is structured in deference to the event. Indeed, by virtue of not being present, absent viewers and listeners are not in thrall to the aura of the event and are thereby better able to see through the façade of rhetoric designed to rally the faithful and excoriate the faithless.

The force of this argument is to suggest that the circumstances of the absent listening and viewing public create participation without involvement. Where the live audience is committed to the event viewers and listeners may take a non-committal stance. It is not that the event is more real and meaningful for the live audience, less real and meaningful for listeners and viewers; rather there are different realities with different effects. The public life of broadcasting does not stand in a secondary and supplementary relationship to a prior and privileged public life based on presence. It has rather created new contexts, realities and meanings.

But, it might still be objected, the audience still remains fragmented, isolated and atomized — trapped in the sphere of privacy. This is to view individuals as figures in a Lowry landscape, with no social life or contact with others. But empirical research points to the manifold ways in which the output of radio and television today serve as topical and relational resources in mundane social encounters and conversations (Morley, 1986, for instance). Precisely because the public life of broadcasting is accessible to all, it is there to be talked about by all. Everyone is entitled to have views and opinions about what they hear and see. This is not the case with most other cultural resources. Bourdieu has shown how culture is a kind of capital which serves to maintain social difference, and his empirical researches cover many aspects of contemporary (French) cultural tastes: painting, photography, cinema, theatre, music, newspapers, food and furnishing (Bourdieu, 1984). But radio and television are significantly absent, precisely because the social distinctions maintained by the cultural distinctions of particular taste publics collapse in the common cultural domain of broadcasting.

In the case of 'high art' and the avant-garde, while the uninitiated and uneducated may regard them as 'rubbish' their opinions have no status because they are not 'entitled' (Bourdieu, 1984: 18 ff). Susan Kippax has shown how, for some women, particularly middle-class unwaged women, the enjoyment of cinema, theatre and the arts has only an inner, personal resonance. In social contexts they express their views tentatively and with diffidence. They do not possess their opinions because they are not entitled to them (Kippax, 1988). Uncommon knowledges and tastes confer uncommon entitlements. But broadcasting is, precisely, a common resource and a common knowledge that excludes none. And thus all are entitled to their views. It is noticeable how everyone, even the very young, have no difficulty or hesitation in talking about what they have recently seen and heard (Palmer, 1988). *Did You See?* is a common way of striking up a conversation or of keeping it going. Broadcasting thus acts not so much as a social cement as a social lubricant, easing social interaction and sustaining it in countless mundane contexts. It is perhaps the one thing (apart from the weather in the UK) that we all have in common as a topical resource.

Thus broadcasting, unobtrusively but no less remarkably, resocializes private life. Certain kinds of programme — soap operas, pre-eminently — are little ritual social events in which families or groups of friends watch together and talk about the programme before, during and after. Gossip is the life-blood of soap operas, as it is of ordinary daily life — 'the living breath of events', as Patricia Meyer Spacks calls it, quoting Faulkner

(Spacks, 1986). Gossip in broadcasting, gossip about broadcasting in the tabloid press and in ordinary conversation — this is the very stuff of broadcasting's interconnection with so-called private life or, as I prefer, ordinary daily life. It points up the quality and character of its communicative ethos. If it seems both ordinary and trivial it is also relaxed and sociable, shareable and accessible, non-exclusive, equally talkable about in principle and in practice by everyone.

VII

I do not then recognize the validity of arguments that broadcasting is a non-authentic or pseudo-public sphere. Nor do I accept those that construe it, in various ways, as an ideological apparatus. Through the work of Stuart Hall and his graduate students at the Centre for Contemporary Cultural Studies, the main way in which the small parish of Media Studies has come to (mis)understand the role of the media is in terms of its 'ideological effect'. The media, so the theory goes, work to produce a social and political consensus that confirms the dominance of existing economic and political institutions and processes, and of existing structures of class, gender and ethnic relations in capitalist societies (cf. Hall et al. 1980; Hall, 1977, 1982). The national press and broadcasting agencies contribute to the reproduction in dominance of the existing economic and political order by underpinning their legitimacy through their complex practices of representation: i.e. through the selective organization and representation of images and accounts of contemporary social reality. In so doing they uphold the interests of powerful social apparatuses and groups by marginalizing or misrepresenting the interests of subordinate social groups; by excluding or distorting oppositional voices; and by producing 'preferred readings' of events which favour the dominant interests.

This led to a focus on 'the politics of representation', taking news and current affairs as favoured sites for the renegotiation of the dominant meaning system. Semiology was recruited to expose the tricks of ideology — the ways in which it naturalized itself as the seemingly obvious and self-evident, as what everybody knows and takes for granted. Barthes provided a basic way of prying apart the first- and second-order levels of meaning in a wide range of cultural 'texts' by showing how symbolic (connotative) meanings were embedded as seemingly natural in obvious, referential (denotative) meanings (Barthes, 1972). A critical semiotics was elaborated to unmask the slipperiness of contemporary bourgeois, patriarchal ideology.

The effect of this approach is to read off all the output of broadcasting as if it works in the same way, as if there were no difference between the 'discourses' or 'practices' of news, documentary, drama, or entertainment. But it has never studied the output of broadcasting systematically as a totality. At best there has developed something like genre studies (of news or soap opera to take the two most obvious cases), at worst there has been a tendency to 'read' off the 'unity' of current affairs television from a single study of a single programme (Hall et al. 1978). But in a sense there is no need for detailed study because television (radio is largely ignored) is everywhere and always the same. Barthes, years after he wrote *Mythologies*, noted ruefully that the techniques of demystification he had there developed had in turn become mystified. Students had learned to distinguish first- and second-order meanings, and expose their petit-bourgeois character, but that was all they had learned, and it wasn't much. Tearing aside the ideological veil had itself become stock phrases, discourse, dogma (Barthes, 1977: 166).

The 'ideological effect' thesis is a one-dimensional critique that, in effect, only needs doing once from a predetermined political template. It collapses any difference or contradiction in the work of broadcasting. As such, broadcasting has no history, no development. There is very little positive to study, and nothing to learn from broadcasting. It cannot produce knowledge or understanding. It cannot transform perception. Any notion that the media might be instruments of enlightenment, as Reith thought of broadcasting, must be delusory. But then, the broadcasters do not know what they are doing: 'unwittingly, unconsciously, [they serve] as a support for the reproduction of a dominant discursive field'. They may have ideas about what they are doing, but these (from the point of view of theory) are irrelevant, for 'ideology is a function of the discourse and of the logic of social processes, rather than an intention of the agent'. Ideology, as discourse, speaks itself through the media (Hall, 1982: 88). What speaks through Stuart Hall, we might wonder, that privileges the knowledge-producing consciousness of the media academic over ignorance-inducing unconsciousness of the media professional? The answer, I suppose, is Theory (Althusser as the voice of Ideology, Foucault of Discourse), but it is one, to my mind, that systematically misunderstands and misrecognizes its object.

VIII

For all its seeming sophistication the Theory of Ideology says something very simple indeed; something not very different from what Leavis was saying in the 1930s: the media are harmful and the function of literary criticism or theoretical critique is to expose them in that light. Such an approach is not reconcilable with any view of broadcasting as a public sphere that works to enhance the reasonable, democratic character of life in public and private contexts. To regard the media as ideological is to regard them as either anti-rational or irrational. But although I reject such characterizations, a major difficulty in discussing the rationality of broadcasting lies in the way that academic debates about rationality are largely contained within the theoretical envelope of the philosophy of consciousness, the so-called western episteme from its provenance in the Greeks to its contemporary terminal state in the aporias of post-structuralism and the intellectual capitulations of post-modernism.

Although Habermas is the most valiant opponent of this latest *trahison des clercs* (this time by abandoning rather than engaging with politics), the terms of his defence of communicative rationality are remote from the actual circumstances of ordinary conversation and mundane social interaction which, I have argued, characterize the communicative domain of broadcasting. I have tentatively tried to ground the communicative ethos of broadcasting in Anglo-American sociology and linguistic pragmatics that take, as their object, mundane daily life, social interaction and talk (Scannell, 1988b). A fundamental kind of human rationality is implicated in this work which attends to the communicative basis of social life and the means whereby it is maintained in ordinary interaction, especially talk. An orientation to co-operation underpins the maintenance of a perspective of normality (Garfinkel, 1984: Ch. 2), the common grounds of intersubjective understanding (Schutz, q.v. Heritage, 1984: 54 ff.) and a communicative intentionality in talk that is grounded in considerations of clarity, sincerity, relevance and informativeness (Grice, q.v. Levinson, 1983: 100 ff.).

Such concerns are closely paralleled in the 'validity claims' that Habermas proposes as the universal grounds of communicative behaviour oriented towards understanding (Habermas, 1979, Ch. 1). My difficulty with Habermas is that he seems to regard consensual understanding as achieved through receptiveness to the best argument (i.e. the most rational one) in ideal speech situations. The ideal speech situation, it appears in John Keane's helpful discussion, is grounded in communicative competence, and the model Habermas has in mind is the classical Greek category of politics as public speaking and acting — 'Socratic forms of communication' (Keane, 1984: 159, 163). But this is to privilege not so much rationality, as rhetorical skill. It is notable about Socrates, for instance, that he always gets the last word and thus always 'wins'. The best argument can be, it is not hard to imagine, a kind of domination and oppression, to which the less articulate must submit. Feminist critiques of how men argue are very much to this point, especially in their observation that listening is as important as speaking (Spender, 1980). For almost all discussion of rational discourse considers it not merely in formal terms (its immanent, logical properties) but as a contestation for the best, the most powerful, the most convincing argument. There is virtually no consideration of rational discourse as social dialogue.

I think Habermas is right to regard communicative rationality as grounded in mutual understanding, but I do not think it is achieved (or achievable) along the lines he proposes, for mutual understanding presupposes cooperativeness as its basis, a willingness to listen, to allow the validity of the other person's viewpoint and, if necessary, a willingness to leave aside what may be the best argument (in terms of clarity, logic, force, etc.) in consideration of the most appropriate decisions in relation to the particular circumstances and the particular persons involved. The skills that are needed for coming to conclusions with which all agree, include tact, thoughtfulness and consideration for others, knowing how and when to listen, etc. Such skills produce agreements that are reasonable (as distinct from rational) and thus acceptable in the eyes of participants. They are the everyday skills that everyone possesses and deploys in ordinary talk and mundane contexts, as distinct from the peculiar communicative competence of philosophers and their peculiar discourses.

Thus, I prefer to characterize the impact of broadcasting as enhancing the reasonable, as distinct from the rational, character of daily life in public and private contexts. In this context, reasonable has the force of mutually accountable behaviour; that is, if called upon, individuals can offer reasons and accounts for what they have said or done. To refuse an explanation, if called for, is unreasonable. To be unable to offer an explanation is unreasonable. Reasonableness is a guarantee and hallmark of forms of private and public life in which people accept mutual obligations to each other, acknowledge that they are answerable and accountable to each other — in short, deal with each other as equals. In such conditions the right to ask for explanations and accounts (where necessary or relevant) is a communicative entitlement.

IX

I have used the term 'communicative entitlement' several times in this article, and it needs clarification. Communicative entitlements presuppose communicative rights. Communicative rights (the right to speak freely, for instance) are enshrined in the written constitutions of some countries, but not in Britain. A minimal notion of guaranteed communicative rights is a precondition of forms of democratic life in public and private. If one party (the state, the police, teachers, parents, husbands) refuse to be answerable for their conduct to the other party (the electorate, suspects, pupils, children, wives), not only is this unreasonable — it denies a communicative entitlement and nullifies a right. Communicative entitlements can be claimed and asserted, within a presupposed framework of communicative rights. Rights of free assembly, to speak freely and (more often overlooked) to listen, contribute to creating formal, minimal guarantees for certain forms of public political and religious life. They seed the possible growth of wider and more pervasive claims from those denied a hearing in manifold public and private contexts, that they should be listened to: i.e. that they should be treated seriously. As equals.

I believe that broadcasting has enhanced the reasonable character and conduct of twentieth-century life by augmenting claims to communicative entitlements. It does this, as I have tried to show, through asserting a right of access to public life; through extending its universe of discourse and entitling previously excluded voices to be heard: through questioning those in power, on behalf of viewers and listeners, and trying to get them to answer. More generally, I have suggested, the fact that the broadcasters do not control the communicative context means that they must take into account the conditions of reception for their utterances. As such they have learned to treat the communicative process not simply as the transmission of a content, but a relational process in which how things are said is as important as what is said. All this has, I think, contributed to new, interactive relationships between public and private life which have helped to normalize the former and to socialize the latter.

In saying this I am not trying to idealize the present system, whose reasonable/rational character is contained within the framework and limitations of mass democratic politics which work, in many ways, to sustain the power of institutional public life over mundane, private life. One way in which the limits of rationality in political debate can clearly be shown emerges from careful analysis of the techniques and protocols of political interviews. When, for the first time, viewers were invited to put questions to leading politicians, in the run-up to the general election of 1964, there was a clear and simple demand for straight answers. 'On the postcards, often underlined, were, again and again, words like "No hedging on this question please" and "please answer Yes or No"' (Goldie, 1978: 271). In the 1960s, broadcast journalists tried hard to prevent politicians from evading their questions, through the use of combative one-to-one questioning. But since then political pressures, David Greatbatch argues, have forced a more cautious stance on the broadcasters who have covered themselves against cries of bias by increasingly preferring the use of panel formats with representatives of several different political positions or views (Greatbatch, 1986a).

In a recent speech at the University of Essex Sir Robin Day complained that politicians no longer answered his questions (El Gabry, 1988). Greatbatch has shown that, although interviewers have sanctions against politicians who avoid answering questions, those sanctions are limited (Greatbatch, 1986b). There is no oath or legal sanction for perjury to oblige political interviewees to tell the truth, and interviewers cannot press relentlessly, as counsel may do in the courts. Such an aggressive line of questioning would violate norms of courtesy and politeness that operate in all more or less cooperative talk. The extent to which politicians can refuse to be answerable and accountable marks the boundaries of open, reasonable and informative discussion on radio and television.

Another way in which those boundaries maintain the inequalities of power between public and private can be seen in the distribution of entitlements to opinions and experiences on radio and television. To have an opinion is to be entitled to comment on events, to have views about them, to assess their significance. To have an experience is to be entitled to describe an event that happened to oneself and to say what one felt about it. In broadcast news public persons are entitled to opinions, private persons to experiences. Public persons (politicians, businessmen, authorities, experts, media reporters and commentators) are routinely called upon to comment on the wider implications of newsworthy events (what they mean for this country, the government, business, etc.). They speak as representatives of institutions, as agents not as persons, and their views have a generalized weight and authority. They are accredited spokespersons, whose views are legitimated and legitimating. Private individuals appear in news, become newsworthy, accidentally and usually disastrously. They are often the victims or witnesses of catastrophes and are interviewed for what they saw or for how it affected them — what it was like (when the ship sank), what it felt like (on learning their children were/were not safe). They are there to authenticate, to embody, the human consequences of events. They speak as persons, their testimony is particular, their newsworthiness has a one-off, unique character.

This arrangement in news of those who are entitled to express opinions and those who are entitled to experiences reinforces the division between public and private, and maintains them as separate. For although public persons may also be entitled on occasion to newsworthy experiences and feelings (Mrs Thatcher when her son was lost in Africa), private persons are not, on occasion, entitled to newsworthy opinions other than in 'vox pops' on Budget Day, etc. If, in news, private life is devalued, it is revalued, I have suggested, in the strategies and tactics of broadcast documentary whose narratives are designed partly in antithesis to those of news. But although the subjects of documentary are entitled to opinions about their experience, and may be invited to express them, those opinions have only a subjective force. They lack the generalizing power of the opinions of public persons.

That power is routinely confirmed in the broadcast formats for the staging of political debate. The classic model, developed by the BBC in the late 1940s, was *Any Questions*, which is still, forty years on, alive and well on Radio 4 today. Its television equivalent is *Question Time*, chaired by Sir Robin Day. These programmes reveal the tactics developed by the BBC for organizing public debate on topical matters of general interest, within the framework of parliamentary democracy. There is a chairperson to control the programme and to perform the complex communicative task of mediating between three audiences — the panel of speakers, the live studio audience who ask them questions, and the absent listeners or viewers. The panel of four is broadcasting's solution to the delicate task of ensuring balanced debate: *Any Questions* used typically to be made up of a Labour and a Conservative MP, a bishop and a 'woman'. Women are always doubly determined in public discussion panels: they are there as 'women' as well as being MPs, authors, academics, etc. They are usually there in the ratio of one to three and it is as rare as snow in August for there to be a majority of female panellists in public debate programmes.

The panellists are licensed opinion-leaders. They are entitled to have views on topics that range from the trivial to the serious. The audience (invited or selected) is cast in a position of subordination vis-à-vis the panel. They are there to be enlightened and informed. They have their opinions too, on *Question Time*, but it is noticeable that they do not have the same status, the same resonance, as those of the panellists. Partly this is because they lack the skills of speaking in public, and hence they seem by comparison to be less clear, less informed and less articulate than the panellists, who are used to speaking in public and know the appropriate rhetorical and performative skills. Again, the effect of this kind of staged public debate is to affirm the power of the opinions of public persons and the powerlessness of the opinions of private persons.

Broadcasting still operates within a particular definition of democracy established back in 1918 by the Representation of the People Act. The limits of representative democracy and of broadcasting's representative public service role within it are essentially the same; power accrues to the representatives, not those whom they represent. More participatory forms of politics and broadcasting are required if people are to play an active part in public life and decision-making, thereby exercising greater control over their own individual and social life. As far as broadcasting goes what is needed are many more properly local radio stations (dozens of stations in London, for instance) and more regional television networks to strengthen rather than vitiate the diversity of identities of place. Moreover, public access and participation in programmes, programming and programme making should be a key feature of decentralized radio and television services.

Such services should enhance but not displace the present system of public service broadcasting in this country and its commitment to properly public, social values. In my view equal access for all to a wide and varied range of common informational, entertainment and cultural services, carried on channels that can be received throughout the country, should be thought of as an important citizenship right in mass democratic societies. It is a crucial means — perhaps the only means at present — whereby common knowledges and pleasures in a shared public life are maintained as a social good for the whole population. As such it should be defended against its enemies.

References

Barthes, R. (1972) *Mythologies*. London: Paladin.

Barthes, R. (1977) *Image–Music–Text*. London: Fontana.

Bausinger, H. (1984) 'Media, Technology and Daily Life', *Media, Culture & Society* 6(4): 343–51.

Bell, E. (1986) 'The Origins of British Television Documentary: the BBC 1946–1955', in J. Corner (ed.), *Documentary and the Mass Media*. London: Edward Arnold.

Booth, J. (1980) 'Watching the Family', in H. Baehr (ed.), *Women in Media*. Oxford: Pergamon.

Bourdieu, P. (1984) *Distinction. A Social Critique of the Judgement of Taste*. London: Routledge & Kegan Paul.

Bridson, D.G. (1972) *Prospero and Ariel*. London: Gollancz.

Cardiff, D. (1980) 'The Serious and the Popular: Aspects of the Evolution of Style in the Radio Talk, 1928–1939', *Media, Culture and Society* 2(1).

Cardiff, D. (1982) 'Styles of Variety', *Radio in World War II: Light Entertainment* (Side One), (AC334). (A teaching cassette accompanying *Popular Culture*, Unit 8, Radio and World War II, U203, Milton Keynes: The Open University.)

Corner, J. (forthcoming) 'Onlooking and Eavesdropping: Rhetorics of Mediation in Early Television Documentary, in P. Scannell (ed.) *Broadcast Talk*. London: Sage Publications.

Dimbleby, J. (1977) *Richard Dimbleby*. London: Hodder & Stoughton.

El Gabry, W. (1988) 'Minister — Please Answer the Question', BA Media Studies dissertation, Polytechnic of Central London.

Elsaesser, T. (1982) Narrative Cinema and Audience-oriented Aesthetics', in T. Bennett et al. (eds), *Popular Television and Film*. London: BFI/Open University.

Garfinkel, H. (1984) *Studies In Ethnomethodology*. Cambridge: Polity Press.

Garnham, N. (1972) 'The Politics of TV Naturalism', *Screen* Summer.

Garnham, N. (1986) 'The Media and the Public Sphere'. in P. Golding et al. (eds), *Communicating Politics*. Leicester: University of Leicester Press.

Goldie, G.W. (1977), *Facing The Nation, Television and Politics, 1936–1976*. London: Bodley Head.

Greatbatch, D. (1986a) 'The Management of Disagreement Between News Interviewees' (offprint). University of Warwick, Department of Sociology.

Greatbatch, D. (1986b) 'Aspects of Topical Organization in News Interviews: The Use of Agenda-shifting procedures by Interviewees', *Media, Culture & Society*, 8(4): 441–55.

Habermas, J. (1979) *Communication and the Evolution of Society*. London: Heinemann.

Hall, S. (1977) 'Culture, the Media and the "Ideological Effect"', in J. Curran et al. (eds), *Mass Communication and Society*. London: Edward Arnold.

Hall, S. (1982) 'The Rediscovery of "Ideology": return of the repressed in media studies', in M. Gurevitch et al. (eds) *Culture, Society and the Media*. London: Methuen.

Hall, S. et al. (1978) 'The Unity of Current Affairs Television', *Working Papers in Cultural Studies* 9.

Hall, S. et al. (1980) *Culture, Media, Language*. London: Hutchinson.

Heritage, J. (1983) 'Analysing News Interviews: aspects of the production of talk for an overhearing audience', in T. van Dijk (ed.) *Handbook of Discourse Analysis*. London: Academic Press.

Heritage, J. (1984) *Garfinkel and Ethnomethodology*. Cambridge: Polity Press.

Keane, J. (1984) *Public Life and Late Capitalism*. Cambridge: Cambridge University Press.

Kippax, S. (1988) 'Women as Audience: the experience of unwaged women of the performing arts', *Media, Culture & Society* 10(1): 5–21.

Levinson, S. (1983) *Pragmatics*. Cambridge: Cambridge University Press.

Matheson, H. (1933) *Broadcasting*. London: Thornton Butterworth.

Morley, D. (1986) *Family Television: Cultural Power and Domestic Leisure*. London: Comedia.

Palmer, P. (1988) 'The Social Nature of Children's Television Viewing', in P. Drummond and R. Paterson (eds), *Television and Its Audience*. London: BFI.

[Peacock Report] (1986) *Report of the Committee on Financing the BBC*. Cmnd. 9284. London: HMSO.

Scannell, P. (1979) 'The Social Eye of Television, 1946–1955', *Media, Culture & Society* 1(1).

Scannell, P. (1980) 'Broadcasting and the Politics of Unemployment, 1930–1935', *Media, Culture & Society* 2(1).

Scannell, P. (1981) 'Music for the Multitude? The Dilemmas of the BBC's Music Policy, 1923–1946', *Media, Culture & Society* 3(3): 243–60.

Scannell, P. and Cardiff, D. (1982) 'Serving the Nation: public service broadcasting before the war', in B. Waites et al. (eds), *Popular Culture Past and Present*. London: Croom Helm.

Scannell, P. (1984) '"A Conspiracy of Silence": The state, the BBC and public opinion in the formative years of British broadcasting', in G. McLennan et al. (eds), *State and Society in Contemporary Britain*. Cambridge: Polity Press.

Scannell, P. (1986) 'The Stuff of Radio: developments in radio features and documentaries before the war', in J. Corner (ed.), *Documentary and the Mass Media*. London: Edward Arnold.

Scannell, P. (1988a) '*Radio Times*: the temporal arrangements of broadcasting in the modern world', in P. Drummond and R. Paterson (eds), *Television and its Audience*. London: BFI.

Scannell, P. (1988b) 'The communicative ethos of broadcasting'. Conference Paper, International Television Studies Conference, London: BFI.

Scannell, P. (1989) 'Public Service Broadcasting: history of a concept', in A. Goodwin and G. Whannel (eds), *Understanding Television*. London: Routledge.

Spacks, P.M. (1986) *Gossip*. Chicago/London: University of Chicago Press.

Spender, D. (1980) *Man Made Language*. London: Routledge & Kegan Paul.

Wolfe, K. (1984) *The Churches and the British Broadcasting Corporation 1922–1956*. London: SCM Press.

Index